SPECTERS OF WAR

SPECTERS OF WAR

The Battle of Mourning in Postconflict Central America

IGNACIO SARMIENTO

THE UNIVERSITY OF
ARIZONA PRESS
TUCSON

The University of Arizona Press
www.uapress.arizona.edu

We respectfully acknowledge the University of Arizona is on the land and territories of Indigenous peoples. Today, Arizona is home to twenty-two federally recognized tribes, with Tucson being home to the O'odham and the Yaqui. Committed to diversity and inclusion, the University strives to build sustainable relationships with sovereign Native Nations and Indigenous communities through education offerings, partnerships, and community service.

ISBN-13: 978-0-8165-5428-7 (hardcover)
ISBN-13: 978-0-8165-5427-0 (paperback)
ISBN-13: 978-0-8165-5429-4 (ebook)

Cover design by Leigh McDonald
Cover art from Jorgelina Cerritos's *13703. El misterio de las utopías*, photo by René Figueroa
Typeset by Sara Thaxton in 10/14 Warnock Pro with Irby WF and Adobe Jenson Pro

Publication of this book is made possible in part by the proceeds of a permanent endowment created with the assistance of a Challenge Grant from the National Endowment for the Humanities, a federal agency.

Library of Congress Cataloging-in-Publication Data
Names: Sarmiento, Ignacio, author.
Title: Specters of war : the battle of mourning in postconflict Central America / Ignacio Sarmiento.
Description: Tucson : University of Arizona Press, 2025. | Includes bibliographical references and index.
Identifiers: LCCN 2024017598 (print) | LCCN 2024017599 (ebook) | ISBN 9780816554287 (hardcover) | ISBN 9780816554270 (paperback) | ISBN 9780816554294 (epub)
Subjects: LCSH: Central American literature—21st century—History and criticism. | Grief in literature. | War and society—El Salvador. | War and society—Guatemala.
Classification: LCC PQ7471 .S27 2025 (print) | LCC PQ7471 (ebook) | DDC 863/.7093587281—dc23/eng/20241031
LC record available at https://lccn.loc.gov/2024017598
LC ebook record available at https://lccn.loc.gov/2024017599

Printed in the United States of America
♾ This paper meets the requirements of ANSI/NISO Z39.48-1992 (Permanence of Paper).

Para Javiera, por hacer que todo tenga sentido

CONTENTS

ILLUSTRATIONS

ACKNOWLEDGMENTS

The publication of *Specters of War* is a professional and personal milestone, and dozens of people have been directly or indirectly part of this lengthy process. I cannot thank my family enough for the unwavering support I have received from them since my early years. Thanks to my mother, Marina, for always looking for possibilities and solutions and never for difficulties and limitations. She supported me without questioning all the decisions that led me to this path, and I cannot thank her enough for being the best parent I could dream of. I also want to thank my brother, Pablo, my aunts, Chichi and Leda, and my cousin, Lia, for their unconditional love and support. I also want to thank my "nana" Leo for all those years she spent raising and taking care of me. Fundamental to my early years were my *nonnos*. In the middle of writing these lines, my *nonna* passed away. May you finally rest and join your beloved Armand somewhere. Thank you both for everything you did for me.

Even before conceiving the idea of this book, I dreamed about writing one. In large part, I owe the wish to become a scholar to my intelligent, encouraging, and hilarious friends from Universidad Diego Portales, with whom we foresaw and fantasized about an academic future over fifteen years ago. David Padilla, Sebastián Germain, Roberto Lazcano, Esteban Cancino, Mark Krarup, and Bastián Hoffmann, thank you for inspiring me to dream big. This is for you. *We* did it. *Los quiero.*

My professional career would not have been the same without the unconditional encouragement I received from mentors and professors in Chile when I was a young (and clueless) college student. There are many people who contributed, in one way or another, to me reaching my academic goals. I heartfully thank Luis G. de Mussy, Carolina Pizarro, Jaime "el maestro" González, raúl rodríguez freire, and Patricio Arriagada for believing in me and my work from the beginning. I must also thank Miguel Ortiz and Ricardo Pino for their guidance during my adolescence, perhaps my most difficult years. Your support and validation made a difference in me. Waldo Alvear also played a crucial role in my early years. He was able to instill discipline in a highly disoriented kid, and I remember him very fondly. In those years, I met people who are still very close to my heart. Thanks to María Ignacia Donoso, Lawrence Brauer, Cecil Honeyman, Gino Balocchi, Catalina Bosh, Tiare del Río, and Martín Serrano for over two decades of friendship.

Like most immigrants, I have learned the importance of building a family away from home. Over the last twelve years, I have encountered numerous wonderful people who have contributed positively to my life through their friendship and *cariño*. From my brief but intense time in Vancouver, I fondly remember my dear friends Josimar Yácuta, Doaa Magdy, Gabby Badica, Sara Bernard, Olga Martínez Díaz, and Bruno Nassi. Special mention belongs to my friend Javier Álvarez Jaimes for his generous hospitality when I arrived in Canada and his everlasting kindness and sense of humor. In New Orleans, my wife and I found the most fantastic, loving, and caring Chilean family we could ever dream of. Ingrid and Vicente became our "adoptive parents" and brought us into the heart of their beautiful family, where we met Vincent and Catalina. Thanks to them, we met our new "extended family," Nelly, Juan Carlos, and Lucero, whose energy and optimistic view of life will never be forgotten. In those "Chilean nights," we met our everlasting friends, Javiera and Craig Patterson, and later on their kids, Lucas and Emmie. I cannot express with words how important all of you were for us in those years and even more since we moved to Western New York. Your unconditional love means the world to us. Even though we left New Orleans over seven years ago, they still welcome us in their home with open arms every time we are in town, which is, frankly, very often.

This book is the result of a very long process that began in 2012 when I moved to Canada to pursue graduate studies thanks to the immense generosity of Miguel Valderrama, Alejandra Castillo, Óscar Cabezas, and Elixabete Ansa. You changed my life in unimaginable ways, and my gratitude will never match what you did for me. My research on the work of mourning in Central America was, in part, inspired by the groundbreaking work of Idelber Avelar. I had the privilege of working under his supervision at Tulane, where I got my PhD with a dissertation that drafted some of the ideas

I develop here more extensively and in new directions. Thanks, Idelber, for your unconditional support throughout the different stages of my career.

My years at Tulane were also some of the happiest, thanks to the stimulating community surrounding me. Special thanks to my former professors, Maureen Shea, always close to my heart, Fernando Rivera, Dale Shuger, John Charles, and Antonio Gómez. Integral to the happy years in New Orleans were the smart and amazing friends I made there: Fernando Salva, Natalia D'Allesandro, Aroldo Nery, Jimena Codina, Boris Martin, Camilo Malagón, Estefanía Flores, Allison White, Angela Rodríguez Mooney, Jesús Ruiz, Sarah Bruni, Daniela Riveros, and Ximena Venturini, among many others. I miss our time together.

The journey that led to the completion of this book took me to many places. I must mention the friends I made during my trips to El Salvador and Guatemala, notably Jessie Álvarez, who welcomed my wife and me into his home when he barely knew us, Eduardo Maciel and Theresa Denger, who contributed tremendously to my fieldwork in El Salvador, and the talented Denise Phé-Funchal, Elena Salamanca, and Alejandro Córdova. I must also mention the numerous "anonymous heroes" that I encountered over the years who facilitated in multiple ways the completion of this book. I have also been fortunate to find good and loyal friends among my academic colleagues in the *centroamericanismo*, such as Mauricio Espinoza, Miroslava Rosales, and María León, among many others. Special thanks to Andrew Bentley, Magdalena Perkowska, Sophie Esch, and Ricardo Roque Baldovinos for their friendship and for reading preliminary versions of some chapters of this book and providing great feedback and constructive criticism. Thanks to them, this book is much better than what I initially wrote.

I also want to thank my colleagues and students at SUNY Fredonia, where I worked for six years before joining the Department of Central American and Transborder Studies at California State University, Northridge, in the fall of 2024. I was immensely lucky to land in a department where I found people who genuinely supported and cared about my academic development. My years at Fredonia would not have been the same without my fantastic colleagues Juan de Urda, Brian Boisvert, and Carmen Rivera. David Kinkela played a significant role in the publication of this book. He carefully read my submission materials and provided his experienced feedback. Although they may not have contributed directly to this book, I want to thank some former students who made me believe I was doing something important by teaching them about Central America. *Mis agradecimientos*, in order of appearance, to Alexandra Wagner, Carl Aldinger, Britt Cranmer, Kristen Bacher, Lucas Paredes, Genesis Paises, Nate Reyes, Claudia Kaplan, and Elizabeth Smith.

Gabriel Corvest, a former student of mine at SUNY Fredonia, played an essential role in the completion of this book. She was my research assistant in the spring of 2022 and was the first filter my writing went through. I cannot thank her enough for all the energy and hard work she put into this project. In addition to proofreading and commenting on the first versions of each chapter, she also contributed tremendously to the tedious process of translating Spanish quotes.

This book is the result of years of research and fieldwork in El Salvador and Guatemala. Tulane University and the Tinker Foundation funded my first trips to Central America. My most recent fieldwork was funded by the United University Professions (UUP), SUNY Fredonia's School of Liberal Arts, and the Research Foundation for the State University of New York.

The process of publishing an academic book could be a painful one. I was fortunate to find in the University of Arizona Press an outstanding group of professionals who contributed to the successful publication of *Specters of War*. Special thanks to Kristen Buckles for her immediate interest in this project and for her encouraging support during this lengthy process.

In February 2013 Javiera Escobar said "yes" when I proposed in Vancouver on a cold and gray evening and jumped into the unknown with me. No one has sacrificed more than her for this project to happen, and I will never be able to repay her unconditional love and support. Thanks for looking after me, ensuring I was eating healthy and varied, and letting me avoid some obligations at home so I could finish my dissertation on time. Thanks for understanding me and believing in me. For believing so much in us and in a life together that you left Chile, and even worse, your sweet New Orleans, to follow me. I owe you everything. *Gracias por hacer que todo tenga sentido. Te amo.*

SPECTERS OF WAR

Introduction

The Battle of Mourning in Postwar Central America

> En este pueblo lo único que hay es muerte, por eso lo celebran tan bien.
>
> —ELENA SALAMANCA, "ÚLTIMO VIERNES"

> Miles son los muertos. Miles son los deudos. La reconciliación de quienes quedamos no es posible sin justicia.
>
> —*GUATEMALA, MEMORIA DEL SILENCIO*

> First of all, mourning. We will be speaking of nothing else.
>
> —JACQUES DERRIDA, *SPECTERS OF MARX*

Central America is a land of ghosts. The region is haunted by the violence and death inflicted for centuries—from the struggles between Mesoamerican Natives to the ruthlessness of the Spanish conquistadors, the creation of the liberal republics, the political violence of the twentieth century, and the proliferation of criminal activities in the early twenty-first century, to name a few. While grief is a somber constant in Central American history, *Specters of War* seeks to explore the most predominant, complex, and controversial cause of sorrow in contemporary El Salvador and Guatemala: the recent internal armed struggles. The Salvadoran civil war (1980–92) and the Guatemalan internal conflict (1960–96) are arguably the most traumatic events of the Central American twentieth century. Combined, over three hundred thousand people lost their lives or disappeared, and millions were victims of forced displacement and nefarious crimes.[1] Under every consideration, the Central American internal conflicts were tremendous experiences of loss that still haunt postwar societies and are fueled by the extensive impunity for the countless crimes and atrocities that occurred during them.

The last three decades have been a period of drastic transformations in the region. The end of the civil wars did not only sink the hopes of radical political changes but also witnessed the rapid integration of the region into the neoliberal regime of accumulation. Shortly after the signature of the peace accords, massive deportation from the United States prompted the establishment of transnational gang organizations that in a few years acquired control of vast territories in countries such as El Salvador, Guatemala, and Honduras (the so-called Northern Triangle), leading to a massive increase in criminal activities and fear in the population. On the other hand, postwar governments did not succeed in improving living and social conditions for their citizens despite the promises and hopes brought by the peace accords. The poverty index has seen little to no improvement, gender violence has persisted and has remained a daily practice, and access to health and education has remained scarce for a large part of the population. On top of all these difficulties, there is the profound pain caused by the internal armed conflicts and the despair of hundreds of thousands of people who await truth and justice, which have not come.

Specters of War offers an interpretation of postwar Central America by analyzing an interdisciplinary corpus. My goal is to provide a nuanced and diversified vision of contemporary societies that is in dialogue with the extensive scholarly work done over the last few decades by trying to skirt the limitations of academic disciplines. *Specters of War* proposes a study of postconflict El Salvador and Guatemala through the in-depth exploration of one particular issue: the work of mourning. Mourning practices and manifestations in postwar Central America are multiple and diverse. As Paul Connerton claims, "Mourning for historical catastrophes extends beyond the sphere of legal and literary texts. It is dispersed across a wide spectrum of genres: in newspapers, cinema, in video, in painting, in photographs, in songs, in plays and festivals."[2] Following this idea, *Specters of War* maps and analyzes different expressions of the work of mourning produced since the 1990s. In particular, this book studies fiction, theater, and sites of memory and reads them against and in relationship with each other to provide an overarching interpretation of the postwar era. It is important to establish that I will use the term *postwar* (*posguerra*) in this book in a twofold way. First, I use it as a historical period that begins in the 1990s after the signing of the peace accords in El Salvador and Guatemala. Second, and this is perhaps more relevant, I define it as an epistemological category that emerges after the traumatic and catastrophic events of the civil wars. The postwar era, as an epistemological fracture, means putting into question traditional notions and discourses of the political vocabulary such as the nation, the community, and the law. I use the concept here in both the historical and the epistemological sense.[3]

Against the common idea that victims have a monopoly on mourning, *Specters of War* argues that mourning is an action conducted by different groups in postwar societies and with different—and even radically opposed—objectives. In addition to the victims and their loved ones' public expressions of grief, this book also pays attention to the forms in which other communities—such as the national armies, the guerrillas, the elites, and the postwar administrations—have engaged in public mourning.

This book demonstrates that the work of mourning has been conducted heterogeneously in Central America since the 1990s. Some communities rapidly grieved their dead and moved forward without making further demands, such as many former guerrillas and soldiers. Some relatives and loved ones of civilian victims continue to express publicly their pain and demand the right to mourn and for justice to be served, as can be observed in the annual march organized by H.I.J.O.S. (Hijos por la Identidad y la Justicia contra el Olvido y el Silencio) in Guatemala and the thousands of families that gather around the Monumento a la Memoria y la Verdad in San Salvador. Others have managed to accept their reality and have left their pain behind. People not directly affected by the war also reflect on how the armed conflicts and their consequences influenced their lives. Nevertheless, even though these manifestations are multiple and diversified, they are not equivalent, whether in their motives or in their social and political strength. If all citizens had the right to mourn their dead publicly without pressure and without putting their lives in jeopardy, if they could demand truth and reparations for their loved ones even without receiving it, this book would not exist. In postwar Central America, mourning the dead is a privilege, not a right.

Specters of War posits that a battle over the work of mourning is underway in postconflict El Salvador and Guatemala. At the core of this struggle is the possibility of expressing and conducting the work of mourning in the public sphere. The main struggles in the battle of mourning concerns who can be cried for, the ways in which people grieve their loved ones, and who takes part or is invited to participate in the process. What is at stake in the battle of mourning is not a version of the events that occurred or the desire to bring to the fore some overlooked story but the possibility of an open, public act of grieving the dead. Also, the battle over the work of mourning not only means that there are multiple communities expressing their pain through different lenses and for diverse losses but also that some of these endeavors—particularly those committed to the victims of the civil wars—are confronted by forces that aim to interrupt or cancel them. Despite the outcome, what matters in this struggle is the work, the process through which mourning is articulated in the public arena.

The battle over mourning occurs in different forms and scenarios. In some cases, the struggle over mourning and the right to grieve translates physically into the landscape through the numerous memorials and anti-memorials that we can find in present-day Central America. In other cases, the debates regarding whether to mourn the dead of the war become an internal struggle that characters in many literary and theatrical works have to address. It could be easy to overlook the common pattern that emerges in many cultural works regarding the work of mourning when these are studied separately. Put together, they become the manifestation of a Stimmung, a "mourning mood" that permeates multiple layers of the Central American social fabric.

The Politics of Mourning

Mourning is a fascinating practice. It is one of the few actions common to almost every living community on Earth but, at the same time, one that offers a myriad of possibilities.[4] While today many can conceive of mourning as a relatively free and private practice that occurs in society, the fact is that mourning is (and has been) severely regulated. This has been borne out in various moments of history, like Solon's regulation on mourning and burial in sixth-century BC Athens, which sought to privatize grief at the dawn of Athens' democracy (the context in which Sophocles's *Antigone* takes place[5]), and the prohibition of *plañideras* (or *lloronas*) in Spain and Latin America during the eighteenth and nineteenth centuries.[6] Even in today's neoliberal world, mourning is heavily controlled. Many countries have specific laws regarding the time lapse between death and burial and the regulation (or lack thereof) of the more delicate matter of time to mourn. In the United States, for example, it is up to the employer's discretion to permit a leave of absence after the death of a loved one. Guatemala's Código del trabajo authorizes three days of paid leave only in case of the death of the spouse, parent, or child. Salvadoran workers only can take two days of leave with pay, but in that country's legislation, the death of anyone who lives in the household qualifies. In Candi Cann's words, "bereavement policies dictate not only how long one mourns, but also *who* should be mourned."[7]

Purposely or inadvertently, we all participate in the political uses of mourning. The politics of mourning is not a postmodern idea but rather a cofoundational element of modern republics. In his classic 1882 conference "What Is a Nation?," Ernest Renan claimed that mourning together was a crucial aspect in the creation of new national identities: "griefs are of more value than triumphs, for they impose duties, and require a common effort."[8] In the context of nation building and nation preserving, mourning can even take on a performative role, as Sara Ahmed suggests, by creating a new subject, "the nation," that can both mourn and be mourned.[9] Jean-Louis Déotte claims that modern citizens, especially in the nineteenth century, live under contradictory dictums regarding mourning. They are invited to actively take part in the common remembrance of the sacrifices and the death of others who gave their life so that they (or "we") can be here. But at the same time there is an imperative to "passively forget," especially the "historical errors."[10] Walter Benjamin makes a similar point in his "Theses on the Philosophy of History," where he argues that historicism always empathizes with the victorious, expressing an *acedia* (indolence of the heart) toward the defeated.[11] The work of mourning has been instrumental in the creation, reproduction, and preservation of the dominant discourses of national communities and national identities in many parts of the world, and Latin America was not an exception. Mourning the "founding fathers," ignoring the death of the "enemy" (for example, the Spanish soldiers and supporters of the crown), and honoring those who made the ultimate sacrifice in the name of the nation to obtain its desired freedom are common practices in everyday life. The ruling powers have politicized mourning in favor of the dominant narratives for centuries—all the while trying to hide its political character by naturalizing it—and they continue to do so.[12]

The second half of the twentieth century opened a new perspective on the political uses of mourning. This time, the goal was not to build the nation but rather to put it into question, especially after the waves of political violence and mass extermination that flooded most of the planet in the aftermath of World War II.[13] As a result, mourning has become a key concept in post-traumatic societies, often working alongside other terms such as the *poli-*

tics of memory and *transitional justice*. Since the late 1990s, the discussion over mourning, and especially the "politics of mourning," has expanded in various directions and to different contexts, from the Arlington Cemetery to the U.S.-Mexico border, from China to Romania, and of course to Latin America.[14]

Regardless of the numerous books and articles that address the issue of mourning in a wide variety of contexts, this topic has yet to be explored in-depth in postwar Central America. Given the uniqueness of the Central American experience—civil wars that ended through peace accords, truth commissions' reports that rapidly became dead letter, amnesty laws that precluded trials for crimes against humanity, the lack of official politics of memory, weak and insufficient reparation policies, and an extended disinterest toward people's pain within different sectors of the population—studying expressions of mourning in the region is a fundamental task.

While in the early twenty-first century mourning can be perceived by some as a discussion mostly within the field of psychoanalysis, the philosophical discussion about this phenomenon can be traced back to Aristotle's *Problems*—particularly to problem 30, where he suggests the connection between the "genius" and the melancholic character—to Fathers of Christianity and many thinkers in the Middle Ages and early European modernity.[15] I do not aim to summarize two millennia of debate, especially because others have already done a much better job than what I could do here.[16] As I will return to the theoretical discussion throughout the book, in what follows, I will elaborate on some central aspects regarding the work of mourning that are functional for my study of postwar Central America.

Mourning is traditionally understood, following Sigmund Freud, as a reaction to some kind of loss, be it that of a person, an ideal, or a place.[17] According to Jacques Derrida, we can also add that mourning is what follows trauma.[18] While I will not base my reading predominantly on Freud's understanding of mourning, it is important to stress some key elements in his definition for the sake of the discussion. Freud argues that when we experience any kind of loss, we should, eventually, withdraw all libido from said object—a difficult task, as he acknowledges—and substitute it with a new one. Once this process is completed, so is the work of mourning and the "ego becomes free and uninhibited again."[19] When someone fails to conduct this process, they can fall into "melancholia," a pathological state in which the subject fully identifies with the lost object and, as a result, the person's ego is represented as "worthless, incapable of any achievement and morally despicable."[20] Freud will return to this topic in *The Ego and the Id*, where he will argue that melancholia is far more complex and common than what he originally thought and that the "exact nature of this substitution is as yet unknown to us."[21] Freud's reflections on mourning became the pillar to one century of psychoanalytic thought, which expanded his ideas into multiple directions. In this context, Nicolas Abraham and Maria Torok's work is noteworthy. They determined that mourning can happen even inadvertently for the subjects, in the deepest parts of the subconscious, revealing itself only through certain linguistic patterns. This procedure, "which lies in replacing a word by the synonym of its alloseme" received the name of *cryptonymy*, the psychic crypt.[22] The psychoanalytical study of mourning led not only to a thorough discussion that still persists but also to the understanding of mourning as a predominantly private issue that falls frequently in the intimate and confidential domain of therapists, support groups, and any other person(s) involved in people's mental health.[23] The above occurs, in part, because of the Freudian understanding of melancholia as a "narcissistic disturbance," as Judith Butler notes.[24] Despite studying the work of mourning, this book does not engage extensively with psychoanalysis, which does not mean that it will entirely omit that field's vocabulary or reject its inheritance—as Derrida says, no one is free of the "Freudian impression." Instead, as expressed above, I am more interested in the politics of mourning and how expressions of grief take shape and interact in the public sphere.[25]

Specters of War is closer to Jacques Derrida's reflection, especially because of his focus on mourning those who died as a consequence of injustice, political violence, and any other form of oppression. Mourning, he posits,

> consists always in attempting to ontologize the remains, to make them present, in the first place by *identifying* the bodily remains and by *localizing* the dead [. . .]. Now, to know is to know *who* and *where*, to know whose body it really is and what place it occupies—for it must stay in its place. In a safe place [. . .]. Nothing could be worse, for the work of mourning, than confusion or doubt: one *has to know* who is buried where—and it is *necessary* (to know—to make certain) that, in what remains of him, *he remains there*. Let him stay there and move no more![26]

Two elements of this definition must be highlighted. First, Derrida frames mourning more broadly than the psychological process elaborated by Freud and defines it as a public act of truth seeking. Identifying, localizing, and fixing the dead in a certain space and time are key elements in this process. As David Appelbaum has noted, mourning means for Derrida, first of all, a "restitution by the gift of a name, a designation."[27] A second major aspect in this definition is the importance of mourning as work, as an *attempt* to conduct the actions described. For Derrida, the work of mourning is an ethical action that seeks to demand justice, one that reaches beyond the legal system (especially the obscure Central American ones) and its laws, which are always the result of violence.[28] Understanding mourning as a demand is crucial in Derrida's scheme, since the possibility of total restitution of the loss, or the complete overcoming of it, it is always an impossible task; it is "doomed to fail."[29] Therefore, "melancholy,"[30] instead of feared, is embraced as the only possibility accessible to us. Mourning is thus much more than a "transitional"—or *transience* as Freud will put it[31]—phase before the overcoming of trauma and the development of a memory of the traumatic past. It is a state, a disposition in itself that might accompany mourners for a duration of time that is likely to be long and indeterminate.

While Derrida does not propose ways of "successfully" completing the work of mourning—which is "in fact and by right interminable, without possible normality"[32]—he refers to the importance of exorcising the ghosts around us, which is perhaps the ultimate goal of mourning those whose lives were lost at the hands of violence. "To exorcise not in order to chase away the ghosts, but this time to grant them the right, if it means making them come back alive, as *revenants* who would no longer be *revenants*, but as other *arrivants* to whom a hospitable memory or promise must offer welcome—without certainty, ever, that they present themselves as such. Not in order to grant them the right in this sense but out of a concern for *justice*."[33] The main goal of the work of mourning for Derrida lies in the possibility of welcoming and embracing the specters—the eternal revenant, the becoming body—promising them our commitment to demand justice in their name. Mourning is never given; it is a task, a debt, and a responsibility the heirs willingly accept. Only once the heirs have accepted this responsibility toward the absent ones, and have therefore engaged in an impossible task of mourning, will they learn how to live with the ghosts, in their company, "[t]o live otherwise [. . .] not better, but more justly."[34] Following the above, *Specters of War* will pay close attention to expressions of mourning that emphasize a demand for truth and justice and also to manifestations of mourning that confront forces that aim to prevent the development of said work. This friction over the work of mourning will be the heart of this book.

A second major aspect *Specters of War* will discuss is the relationship between mourning and community. These two terms are closely connected in philosophical and theoretical discussions.[35] In particular, this book aims to trace the form in which people, with or without direct connections to victims of violence, establish what I will call a "community of mourners." I follow Judith Butler when they argue that grief, instead of being a private and depoliticized practice, "furnishes a sense of political community of a complex order, and it does this first of all by bringing to the fore the relational ties that have implications for theorizing fundamental dependency and ethical responsibility."[36] Thus, the act of grieving "is the thrall in which our relations with others hold us, in ways we cannot always recount or explain."[37] Even though it could be obvious to some that there is no grieving without a community that mourns someone's death, Butler sheds light on the "frame" that ultimately decides the value of a life, the power that distinguishes when a life is grievable. "Grievability," Butler asserts, is not a right but rather "a presupposition for the lives that matter."[38] Mourning, following this idea, always presupposes a battle between humanization and dehumanization—what Butler calls, using Levinas's words, seeing "the face" of the other.

Building on the above, I will use the term *community of mourners* in this book to refer not only to the sense of collectivity that emerges in certain contexts to mourn a dead person acknowledged as one of "them" but also to refer to a political community that, consciously or not, demands the restoration of humanity for those who have been victims of political repression and violent deaths. This is a community without proper names that can even exist in secrecy, in which anyone who feels a responsibility toward the dead can participate. This community belongs, in part, to what Butler calls the enigmatic dimension of mourning, "the experience of not knowing incited by losing what we cannot fully fathom."[39] We must not lose sight of this dimension. The work of mourning is not only an at times silent and oblique path but can also involve "a new experience of secrecy and a new structure of responsibility as an apportioning of mystery."[40] Mourning and taking part in a community of mourners can happen even inadvertently or without knowing why or how.

Mourning is a process in constant contradiction. Engaging in an ethical and inclusive work of mourning, especially in Central America, is to knowingly take on an impossible task. However, as *Specters of War* demonstrates, the promise of an undeniable failure is not an impediment for some mourners to assume their responsibility as heirs of those who lost their lives under the most inhumane circumstances. Contradictory as it may sound, to "succeed" in the work of mourning, as Derrida suggests in his eulogy to Louis Marin, it might well mean to *fail*, "to fail *well*."[41] This means assuming mourning not necessary as a liberating or redemptive action but as the compulsory one, the unavoidable one.[42]

Based on the above, perhaps it would be correct to consider postconflict Central America as a melancholic epoch, one in which people, or at least a portion of the population, are engaged in an unfinishable grieving process that they cannot or do not want to complete. But as the baroque did—at least the German and Spanish baroque, following Walter Benjamin (*The Origin of German Tragic Drama*) and Ángel Álvarez Solís (*La república de la melancolía*)—a melancholic period can bear witness to the decay of political and social institutions but can also be a time of great intellectual productivity. This is the case of postconflict Central America. The perpetual work of mourning, rather than paralyzing, is a force that moves artists, writers, intellectuals, and civil society to mourn even under the most oppressive circumstances.

Unconcealing the Battle over Mourning

How Central Americans deal with the recent traumatic past has been the subject of study of numerous scholars in multiple disciplines, including literary and cultural studies, historiography, sociology, and anthropology.[43] *Specters of War* draws from this extended scholarly work and aims to propose a new interpretation of postconflict societies: the battle of mourning. Understanding mourning as a site of struggle allows a better comprehension of postwar times because it enables us to observe the nuances and conflicting forces within the multiple acts of grief that occur in the public arena.

The work of mourning has often been investigated in great proximity to (and sometimes completely subsumed by) the labor of memory.[44] Against this trend, this book does not reflect on mourning as a necessary step or as a path to develop a historical or social memory of the civil wars. Instead, *Spec-*

ters of War seeks to think from and through the work of mourning, studying not only its manifestations but also its political and ethical possibilities. In other words, I use mourning as a *lens* that allows the interpretation of a diverse corpus regardless of their political or aesthetic objectives and context of production.

Although memory and mourning are close concepts, they are not synonyms or interchangeable terms. Like mourning, *memory* has been defined in multiple ways by numerous authors.[45] Memory scholars agree (for the most part) that memory is directly connected to the management of a past reality or event(s) in the present.[46] Keeping the absent presence of past events is not a natural action but rather the product of a relatively conscious and active process. "[M]emory is life," claims Pierre Nora.[47] Memory has an inherent reverse: forgetting.[48] The latter emphasizes memory's political force, especially in the aftermath of traumatic events, since it represents, in Andreas Huyssen's words, "the attempt to slow down information processing, to resist the dissolution of time in the synchronicity of the archive, to recover a mode of contemplation outside the universe of stimulation and fast-speed information."[49] We can also add that memory, especially in post-authoritarian contexts, is directly connected to the experience of truth telling (and it is there that we find its connection with *testimonio*[50]), resisting the erasure of the violent past and fighting for the visibility of the victims' narrative. As a consequence of aiming to establish the truth, narratives of memory are always subject to claims that they lack trustworthiness or veracity, as the well-known controversy regarding Rigoberta Menchú's testimonio sadly exemplifies.[51]

One major difference between mourning and memory is the existence (or at least the desire) of a coherent and fixed narrative. As Werner Mackenbach and Julie Marchio claim, "a public and collective memory is impossible without a tale, without a fixed narration that can be transmitted and communicated."[52] In the work of mourning, on the other hand, narratives (especially transparent and direct ones) are scarce. In Idelber Avelar's words, "Mourning and storytelling are, even at the most superficial level, coextensive with another: the accomplishment of mourning work presupposes above all the telling of a tale about the past."[53] Thus, while communities engaged in the labor of memory work tirelessly to produce a narrative about the past, the unfinished work of mourning creates a resistance to processing trauma and therefore to producing a tale about it. Resistance in this case does not mean absolute silence but instead the production and circulation of fragmentary and oblique narratives regarding the traumatic events of the civil wars.

What many of these narratives resist is the linguistic strategy that seeks to dilute and metaphorize the tragic experience from which they are born. Following Avelar, any confrontation of trauma "must labor on that resistance to all language and to all narrative."[54] The above means that we need to understand many contemporary narratives as narratives of mourning, and that we must therefore read them as part of an ongoing individual and/or collective grieving process. I propose that the lack of a coherent and organized narrative regarding the war in many of the sources I will analyze here might be related to an unfinished work of mourning that hampers, consciously or not, a direct and transparent approach to the harrowing events of the internal armed conflicts. The materials studied here—with the exception of some memorials and museums—do not seek to preserve a form of memory from oblivion or try to convince us about something. More humbly, we could say, they just want to express their ongoing pain—one that is often overlooked—and demand their right to mourn.[55]

The hypothesis of the "battle of mourning" dialogues with one of the predominant propositions in postwar Central America, the "battle over memory." Elizabeth Jelin claims that memories become objects of dispute in post-authoritarian contexts, which are often mediated and framed by relationships of power. In the battle over memory, following Jelin, "memory entrepreneurs" seek social recognition and legitimization of their narrative of the past, fighting to keep their narrative visible and politically active.[56] Many scholars have convincingly argued about the existence of a battle over memory in postwar Central America. Werner Mackenbach, for example, claims that the struggle over memory in the isthmus is not restricted to certain forms or contexts and that these struggles can be observed in a variety of narratives, including but not limited to literature, memoirs, testimonios, and truth commissions' reports.[57] A common trend among memory studies scholars consists in grouping and classifying the narratives, attitudes, and perspectives regarding the traumatic past.[58] Central Americanist scholars often follow a similar method. The approach of academic and social activist Ralph Sprenkels is noteworthy, as he identifies five "heuristic proposals" that administer memory in postwar societies. These positions are (1) imposed oblivion, (2) war among brothers, (3) revolution, (4) anticommunism, and (5) disillusionment. All of them, Sprenkels posits, "coexist and, on occasions, compete for the postwar Central

American public space."[59] In a similar fashion but within a national frame, Eric Ching argues that there are at least four "memory communities" in postconflict El Salvador: (1) the civilian elites, (2) the military officers, (3) the guerrilla commandants, and (4) the rank-and-file actors. These "memory communities," like Sprenkels's "heuristic proposals," are in a constant struggle for visibility and circulation, wishing to ultimately become the most accepted narrative of the past.[60]

The battle over memory in postwar Central America is a reality, and I do not aim to deny its existence or its significance. *Specters of War*, however, takes a different approach and claims that on a more subterranean level there is also a struggle over the right to mourn. In the battle over mourning, the expressions of sorrow can hardly be grouped. It is, we could say, more rhizomatic, unstable, unpredictable. As this book will demonstrate, the struggles over mourning can even take place within one individual or family, revealing that mourning is an ongoing conflict even at the most intimate level. While there can be some commonalities among the manifestations of mourning (as I will explore in chap. 1), they do not embody a unified, coherent tale of the past and therefore do not integrate a major narrative or project. The above is indeed detrimental for participants, especially for those engaged in mourning the civilian victims of the war. Nevertheless, the participants in the battle of mourning do not aim to impose their grief over others. Some of them even assume defeat as the anticipated outcome. Yet this does not prevent them from continuing to mourn actively. Many actors in the battle of mourning only seek a very humble objective: to grieve their dead.

In the first two decades of the twenty-first century, some literary critics have reflected on the work of mourning in postwar Central America. Arturo Arias, Beatriz Cortez, and Ricardo Roque Baldovinos, to name a few, agree that the work of mourning is a pending task in postwar societies.[61] However, this ongoing process is often seen and portrayed in a negative light, as if mourning was something we should rapidly overcome in order to get back on track. Arturo Arias, for example, argues that the work of mourning in postwar fiction is a failed task. For him, the absence of direct references to the internal conflicts and their consequences in postwar literature means "an ethical refusal to assimilate the past, assimilate the dead, assimilate political defeat within a coherent and explanatory historical narrative."[62] Following this thread, Arias claims that postconflict fiction makes the dead of the war vanish from its pages, triggering a "second disappearance" by questioning their sacrifice, resulting in a negation of "their place in history, in public memory, and in memorialization through mourning."[63] Beatriz Cortez also claims that the work of mourning is an unfinished task, although she develops a different argument. Cortez posits that the work of mourning is a "postponed" process in Central America, among other things, because of the lack of politics of memory that contribute to the preservation of the dead in social memory (e.g., through sites of memory). Cortez's conclusion is thought provoking: "Perhaps the work of mourning that we have not experienced goes way beyond the recent massacres and the recent crimes against humanity. Perhaps it can be traced back to the critical moment of the formation of Central American identity [. . . , one] that negated since then the atrocities suffered by the Indigenous peoples. Perhaps mourning is already two hundred years delayed and still awaits its inauguration."[64] Although the literary corpus I will study here is more recent than the one analyzed by Arias and Cortez, I agree with them about the unfinished condition of the work of mourning in many of these works. However, unlike Arias, I read this prolonged process not as the result of a lack of interest but as a consequence of the political forces that aim to either prevent the work of mourning from happening or that seek to accelerate and close the grieving process as soon as possible to serve their political interests. I claim that an ethical imperative to mourn is expressed in numerous works of literature in the postwar period even if that means avoiding any references to the internal conflicts. Unlike Cortez, I do believe that the work of mourning was inaugurated a long time ago. Nevertheless, the distance between initiated and accomplished is immeasurable, if not unsurmountable. The work of mourning has been indeed a lengthy (and perhaps never-ending) process. However, as Butler reminds us, mourning "may be understood as the slow process by which we develop a point of identification with suffering itself."[65] As *Specters of War* will demonstrate, public expressions of grief are a predominant form of political engagement and of demanding justice.

In *Más allá del duelo*, Yansi Pérez claims that mourning has been "the privileged conceptual tool" to study issues of memory in postwar Central America.[66] However, Pérez does not cite any example of this alleged predominant lens—as of March 2024, no book has been published on this issue, and only a handful of articles address it in depth—and her claim is based in the common overlapping and conflation between mourning and memory I discussed above.[67] Most importantly, ignoring the multiple expressions of mourning based on their alleged "lack of novelty" is not a persuasive argument. Pérez's reading is nonetheless compelling—and I will return to it in chapter 3—because it seeks to offer new concepts to think about contemporary cultural works, such as abjection, or a "humorous" understanding of mourning.[68]

Specters of War adds to existing scholarship by proposing an interwoven reading of multiple sources that have not yet been studied interconnectedly in depth. Also, by understanding mourning as a site of struggle, this book seeks to study not only how people grieve but also the visible and invisible forces that aim to prevent or defer the mourning process of others. In this battle, positions are not always well defined, exceeding and even contradicting, at times, the creators' and authors' declared intentions. To explore and map these multiple attitudes toward the work of mourning, I have chosen a corpus that allows me to present some of the various faces of the grieving process in postwar Central America. The opposing views about who can be mourned and how they can be mourned are evident when different memorials and museums built since the late 1990s are contrasted, as I examine in the opening chapter. I have decided to dedicate the rest of the book to focus on works that express a demand for justice or a commitment to facilitate the mourning process of others—although they often have to confront forces that aim to interrupt the developing of said work. This ethical position is present in the dramaturgy of Jorgelina Cerritos and in the literary works of Claudia Hernández, Mónica Albizúrez, and Eduardo Halfon, which I study in chapters 2, 3, 4, and 5, respectively. These sources demonstrate that grieving the dead and participating in an active work of mourning is far from being a passive action and becomes instead a form of struggle.

Mourning as Resistance

While the primary and immediate objective of the struggle over the work of mourning is, predominantly, grieving the dead and the losses of the recent civil wars, most of the sources studied here (with the exception of some memorials and museums) engage, in one way or another, with the social, economic, and political transformations introduced in the region in the aftermath of the peace accords. Scholars from different disciplines have proven that the end of the armed conflicts facilitated the reconcentration of economic and political power in local elites' hands thanks to neoliberal reforms.

Ricardo Roque Baldovinos phrases this idea very well when discussing the cliché that the civil war in El Salvador concluded without winners or losers: "The main winner was (not the army, of course) but the capital."[69] Unsurprisingly, the economic elites have used their regained power to take an active role in the denegation of justice.[70] Following Sergio Villalobos-Ruminott, the aftermath of the Central American civil wars meant a symbolic "update" of both the social contract and the promises of the new republics in the early nineteenth century. But the context is now radically different, "where we experiment an exhaustion of state sovereignty, and, therefore, its transnational and corporative transmutation."[71] In this context, I understand the ongoing work of mourning embodied in some of the materials studied here as a disruptive force that seeks to suspend (or at least slow down) the neoliberal machine that forces citizens to rapidly forget the hundreds of thousands of people who died during the internal conflicts. Against the forced incorporation of citizens' lives into the never-ending productivity discourses of the neoliberal world, some of the materials studied here use the unfinished work of mourning as a creative pause. As Slavoj Žižek claims, sometimes the "only truly 'practical' thing to do is to resist the temptation to engage immediately and 'wait and see' by means of a patient, critical analysis."[72]

Many of the participants in the battle of mourning accept the impossibility of any substitution, restitution, or metaphor that could enable them to overcome their loss. While that means many communities live in perpetual pain, I do not read this situation as a destructive process but rather as a space of political and ethical production. Following Idelber Avelar, the apparent "paralysis of mourning" may work as "an affirmative practice with clear political consequences."[73] In this regard, the promise to remain faithful to the dead, to mourn and welcome them, is not, as Derrida stresses, "to remain 'spiritual' or 'abstract,' but to produce events, new effective forms of action, practice, organization."[74] The resistance to concluding the grieving process can become a space of political participation through the creation of communities of mourning that embrace and welcome the dead, resisting their codification, commoditization, and potential oblivion in the logic of the official postwar narratives that aim to close any grieving process with the fast speed of the neoliberal commodities market.[75] The specters of the civil wars are a threat to the status quo imposed in postwar El Salvador and Guatemala.

In Central American societies, mourning is always at risk of being coopted by the ruling powers. As I will further elaborate on in chapter 1, this is, in part, what happened for decades in El Salvador, where the new political duopoly that emerged after the signing of the peace (the Frente Farabundo Martí para la Liberación Nacional [FMLN] and Alianza Republicana Nacionalista [ARENA] parties) sought to limit expressions of grief only to the former groups in combat as a way to promote "national reconciliation." Nonetheless, as Marc Nichanian reminds us, "Political reconciliation is always a manipulation of mourning."[76] In this context, the goal for many writers, creators, and communities in general is developing a work of mourning that demands justice and creates a sense of collectivity and ethical responsibility that becomes inapprehensible for the mainstream political powers. In other words, the challenge is to imagine and conduct a mourning process that can escape the sacrificial logic that gave rise to the Central American republics in the early nineteenth century, which has also been at the core of the reconciliation and impunity narratives in postwar times. Embracing an unfinished work of mourning means, in some cases, imagining and claiming for another form of politics and democracy beyond the violence, limitations, and exclusions imposed by the political vocabulary of the liberal republics over two centuries ago.

Despite dealing with spectrality, mourning, and death, this is a book about the living. The specters of the war are only a concern for those of us who still walk the Earth. There is no spectrality without a living individual or community that perceives their presence, that feels "watched, observed, surveyed" by them.[77] Only the living can bury and grieve the dead, build a community of mourners that engages in an ongoing demand for justice and truth, and accept to live in an asymmetrical relationship with the specters. The spectral oath can only be accepted by us.[78]

The Organization of This Book

Specters of War tries to overcome some of the difficulties that scholars from multiple disciplines face when approaching postwar Central America. On the one hand, historians and social scientists require archives, whether physical records (statistics, official cables, published memoirs and testimonies, newspapers, etc.) or the voices of witnesses (oral histories, ethnographies, etc.). If a voice cannot be found, they cannot just invent it (or at least they should not do so). Erik Ching reflects on this point in the conclusion of *Stories of Civil War in El Salvador*, clarifying that to the date of his research, many communities were not represented in written memoirs or testimonies, including but not limited to nonconservative elites, conservative priests who opposed the liberation theology, the U.S. military or diplomats, and more importantly, the thousands of people who remained politically neutral or did not support the guerrilla.[79] Literary and cultural studies scholars are no less limited by their sources, even though their interpretative range is wider. Writers, and artists in general, can produce works on their topic of preference and choose these works' point of view. Still, many literary scholars have accused postwar fiction of avoiding the topic of the civil wars and their consequences. As Beatriz Cortez rightfully claims, even in the most "committed" postwar literature, the leading characters and narrators are easily identified with ladino—and, too often, privileged—voices.[80]

Specters of War aims to create bridges among theories, methodologies, and sources, with the aim of providing a more complex and far-reaching picture of postconflict Central America. In this regard, *Specters of War* seeks to fill some of the voids identified by previous scholarship. For example, postwar fiction does present many examples of narrators who, despite belonging to the elite, critically approach the role of the army and the governments during the civil wars (elements that Ching did not find in written memoirs). On the other hand, some places of memory embody the voice of the victims and demand justice, which many literary works fail to do—or do it more obliquely. Today, theater represents one of the most direct and confrontational approaches to civil war violence and the work of mourning produced in the arts. By themselves, these manifestations can be praised or criticized. However, when we put them together and study them side by side, we observe new perspectives and nuances, and the battle over mourning rises in front of our eyes.

Mostly because of methodological and theoretical issues, history and social sciences publications that study postwar Central America often privilege a local or national perspective on this matter.[81] Literary and cultural criticism, on the other hand, has favored a panoramic approach to the isthmus.[82] *Specters of War* proposes an intermediate approach. Since I build an argument grounded on a historical reality—the common experience of the internal conflicts in El Salvador and Guatemala—I do not aim to propose an interpretation that could also be valid for other contexts that did not have the same experience (like Costa Rica or Honduras). This does not mean that there is no battle over mourning in other contexts within or outside Central

America. On a smaller scale, *Specters of War* follows the path of Ana Patricia Rodríguez's *Dividing the Isthmus* in its goal of reading "selected texts across national divides, drawing connections between them while producing other transisthmian and transnational cultural and literary spaces."[83] Thus, while acknowledging their historical differences and experiences, *Specters of War* analyzes Salvadoran and Guatemalan societies and cultural productions through a common hypothesis that I believe to be valid for both cases.

For methodological reasons I have restricted my study to sources produced in the span of just over three decades, from the 1990s to the early 2020s. This does not mean that the book's argument is less valid for the years preceding this period–I firmly believe that the work of mourning, as a "mood," is manifest before the official end of the conflicts—but I have focused on the period that has produced the most expressions of sorrow.[84] Also, this book is organized around the sources it discusses. This will allow me to study each of the materials in its own dimension and expectations, avoiding disciplinary difficulties and contradictions. Because of this, I have decided to address the discussion within certain disciplines more in-depth in the first pages of specific chapters (particularly in chapters 1–3).

Specters of War opens with "Sites of Memory, Sites of Mourning: Memorialization in Postconflict Central America." This chapter is the result of fieldwork conducted in El Salvador and Guatemala between 2015 and 2023. I spent part of the summers of 2015, 2017, and 2019 in El Salvador, traveling between San Salvador, Morazán, La Libertad, and Chalatenango. In the summers of 2017 and 2019, I also conducted fieldwork in Guatemala City and La Antigua. In the spring of 2023, I made my last field trip to El Salvador and Guatemala before submitting the final version of this book for review. During these trips, I visited numerous memorials, museums, and sites of memory that engage with the internal conflicts, and this chapter offers a comparative analysis of some of the most representative ones. The chapter is divided into three parts. First, it offers a theoretical and historical discussion of the links between mourning and memorialization, highlighting their major roles and challenges in postwar Central America. Then, the chapter provides a panoramic gaze into some of the most relevant sites of memory in Guatemala City, stressing the great contributions of Casa de la Memoria Kaji Tulam and the Archivo Histórico de la Policía Nacional to the works of mourning and memory. The central part of the chapter proposes a reflection on some of the most important sites of memory, museums, and memorials that deal with the civil war in postconflict El Salvador, particularly the El Mozote memorial, the Museo de la Revolución, the Monumento a la Memoria y la Verdad, the Museo de Historia Militar, the Proyecto de Paz y Reconciliación, and the Parque Escultórico a la Reconciliación. The chapter's ultimate goal is to demonstrate that the battle over the work of mourning is not limited to intimate expressions of grief but that it also translates physically into the memorialization projects that have been developed in both countries since the 1990s. This chapter also argues that, with considerable nuances in form, power, and visibility, various communities in postwar Central America have conducted a public work of mourning over the last three decades. This includes parties that have made significant efforts to impede the mourning of others, such as the national armies, the postwar governments, and even the guerrillas. All of them mourn. But the difference is in *how* they do it and *who* is invited to participate in the process.

Chapter two, "Staging Mourning in Postwar El Salvador: Jorgelina Cerritos's *Ensayos sobre la memoria*," pays attention to the contribution of theater and performance to the work of mourning in postwar societies. The chapter's main focus is the analysis of Jorgelina Cerritos's trilogy *Ensayos sobre la memoria* (2010–17). I argue that these plays embody some of the main conflicts within the battle over mourning. For example, we observe in them a clash between characters who wish to mourn and those who seek to interrupt the grieving process. On some occasions, the struggle regarding whether to mourn even takes place within one character, demonstrating that the battle of mourning does not necessarily occur externally but also internally. Bearing in mind the declared aim of these plays to contribute to the historical memory in postwar El Salvador and to the building of a new national identity, I consider that these plays become a failed project because the ongoing and endless work of mourning prevents them from achieving their goal of producing a narrative about the war and its consequences. Despite that, the plays portray an encouraging scenario in which the characters, and more importantly the audience, are invited to engage in a public and communal grieving process.

Specters of War's last three chapters study postwar fiction. While grief is a predominant topic in recent literature, I have decided to focus on three authors who offer a novel approach to it and whose fiction contributes to the understanding and visibility of the battle over mourning. Chapter 3, "What to Do with the Dead? The Specters of War in Claudia Hernández's

De fronteras," provides a close reading of Hernández's *De fronteras* (2007), one of the richest and more complex explorations of the work of mourning in postwar literature. I argue that Hernández's book engages with the work of mourning from multiple positions, portraying different mourning figures and their struggles to conduct their grieving process. Through the analysis of corpses and missing limbs in the stories, Hernández's characters engage in a constant struggle to mourn others within their possibilities and moved by an ethical drive. Against them there is often a powerful but silent force that aims to prevent that mourning from happening, which only reveals itself toward the end of the book.

Chapter 4, "*Somos la masa silenciosa*: Archival Work and the Work of Mourning in Mónica Albizúrez's *Ita*," draws connections between the 2005 finding of the National Police Archive and the work of mourning in postwar Guatemala through the reading of Albizúrez's debut novel *Ita* (2018). With a profound historical component, *Ita* invites us to consider the deep impact of the Guatemalan internal conflict from the point of view of the groups that did not engage directly in the armed conflict but were supporters of the army, what the novel calls "la masa silenciosa." While approaching the violence of the civil war and the National Police Archive from the point of view of an upper-class family could seem initially problematic, I read this novel as an effort not to avoid but to focus on the country's inequalities and the atrocities of the armed conflict. Through this process, I propose, *Ita* makes a claim for a national communion through grief.

Specters of War closes with "Eduardo Halfon: A Global Struggle for Mourning." This chapter offers a reading of Eduardo Halfon's oeuvre and proposes that the work of mourning lies at the core of it. In the first section, the focus is on the symbolic loss of the father and how his spectral presence connects with the struggles over the work of mourning. The second section studies how the Shoah and the Guatemalan internal conflict are portrayed in Halfon's fiction. While Halfon himself is not a direct victim of these atrocities and he never poses as such, his fiction feeds from them through his family history and his infancy in Guatemala. As a result, Halfon builds a narrative of mourning that transcends generations and travels across the oceans, ultimately developing a literature that lives in perpetual mourning.

Finally, it is important to make a note about the translations. I have decided to preserve most of the direct quotes from the literary and dramatic texts I analyze in this book in Spanish. The goal is to avoid any potential discussion about the translation and focus on the actual citations. An English translation of each quote will be found in the corresponding endnote. On the other hand, I have translated most quotes from academic, theoretical, and journalist texts (including some paratexts) into English to smooth the book's readability. Unless otherwise noted, all translations are mine, with Gabriel Corvest's assistance.

* * *

Jacques Derrida claimed that "one cannot hold a discourse *on* the 'work of mourning' without taking part in it,"[85] and I believe he was right. This book, and all the years it took me to complete it, have been part of a personal mourning process. Albeit I have not been a direct victim of any act of state terrorism, mourning and responsibility, as Derrida reminds us, exist beyond proper names and appropriation. We can accept the responsibility toward the injustice of violent death, torture, and disappearance even when, as we say in Spanish, *ese muerto no es mío* (that dead one is not mine). I believe, along with many others whose work I discuss in this book, that all dead ones are ours. And it is our responsibility to accept them, welcome them, and mourn them.

CHAPTER 1

Sites of Memory, Sites of Mourning

Memorialization in Postconflict Central America

This chapter explores memorialization projects in postwar El Salvador and Guatemala. This topic is particularly relevant because, unlike cultural productions, such as the theater and fiction that will be studied in the following chapters, memorials, sites of memory, and museums are inscribed in the public landscape and as a result often enjoy larger visibility. Thus, independently of citizens' religious beliefs and cultural, political, economic, or social capital, they often interact with different forms of memorialization in their daily lives even without noticing it. Studying processes of memorialization is relevant because despite the common assumption among academics and practitioners that memorialization is anything but neutral or apolitical, these sites are considered by many to be a reliable source of truthful information.[1]

Memorialization in postwar El Salvador and Guatemala has been a controversial issue since the signing of the peace accords. The building (and also the absence) of memorials, museums, and sites of memory results from the struggle between power factions vying for visibility and legitimacy in postwar societies. In their study of postwar Guatemala, Steinberg and Taylor claim that landmarks and memorials can tell the observer not only who won the discursive battle of the internal armed conflict but also about the "continuing struggle for power."[2] Thus, what is at stake in the memorialization battle is not only who or what is memorialized but also who has the authority to memorialize.

Despite the overt recommendations made by the truth commissions, as of 2023 none of these countries has an official state-sponsored memory museum or memorial, as we find in other Latin American countries such as Chile and Argentina. Also, very little has been done overall to memorialize and honor the victims of the armed conflicts with the exception of some questionable or irrelevant projects that are discussed in the following pages. While someone not familiarized with Central America may be surprised at the almost nonexistent politics of memory, the truth is that this absence is well aligned with the general disinterest expressed by almost all postwar administrations. For example, human rights violations were systematically denied by postwar governments in El Salvador and Guatemala for over one decade after the end of the wars. Only in 2009, thirteen years after the signing of the peace accords, did Guatemalan president Álvaro Colom apologize concretely in the name of the state for the crimes committed during the internal conflict. (Previously, in 1998, President Álvaro Arzú offered a vague apology on the second anniversary of the peace accords, where he stated "yo pido perdón al pueblo de Guatemala por nuestras acciones u omisiones, por lo que hicimos o dejamos de hacer." In 2005, Vice President Eduardo Stein apologized only to the relatives and victims of the 1982 massacre of Plan de Sánchez, during Óscar Berger's presidency, following the sentence of the Inter-American Court of Human Rights. The absence of the president in such an important event cannot go unnoticed.)[3] In 2011, Colom also apologized specifically to the victims of the massacre of Dos Erres, which took place in December 1982. Nevertheless, asking forgiveness in the name of the state did not introduce any lasting transformation either in terms of furthering transitional justice or in public opinion.

Starting in 2009 a handful of trials against high-ranking officials took place in Guatemala, but only a small number of them were convicted, and in only a few cases did the sentences involve reparation to the victims.[4] The most noticeable case is arguably the trial of General Efraín Ríos Montt, Guatemalan dictator from March 1982 to August 1983, accused of genocide. During Ríos Montt's administration, the army conducted the most ruthless slaughtering of the civilian population, especially targeting Indigenous communities.[5] In 2013 Ríos Montt went to trial for several massacres that had occurred in the Ixil region.[6] Guatemala's Supreme Court found Ríos Montt guilty, acknowledging the existence of a genocide against the Maya population during his administration, and sentenced him to eighty years in prison.

Nevertheless, the trial was annulled a few days later for alleged flaws in the process, and Ríos Montt only remained under house arrest. New attempts to bring him to justice were made in 2015 and 2017, but none of them succeeded. Ultimately, Ríos Montt died, at age ninety-one, in 2018.[7] Large segments of Guatemalan society seem unperturbed by all this. After the death of approximately two hundred thousand people and the juridical confirmation of the genocide against the Indigenous population, several powerful voices (including former presidents and presidential candidates) still claim that *no hubo genocidio* (there was no genocide) during the internal conflict.[8]

The situation in El Salvador is no less disheartening. Only in 2010, eighteen years after the signing of the peace accords, President Mauricio Funes, the first FMLN president since the end of the war, asked for forgiveness in the name of the state for the crimes committed by the army during the internal conflict. Nevertheless, he specified that apologizing for war crimes did not mean seeking justice for the victims.[9] Although transitional justice in Guatemala is scarce, there is more progress than in El Salvador, where the amnesty law remained in effect until 2016, but as of 2023 no case has been successfully prosecuted. The only person condemned for human rights violations during the Salvadoran civil war is former vice president of public security, Colonel Inocente Montano Morales, who stood trial in Spain, not in El Salvador, for the murdering of six Jesuit priests and two women in the Central American University in November 1989. He was sentenced to 133 years in prison in 2020.[10]

The victims of the Central American civil wars are barely acknowledged by postwar administrations. Therefore, a politics of memory and projects of memorialization seem, unfortunately, a far-fetched idea even three decades after the end of the armed conflicts. The following pages will explore how some locations in postconflict Central America play an active role in the rich and complex web of memorialization and how they participate in the battle of mourning.

The tasks of grieving, humanizing, honoring, and remembering the dead have primarily been carried out by civil society organizations. In Diane M. Nelson's words, this includes "DIY (do-it-yourself) projects—of memorials, reports, and other forms of commemoration."[11] It would be incorrect, however, to say that the political parties, the former guerrillas, and the national armies do not mourn their dead. They do. But they have little interest in building a far-reaching community that can come together and grieve the dead, privileging instead a self-centered narrative that often seeks to justify the biggest atrocities. While I will consider several aspects in the analysis of these sites—such as their rhetoric, aesthetics, and historicity—my focus will be on how these places undertake (or avoid) the task of mourning the civil war's losses. This chapter opens with theoretical and historical considerations regarding the construction of museums and memorials and their inherent connection to the work of mourning. The second part offers an overview of memorialization in postwar Guatemala, particularly in Guatemala City. The third and final section, which is also the lengthiest, provides an in-depth study of six sites of memory in present-day El Salvador.

Memorialization: A Historical and Theoretical Approach

Memorialization is everywhere. In streets, in plazas, in high schools, in universities, in public buildings. Almost everywhere we go, we encounter some form of memorialization. Most of the public schools are named after someone; many libraries (especially in the United States) are "memorial libraries"; and almost all street names commemorate a person or an event (even in cities that use a numeric system, like Guatemala City, some major avenues have parallel memorial names). In the first decades of the twenty-first century, memorialization has become a polemic topic. Many people around the world are voicing their opinions about the processes of historic memorialization that have contributed to shaping modern societies worldwide. This has meant, in some context, the destruction or resignification of certain monuments and sites, like the removal of former Confederate generals' statues, the vandalization of statues of Columbus in many parts of the American continent, and the renaming of Plaza Baquedano to "Plaza de la Dignidad" during the 2019 protests in Chile.[12] Despite their undeniable yet generally overlooked presence in our daily life, memorialization practices have significantly mutated over time.

The memorialization process is historically linked to the relationship between memory—either what, following Maurice Halbwachs, we could call "collective" or "social" memory—and death. Accordingly, sites of memory are inevitably sites of mourning, as the title of Jay Winter's book, *Sites of Memory, Sites of Mourning,* suggestively claims. In his study of memory in early modern Europe, Peter Sherlock makes clear that the struggle over memory existed much before the atrocities of the twentieth century. He argues that in the wake of the Protestant reform in the sixteenth and seventeenth centuries, Western Europe experienced a "revolution" in memory. According to Sherlock, one of the most accepted meanings of *memoria* in early modern Europe "revolved around the relationship between the living and the dead."[13] During this epoch, Sherlock continues, Europe was "replete with deliberately created memories and invented commemorations, designed as responses to the Reformation with its attendant loss of an established narrative for the past and to the beginnings of the disenchantment of the world."[14]

In the late eighteenth and early nineteenth century, the birth of new republics in Western Europe provoked a radical shift in memorialization practices. In this new era, some states established an official policy toward memory, memorialization, and the use of public space. In his seminal work on sites of memory, *Les lieux de mémoire*, Pierre Nora posits that during this period, history (and the professionalization of historiography), memory, and the nation had a natural symbiosis at different levels, including scientific, pedagogic, practical, and theoretical connections.[15] In other words, the birth of the new republics and nations (discursively homogenous with a shared past and a common culture) also meant establishing a specific memory common to everybody who belonged (or longed to belong) in the nascent community. When memory becomes a crucial aspect for building the nation-state, memorialization allows the connection between abstract ideas of memory and history with soil. Modern forms of memorialization did not elude its relationship with the dead. In his study of memorialization practices in the United States, David Jacobson comments that memorialization is "the 'dead hand' of the past" that organizes public space and determines "who 'belongs' to the nation and on what terms."[16] Monuments, Jacobson argues, delineate "the space, as well as the tie to the land, through which citizens individually would understand the bounds of (their) nationhood. They captured the 'spirit' of the nation."[17]

In many respects, memorialization practices in the Latin American republics of the nineteenth century were not much different, at least in spirit, from their counterparts in Europe and the United States. During the first half of the nineteenth century, some Latin American governments began the construction of state-owned institutions dedicated to spreading scientific and historical knowledge to the public. Following the European trend, some states invested in scientific development that led to the creation of museums of natural history. This, according to Lopes and Murriello, was another form of investment in the creation of the nation.[18] Examples of the above are the Museo Nacional de México (1825), which replaced the Gabinete de curiosidades established in the last decades of the colonial administration,[19] and the Museo Nacional de Historia Natural (1830) founded in Chile by French naturalist Claudio Gay.[20] This process took place a few decades later in Central America, when some isthmian countries eventually paid attention to the role of museums in the building of a national identity. Examples of this are the Museo de Historia Natural (1883) in El Salvador (today Museo Nacional de Antropología Dr. David J. Guzmán),[21] and the Museo Nacional founded in Costa Rica in 1887.[22]

Xavier Cuenin claims that Central America experienced a boom in memorialization beginning in the 1880s, under the so-called liberal regimes, when different governments began to designate heroes and national celebrations that supported the invention of the Central American *patrias*.[23] A good example of this is the adoption of Francisco Morazán, former president of the Federal Republic of Central America and Central American Unionist leader, as a national figure in different isthmian countries. In 1882, during the fortieth anniversary of his death, Honduran president Marco Aurelio Soto ordered the building of a statue of Morazán and the busts of other *padres de la patria*, including José Cecilio del Valle, José Trinidad Cabañas, and José Trinidad Reyes. The same year, in El Salvador, President Rafael Zaldívar also ordered the building of a statue to honor Morazán and placed it in the Francisco Morazán Square in downtown San Salvador.[24] I will not discuss here the implications of embracing Morazán despite the failure of the Unionist cause. For this book's purposes, it is important to stress that many Central American governments agreed that Francisco Morazán was a figure who deserved to be publicly grieved and remembered not only because of his contribution to the Unionist cause, which ultimately failed, but because mourning him was another form of strengthening the rising national identities.[25] The above reaffirms the idea that during the first century of independent life, memorialization was primarily an official and state-sponsored praxis, becoming a "self-aggrandizing locus for national memory."[26] Although today we know very well that the long-term process of official memorialization led to the establishment of silence and oblivion regarding certain communities and groups—such as women, Native populations, and people of African descent—its true concealment may not be fully revealed yet.

Memorialization practices in Europe and the Americas began to be challenged in the second half of the twentieth century when the systemic extermination of human beings became a standard state policy in several countries throughout the world. I will not contribute here to the extensive bibliography regarding this issue. However, it is important to highlight that since the 1980s, when we observe a considerable effort to memorialize the victims of the Holocaust, mostly in Europe and the United States, there has been a deep ongoing discussion regarding the role of museums, memorials, and sites of memory in postcatastrophic societies.[27] This new impulse sought to remember, grieve, and honor those who died because of the biggest atrocities committed by mankind—atrocities that often took place in the name of the nation and national community. In Amy Sodaro's words, "these new memorials are intended to remember and teach the lessons of the horrors of past conflicts, violence, and genocide, to ensure that that which society might most like to forget is never forgotten."[28] These new forms of memorialization also aim to bring to the present the absences left by the catastrophic past "through material and imagined settings that appear to be relatively permanent and stable in time."[29] This turn opened a long-ignored distinction between remembering, honoring, and memorializing. In this regard, James Loewen warns us that some "memorials heroify people who should not be forgotten, but who should never have been *commemorated*."[30]

In Latin America, the major shift in memorialization practices dates from the 1990s, after the end of civil wars and authoritarian regimes throughout the region. Chile and Argentina are perhaps the most well-known examples of the so-called memorialization boom. In 1997, seven years after the "return" of democracy, Villa Grimaldi, a former clandestine detention and torture center located in Santiago, Chile, became the first site of memory in the post-Pinochet era. By 2017 Chile already had forty registered sites of memory.[31] In Argentina, the Museo de la Memoria de Rosario was inaugurated in 1998, fifteen years after the end of the dictatorship. In 2006, under the Néstor Kirchner administration, the Argentinean state created the "Federal Network of Sites of Memory," and by 2015, thirty-five sites of memory were open to the public throughout the country.[32] Although Central America has also transited an arduous path in the elaboration of sites of memory, it is arguable that these endeavors, especially in El Salvador and Guatemala, are still far from accomplishing what has been achieved in the Southern Cone in terms of the labor of memory and transitional justice.

In societies where the state predominantly monopolizes memorialization, alternative private and public forms of remembering often emerge. Candi Cann investigates some examples of these alternative forms of memorialization in *Virtual Afterlives,* where she explores new practices of coping with grief such as tattoos, car-decal memorials, and internet and social network memorials. She claims that this is a response to the lack of public space to conduct bereavement, "which forces people to create and adopt alternative forms of mourning to help them navigate public space with their altered status as grieving individuals."[33] As we will see in the following pages, one of the main features of the memorialization process in postconflict Central America is the constant challenge of state monopoly to civil war memorialization.

Since this chapter will particularly examine how memorialization projects engage with the task of mourning, we must mention that these efforts are always mediated by affects. Grief, as Erika Doss says, "is the most evident affect employed in the making of memorials and their meanings."[34] Without a certain form of affect, neither the labor of memory nor memorialization would exist. In Kaitlin Murphy's words, sites of memory "do not themselves autonomously remember but rather are constituted through affective, corporeal practices of remembering."[35] In other words, for a site of memory to perform a labor of memory—and also a work of mourning—it must be "mediated by human engagement with those places."[36] The "human engagement" needed to give meaning to sites of memory takes us back to the communitarian aspect of the work of mourning previously discussed in the introduction. The "community of mourners," as this chapter will demonstrate, is involved in a reciprocal move in which they produce sites of memory, but also they can be produced and sustained as grievers through the existence of these sites. The creation, participation, reproduction, and sustainability of this community is fundamental not only for the emergence but also for the preservation of any site of memory.

Ultimately, we should not forget that sites of memory are places that, like everything else, are susceptible to the passage of time. In his study of war memorials in Europe, Jay Winter synthesizes what he calls the "trajectory of decomposition" in the memorials' meaning, "[o]nce the moment of initial bereavement has passed, once the widows had remarried, once the orphans had grown up and moved away, once the mission of veterans to ensure that the scourge of war would not return had faded or collapsed, then the meaning of war memorial was bound to change."[37] The historical condition of sites of memory forces us to be aware of their stages and development, of their potential reinterpretation and appropriation by agencies or organizations that initially did not participate in the memorialization process, and in some cases, of their path to becoming meaningless sites, or even worse, to be destroyed.

Memorializing in Guatemala City

The following pages explore the continuous battle over memorialization in Guatemala through an overview of sites of memory in Guatemala City. A good starting point for this is the Parque Central, Guatemala City's main square, in Zone 1. During the signing of the peace accords in December 1996, a monument called Flama de la paz (Peace Flame) was erected in the middle of the square with the promise of always burning to remember the "anonymous heroes of the peace." Although it is unclear who the "heroes of the peace" were, the flame, the legend, and one peace dove were seemingly enough to build one of the first memorials of the postwar era. During their 2001 and 2002 observations, Steinberg and Taylor noted that the memorial was "hardly noticeable against the backdrop of the National Palace, which continues to be guarded by troops in combat fatigues carrying automatic weapons."[38] Over time, the memorial deteriorated. The flame was not always burning, and graffiti was scribbled on its case. In 2004 President Óscar Berger decided to move the flame inside the National Palace—on the north side of the Parque—to take better care of it. The flame was lighted on October 1 in the presence of His Holiness the Dalai Lama and Nobel Prize winner Rigoberta Menchú, among others.[39] Although the flame has a central place in the palace (fig. 1), located in a quad called Patio de la Paz, visitors to the palace receive no context regarding it, turning it into a meaningless memorial for anyone who is not aware of Guatemala's recent history.[40] Even if we trusted Berger's good intentions regarding peace, relocating the flame inside the palace was an ambiguous message, mainly because the flame now lies inside the building where thousands of orders to arrest, torture, and slaughter were dictated daily during the war. Moreover, the Government Palace witnessed several coups and (very likely) the illegal detention and torture of an undetermined number of people.[41]

On the eastern side of the park, right next to the National Palace, lies the Metropolitan Cathedral. This site is highly relevant in the memorial-

FIGURE 1 Flame of Peace, National Palace, Guatemala City, Guatemala. Photo by Javiera Escobar Yametti.

ization process, for the Guatemalan Catholic Church has had a crucial role in the postwar era.[42] In the Cathedral, Archbishop Juan Gerardi presented the findings of the Recuperación de la memoria histórica (REMHI) report, *Guatemala: Nunca Más,* on April 24, 1998—which cost him his life two days later. In 1999 the names included in the REMHI report along with the names of several massacres were engraved in the Cathedral's pillars (fig. 2). The latter was a bold statement that brought the infamous atrocities of the armed conflict to the heart of the city and placed them right next to the site where the criminal orders had emanated. Twenty years later, however, the names of the dead are hardly seen from a far distance, and many of the blocks that hold the victims' names are in poor condition. Their identities are still there, but their visibility in one of the city's most important buildings is in constant jeopardy.

Zone 1 also hosts several other small memorials that pay homage to the victims of the internal conflict. For example, on the floor of the Portal del

FIGURE 2 Engraved pillar of the Cathedral of Guatemala, Guatemala City, Guatemala. Photo by Javiera Escobar Yametti.

Comercio lies a plaque that remembers the assassination of student leader Oliverio Castañeda in 1978. Also, there is a plaque that pays homage to poet Otto René Castillo (assassinated by the Guatemalan army in 1967) inside the Instituto Central Para Varones, and in Parque San Sebastián, there is a memorial that remembers Archbishop Juan Gerardi. All these sites, although at times discrete and overlooked, engage in the ongoing struggle over mourning and memorialization in contemporary Guatemala.

While the attempts to hold the memory of the victims of state terrorism have been far from victorious, it is crucial to highlight the efforts that several people and civil organizations have gone to in order to memorialize in a country where seeking justice for political crimes involves putting one's life at risk. In this regard I would like to address more in depth two sites that battle daily to challenge the common understanding of which lives deserve to be grieved and which ones should be forgotten. These places are the Casa de la Memoria Kaji Tulam and the Archivo Histórico de la Policía Nacional (AHPN).

The Casa de la Memoria Kaji Tulam is the first (and only, at the time of writing) memory museum in Central America to address the civil wars.[43] The museum was established in 2014 by the Centro para la Acción Legal en Derechos Humanos (CALDH), an organization created in the 1980s to fight against human rights abuses. This museum does not receive any state funding, and the people working there are constantly at risk of being threatened or even attacked by civilians and state forces, which demonstrates the delicate position of civil society in the memorialization process.[44] Casa de la Memoria is situated in what I call the "memory neighborhood" in Guatemala City because it is located across from the Holocaust Museum of Guatemala (which *does* receive support from the Guatemalan government) and just one block north from Archbishop Gerardi's memorial in Parque San Sebastián.

Casa de la Memoria is not a traditional memorial museum. Unlike other similar sites in Latin America that focus predominantly on the "repressive period,"[45] this museum offers a complete reinterpretation of Guatemalan history from the perspective of Indigenous communities and women. Casa de la Memoria's tour opens with a room entirely dedicated to Maya worldview. There, visitors can consult their Maya horoscope and learn about the Maya calendars. When visitors advance to the second room—which describes the Spanish conquest—they must walk underneath several white swords that represent the violence of European colonization. This room exhibits paintings that represent the extermination of the Native population and gallows that stress the fatal ending of millions of Indigenous peoples. The room also provides a historical account of the Spanish invasion, highlighting the violence suffered by Native communities and the genocide conducted by the invaders. The museum makes important connections between the Spanish violence and Guatemalan structural racism. For instance, one of the plaques says that racism, violence, terror, and land dispossession were some of the fundamentals that contributed to the extermination of the Native population during the conquest. All these elements, "have perpetuated in the history of Guatemala, maintaining the oppression against Native people until the present."[46]

In the successive rooms, Casa de la Memoria continues narrating the history of Guatemala—the independence, the 1944 revolution—stressing the role of the traditionally concealed population in the liberal discourse—mostly women and Indigenous peoples. The museum presents the history of some important women in Guatemalan history in a very remarkable way. In some rooms, visitors find a discreet closed door. When the door is opened, the story of a veiled subject emerges, such as high school teacher María Chinchilla as well as Indigenous women during the internal conflict.

The final section of the tour is dedicated to the internal conflict and its aftermath. The museum's discourse is grounded in symbolic elements rather than historical objects. For example, the first room represents the early years of the war and displays toppled chairs, tables, and a bed, mimicking a house that was attacked by the army in search of weapons, guerrillas, and dissidents (fig. 3). Then, visitors enter a room where Indigenous clothing creates a whirlwind that represents the transformation and destruction of people's lives. After visitors walk through a black tunnel with thousands of victims' names, the tour ends with a room dedicated to postconflict Guatemala. This room displays pictures and testimonies of deceased and surviving victims of the internal conflict (like Otto René Castillo, Archbishop Gerardi, and Oliverio Castañeda), mentioning the importance of their sacrifice to build a more just Guatemala. The latter section also includes different interactive features, primarily oriented toward children and the youth, which function as a symbolic act of their commitment to peace, democracy, and justice. For example, a hand on the wall with the message "Things only change when you change," invites visitors to push it. When they do it, the room illuminates, and positive messages are displayed on the walls. By the end of the tour, there is a wall where visitors can leave their messages and thoughts about the war and Guatemala's history.

At the end of the tour, visitors can enter a room that houses temporary exhibitions. In my 2019 visit, the room displayed an artistic intervention facilitated by H.I.J.O.S.—the acronym for Hijos e Hijas por las Identidad y la Justicia contra el Olvido y el Silencio, an organization that brings together children of assassinated and disappeared people during the internal conflict. H.I.J.O.S. uses art as a tool to prevent oblivion. This exhibition displayed, among other elements, a large quilt that holds the names of thousands of victims of state terrorism during the internal conflict. Each name is knitted by hand into a small square added to the larger quilt that covers the roof and one of the walls. The quilt as a tool of memory must not go overlooked. First, it is a creation often made by women, who represent the most visible face of political violence in Guatemala–the powerful image of dozens of Maya women giving their testimonies in Ríos Montt's trial is the perfect example. Second, as Paul Connerton reminds us, quilting embodies the fragility of this

FIGURE 3 Casa de la Memoria Kaji Tulam, Guatemala City, Guatemala. Photo by Javiera Escobar Yametti.

memory. Unlike memorials made of stone or bronze, which symbolize eternity, cloth "is fragile, it fades and frays, it needs mending."[47] The names sewn in these quilts expose not only the brittleness of life, but also the looming threat of their memory being erased forever.

Casa de la Memoria is not only an insightful and thoughtful memory museum; it is a novel, revolutionary concept of a memorial museum. This institution not only memorializes and mourns the victims of the recent Guatemalan internal conflict but also the millions of people who lost their lives during the last five hundred years. The most compelling feature of Casa de la Memoria is the reinterpretation of Guatemalan (ladino) history, which is the dominant narration in the country, as can be found in the National History Museum. By doing this, the museum articulates a new notion of community that challenges the liberal-ladino perspective. This new vision does not praise the conquest nor the independence nor the building of a "Guatemalan" identity or tradition. Quite the contrary, it stresses the violence suffered by the Indigenous communities, women, and poor ladinos. By reshaping the notion of community, Casa de la Memoria performs a profound and meaningful work of mourning. The museum invites visitors to grieve not only the losses of the war but also the millions of cadavers that inhabit Guatemalan history. All of them, Casa de la Memoria claims, are one of *us*. Their lives deserved to be lived, and therefore their death must be grieved. Thus, holding their memory is presented here as a natural outcome, an ethical and moral obligation that must be assumed by the community.

A second major site under consideration in Guatemala City is the Archivo Histórico de la Policía Nacional (AHPN), located in Zone 6. What today is the AHPN used to be an army warehouse that contained thousands of weapons and explosives that accidentally detonated in June 2005, resulting in a massive fire. When Edeliberto Cifuentes, head of the Procuraduría de Derechos Humanos (PDH), inspected the place a few weeks later to make sure all hazards were removed, he found millions of documents in poor conditions. "When Cifuentes asked the ranking PNC official there, Ana Corado, what sorts of papers these were and in what quantity they could be found, she replied, simply, 'These are the archives of the National Police.'"[48] The archives of the National Police, the existence of which was systematically denied for decades, were suddenly in front of the human rights *procurador*, and from then on, it went through a tortuous and complex but also hopeful process of cataloging and preservation.

Since its finding, the main source of support for the AHPN came from the United Nations Development Programme (UNDP). Thanks to their assistance, dozens of professionals and volunteers managed to organize and put together the scattered records. While the AHPN is primarily an archive that contains nearly eighty million documents about political crimes and human rights abuses, this site also works as a place of memory. In 2011 the AHPN took part in the endeavors to boost memorialization in postconflict Guatemala, and "the site was transformed, most powerfully by the repurposing of the pitted, barbed wire–topped concrete perimeter walls into canvases for dozens of brightly painted murals."[49] The murals portray different dreams and references to the internal armed conflict. For example, many of them express messages that relate to the AHPN by painting documents that explicitly refer to the national police archives. One mural, painted by "EV," portrays Lady Justice emerging from scattered documents on the floor. Another one shows kids forming the word *memoria* with single-page documents. Other murals have messages such as *justicia, paz, vida, esperanza* (justice, peace, life, hope). Personally, one of the most striking murals is one that portrays a mother and her children in the center of the image. The mother is holding her baby in her arms, and her daughter is standing next to her. They are crying next to a dead man (presumably the husband/father). On the left side of the painting, there is a tiny and young soldier (seemingly the assassin) holding his rifle and aiming at the women. In the background, a smoking green volcano houses this horrific scene (fig. 4). The grieving family, next to the soldier's insensibility, symbolizes a country that mourns in front of people who express their utmost contempt regarding the pain of others.[50] The murals add an affective component that challenges Guatemala's status quo. The relevance of the AHPN murals, following Murphy's reflection on visuality and memory, is that they can "trouble, shape, reinforce, and challenge individual and cultural memory

FIGURE 4 Mural painted outside the AHPN, Guatemala City, Guatemala. Photo by Javiera Escobar Yametti.

because they both give material form to personal and shared narratives and function as truth claims about the past."[51]

In addition to the exterior murals, the archive offers a modest exhibition inside its walls. Among other things, visitors find a portrayal of the situation when the PDH people arrived in 2005. An open door reveals thousands of documents on the floor that mimic the pitiable conditions in which the documents were found (including a plastic mouse and a stop sign). Behind them, there is a large photograph that depicts the situation when they found the warehouse containing the real documents. The exhibition also includes elements such as typewriters, copies of documents, furniture, information about the archive, and pictures of the archivist work. The murals and the exhibition do not only complement the archive, they also actively engage in the struggle over mourning and memorialization in postwar Guatemala. Unlike Casa de la Memoria, the building that today hosts the AHPN had crucial importance during the internal conflict, and therefore the connection between the affective, historical, and spatial dimensions is overt. Thus, while the archive is doubtlessly the protagonist, recent additions have enabled this site to be included in the incipient—or better, virtual—Guatemala City's "memorial route."[52]

In the introduction to *Memory, Mourning, Landscape,* Kate McLoughlin combines the reflection on memory and mourning with cultural geography to propose the interweaving of notions of memory, mourning, and landscape in sites of memory. She posits that when put together, these terms "draw a vertical, temporal axis (revisiting the past and carrying it into the future) and a horizontal spatial axis (grounding the first two activities)."[53] Following this idea, we can say that at the AHPN, the temporal axis that remembers state terrorism connects with the spatial dimension of a site that housed highly systematized information of said violence and the unknown fate of thousands of political detainees. The combination of the archive of political violence, grassroots murals, and the exhibition results in a strong claim for justice that goes beyond the obscurity of the Guatemalan judiciary system. Rather, it works as a demand before the impossibility of just compensation for the harm inflicted. The AHPN combines, willingly or not, different forms of a permanent work that has no foreseen end: archival work, work of memory, and the work of mourning.[54]

In 2019, in a highly controversial decision, the control of the National Police Archive was transferred from UNDP to the Guatemalan state, particularly to the Ministry of Culture and Sports. Many feared, with good reasons, that the state would use its control of the archive to boycott its conservation, cataloging, and access. Some of these fears were partially confirmed when the Ministerio de Gobernación, which controls the National Civilian Police, requested an active role in the administration of the AHPN. Fortunately, these efforts did not succeed, and the archive still remains under the control of the Central American Archive, which is controlled by the Ministry of Culture and Sports. In 2020 the AHPN was declared a National Cultural Heritage.[55]

* * *

It is clear that despite its limited visibility and modest budgets, different civil organizations are doing hard work to develop memorialization practices in contemporary Guatemala and to grieve the dead of the internal conflict. The great absence here is undoubtedly the Guatemalan state, which has not shown any concern for the memorialization of civil war victims and apparently has no problem with the army praising the Kaibiles in the Museum of Military History.[56] A great example of the Guatemalan state attitude regarding memorialization and the civil war can be found in the Museum of National History. This museum was created in 1976, during General Laugerud García's administration, and does not include a single word regarding the internal conflict. The museum's tour ends with the 1954 CIA-sponsored coup against President Jacobo Árbenz. Curiously, the museum is in relatively good health after being renovated during the COVID-19 pandemic and reopened to the public in 2021. Graphics are in good shape, and the museum incorporates contemporary perspectives, like the role of some women in Guatemala's history. It simply seems that from the perspective of the official institutions, the internal conflict does not deserve a site in Guatemalan history.

Memorialization and the Battle of Mourning in Postwar El Salvador

A tour across El Salvador suggests that civil war memorialization is, to a certain extent, more developed than in its neighbor Guatemala. Regardless of their modesty, it is not uncommon to find several forms of memorialization when one traverses San Salvador or visits different areas throughout the country. Nevertheless, the above does not mean that this process has brought dignity to the civil war's victims or that it has contributed to transitional justice or established robust politics of memory. Quite the contrary, a careful analysis of memorialization practices in postconflict El Salvador reveals that most of the contemporary struggles about justice, political violence, democracy, and mourning translate to the memorialization process.

Memorialization was an important recommendation made by the Truth Commission for El Salvador in its 1993 report *De lo la locura a la esperanza.* Regarding moral reparation to the victims, the commission suggested: (1) the building of a national monument in San Salvador with the names of all the identified victims of the conflict, (2) acknowledging the honorability of the victims and the crimes that were committed toward them, and (3) establishing a national holiday to remember the victims.[57] Despite the recommendations, the Salvadoran state–controlled by rightwing party ARENA from the end of the war until 2009–did virtually nothing in terms of reparation to the victims and the labor of memory. The latter, as Annette Hernández argues, imposed silence as the primary state official policy in postwar El Salvador, something that only changed moderately when the FLMN won the 2009 presidential election.[58]

Whereas the truth commission's recommendations regarding victims' memorialization were ignored almost completely, it would be erroneous to say that the Salvadoran state did not foster any politics of memorialization and heritage development after the end of the war. As Robin DeLugan demonstrates, in the years following the signing of the peace accords, "there were simultaneously occurring state-led projects to represent the nation and rebuild national society."[59] Nevertheless, the state-sponsored museography and heritage projects did not aim to memorialize civil war victims. Instead, their goal was to strengthen the idea of national community and the concepts of national identity that were profoundly affected during the armed conflict. In this context, the conflict was presented as a "fratricidal war" and a temporary *locura* (explicit in the truth commission report's title). The official efforts to strengthen the national community in the postwar era were also supported by the construction of public buildings oriented to tell the history of "the people" of El Salvador. For example, the Museo Nacional de Antropología Dr. David J. Guzmán (MUNA) reopened in 2001 after the old building collapsed in the 1993 earthquake. In the years following the peace accords, the Salvadoran state also developed a touristic infrastructure around archaeological sites such as Joyas de Cerén, designated UNESCO World Heritage Site in 1993.[60]

The first state-sponsored postwar memorial in El Salvador was the Monumento Cristo de la Paz. The monument was inaugurated in 1994 during Alfredo Cristiani's administration to welcome the athletes participating in the 5th Central American Games. The monument is located on the Comalapa highway, just outside the capital city, and it was built to be seen when driving from El Salvador's international airport to San Salvador. It displays a three-meter Jesus Christ figure releasing a peace dove. Underneath Jesus, in the supporting structure, lies the sentence *la paz sea con vosotros* (may peace be with you). The Cristo de la Paz was created by Salvadoran sculptor Rubén Martínez, who in 1990 created the Monumento a la Constitución (better known as "la Chulona," the naked woman) to honor the 1983 constitution (a symbol of ARENA and the army). A curious feature of the Monumento Cristo de la Paz is that the sculpture was created with gun shells and weapons used in the armed conflict. As Elena Salamanca proposes, this figure opened a new era in the history of Salvadoran sculpting in which the use of certain materials allowed the connection of these pieces with the immediate national reality.[61] The employment of elements used in the civil war allows the Cristo de la Paz memorial to bring together both the Salvadoran army and the former guerrillas in one site. Nevertheless, the civilian victims of the conflict and the millions of displaced people were overtly excluded from this memorial. The latter is unsurprising considering that this monument was built only two years after the end of the war, when the country's political stability was still in jeopardy. Nevertheless, what for many in 1994 was the starting point of a new, promising era, is today a reflection of the poor labor of memory conducted in postconflict El Salvador.[62] The absences we observe in this memorial became the rule in the state-sponsored memorialization process that will take place over the following three decades.

Before the Salvadoran state's disinterest in undertaking significant actions regarding memorialization toward war victims, several civil society organizations had taken up the torch to honor their dead. The combination of both the lack of an official narrative of the war and civil society initiatives results in a situation in which each memorial, museum, or site of memory embodies its own discourse without necessarily engaging in national or local community narratives. A thorough analysis of these sites reveals that despite their supposed equivalence under the umbrella term *sites of memory*, each place mourns and remembers not only different people (from guerrillas to civilians and army soldiers) but also in different forms. Furthermore, while some sites undertake an active and inclusive work of mourning, others openly accept that their grieving process is over or restrict others from participating in it. Some of the sites also reinforce the official ideas of forgetting and impunity. The coexistence of all these sites across the country makes apparent the existence of a battle over the work of mourning. This struggle is not based on imposing a certain form of doing things on others; instead, this is a struggle over expressing and conducting the work of mourning in the public sphere. What is at stake in this battle is not exclusively who is mourned but *how* people mourn and *who* is invited to take part in this process.[63]

An illustrative example to introduce the idea of the battle of mourning in postconflict El Salvador is the memorialization of Roberto D'Aubuisson and Schafik Handal. D'Aubuisson was the founder of the rightwing party ARENA, presidential candidate for said party in 1984, and mastermind of the assassination of Monseñor Oscar Romero in 1980. Schafik Handal, on the other hand, was the secretary of the Salvadoran Communist Party, guerrilla leader during the civil war, and FMLN presidential candidate in 2004. D'Aubuisson died from cancer in 1992 at age forty-two, whereas Handal died in 2006, at age seventy-five, from a heart attack. Both leaders have been strongly memorialized by their followers in recent years despite their active participation in the political violence of the 1980s. Ralph Sprenkels argues that "partisans project them as extraordinary citizens, of impeccable moral standards, visionaries and lovers of freedom, victims of persecution and slander, gifted speakers, close to the people and loved by the people, willing to endure every imaginary sacrifice for their ideals."[64] Today, both adversaries have their respective memorials in San Salvador, where followers can grieve and pay homage to their deceased leaders.

When D'Aubuisson died in 1992, only a few weeks after the signing of the peace, he was publicly and nationally mourned by his associates from the ARENA party and by thousands of civilians. President Cristiani declared three days of national mourning and posthumously awarded him the Order of Merit Dr. José Matías Delgado.[65] In 2006 a memorial located in a roundabout in Antiguo Cuscatlán was erected to honor D'Aubuisson by disgraced ARENA president Antonio Saca (imprisoned in 2018 for diverting state funds). The monument consists of a white pole surrounded by plaques with nationalistic messages like "Patria Sí, Comunismo No," "Primero El Salvador, Segundo El Salvador, Tercero El Salvador," and "Presente por la Patria." The memorial presents D'Aubuisson as a patriotic national hero who devoted his life to defending his beloved El Salvador. Nothing is said here, of course, about the death squads he created during the civil war or his role in Monseñor Romero's assassination.[66]

Since its creation, D'Aubuisson's memorial has been subject to a barrage of criticism and vandalism, which did not stop ARENA members (colloquially called *areneros*) from honoring their deceased leader. In 2007, ARENA representatives tried to decorate D'Aubuisson as *hijo meritísimo* (merit son) of El Salvador, which ultimately failed.[67] In 2014, San Salvador mayor Norman Quijano renamed a major avenue in the city after D'Aubuisson, which provoked fierce criticism, including the online campaign #NingunaCalleLlevaráTuNombre. The "Mayor Roberto D'Aubuisson Street" lasted only a few months until mayor Nayib Bukele (who became president of El Salvador in 2019) restored the street's original name in May 2015.[68]

On the other end of the spectrum lies the FMLN leader Schafik Handal. Despite his "hardline" leadership during the civil war, Handal is a respected figure in El Salvador today and the "most emblematic figure of the Salvadoran leftwing."[69] Handal's mausoleum in the Cementerio de los Ilustres is highly decorated and frequently visited by people to pay their respects and leave flowers. In March 2010, with the FMLN in office for the first time, the Casa Museo Schafik Handal was inaugurated, which offers visitors an insight into Handal's life and political career. In 2011 a memorial was built in his honor in the municipality of Mejicanos in northern San Salvador. Like D'Aubuisson's memorial, Handal's is located at a busy roundabout, and thousands of people see it every day. Analyzing Handal's memorialization, Carlos López Bernal argues that his death represented an essential step for the FMLN toward their unity as a political party, and his legacy and figure played a vital role in the 2009 presidential elections.[70]

D'Aubuisson's and Handal's memorialization exemplifies the complexities of the work of mourning in postwar El Salvador. Beyond the present-day political leveraging of their lives, deeds, and memory, both the far right-wing and the former revolutionaries feel entitled to grieve their dead—a privilege that is denied to those who still ignore the fate of their loved ones. It could even be said that both Handal's and D'Aubuisson's mourners have arrived at a sort of peace. Both leaders died surrounded by friends and family, and funeral rites were properly undertaken. The memorialization of these two radically opposed figures suggests that such work can only take place with official compliance when it does not challenge the postwar status quo. Perhaps even more problematic is that by sponsoring the memorialization of these two persons, the Salvadoran state narrows the options to two alternatives, as if there were no possibility of grieving outside the political duopoly established after the peace accords. Thus, through public mourning, Handal and D'Aubuisson are equated in the public sphere, as if grieving them would allegorically satisfy the Salvadorans' will of mourning the losses of the civil war. Notwithstanding the apparently completed work of mourning portrayed by the official postwar political parties, civil society and local organizations resist the closure imposed on them.

In the following pages, I will analyze how specific sites of memory, memorials, and museums engage with the work of mourning in postwar El Salvador. From more than ten major sites that participate in this struggle in present-day El Salvador, I have selected six: three in San Salvador, and three in the province of Morazán, in eastern El Salvador. Reasons for selecting one over the other are always subjective and even unjust, but I believe the chosen sites exemplify the different directions in the work of mourning that have taken place in El Salvador in the three decades following the peace accords. I have decided to focus on these two areas because San Salvador and Morazán contain most of the civil war–related monuments, memorials, and museums. While this concentration is unsurprising in the case of San Salvador for being the capital city, Morazán is a less obvious choice of focus for someone not familiar with El Salvador's history. Morazán was a region predominantly controlled by the guerrillas during the civil war and hosted many violent combats and massacres. After the end of the war, the Promotora de Turismo (PRODETUR) company was created to promote Morazán as a tourist destination and to protect the environment.[71] Once a "red zone," Morazán is now—not without irony—marketed as the "Ruta de la paz" (Peace Route), one of the seven touristic routes promoted by the Salvadoran Tourism Ministry. The former battlefields, according to *Infoguía El Salvador*, have "been transformed into peaceful surroundings full of natural beauty, with crystalline rivers, waterfalls, and ideal camping and hiking sites."[72] Also, I have decided to overlook sites that have been thoroughly discussed and praised by numerous scholars, such as the Museo de la Palabra y la Imagen (MUPI) in San Salvador.[73] I have also excluded sites that are currently under development, despite how promising they are regarding the work of mourning, like the powerful memorialization process currently occurring in Arcatao.[74]

In San Salvador, I study the Monumento a la Memoria y la Verdad, the Parque Escultórico a la Reconciliación, and the Museo de Historia Militar. In Morazán, I analyze the Museo de la Revolución, the El Mozote memorial, and the Proyecto de Paz y Reconciliación. While each of these sites develops its own discourse and relates differently with the work of mourning, I have decided to pair the places that offer certain similarities in their mourning process for reasons of argument. As a result, the following pages will be divided into three parts. The first part will analyze the Museo de la Revolución and the Museo de Historia Militar. The second part will examine the Monumento a la Memoria y la Verdad and the memorial at El Mozote. Finally, in the third part I will study the Proyecto de Paz y Reconciliación and the Parque Escultórico a la Reconciliación. In the analysis of the aforementioned sites, I am particularly interested in two things. First, how these places engage with the work of mourning in their respective contexts, and second, how these sites create or support a community of mourners around them.

Martyrs and Heroes

There are many parallels in the way different factions grieve and remember their dead. Erik Ching argues that notwithstanding the side in which people positioned themselves in the postwar era, their narratives often share similarities in form and structure. An example of the latter can be observed in testimonies of rank-and-file soldiers who, according to Ching, "may have fought against the rank-and-file guerrillas during the war, but they narrate their experiences more like them than their former army officers."[75] Something similar happens, with many nuances nonetheless, when both the army and former guerrillas create their respective museography projects. The following pages explore how the work of mourning is portrayed in the Museo de la Revolución in Morazán and in the Museo de Historia Militar in San Salvador.

The Museum of the Revolution

The Museo de la Revolución was created in the village of Perquín (Morazán province) by former guerrilla members in December 1992, eleven months after the signing of the peace accords. According to Felipe, one of the owners and guides, the site was created with two clear objectives: to keep the memory of thousands of men and women who lost their lives nationwide during the civil war, and to serve as a historical reference for future generations.[76] The museum has two buildings that host indoor exhibitions, and there are several elements on display outdoors.

The tour begins in the major indoor exhibition, which is divided into four sections (one in each room). First, visitors enter the largest room, which hosts dozens of pictures on the walls. This room aims to provide historical background on the popular struggle in El Salvador and inform visitors about the years of the civil war. The room includes pictures of La matanza of 1932, when dictator Maximiliano Hernández's regime slaughtered over thirty thousand people during a popular uprising, alongside pictures of the armed conflict and the situation in El Salvador during the 1970s and 1980s. The above, as Leigh Binford argues, supports oppression and resistance as the master narrative of the museum, narration in which the FMLN embodies a popular struggle that initiated in 1932.[77] Despite its intentions, the exhibition provides very little information about the civil war and its causes. Many pictures are displayed without any context. The few written pieces in this room are transcriptions of revolutionary songs, poems, or speeches. For example, one of the walls is dedicated to the "Heroes and Martyrs" of the revolution. There, we see dozens of pictures of guerrillas who lost their lives during the internal conflict. In many cases, however, the black-and-white pictures are anonymous, and the identities of the "heroes and martyrs" are concealed (fig. 5). The same occurs with the pictures that portray protests and poverty in the country, which do not inform visitors of the year or place in which they were taken. The second room, the smallest in the building, exposes multilingual posters of international solidarity with the people of El Salvador—the majority calling for a stop to U.S. military aid and bombings. The third room is dedicated to life within the guerrilla camps, showing daily activities (training, literacy campaigns, harvesting) and highlighting the participation of women in the struggle (such as Comandante Guadalupe Martínez) (fig. 6). It also exhibits weapons, communication devices, and other artifacts used during the war. Finally, the fourth room exhibits weapons used by both the guerrilla and the national army and displays pictures of the peace process.

When visitors exit the first part of the exhibition, they are faced with the remains of five aircrafts. One of them represents the most precious guerrilla's prize from the civil war era: Colonel Domingo Monterrosa's helicopter

FIGURE 5 Anonymous dead guerrillas honored at the Museo de la Revolución, Perquín, El Salvador. Photo by Javiera Escobar Yametti.

FIGURE 6 Anonymous guerrilla women honored by the Museo de la Revolución, Perquín, El Salvador. Photo by Javiera Escobar Yametti.

FIGURE 7 Debris of Colonel Domingo Monterrosa's helicopter, Museo de la Revolución, Perquín, El Salvador. Photo by Javiera Escobar Yametti.

(fig. 7). Colonel Monterrosa, commander of the BIRI Atlacatl Battalion, is infamous for leading the massacre of El Mozote in December 1981, which took place just a few kilometers from the museum. Monterrosa was killed along with thirteen other people on October 23, 1984, by the Ejército Revolucionario del Pueblo (ERP) in a Trojan Horse–style operation.[78] The outdoor section also displays bulletproof cars given to the guerrilla leaders by the Mexican and French governments in 1982 and 1992, respectively, and a hole left by a U.S.-made bomb dropped by the Salvadoran army in 1981.

After exploring the outdoor exhibits, visitors may enter the second building, which is dedicated primarily to displaying artifacts used by Radio Venceremos, the guerrilla mobile radio station, including Vikingo 5 (one of the pieces of radio equipment), Betamax players, and a small television were guerrillas used to watch the news and Cantinflas's movies, according to one of the guides. The walls display, among other elements, pictures of Radio Venceremos presenters, revolutionary music groups such as Los Torogoces de Morazán, and a printed version of Roque Dalton's "Poema de Amor." After completing the tour, for an extra fee, visitors can explore the "Campamento guerrillero," a reenactment of a guerrilla camp where tourists can have their picture taken with a rifle and guerrilla clothing.

The museum relates in many ways with the task of mourning. On the surface, the museum appears to reject the idea of mourning as an active and ongoing process, and it embraces mourning as an accomplished task instead. Very little in this museum invites visitors to think critically about human rights violations, the current situation of the country, and the role of the FMLN in the postwar era. In its relationship with loss, the museum exploits the martyrdom discourse, something common in many civil war–related memorialization projects in Central America. Martyrdom, following Anna and Brandt Peterson, frames "survivors' relations with their dead, giving them meaning that made the loss more bearable."[79] In this sense, the dead comrades are grieved and celebrated at the same time. They are presented as role models for future generations, as the plaque next to the "Heroes and Martyrs" pictures cries, "so the new generations will never erase from their memory the historical experience and value the example of the heroes and martyrs who gave their lives to reach a better society." The "martyrdom" of the guerrilla, as depicted here, follows what Jon Sobrino called the "Socratic dimension" of martyrdom. This means, "the will of transforming reality [. . .] without avoiding the consequences of directly confronting the powers of the world."[80] The martyrdom of the FMLN combatants, along with the exhibition of guerrillas' prizes (e.g., Monterrosa's helicopter) and other elements that stress the guerrilla's cleverness to fight a war against a better trained, armed, and funded enemy suggests that the Salvadoran civil war is a closed era. Visitors will not find claims for justice or lamentations for the meager change that the end of the war brought to the country's poorest, including former guerrillas. Instead, they are presented with a heroic tale of the war, a settled narrative in which the dead seem to be at peace thanks to their willing sacrifice and the homage paid to them by the museum.

The Museum of the Revolution also serves as a site of burial. Next to the hole left by the bomb mentioned above, visitors can see the tomb of Rodrigo Cifuentes Carmona, known as José Luis "el Chileno." Carmona was a member of the Movimento de Izquierda Revolucionaria (MIR) in Chile, who joined the Salvadoran insurgency as many other internationalists did. He died as a consequence of a bomb in 1988 and was buried in the mountains of Perquín. When the museum was inaugurated, José Luis was relocated within it. In 2010 his mother, Silvia, traveled from Chile to El Salvador, performed

FIGURE 8 Tomb of Rodrigo Cifuentes Carmona (José Luis, "El Chileno"), Museo de la Revolución, Perquín, El Salvador. Photo by Javiera Escobar Yametti.

funeral rites, and placed a plaque in her son's grave (fig. 8).[81] The presence of a tomb within the museum contributes to the idea that all mourning rites have been performed, and the only pending task is to transmit the tale of the revolution and the guerrillas (their bravery, social commitment, and cleverness) to future generations.

Nevertheless, if we dig deeper, we find an alternative phantasmagoric story that haunts the Museo de la Revolución. I did not realize this until my second visit in August 2019, when on my way out a young man asked me if I had any further questions. Since I was there for analyzing the museum in preparation for this book, I asked him whether there was any reference to Roque Dalton, as I did not recall seeing any. He seemed confused and called an older man over to speak with me. He gave me an uncomfortable look when I asked about Dalton and invited me to sit down with him at a picnic table. He told me that since Roque Dalton was still a controversial figure for the FMLN because of his unsolved assassination, they have deliberately overlooked him in the museum. Dalton's only reference is in the poem located in Radio Venceremos' room, which has no picture of the guerrilla poet. The reason for this, he claimed, was to prevent hate and discussion among the new generations. What is curious about this choice is that "Poema de amor," following Yansi Pérez, is not a docile poem. Although it has been read as an expression of the Salvadoran identity, ultimately it shows the scabrous and miserable side of the Salvadoran reality.[82] Apparently, the museum strictly followed Dalton's words: "when you've heard I have died, do not pronounce my name." However, as Elena Salamanca claims, "He asked for silence and we gave it to him. But we gave it to him in a manner bereft of justice."[83] Roque Dalton's specters, visible through their concealment, shed light on the vacuums and holes in the museum's script and reveal a subterranean, hidden narration that forces us to reconsider the work of mourning in the Museo de la Revolución. The lack of a transparent and honest narrative that presents a comprehensive history of the war, in addition to the museum's many silences, enables us to consider the existence of an underlying work of mourning, one that even its creators could be unaware of.

There exist at least two antagonist discourses regarding the work of mourning in this museum. On the one hand, the museum inscribes the dead under the martyrdom discourse, which enables them to give sense to their comrades' sacrifice. Following this thread, mourning is presented as an accomplished task, one they can speak about in a transparent manner with visitors. On the other hand, the lack of a coherent narrative of the war along with the absence of a critical view of the guerrillas and their crimes (or "mistakes," as they often call them) suggest that some issues remain unanswered. Indeed, a key feature of unresolved trauma—and therefore of an ongoing work of mourning—is the impossibility of articulating a coherent, transparent narrative of the past. As Idelber Avelar argues, "the accomplishment of mourning work presupposes the elaboration of a story about the past."[84] Thus, despite its intentions, the Museo de la Revolución makes its unfinished work of mourning visible through its apparent completion. The omission of one name, Roque Dalton, is enough to reveal the unsaid.

The coexistence of two opposite discourses, one explicit, and a second one only visible through its disguise, reveals that the battle over mourning is a process that does more than simply confront people holding different political positions. This battle can also take place within factions with alleged clear positions and even within small communities. In this case, the Museo de la Revolución decides who deserves to be grieved and what deaths are better kept in silence as an inner and unresolved sorrow.

The Museum of Military History

The Museo de Historia Militar was created by presidential decree by Alfredo Cristiani on June 16, 1993. The museum's goal was to recognize the army's "glory and heroism" throughout Salvadoran history, including their recent "sacrifices" against those who "tried to destroy the Republic."[85] The Museo de Historia Militar is a perfect example of how postwar administrations, particularly ARENA presidents, invested in memorialization in the postwar era. However, the goal never was memorializing civil war victims but rather emphasizing national identity and the army's crucial role in El Salvador's history.

Despite its official support, the museum was not inaugurated until 2002, under Francisco Flores's administration, when it opened its doors to the public in the Ex-Cuartel El Zapote, across from the former Presidential House in San Salvador (in 2003, the site was complemented with the inauguration of the Plaza Central del Complejo Recreativo Cultural San Jacinto, which serves as a recreational space). In January 2003, less than six months after its opening, the Salvadoran government declared the building that houses the museum "Bien Cultural" (Cultural Heritage).[86] The museum was overtly aligned with ARENA and the army's political views. An example of this was the creation of a room exclusively dedicated to honor Colonel Domingo Monterrosa. Interestingly, and despite some initial statements, the FMLN did not take any action regarding the museum during their ten years in office.[87] According to 2023 data, the Museum of Military History is among the most visited museums in the country.[88]

Unlike other state-sponsored museums, such as the MUNA or the Museum of Natural History, the Museum of Military History is free. However, visitors must present an official identification at a military checkpoint before entering the museum, which must be uncomfortable, to say the least, to many Salvadorans. Before reaching the museum's main entrance, visitors are welcomed by a raised-relief map of El Salvador, unveiled in 2005 by former president Elías Antonio Saca (Saca's involvement in both D'Aubuisson's memorial and here should not go unnoticed). The map presents visitors with a material representation of the Salvadoran nation, an idea that will be systematically reinforced throughout the museum's script. The museum consists of indoor and outdoor exhibitions. In the outdoor section, visitors will find tanks, military vehicles, helicopters, and airplanes used by the army at different moments in history. The indoor exhibition offers a chronological history of El Salvador from the Spanish conquest of the American continent to the present.

Before moving forward with the analysis, I must make a note. I visited the museum for the first time in July 2019. One month earlier, on June 1, 2019, Nayib Bukele, who had been in office for two months, tweeted the order to remove everything related to Domingo Monterrosa (including his name) from military institutions.[89] Therefore, the "Sala Tcnel. Domingo Monterrosa Barrios 1980–1992" was closed when I visited the museum, but the rest of it remained as it was originally designed. When I returned to the museum in March 2023, I noticed significant modifications that were clearly mandated by Bukele's government. While discouraged by this at first (my analysis of the museum was already drafted), the changes introduced in the years following my first visit are significant from the point of view of mourning. Because of this, I have decided to divide my analysis into two parts. First, I will discuss the script of the museum as I observed it in my 2019 visit, which represents the army's original perspective, and then I will comment on the modifications introduced by Bukele's administration and how they affect the work of mourning.

THE MUSEUM IN 2019

In 2019 the most relevant rooms for this book's purposes were the last two of the tour, which were dedicated to the civil war and the postwar period. The museum presented the civil war not as an internal conflict but rather as a defensive campaign against an alleged foreign enemy who is not identified. The army's position regarding the civil war was explicit when visitors reached the room dedicated to the armed conflict, called the "1980–1992 Military Campaign Room." This room, as the plaque at the entrance stated, "is dedicated to the members of the Armed Forces that defended with honor and loyalty the country's institutionality during the internal conflict that took place between 1980 and 1992." While both *campaign* and *internal conflict* were used, the museum made evident its preference for the former. Thus, the civil war did not differ much from the 1969 war with Honduras, outlined in the previous military campaign room, which is also narrated—although this time correctly—as a struggle against a foreign enemy.

Like the Museum of the Revolution, the Museum of Military History offered a minimalist narrative of the internal conflict. The 1980–1992 Military Campaign Room exhibited a collection of artifacts corresponding to the civil war era, including photographs and awards of the infamous Atlacatl Battalion, next to memorabilia, uniforms, and arms. Unsurprisingly, this room concealed any guerrilla military achievement. While the Museum of the Revolution exhibits Monterrosa's helicopter with pride, the military museum honored the people who died because of guerrilla actions without naming their cause of death. An excellent example of the latter was the picture of Sergeant José Armando Azmitia Melara (a graduate of the School of the Americas who participated in different massacres, including El Mozote), who died alongside Monterrosa when the ERP blew up their helicopter in 1984. Notwithstanding, the plaque that accompanied the pictures omitted the circumstances of his death, just saying "[Sergeant Azmitia] died on October 23, 1984, in an aerial *accident* in the area of Joateca, department of Morazán" (my emphasis). Beyond weapons, memorabilia, pictures, and uniforms, the room did not include anything that informed visitors about the causes of the war and its development. In general, it can be said that the room's primary goal was honoring those who died during the "military campaign" without telling why or how they died, a feature we already observed in the Museo de la Revolución.

Whereas the 1980–1992 Military Campaign Room overlooked any information or explanation regarding the civil war, the Peace Accords of 1992 Room welcomed visitors with a plaque that broadly explained the peace accords and stressed the army's role in the process. In line with this, the room exhibited a recognition given to the army by the United Nations on the tenth anniversary of the peace: "the General Secretary of the United Nations publicly expressed that the Armed Forces of El Salvador were the governmental institution that better accomplished the acquired agreements." While the FMLN and the Salvadoran government were entirely ignored in the 1980–92 campaign room, the peace accords room included the different factions that participated in the civil war, which is now called "the armed conflict." Here, the museum displayed pictures and official documents including the final declaration that put an end to the armed struggle. One of the most intriguing documents exhibited in this room was the "Parte de la Fuerza Armada a la Nación Salvadoreña." This document was given by the army to President Cristiani in an official ceremony on January 31, 1992. In said declaration, General Gilberto Rubio claims that from that date on, the Armed Forces would end the military campaign undertaken to stop communists' aggression, thus fulfilling their constitutional mission of defending national sovereignty. Rubio claims that the mission "was successful thanks to the heroism, courage, sacrifice, and professionalism of the Salvadorian soldier."

The Peace Accords of 1992 Room also presented a problematic timeline of the civil war that aimed to explain the development of the conflict. This timeline was located a few meters above the visitors' heads and went around the room. It mentioned more than twenty events that, according to the museum, were central in the narration of the Salvadoran civil war. Some of these events were the 1979 General Romero's coup d'état, the murder of Monseñor Romero in 1980, the visit of the Pope John Paul II in 1983, the death of Colonel Monterrosa in 1984, the boycott of public transportation in 1987, the FMLN's "Ofensiva hasta el tope" in 1989, and the signing of the peace accords. The majority of the "negative" events mentioned correspond to guerrilla actions. For example, the timeline included the FMLN unification in 1980, the final offensive of 1981, the destruction of national infrastructure, the murder of American marines in 1985, the kidnap of thirteen mayors in 1985, the FMLN no-show to the 1986 peace conversations in Sesori, and the boycott of the 1989 elections.

There is little doubt that the selection of events justified the army's actions and supported the version of the military campaign introduced in the previous room. However, the timeline by itself provided very little information about the events described and their perpetrators. The museum said that a bridge was destroyed, marines were killed, and public transportation was boycotted, but it does not describe who took part in these actions. From the army's point of view, all wrongdoing during the war was made by the guerrillas, and thus we can think of the timeline as self-explanatory. However, from a museography perspective, the timeline failed to provide any relevant information concerning the civil war. For this reason, it is important to highlight what was excluded from the timeline. First, as in the campaign room, the circumstances involving Monterrosa's death are concealed. The timeline said only that "Col. Monterrosa died on October 23, 1984." Once again, this demonstrates how the army resists giving the ERP any credit for Monterrosa's assassination. More blatantly, the timeline omitted all the massacres carried out by the army (El Sumpul in 1980, El Mozote in 1981, El Calabozo in 1982, to name just some of the most well known) alongside the assassination of the six Jesuit priests and two women in 1989 at the Universidad Centroamericana, among other atrocities and war crimes.

It is important to stress that despite being part of the same curatorial project, both the campaign and the peace accords rooms offered dissimilar narratives of the internal conflict. While the campaign room presented the war as a one-sided defense of national sovereignty against an unspecified enemy, the peace accords room mentioned for the first time the factions of the war, subsuming the army into the national government. Notwithstanding the different approaches, both rooms had something in common: they were not able to articulate a coherent and comprehensive narrative of the civil war. This opens the possibility for at least two not necessarily mutually exclusive interpretations. First, the curatorial team considers the civil war to be well known by the population, and therefore everything in the museum is self-explanatory and needs no further explanation. Second, despite its central role in the conflict, the army cannot fully articulate today a comprehensive discourse that explains the war from their perspective. As a result, it contin-

FIGURE 9 Museo de Historia Militar's main entrance, San Salvador, El Salvador. Photo by Javiera Escobar Yametti.

ually falls into repeating the idea of a "defensive campaign" during the armed conflict. Whatever the answer, it is well known that the army has much more to lose when it comes to the atrocities of the civil war. Perhaps because of that, the less information provided, the better for them.

THE MUSEUM IN 2023

Four years following my initial visit, it was clear that Nayib Bukele's government severely intervened in the museum (as in the armed forces in general). The first thing I noticed when I entered the museum was a frame with a picture of Bukele surrounded by smaller pictures of Salvadoran high-ranking officers, who make up El Salvador's High Command of the Armed Forces, establishing that all state forces are under the authority of the civilian government. The subordination of the army to the civilian mandate has also affected the museum's curatorial stance.

The rooms dedicated to the civil war (the military campaign and the peace accords rooms) had been blended into one, utilizing the space that previously housed the Civil War/Military Campaign room. The one dedicated to the peace accords had been closed. Many things were lost in this transition. Most notoriously, the names of all the soldiers, commanders, and generals that were remembered and honored by the army in the civil war room have been removed. The praising and memorabilia of the BIRI Atlacatl Battalion have also been eliminated. Some photographs were kept, but there is no indication of who the people in them are. The back of the room, now dedicated to the process of peace, displays pictures of Alfredo Cristiani and Juan Napoléon Duarte and paintings made by kids in the first years of the postwar era. Nevertheless, there is barely any information about the war or the process of peace. The problematic timeline is not there anymore. Although many of the changes introduced into the museum are positive, such as the removal of the celebratory images of the Atlacatl Battalion, it is also true that the museum considerably debilitated its (already weak and questionable) discourse regarding the civil war. In its original form, the military museum at least presented some ideas that a relatively informed visitor could grasp. In its present version, the civil war and the peace process have been relegated to an irrelevant position, which is Bukele's view of the armed conflict.

The modifications introduced in recent years have significantly affected the way the army used to grieve their dead. Before 2019 the army mourned the deceased soldiers in a similar way as the former guerrillas. In the 1980–1992

Campaign Room, a banner presented several passport photos and names of some deceased military members during the war. These dead soldiers were portrayed here as national heroes who devoted their lives to defending *la patria* and willingly made the ultimate sacrifice. In 2023 the only remaining form of honoring deceased soldiers is the monument called Tumba del soldado héroe de transmisiones, placed at the entrance to the museum. This memorial honors the soldiers who died during the 1980s while working in communications. The monument includes a list of over fifty soldiers who "offered their lives to *la patria* as a model for future generations." Once again, we do not learn how or why they died; we must accept the general statement that they did it with honor and for the sake of El Salvador. While the army tries to continue honoring their dead, it is apparent that they are not interested in seeking justice or revenge. Borrowing James Tatum's words, "mourning the dead of one war becomes training for cadets who will fight the next."[90] The soldiers' deaths are inscribed within the logic of the war (any war, not only the civil war), and hence once the conflict is over, all dead become heroes. Mourning is, at least discursively, rapidly accomplished.

* * *

By contrasting these two museums, it is possible to observe that despite their radically opposing perspectives, the way in which they address the work of mourning—at least at the superficial level—is fairly similar. Both the army and the former guerrillas have codified their dead in a system that makes their death a meaningful act. Nevertheless, what is problematic in this endeavor is that both soldiers and guerrillas seem to have died for nothing concrete, at least according to the Museo de la Revolución and the Museo de Historia Militar. When visitors leave these sites, they may understand that the dead are "martyrs" or "heroes," but both museums lack a narration that can historize and further explain the reasons behind their deaths. What I claim is that the codification process of the combatants' death is both extensive and superficial. While dead guerrillas generally fall under the category of "martyrs" and deceased soldiers are "heroes," these categories aim to be self-explanatory to the audience. They are called repeatedly martyrs and heroes, but why? That is a question to which neither of these places can adequately respond. Perhaps, seeking an answer to this question might mean opening a grieving process that is, at least superficially, closed. The meaning, albeit empty, is given and accepted, and no further tears seem to be necessary for these dead. Perhaps because of this, the military museum has been able to incorporate the modifications ordered by the government since 2019.

Ultimately, it is important to stress that while both museums propose a finished work of mourning, their respective narratives are far from being inclusive and open to other parts of society. The Museum of Military History does not recognize the enemy as someone who deserves to be grieved, and therefore no mention of guerrilla or civilian victims is made. By the same token, the Museum of the Revolution celebrates the death of army members (Monterrosa is the perfect example) and allows no room for the enemy to be mourned. Whereas the latter may not be surprising, it does make evident how the community of mourners also shapes a social situation in which no faction can recognize the other's humanity and right to mourn. As a result, the "completed" mourning embodied by these sites does not engage in the process of bringing other people together to mourn the deceased. Instead, they exhibit their allegedly accomplished work with pride, but they always make a clear distinction between them and the rest of the society that does not participate in said work. Thus, although these places present themselves as sites that have completed the process of mourning, they fail to welcome and incorporate other people with different views into their apparently successful work.

Grassroots Memorials: Fighting for the Right to Mourn

The Monument to Memory and Truth

On December 6, 2003, the Comité Pro-Monumento a las Víctimas Civiles de Violaciones a los Derechos Humanos, a collectivity of ten civil society organizations, inaugurated the Monumento a la Memoria y la Verdad in the Cuscatlán Park in the heart of San Salvador. The Comité was created in 1997, mostly by women, and its goal was to memorialize the victims of the civil war, a task neglected by the Salvadoran state.[91] The memorial is eighty-five meters long and three meters high, and it was inspired by the Vietnam Veterans Memorial in Washington, D.C., designed by Maya Lin.

The Monumento a la Memoria y la Verdad is the result of more than six years of work. Its objective is to dignify and establish the truth about the death of thousands of civilians during the civil war and to contribute to the almost nonexistent politics of memory in the country. In achieving that objective, the Comité aimed to comply (albeit unofficially) with one of the central recommendations made by the truth commission: the building of a memorial to honor the victims of the armed conflict. When the first portion of the memorial was inaugurated, it listed 25,625 names. In 2005 it was complemented with a relief mural created by Julio Reyes, "el tigre," that depicts the years of the Salvadoran civil war. The memorial had a great reception among the victims' relatives, and thousands of people asked the Comité to also include their dead loved ones. As a result, in 2008, a second phase of the memorial was inaugurated, adding 3,169 names and also 194 massacres that occurred between 1970 and 1992.[92] The monument is organized chronologically, by year, from the 1970s to the early 1990s. A noteworthy feature is that the names are grouped into two categories, "homicides" and "disappeared," giving visibility even to those whose bodies were never found.

Like similar war memorials worldwide, the Monumento a la Memoria y la Verdad is a cenotaph, the largest one in El Salvador. Still, for many people, this memorial becomes "a kind of cemetery where people can bring flowers [*enflorar*] [, . . .] reterritorializing the meaning of the place."[93] The Monumento, as cenotaph/cemetery, is also a place where the dead's relatives and friends can "visit" them, and it is here where hundreds of people gather every November 2, the Día de los Difuntos, and for some, the unofficial "Day of the disappeared," to honor the deceased.[94]

The Salvadoran state declined to provide any funding for the project. However, this did not stop the Comité, which raised money from individuals and groups willing to contribute to its construction.[95] In many respects, as Annette Hernández Rivas suggests, the Monumento was a "counter-memorial" since it defied everything the Salvadoran state had done in terms of memorialization for the victims of the war, which at the time was next to zero.[96] No representative of Francisco Flores's government from the ARENA party was present at the inauguration. The highest authority to attend the ceremony was San Salvador's major, the FMLN militant Carlos Rivas Zamora, who said the memorial should "seal" all the injustices that took place in El Salvador,[97] reinforcing the ARENA-FMLN's impunity discourse adopted since the peace accords. After the inauguration, the Comité sought to include a visit to the memorial in the national education curriculum, but the Ministry of Education denied their request.[98] Perhaps, the most crucial struggle between the Comité and the Salvadoran state was the designation of the memorial as "Protected Heritage" (Bien cultural protegido), which would

FIGURE 10 Monumento a la Memoria y la Verdad, San Salvador, El Salvador. Photo by Javiera Escobar Yametti.

have forced the state to take responsibility for the memorial and its care. The government denied this petition for years until 2013, when Mauricio Funes's administration finally recognized the memorial as national heritage.

The Monument to Memory and Truth is one of the most relevant places of memory in postwar El Salvador and one of the few sites that facilitates the work of mourning in the country. Unlike the Museum of the Revolution and the Museum of Military History, the Monumento a la Memoria y la Verdad invites all relatives and friends of civilian victims to join and mourn together. The key to making this site a place of reunion is the civilian status of the dead. After arduous discussion, the committee decided to acknowledge everyone who did not die in combat as a "civilian victim." For example, the memorial includes the names of the twelve people who died in the FMLN ambush in a restaurant in Zona Rosa in 1985, where four U.S. marines who were in the country supporting the Salvadoran army were killed. This criterion allows for a common ground in which people from different factions and political beliefs can come together and mourn their dead. Also, the memorial rejects the heroification of certain figures and does not privilege any of the dead

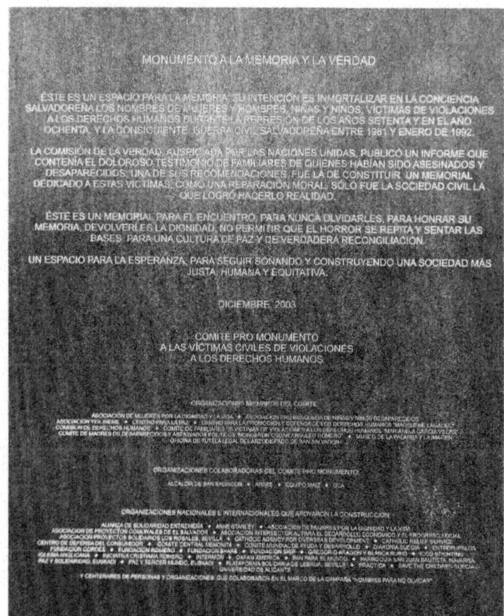

FIGURE 11 Dedicatory plaques to the civilian victims of the Salvadoran civil war, Monumento a la Memoria y la Verdad, San Salvador, El Salvador. Photo by Javiera Escobar Yametti.

FIGURE 12 Dedicatory plaques to the civilian victims of the Salvadoran civil war, Monumento a la Memoria y la Verdad, San Salvador, El Salvador. Photo by Javiera Escobar Yametti.

over others. Thus, Monseñor Romero's and Roque Dalton's names are inscribed in the same size and font as everyone else. As a result, the memorial builds a community of mourners that goes beyond the ideological division (as the army and guerrilla museums do) and proposes a site in which all mourners of civilian victims are welcome to grieve and participate on equal terms regardless of their ideology.

The Monumento has its limitations, albeit some of them are far from the creators' control and are the result of the lack of state support. The first problem is its visibility. Unlike D'Aubuisson's and Handal's memorials, the Monumento cannot be seen from outside the park. Even more, someone walking through the Cuscatlán Park might easily overlook the memorial because of its relatively hidden location. Also, between 2017 and 2019, the park was closed for remodeling, and therefore the most important civil war memorial was inaccessible to visitors. These included victims' relatives, who were not able to *enflorar* the cenotaph for the Día de los difuntos in 2018, which doubtlessly affected hundreds of mourners.[99] In the park's recent remodeling, the memorial did not gain any special attention. If any, there is a footbridge that connects the park with the outside avenue that passes over the memorial, but the consequences of this in terms of exposure are not yet determined. On a symbolic level, it is still debated whether the names of combatants who died during the civil war should be inscribed in this memorial. Perhaps that may contribute to a project of national mourning and eventually national reconciliation. However, having the names of war criminals next to their victims is something not many people are willing to accept.

Despite any potential discussion about who deserves to be included in the memorial and its limitations, the Monumento a la Memoria y la Verdad's decisive role in the process of memory and mourning in postwar El Salvador is undeniable. This site invites visitors to reflect and relatives and friends of the dead to mourn. By doing so, the Monumento calls for action in the public sphere in a country where mourning is intended to be reduced to the minimum work possible.

Grieving the El Mozote Massacre

Two hundred kilometers from San Salvador, in the *departamento* of Morazán, lies the hamlet of El Mozote. During the early 1980s, Morazán was considered a "red zone" controlled almost entirely by the guerrillas, and many local communities, willingly or not, supported or joined the Ejército Revolucionario del Pueblo (ERP). Before December 1981, El Mozote was an important economic center in the region and had an active social life. According to Binford, "as El Mozote grew in economic importance, it developed into an embryonic village with which residents of surrounding hamlets identified."[100] Nevertheless, El Mozote's history of economic development was abruptly truncated by the infamous and bloody actions carried out by the Salvadoran Army in December 1981 during the so-called Operation Rescue. This "was a meticulous operation intended to drain the civilian 'water' from the sea and thereby strand the guerrilla 'fish.'"[101]

On December 9, 1981, soldiers of the BIRI Atlacatl Battalion, an elite unit of the Salvadoran National Army trained by the United States in the School of the Americas, attacked the village of Arambala and killed several males who were on a "blacklist." The following day, the troops moved to El Mozote, where they spent the night. On December 11, the army conducted the largest massacre in the history of the Salvadoran civil war. In addition to Arambala, the army attacked six villages: the *caseríos* of El Mozote, Ranchería, Los Toriles, and Jacote Amarillo, and the *cantones* La Joya and Cerro Pando. They also attacked a cave in Cerro Ortiz. The slaughtering is known as the El Mozote Massacre not only because El Mozote was the best-known hamlet in the area but also because most of the victims died in El Mozote. The exact number of losses is still unclear. The 1991 Tutela Legal report enumerated 794 victims in all the villages, but the number of victims rose to 819 in the 2008 report.[102] In 2017 the Salvadoran state established an updated official number of 978 and fixed the total number of victims (including relatives, survivors, and displaced) at 1658.[103]

Despite the brutality of the events and the first accounts provided by Radio Venceremos, the *New York Times*, and the *Washington Post*,[104] both the Salvadoran and the U.S. governments energetically denied the massacre and the army's involvement in it, calling the reports nothing but communist propaganda. José Napoléon Duarte, Salvadoran head of state at the time, claimed that the alleged killing "was a 'guerrilla trick' meant to smear his government at the very moment when the United States Congress was considering aid to El Salvador."[105] The massacre remained almost completely concealed until the end of the war. Over a decade later, in 1992, the Argentine Forensic Anthropology Team conducted the first exhumations in the area. They found "more than 141 skeletons inside of one site, from which 134 corresponded to children under ten years of age, as well as substantial bullet fragments and spent gun cartridges."[106] In future excavations, hundreds of other skeletons will be found. Notwithstanding the evidence, the massacre was systematically denied by all postwar ARENA administrations. Only on January 16, 2012, during the commemoration of the twentieth anniversary of the peace accords, President Mauricio Funes acknowledged the Salvadoran army's participation in the massacre and asked for forgiveness in the name of the state.[107]

Because of the amnesty law in effect from 1992 to 2016, the victims had no recourse to a legal process in El Salvador for over three decades. In 1990 Tutela Legal, a human rights organization, presented the first motion to have a trial against the Salvadoran state at the Inter-American Court of Human Rights. After a tedious and lengthy process in which the Salvadoran government declined to follow the IACHR's recommendations, the court held a trial in 2011, *Caso el Mozote y lugares aledaños vs. El Salvador*. In its sentencing, decided on October 25, 2012, the IACHR found the Salvadoran Army guilty of human rights crimes and condemned the Salvadoran state to make compensations to the victims' families, among other obligations.[108] Nevertheless, only on September 2, 2016, did the government of Salvador Sánchez Cerén publish a decree informing the specific tasks the state would perform to comply with the IACHR's decision ("Decreto No. 53"). In 2018, when the Court supervised whether the Salvadoran state had complied with the resolution, it found that only two out of the twelve points were followed, one of them being "publishing the sentence and its official summary."[109] In recent years, the case has taken new paths, and for the first time the U.S. government agreed to collaborate with the investigations. The final sentencing regarding the El Mozote massacre has yet to be decided.[110]

Memorialization practices and public mourning in El Mozote began in 1991 when a group of priests conducted the first open-air memorial service in the area.[111] People from the Central American University (UCA) installed the first memorial in the hamlet's square. The monument, which at the time was a cenotaph, consisted of "a metallic sculpture representing a family, the figure of a woman, a man, a small boy and a girl holding hands," which became a symbol of the massacre.[112] In 1994 the metallic sculpture experienced a profound transformation in its memorialization goal. After the exhumations conducted by the Argentine Forensic Anthropology Team, hundreds of corpses were buried under the sculpture, and a new memorial wall with the names of the victims was built. Thus, the memorial, once a

FIGURE 13 Memorial at El Mozote, El Salvador. Photo by Javiera Escobar Yametti.

cenotaph, became a tomb for hundreds of people slaughtered in the massacre, facilitating the work of mourning for some of the victims' families. In 2001 new human remains found nearby were also buried in the site.[113] When Rufina Amaya, the sole survivor of the killings and a tireless activist, died in 2007, she was also buried underneath the monument following her wishes (fig. 13).

El Mozote's memorialization process coincided with the repopulation of the area. After the massacre, El Mozote became a ghost town. People did not return to live in the zone until 1992, when groups of refugees coming from camps in Honduras returned to El Salvador and began to repopulate this desolated region.[114] However, many returnees did not have any relationship with the slaughtered inhabitants of El Mozote. The latter, alongside the returnees' own pain, added an extra layer of complexity to the memorialization process.

The year of 2006 is significant for the memorialization in El Mozote. Until then, Catholic priest Rogelio Ponceele was the undisputed authority regarding commemorations and monuments, and locals had little voice in this work. In 2006, the priest Juan José del Cid took spiritual control of the area, facilitating grassroots memorial projects.[115] For the twenty-fifth anniversary of the massacre, the local community decided to paint murals on the hamlet's chapel. The original chapel was destroyed during the massacre, but in 2001 it was rebuilt in the same location. Argentine artist Claudia Bernardi, who accompanied the forensic process led by the Argentinean forensic team, was asked to conduct this project. The goal was to have the community decide what to paint in the mural, which led to serious debate. According to Bernardi, the community was divided. Half of them "wanted to paint the massacre itself; half of the community refused to accept that the massacre ever existed."[116] Finally, the community agreed to paint a mural that included both the history of El Mozote before the war and how they envisioned the hamlet's future, avoiding any reference to the massacre.

At first sight, the double temporality of the mural is not entirely clear (fig. 14). However, with some aid, observers can notice that there is a path in the middle of the mural that connects El Mozote's past and future. Also, the colors used to portray the past are slightly darker than the ones used to paint the hamlet's future. The past, located on the right of the mural, is portrayed as a peaceful and nonproblematic period in which people harvested the land and went to church. This representation of the premassacre period has not avoided criticism. Alarcón and Binford claim that the mural does not evidence "the poverty that compelled most people to leave the region periodically to work as cheap labour under highly oppressive conditions."[117] The left side of the mural portrays the hamlet's aspirations: noteworthy is the bilingual school and children reading the history of El Mozote while studying on a Wi-Fi-connected laptop. While criticism of the mural is entirely valid, from a mourning perspective, we must consider the impact of creating the mural as a form of community engagement and trauma healing. Recounting her experience, Bernardi says that the mural served the purpose of bringing together current inhabitants of El Mozote even though they did not agree at first on how to represent the hamlet's history. "At times," Bernardi describes, "I counted fifty-five people painting together on the large field of the mural."[118] Regardless of the results, such a number of people painting in a hamlet that only housed a couple of hundred inhabitants gives us a clear perspective of the high level of community engagement carried out for this project. All of them, even newcomers, seemed to have developed a strong connection with the land that now hosts them. In this light, the high level of engagement

FIGURE 14 Mural painted by the community of El Mozote with the guidance of Claudia Bernardi, El Mozote, El Salvador. Photo by Javiera Escobar Yametti.

regarding the tragedy of El Mozote is much more important than depicting the massacre itself on the chapel's wall.

Whereas the north side of the chapel portrays memories and dreams of El Mozote's inhabitants, the south side is dedicated to the children who died in the massacre. In an adjacent patio is located the "Garden of Reflection—The Innocents" (*Jardín de reflexión—Los inocentes*), which was also part of Bernardi's work. On that site, 140 children's cadavers under the age of twelve were found in the 1992 exhumation. In my August 2019 visit, the "Garden" consisted of a cordoned-off section that displays the original floor of the chapel, where it is allegedly still possible to see the children's blood.[119] Also, there is written information regarding the massacre (one of the few written narrations of the massacre found in the memorial) and pictures of Rufina Amaya and Dr. María Hernández (Tutela Legal's director until 2007). The main piece of the "Garden" is the "Mural of the Light," a mosaic mural that covers the chapel's south wall. The mosaic depicts children surrounded by butterflies playing outdoors under clouds, the sun, and a rainbow (fig. 15).

FIGURE 15 Jardín de Reflexión—Los inocentes. Mural created by the community with the guidance of Claudia Bernardi to commemorate the children assassinated by the Atlacatl Battalion, El Mozote, El Salvador. Photo by Javiera Escobar Yametti.

Akin the Museo de la Revolución, the El Mozote memorial labels the victims of the massacre as "martyrs." While the word *martyr* is not overtly visible to visitors, it is repeatedly used by the guides. As previously explained, the word *martyr* is habitual in postwar El Salvador to refer to victims of state terrorism, especially considering the profound impact of the liberation theology in the revolutionary process. Analyzing the existence of "postwar memories" in El Salvador, Carlos Gregorio López Bernal proposes the existence of a "martyrial memory," which is a form of memory that alludes predominantly to repressive actions carried out by the state against unarmed victims. However, it is also used to describe guerrillas who died in combat fighting an enemy superior in number and weapons.[120] Although inscribing the dead under a martyrial logic always faces the risk of overcoding the dead to provide meaning to what otherwise may be meaningless—especially if we consider that approximately half of the victims in El Mozote were children—the use of the word *martyr* in this context has a different meaning from the one given in the Museo de la Revolución. In El Mozote, martyrdom works as an identity that fuels a collective demand for justice and to establish the truth about the horrifying deeds that took place in December 1981. It is, in other words, a productive category, and not a stable term, as it is used in the Museo de la Revolución. In my August 2019 visit, amid the discussion of the new amnesty law in El Salvador, doña Delfina, one of the leaders and the spokeswoman of the memorial, told me that the community was against the amnesty laws since they were still seeking reparations for the massacre. During the 2018 visit of representatives of the Inter-American Court of Human Rights, doña Delfina expressed the thought that "nosotras ahora somos luchadoras y peleonas, vamos a seguir exigiendo justicia."[121] El Mozote's "martyrs" are not passive dead who should be praised for their brave actions. Instead, they are presented as victims of state terrorism whose names are inscribed on a wall visible for everyone who visits the memorial so that their memory is not forgotten in the hopes that one day justice will be given to them.

There are, indeed, some complexities in the mourning process in El Mozote. For instance, there has been a thorough discussion among current inhabitants regarding in what manner (and how much) they want to participate in the memorialization process. In this context it is important to reiterate that after the massacre the hamlet was uninhabited until the early 1990s, when groups of refugees returned to repopulate the area. Hence, people currently living in El Mozote do not necessarily have a personal connection with the massacre (some of them did not even know about it) and remember the hamlet as a quiet and ideal place. Religious beliefs also mediate the situation with debates between conservative and liberal Catholic priests. The growing presence of an Evangelical community also jeopardizes how the work of mourning is conducted in the hamlet.[122]

The ruling of the Inter-American Court has incorporated the current inhabitants of El Mozote into a work of mourning that was not entirely theirs in the beginning (or at least not everyone's). Many of the people who first occupied this land after the peace accords were refugees dealing with their own losses, and therefore it is unsurprising that some of them decided not to become involved in the massacre's memorialization process (or that many of them denied the existence of the massacre itself, which was the official version for decades). Nevertheless, over time, with the development of tourism and memorialization, and also with the funds allocated as reparation (always too limited), the connection between the hamlet's inhabitants and the memory of the massacre strengthened. I am not suggesting that their sorrow is not real or that the community accommodates the changing circumstances out of selfish interest. What I am proposing is that in recent years it is the massacre's memorialization process, more than the massacre itself, that has built a community of mourners in El Mozote.

Today, many of El Mozote's inhabitants grieve the dead as their own even if they were not blood related or never met. Bernardi expresses this perception when working with the community in 2006: "Who could expect that in this place of death a community would come together to paint a mural of remembrance."[123] What makes the event "unexpected" is not a community of people mourning their dead but rather the unique emergence of a community of mourners who do not have a conventional connection with the dead. It would be simplistic, and even unethical, to propose a straightforward explanation for this singularity. Despite the relatively small number of the hamlet's inhabitants, each person has their own different and personal reasons to join the community of mourners. While it can be said that some may have been attracted to take part in the process because of the (direct or indirect) economic reward, many others probably feel an emotional connection with the massacre that took place on the same ground where they now live. Some members of the community are also relatives of the people who were slaughtered by the army in those infamous days of December 1981.

One final layer in the memorialization process is the role of the Salvadoran state. At first, the memorialization process was conducted entirely by civil society (such as the Central American University and local priests) without any governmental participation or interference. However, after the 2012 sentence of the Inter-American Court of Human Rights, the state "added" itself to the memorial in 2016 with a plaque saying that "en cumplimiento de la sentencia y reparación a las víctimas nos suscribimos." In 2017, during Sánchez Cerén's government, the Salvadoran state produced a documentary film entitled *El Mozote nunca más*, following the Inter-American Court's sentence that mandated them to produce a documentary saying that the massacre was executed by the Atlacatl Battalion. The documentary was launched in December 2017 on Channel 10 and screened in El Mozote's main square.[124] A few days later, on December 17, the documentary was streamed through the Government of El Salvador's Facebook page, where it has been watched over one hundred thousand times as of June 2023.[125]

In recent years the memorial has also been affected by Nayib Bukele's government. In December 2020, the Salvadoran president traveled to El Mozote to say, in front of hundreds of relatives of the victims, that the war was a farce, and promised new public works in the hamlet.[126] On March 4, 2022, without consulting with local residents, the Human Rights Association of El Mozote, or the municipality of Meanguera, the National Direction of Municipal Works (DOM) showed up and informed villagers that they would begin works in El Mozote's main square, where the memorial is located, triggering perplexity and discontent among the residents.[127] In my 2023 visit, doña Delfina proudly told me how they stood up and defended the memorial. Still, in the end, they had to agree to certain changes imposed by the government, like the demolition of the acoustic shell built only a few years earlier, and most importantly, the building of a state-sponsored memorial. The two main additions were a fifteen-meter timeline of the civil war and the building of an "interactive" white cube. The new memorial has been criticized by local residents since it was announced in December 2021, among other things, for not focusing on justice and reparation for the victims.[128]

The El Mozote memorial is no doubt a complex site where different social, economic, and memorialization perspectives meet and, at times, clash. The memorialization process has as of today over thirty years of history. Many things have taken place during the last three decades, and we can foresee many transformations occurring soon. It is also true that most of the things that have taken place in El Mozote in the recent decades were shaped by the neoliberal transformations initiated by the ARENA governments. Following Binford, "development interventions in El Mozote have been inscribed in neoliberal forms of governmentality that promote private property, the market, and individual enterprise over communal property, the state, and collective enterprise."[129] Still, from a mourning perspective, El Mozote is one of the most active and community-engaged memorials in El Salvador. The site is, despite all valid criticism, a place of lament but also a place of work. Many years before the Salvadoran state asked for forgiveness (without justice), the community decided to look for their dead relatives and friends to grieve them. The burial of a portion of the victims in the memorial previously built, and converting the cenotaph into an actual tomb, is a powerful move toward the work of mourning because, as Derrida reminds us, mourning "consists always in attempting to ontologize the remains, to make them present, in the first place by *identifying* the bodily remains and by *localizing* the dead."[130] The exhumation, identification, and burial of the dead in a site that previously remembered the dead could not be anything but a positive step toward mourning. Nonetheless, this is an incomplete process, since many people still have not found their relatives' bodies, and all of them are still waiting for justice and reparation.[131] But incomplete does not mean passive. The thousands of people that visit the site each year, in addition to the hundreds of people that participate in the walks to El Mozote for the anniversary of the massacre every year or during Perquín's winter festival, among other events, take part in a tireless, collective mourning process that fights for visibility and invites others to keep working.

* * *

Both the Monumento a la Memoria y la Verdad and the memorial at El Mozote are arguably the most important memorialization initiatives in postwar El Salvador. They share many things in common; namely, they were grassroots memorials erected with no state funding, and in their origin, they fought to establish truth that was systematically denied by the Salvadoran state. However, the relevance of these sites for the purpose of this book does not lie in their importance regarding keeping the memory of the dead alive or telling the truth about the atrocities carried out during the civil war. Instead, I highlight these memorials because of their active role in the mourning process in the public sphere and for their essential function in developing communities of mourners that exceed the intimate and familiar circle. The creation of these sites and the mourning activities that take place in them at different times of the year enable the visibility of the work of mourning in the Salvadoran public sphere and invite different sectors of society to participate in it.

Countermourning: Reconciliation, Oblivion, and Impunity

Finally, I will analyze two places that could be considered "countermourning" sites: the Proyecto de Paz y Reconciliación, in Morazán, and the Parque Escultórico a la Reconciliación, in San Salvador. These sites demonstrate that discourses of oblivion and impunity are also present in alleged memorialization projects, highlighting the existence of radically opposed attitudes toward the work of mourning.

The Project of Peace and Reconciliation

One kilometer away from El Mozote's square lies the Proyecto de Paz y Reconciliación, which is often mentioned in the tours to El Mozote as the next site to visit. This place, inaugurated in 2016, was conceived by a German priest living in Ecuador and built by an Ecuadorean architect and an Irish Catholic engineer on a piece of land owned by a Salvadoran priest currently living in New Jersey.[132] It is apparent that the nearby communities (including El Mozote's inhabitants) had little to no participation in this monument besides providing labor in its construction.

The Proyecto de Paz y Reconciliación is located on the top of a hill surrounded by vegetation. Visitors are welcomed by a sign that informs them that the site is a "response from Christian faith to the cruelest genocide that occurred in this place." The "cruelest genocide," visitors should guess, is the massacre at El Mozote, which is never mentioned in this monument.

The site has five sections in total. The first and foremost part "remembers" the victims of the massacre. (I am deliberately using quotations marks here in their two common uses. First, as a quotation, and second, to denote that something must not be fully trusted.) When visitors first approach the central section, they see two plinths sculpted in low relief on each side of the main entrance. The one on the right exhibits a Pietà very similar to Michelangelo's work, and on the left there is a crucified Jesus accompanied by the Virgin Mary and John the Apostle. The central piece of the section is approximately ten meters tall. From bottom to top, it includes sculptures of Martin Luther King Jr., Mahatma Gandhi, Mother Teresa of Calcutta, and Pope John Paul II. Above them, there is a sculpture of Jesus Christ with open arms and the sentence *La paz os dejo la paz os doy* (Peace I leave with you, my peace I give to you) underneath him. Above Jesus's head there is a crown, and over it a reproduction of the sculpture of the family that remembers El Mozote's victims (fig. 16). The Proyecto also has a children's playground and a small square that pays homage to Monseñor Romero (which also offers a panoramic view of the area). Finally, it has a spiritual center and a replica of the chapel where Saint Nicholás de Flüe lived in Switzerland in the fifteenth century.

FIGURE 16 Proyecto de Paz y Reconciliación, El Mozote, El Salvador. Photo by Javiera Escobar Yametti.

Despite the intentions inscribed in the welcome message, there is scarce connection between the Proyecto de Paz y Reconciliación and the massacre of El Mozote. Rather, this project contradicts the claims for justice and the work of mourning carried out by the El Mozote memorial by omitting any concrete reference to the killing besides the vague expression "the cruelest genocide." The Proyecto goes even further and resignifies the famous black sculpture that represents the victims of El Mozote by claiming that this figure symbolizes the role of the family as "the main educator of peace." Through this voiding process, the project aims to erase the political violence and state terrorism carried out in the area during the civil war to privilege an ahistorical discourse of peace. This is reinforced through an analysis of what is included in the memorial. For example, the people depicted in this site, with the exception of Pope John Paul II and perhaps Mother Teresa of Calcutta, were completely unknown to the local people.[133] Still, for the Christian developers of the project, these universal "figures of peace" can fix, almost by magic, the atrocities carried out by the army in the area, making it even unnecessary to utter what happened nearby that deserves this site in the first place.

Although it would be easy to dismiss this place for its disconnection with local reality, the truth is that this site also plays a role within the battle of mourning. This monumental building, which is often included as part of the tour to El Mozote and surpasses the visibility of the El Mozote memorial on Ruta de Paz's official website,[134] embodies the aseptic condition of peace and reconciliation that has officially been established in postwar El Salvador. The Proyecto de Paz y Reconciliación is an overt call for peace, but it fails to explain why peace is needed. Unlike the case of the Museo de la Revolución, where silence can be interpreted as a subterranean work of mourning for the FMLN's crimes and "mistakes," silence in this context represents the erasure of the past, an effort to conceal the civil war, its causes, and its violence. This site argues that mourning is no longer needed. More importantly, its sole presence in the area aims to stop (or at least counterbalance) the active work of mourning that is taking place only one kilometer away. To achieve its goal, the Proyecto de Paz y Reconciliación does not hesitate to reinterpret the massacre of El Mozote for its own agenda, promoting impunity and forgetting disguised as peace.

The Reconciliation Sculpture Park

On January 15, 2017, the eve of the twenty-fifth anniversary of the peace accords, FMLN president Salvador Sánchez Cerén inaugurated the Parque Escultórico a la Reconciliación, located on Boulevard Monseñor Romero, in San Salvador. The park, destroyed in early 2024, had four sections. The most important one was the Monumento a la Reconciliación, which consisted of two elements. First, the ten-meter-tall naked torso of a blue woman, the Mater Civis, *la patria*, who pointed an accusatory finger in the direction of the second part of the monument, the seven-meter-tall sculpture of a guerrilla and a soldier who walked toward the future (and away from the naked woman) with their arms around each other while releasing nine peace doves. The second section was a sixteen-meter relief mural called *Huellas del Jaguar* (Jaguar's footprints), which aimed to tell the history of El Salvador, from its Indigenous origins—with representations of maize and Quetzalcoatl—to the present day. This included the 1811 revolt and distinguished Salvadorans such as María de los Ángeles Miranda, President Óscar Osorio Hernández, Alberto Masferrer, and Roque Dalton, among others. Of all the people, the principal figure was Monseñor Romero, whose face was two or three times larger than the others, and who was also located above the rest. The third section, located underneath the sculptures of the naked blue woman and the combatants was the Plaque of the Peace Signatories. The plaque was a large-scale reproduction of the signatures of all those who signed the peace accords on January 16, 1992, including FMLN leader Schafik Handal, President Alfredo Cristiani, and UN representative Cristián Salazar. The last section was a path that connected the different areas of the memorial, called the "Path to Reconciliation."

The project, developed without public or community consultation by the Ministry of Public Works, aimed to "unify Salvadoran society" and "prevent future generations from repeating the mistakes of the past."[135] Nevertheless, the monument faced public criticism even before its inauguration. Rome-based Salvadoran sculptor Napoléon Alberto developed the original mock-up, but the sculptures were built by Taller de Fundición Vielma in Mexico without Alberto's supervision. The artist expressed his dissatisfaction with the final work saying that the monument was "crude" (*tosco*), rigid, and with many anatomical and proportional defects. Film director Jorge Dalton, Roque Dalton's son, said that the monument was "horrific" and that the blue doll looked like an extraterrestrial figure out of a bad comic book (fig. 17).[136]

Beyond the understandable aesthetic condemnation, the fundamental citizens' criticism was the building of the monument without truth or justice and, of course, without peace. Another critical issue with this memorial was its utter silence regarding the violence of the civil war. As Rachel Hatcher points out, the monument was a celebration of the peace accords and its actors, and therefore it silenced "the repression, death, and violence that necessitated peace negotiations in the first place. Taking this to an extreme, there was no war and no victims who need to be remembered."[137] According to Eduardo Maciel, the Monumento a la Reconciliación reinforced what he calls the "January metaphor." Maciel proposes that this metaphor is the representation of the "victors" (the former guerrilla commandants, high-ranking military officers, and prominent politicians from both the FMLN and ARENA) who continued to hold and exercise their political power in the years following the end of the civil war. In other words, this metaphor consists of those who claim that the war ended "without winners or losers" but whose political power was never at risk in the political transition.[138]

Similar to what we observe in the Proyecto de Paz y Reconciliación, the Parque Escultórico a la Reconciliación lacked a coherent narrative of the civil war. The relief mural, the only section of the monument that aimed to

FIGURE 17 Monumento a la Reconciliación, San Salvador, El Salvador. Photo taken in 2019. Photo by Javiera Esocbar Yametti.

tell a story, squeezed two hundred years of history into the low relief facing dozens of people without contextualization. Apparently, its ultimate goal was inscribing the FMLN as the continuator of popular struggles and resistance in El Salvador's history.[139] Nevertheless, this memorial ignored the circumstances that gave rise to the FMLN, and by doing so the monument not only revealed its emptiness but also profoundly disrespected those who died so that the survivors could be alive at the time to congratulate themselves. The Parque Escultórico a la Reconciliación did very little in terms of the labor of memory. It did not remember anyone who was "forgotten" in history; neither did it offer an explicit narrative of the war nor support the civil war's victims and their families. Nevertheless, this controversial site did actively participate in the battle of mourning. By erasing the dead, the violence, the suffering, and the sorrow, the Parque appealed to a definite closure to the work of mourning. This site was an invitation to leave grief behind and focus on the promising future that can be reached through (unpunished) reconciliation.

The Reconciliation Sculpture Park has been another victim of Nayib Bukele's government. On June 4, 2020, during a public address in the context of the COVID-19 crisis, Bukele ordered the Minister of Public Works to dismantle the park for being a "horrible monument."[140] On December 30, 2021, almost two years later, the dismantling began, only to be interrupted a few hours later for unclear reasons (fig. 18).[141] I visited the park in March 2023, when it was already officially closed but nothing impeded access. The structure was still in place, although some elements were removed, like the doves, and others were destroyed, like the name of the park. On January 4, 2024, the Ministry of Public Works finally executed the destruction of the Mater Civis. Minister Romeo Herrera Rodríguez clarified that the order was only to destroy the blue sculpture and that the government would build a new monument in the same place within a few months.[142] As of March 2024, that had not occurred. Instead, on February 24, 2024, the former memorial made its debut as an open-air cinema with the screening of the 2001 film *Shrek*.[143]

Both the Proyecto de Paz y Reconciliación and the Parque Escultórico a la Reconciliación are perfect examples (albeit not the only ones) of how certain sites claim for the end of the work of mourning in postconflict Central America. Like the amnesty law that was in effect from 1993 to 2016 (and the

FIGURE 18 Initial destruction of the Parque Escultórico a la Reconciliación, San Salvador, El Salvador. Photo taken in March 2023. Photo by Javiera Escobar Yametti.

failed 2020 Law of National Reconciliation), these two sites adopt the term *reconciliation* as a form of promoting impunity and demand the closure of the work of mourning in postwar El Salvador. The term *reconciliation*, as Hatcher argues, is used in these examples in a very narrow and limited sense because it only applies to the factions that fought against each other in the war and that ultimately signed the peace accords.[144] The term does not even include everyone who participated in the war, since many rank-and-file former combatants reject the state-led reconciliation and criticize it for being a "top-down process that negates individual and community desire for social and economic justice."[145] Also, what this notion of reconciliation conceals are the tens of thousands of noncombatants who died because of state terrorism and political violence and whose lives and deaths did not seem to matter either back then or now.

It is important to note how the official position of the Salvadoran state has not varied significantly regardless of the rotation of political parties in power (at least in the 1992–2019 period; I will comment on Bukele's attitude toward memorialization in the conclusion to this chapter). While presidents from ARENA and the FMLN were in office, the state showed no interest in mourning the dead who did not belong to the factions in combat during the civil war. To an even greater extent, the Salvadoran state also sought ways to prevent the relatives of the dead from conducting their mourning process (as we observed in the refusal to build a memorial to the war's victims). While the thousands of combatants who died during the civil war are often not mourned or acknowledged in the present day except under the use of general terms such as *heroes* or *martyrs*, depending on their affiliations, they are expected to be mourned under allegoric rituals, like those directed toward Handal and D'Aubuisson. For the once ruling parties of El Salvador, only they deserve burial rituals and public mourning, and they decided to stop grieving a long time ago.

Conclusion

This chapter demonstrates that there is no one clear path in the civil war memorialization process in postconflict Central America. Instead, different civil society organizations, communities, and states have developed their own initiatives, and as a result, today we witness several memorials and museography projects that provoke dialogue and debate. As we have observed, each of these sites embodies its own unique discourse, contradictions, and work of mourning regardless of their similarities.

A fundamental issue I have considered when studying these sites is the foundation and preservation of a community of mourners. The latter is an essential issue in the discussion on mourning because, as I have discussed in the introduction following Judith Butler's reflection, the public work of mourning always presupposes the existence of a community that recognizes the dead as their own, thus building a political community that acts in the public sphere. Therefore, the potential to expand the limits of the community of mourners is directly related to the possibility of gaining visibility and political force through the inclusion of new participants and subjects who identify with the pain experienced by others. That is why I posit that the Monumento a la Memoria y la Verdad and the memorial in El Mozote are not only the two most important sites of memory in postwar El Salvador but also among the biggest catalyzers of the work of mourning in the country. These two sites have the particularity of having flexible boundaries (unlike, e.g., the Museo de Historia Militar), and thus they welcome everyone who wishes to join them and mourn the dead together, even without blood or affective ties in life. The active work of mourning embodied by the Monumento a la Memoria y la Verdad and El Mozote memorial bears witness to an active, productive process that refuses to stop grieving before the impassivity of the Salvadoran state. For the mourners who gather around these places, the dead are not fully dead; there is no eternal rest for them yet. The bodies, whether they have been found and buried or are still disappeared, are put to work by their relatives and loved ones and by any person who believes that their lives were worth living and their death is worth grieving.

On the other hand, it is evident that the Central American states have little interest in maintaining an open work of mourning for the victims of the civil wars. The successive postwar administrations have opted to ignore the sorrow of the dead's relatives to privilege an accelerated closure regardless of the corpses' fate, often ignored, and the impunity for war crimes. This is explicit in the memorialization initiatives developed by ARENA, the former guerrillas, and the Salvadoran army. They have chosen to signify their dead as "heroes" and "martyrs" within their internal narratives of the civil war, even if that means—as we can observe in the Museo de la Revolución—to swallow their own guilt regarding crimes they shamefully regret.

In 2019 the Salvadoran state took a radical new direction under Nayib Bukele, who called himself "the end of the postwar." Instead of continuing the FMLN discourse regarding forgiveness and, to a much lesser degree, memory, Bukele chose silence. On January 26, 2020, for the first time in twenty-eight years, there was no official ceremony to commemorate the signing of the peace accords. That position continued in the following years, becoming particularly evident during the thirtieth anniversary of the end of the war, in 2022. While Bukele has not offered any clear directions regarding the politics of memory, he has intervened in numerous memorial projects, from the army to the FMLN and ARENA, but he seems more concerned with their destruction (or reduction, at least) than with their resignification with the victims in mind.[146] As of today, Salvadoran civil society organizations and local communities seem to be the only ones who believe that the dead deserve proper and public mourning, memory, and justice.

Ultimately, it is essential to stress the historical condition of the memorials and museums studied here. All these sites were created between 1992 and 2017, and thus are still affectively engaged with civil war survivors and victims' relatives. However, despite their original intentions, it would not be surprising if the meaning and importance of these places mutated over time, or even for us to witness the destruction of any of them, as Bukele has done. Following Jay Winter, with the passage of the years and decades, sites of memory are susceptible to acquiring other meanings "derived from other needs or events," and they might even have "no meaning at all."[147] The fate of these sites is thus unpredictable. A good example of how memorials' meanings can easily be transformed in just a few decades is the case of the Monumento a la Constitución (better known as "la Chulona"), in San Salvador. This monument was inaugurated in 1990 by the Legislative Assembly, with Roberto D'Aubuisson as the Assembly's president, to honor the 1983 constitution (written by the Constitutional Assembly, led by D'Aubuisson himself). Despite the strong connection of this monument with the army and ARENA in its inception, the original meaning of this memorial is virtually lost. Official sources do not agree on its inauguration date, ordinary citizens ignore the origin of the monument, and more recently, feminist organizations have chosen this site as the loci of their public manifestations against gender-based violence. In December 2021, Alejandra Gavidia, Miss El Salvador, dressed as "la Chulona" during the Miss Universe competition to denounce violence against women in El Salvador.[148]

Whether the sites studied here will face the same fate as the Monumento a la Constitución is in the civil society's hands. It is up to the Salvadoran and Guatemalan citizens to choose and accept their inheritance. Nevertheless, what is known for a fact is that as of the early 2020s, all these sites, willingly or not, participate in a public battle over the work of mourning in post-conflict Central America. This battle, far from having winners or losers or imposing someone's view on others, is a struggle over something so personal and collective at the same time, the right to grieve.

CHAPTER 2

Staging Mourning in Postwar El Salvador

Jorgelina Cerritos's Ensayos sobre la Memoria

> No ha pasado suficiente tiempo para que, en todo este país, haya alguien de cualquier edad que no tenga pesadillas de la guerra.
>
> —JORGELINA CERRITOS, *13703. EL MISTERIO DE LAS UTOPÍAS*

This book posits that mourning takes several forms in the Central American public sphere. One of these expressions has the peculiarity of bringing a willing audience together to witness its manifestation: the artistic performance. Although visual and performative arts are far from being extensively developed in Central America, in the last few decades, numerous artists have explored how political violence and state terrorism have affected the lives of millions of people in the region and how their lament continues to be ignored. This chapter explores how Salvadoran theater, specifically the plays created by Jorgelina Cerritos, has embodied, symbolized, and staged El Salvador's traumatic past, thus participating in the battle over the work of mourning.

The dramatic arts and the work of mourning have been intertwined since the golden age of Greek theater in the fifth century BC. In his classic book, *The Origin of Tragedy,* William Ridgeway claims that the earliest dithyrambs, athletic feats, horsemanship contests, and tragic dances were "part of the same principle—the honouring and appeasing of the dead."[1] Similarly, Susan Letzler Cole suggests that tragic drama, from ancient Greece to the present, works as an "artistic transformation of the impulse to mourn," adding that "[t]he grave is the birthplace of tragic drama and ghosts are its procreators."[2] Unsurprisingly, dramatic arts have also been the starting point of numerous contemporary reflections regarding the work of mourning. Walter Benjamin's *The Origin of German Tragic Drama* (*Ursprung des Deutschen Trauer-*

spiels), a seminal book on the work of mourning in the twentieth century, is a perfect example of how dramatic arts and mourning nourish one another not only in ancient Greece but also in early modern European literature. A more recent example is David McIvor's *Mourning in America*, where the author traces his idea of the "democratic work of mourning" back to the Great Dionysia in the fifth century BC, specifically, to Aeschylus's *Oresteia*.

The history of Latin American theater is not too far from the tradition described above. Perhaps one of the most noteworthy examples is the abundance of adaptions of Sophocles's *Antigone* on Latin American stages. Following Juan González Betancur, the reworking of *Antigone*, the mourning character par excellence, is a response to the tragic destiny of the region.[3] In recent decades, Latin American theater has explored numerous paths to approach the political violence and state terrorism of the late twentieth century. These works often incorporate new trends in the dramatic arts, such as performance, documentary theater, postdramatic theater, and biodrama, among other influences. Maximiliano de la Puente claims that the overall goal of these works is not to objectify the atrocities of military dictatorships and civil wars but rather to resignify how that era is portrayed in the present.[4] As this chapter will demonstrate, Central America has not been absent in the development of the so-called Latin American *teatro de la memoria*.[5]

In its most comprehensive definition, performance has had a significant role in postauthoritarian Latin America, especially regarding efforts to heal from trauma and demands for justice. The Madres de Plaza de Mayo, for example, who have tirelessly sought truth and justice for their disappeared loved ones since 1977, are, in Diana Taylor's words, "the most emblematic of trauma-driven performance protest" in the region.[6] With much less visibility and support but no less enthusiasm and determination, we can also find examples of trauma-driven performance protests in Central America. One of the largest organizations to conduct an annual demonstration is H.I.J.O.S. Guatemala, which marches every June 30th throughout Zones 1 and 2 in Guatemala City visiting some of the sites studied in the previous chapter. In terms of artistic performance (what Taylor calls "denunciation-driven performances"), the compelling work of Guatemalan artist Regina José Galindo must not go unmentioned. In one of her most powerful works, *La verdad* (2013), Galindo sits on a chair while she reads testimonies of Maya women who suffered state violence during the internal conflict. All the while, a dentist injects her with anesthesia every ten minutes, numbing her mouth and causing her to slur her words. Among other things, this performance exposes the clash between the truth about the atrocities committed during the civil war and the attempts to silence the victims, their testimonies, and their claims for justice. Through this procedure, as Emanuela Jossa argues, Galindo can bring the victims to the fore in a society that constantly denies their pain.[7]

The power of performance lies in its capacity to irrupt in the public sphere and disrupt societies' "apparent calm."[8] Kaitlin Murphy argues that performance can create "real effects *through* circulation, whether through engagement with audiences, embodied ritual [. . .] or as proxy for the missing and the dead."[9] In postconflict Central America, the dramatic arts have taken on an active role in the battle over the work of mourning. To further explore the above, this chapter investigates how issues of mourning have been discussed and incorporated into postwar theater, particularly in the work of Salvadoran playwright Jorgelina Cerritos. This chapter claims that Cerritos has undertaken what is arguably the most ambitious project about the work of mourning in Central American dramatic arts, bringing struggles over grief, memory, and justice to numerous stages.

A Brief History of El Salvador's Theater

The history of the dramatic arts in El Salvador proceeds through ups and downs. El Salvador's first theater was inaugurated in 1842. However, buildings created exclusively to host artistic events were not constructed until the early twentieth century with the inauguration of the Teatro Francisco Gavidia (San Miguel, 1909), the Teatro Santa Ana (Santa Ana, 1910), and the Teatro Nacional de El Salvador (San Salvador, 1917). Historians of Salvadoran theater often divide its contemporary history into six parts: (1) the first half of the twentieth century, (2) the early 1950s (following the 1948 revolution), (3) the emergence of the Teatro Universitario in the late 1950s, (4) the creation of the Bachillerato en Artes (in the late 1960s), (5) the civil war period, and (6) the postwar period.

The first half of the twentieth century represents the consolidation of dramatic arts in El Salvador. In addition to the inauguration of the theaters listed above, we should mention the publication of Francisco Gavidia's plays (the first prominent Salvadoran playwright) and the 1929 foundation of the Escuela de Declamación y Prácticas Escénicas.[10] This period coincides with the development of a Salvadoran national identity following the second failed attempt at establishing a Central American federal union (1921–22), which was strongly supported by artistic works.[11]

The 1948 revolution provided solid support for the arts. On January 1, 1951, Óscar Osorio's administration created the Dirección General de Bellas Artes. Nevertheless, the revolutionary government failed to achieve its original goals to fully develop an artistic scene partially because of the lack of physical space to stage the plays. Notwithstanding, it is important to bear in mind, as Ricardo Roque Baldovinos points out, that the Bellas Artes project was conceived from a Eurocentric perspective, reproducing the idea that the arts are a luxury reserved only for the elites.[12] Spanish actor Edmundo Barbero was director of the Bellas Artes' Theater Department, and most of the plays followed the Spanish acting models of the late nineteenth century.[13] In 1956 the National University of El Salvador (UES) created the Teatro Universitario under the direction of André Moreau. According to Alejandro Córdova, one of the highest merits of the Teatro Universitario was its staging of Álvaro Menen Desleal's *Luz negra* (1962), "perhaps the most important play written in the twentieth century in El Salvador,"[14] which was presented over a hundred times, an unprecedented number in Salvadoran theater. Interestingly enough, *Luz negra*, a classic of Salvadoran theater, explores similar topics to Cerritos's trilogy. In this play, a hustler and a revolutionary are sentenced to death and decapitated in the main plaza of an unnamed town. The disembodied heads talk throughout the play while lying on the ground, wishing to be heard and found before they disappear forever. Despite the initial theatrical success, the Teatro Universitario rapidly lost funding and support because of the National University's military intervention in 1972.

One of the most significant transformations in the history of dramatic arts in El Salvador occurred in 1968, when education minister and dramatist Walter Beneke conducted a wide-reaching educational reform and created the most ambitious state-funded project in El Salvador's cultural history: the Bachillerato en Artes. The Bachillerato was a public educational institution dedicated to training youth in different artistic areas. They offered specializations in music, visual arts, and drama. The program hosted its first cohort in 1970 after nationwide recruitment. According to Roberto Salomón, the first director of the Bachillerato's theater section, the program's objective was to form El Salvador's "future actors, directors, and playwrights."[15] In 1975, because of another intervention of the National University, the program lost its initial momentum and was partially dismantled as faculty and students resigned, often leaving their artistic training to join the revolutionary forces.[16]

The civil war collapsed the (relatively weak) structural support given to the dramatic arts—and arts in general—throughout the twentieth century. One of the few theater companies that survived the war was Sol de Río, founded in 1973 by a group of students of the Bachillerato. During the 1980s the so-called Teatrillo emerged in guerrilla-occupied zones. According to Salomón, this kind of theater served ideological purposes, seeking to consolidate communal relationships by representing "the evil capitalist and the corrupt politician exploiting the peasant and the worker who give them their dues."[17] The signing of the peace accords in 1992 opened new opportunities for Salvadoran theater. In 1993 Sol de Río organized the first Festival of Central American Theater, facilitating exchange and collaboration within Central American dramatic arts and increasing their visibility at the end of the twentieth century. The 1990s was also a time for rebuilding training in the dramatic arts. An excellent example was the Escuela del Arte del Actor, created in 1998 under the direction of Filander Funes, a former student of the Bachillerato who later studied in the Soviet Union. Among the students of this project's first and only cohort was a young woman called Jorgelina Cerritos.

The twenty-first century has witnessed the emergence of a new era in Salvadoran theater. For example, in 2003, the Escuela de Arte Teatral was inaugurated with the support of the Council of Culture of El Salvador. The building of new theaters, such as the Teatro Luis Poma, and the creation of new universities (all of which were private) have opened new possibilities for learning about and performing theater. Additionally, dozens of new theater companies have been created since the early 2000s, such as Grupo de Teatro Hamlet, La Cachada Teatro, and Moby Dick Teatro. All of them, along with Jorgelina Cerritos's Los del Quinto Piso, are shaping the new face of Salvadoran theater.

While the emergence of new theatrical groups has contributed to the diversity of this art, it is arguable that the dominant trend in postwar Salvadoran theater is the so-called *teatro de la memoria*. An overview of some recent plays clearly reveals that civil war violence and its repercussions for people's lives have become major topics in the work of numerous creators. One of the first plays to tackle the civil war in postconflict El Salvador was Carlos Velis's *San Salvador después del eclipse*. It was staged in June 1992 and is considered the first play of the postwar era. The play, a Salvadoran reinterpretation of Argentinean playwright Nelly Fernández Tiscornia's *Made in Lanús* (1986), portrays the reunion of two couples. One couple (Beti and Chepe) stayed in El Salvador during the war, while the other (Alfredo and Estela) fled and settled in the United States. Estela and Alfredo's return occurs shortly after the signing of the peace accords. For Alfredo, their travel is shaped by nostalgia. For Estela, it is shaped by refusal. Either because it is an adaptation or because of the historical moment, the play does not openly address the atrocities of the civil war, but it makes it very clear that all the characters were engaged in guerrilla actions. The couple's return is a journey toward the past filled with nostalgia and pain. The end of the play (unlike the other plays I will discuss below) transmits an optimistic message about the present situation in El Salvador, inviting the audience to commit and take an active role in the new era of peace that began in January 1992.[18]

A pioneer play regarding issues of memory and mourning in Salvadoran theater, especially when it comes to openly speaking about the atrocities of the war, is Harry Castel's (Jennifer Valiente's pen name) *Santa María de la espera*. Staged for the first time in 2010 at the National Theater of El Salvador, the play presents the tragic story of María and Marta. These two women are the mother and girlfriend, respectively, of Lázaro, a young man who disappeared during the FMLN's "Ofensiva hasta el tope" in November 1989. The two women await for their loved one to return and reappear, even as a cadaver, to give closure to their infinite sorrow.[19] This play anticipates some of the topics and discussions present in Cerritos's trilogy, especially regarding the suffering provoked by the disappearance of people during the internal conflict and the emotional distress of the relatives.

Another good example of *teatro de la memoria* in Salvadoran dramaturgy is José Napoléon Rodríguez's *Muerte en la consagración o la consagración de la muerte*, published in 2015. This play takes place in the late 1970s in the context of the guerrilla uprising in El Salvador. The play has two distinctive moments. First, we observe the social exclusion and political violence poor peasants face at the hands of the authorities and the elites. In the background, Monseñor Romero's words resonate and touch people's hearts until he is assassinated by the *máscaras*, which embody the death squads. In the second half of the play, Rodríguez, in a typical Shakespearean move, incorporates theater within the theater. Two workers who have survived the massacre during Monseñor Romero's wake enter a theater in search of help and refuge. They are initially aided and hidden by the actors, and when the police leave, they are invited to join the play as extras. However, it is rapidly revealed that the play's director (who also happens to be one of the directors of the Bachillerato en Artes, and therefore an employee of the Ministry of Education) and the actors are supporters of the Salvadoran army. Finally, the director hands the workers over to the *máscaras*, who kill them. This play provides readers and spectators with a vision of social exclusion and the political violence in the 1970s that led to the assassination of Monseñor Romero and to the civil war. At the same time, the play introduces harsh criticism of the role of theater during those volatile times.

One last work that must not go unnoticed is Alejandra Nolasco's *Los ausentes*, staged for the first time in 2017. In this solo act, Nolasco interprets Milagros, a character who embodies the never-ending mourning in El Salvador. Milagros's brother disappeared during the civil war and, in the postwar era, her eighteen-year-old son was kidnapped and assassinated because he did not pay the gang's extortion fee of sixty dollars. The first half of the play presents, through dialectic scenes, Milagros's intimate sorrow and rage vis-à-vis the cynicism and superficiality of Salvadoran society symbolized in a clumsy prime-time television show. In the second half, Nolasco transmits Milagro's unimaginable grief and sadness through her body and movements. In one of the play's most powerful moments, Milagros repeatedly yells at her missing son, "¡Hasta que no te encuentre no te doy descanso!" Nolasco's *Los ausentes* is a powerful piece that takes up the pain of the civil war and connects it with El Salvador's present-day violence, which, as the play makes apparent, has contributed to deepening the sorrow of Salvadoran society.

Over the last few decades, Salvadoran theater has continuously attempted to approach and explore issues of historical memory, political violence, and mourning. In this context, even though Cerritos's plays are not the only ones addressing these issues, the *Ensayos sobre la memoria* trilogy is the longest-standing project–and perhaps the most ambitious–theatrical work to explore El Salvador's recent past.

Jorgelina Cerritos and the *Ensayos sobre la memoria*

Jorgelina Cerritos, born in 1974, is one of the most relevant Salvadoran playwrights of the early twenty-first century. She graduated with a psychology degree from the Universidad Nacional de El Salvador, and in 1998 she joined the only cohort of the Escuela de Arte del Actor. Cerritos dedicated the first years of her career to creating children's theater with substantial success. She won the National Prize for children's theater on three occasions, becoming, in 2004, "Gran Maestre" of Salvadoran literature. In 2010 Cerritos acquired international recognition when she obtained the prestigious Casa de las Américas Prize for the play *Al otro lado del mar*. In 2011, the jury of the V Premio de Teatro Latinoamericano George Woodyard, organized by the University of Connecticut, unanimously awarded Cerritos the first prize for the play *Vértigo 824*.

In 2007 Cerritos and Víctor Candray began the process of forming a theater company. They invited Rafael Pineda, trained by Cerritos, and together they created Los del Quinto Piso. The name of the group comes from accidental circumstances. They rented the fifth floor in a semi-abandoned building near Parque Cuscatlán in San Salvador. Since they were some of the few occupants of the building, they were often called "los del quinto piso" by the few people working there.[20] Between 2010 and 2017 Jorgelina Cerritos and Los del Quinto Piso undertook one of the most exciting projects in postwar Salvadoran theater, the writing of the trilogy *Ensayos sobre la memoria*. In Cerritos's words, their goal was "to contribute to the reconstruction of memory from the dramatic and theatrical word."[21] The notion of *ensayo* works for them "as a synonym of trial, like what we do in theater, not in the sense of a literary genre."[22] The trilogy's first play, staged in 2013, is *La Audiencia de los confines. Primer ensayo sobre la memoria*. Then, in 2016 the group presented *Bandada de pájaros. Segundo ensayo sobre la memoria*. The final play of the trilogy, *13703. El misterio de las utopías. Tercer ensayo sobre la memoria*, debuted in 2017. The plays embody an exploration of the complexities and nuances of the traumatic experiences of the civil war, which resound through to the present day. It is worth mentioning that all the dramatic texts were published by Índole Editores, an independent Salvadoran publisher, and became available to the public around the same time that the plays debuted.

Cerritos's *Ensayos sobre la memoria* trilogy is a perfect example of how the battle of mourning unfolds in contemporary Central American dramaturgy. These plays engage in the struggles over mourning in at least two ways. Thanks to the publication and staging of these plays in El Salvador and other Central American countries, political violence, impunity, and grief have been resurrected on the stage. This chapter also argues that these plays embody the struggle over mourning at the core of their plot. We constantly observe in this trilogy the duality between characters who wish to know, remember, and mourn juxtaposed with those who would rather leave the past behind. How these characters relate and react to the shared experience of loss portrays the struggles faced by millions in postconflict Central America.

The Truth Will Not Make Us Free: Perpetual Mourning in *La Audiencia de los confines*

La Audiencia de los confines. Primer ensayo sobre la memoria was staged for the first time in Cuba in 2013, under the direction of Alina Narciso, during the 6th Bienal de Dramaturgia Femenina, La Escritura de la Diferencia. The audience's reception of the play was overwhelmingly positive, and it was awarded first place. Historically speaking, the Audiencia de los Confines evoked in the play's title was the Supreme Court of the Captaincy General of Guatemala (also known as the Kingdom of Guatemala), created in 1542 during the Spanish colonial period. In the prologue, Cerritos explains that in a country that has seen as many injustices as El Salvador, theater works as a tool "to force us to an Audiencia—half farce, half true—of our own past."[23] Thus, from the title and the prologue, the readers and spectators understand that the possibility of justice is at stake in this play, or rather, the demand for justice in postwar El Salvador.

La Audiencia de los confines is a play with three characters: Carola, Mauro, and Alonso. They inhabit the "eternal night," waiting for dawn. For reasons that are unclear, the characters know about a prophecy. Three bell rings will announce the beginning of the Audiencia de los confines and finally usher in the dawn. The play opens with the characters discussing whether they have heard the bell. Then, the three characters adopt new identities, and the Audiencia begins. Carola becomes "the Truth," Mauro "the Memory," and Alonso "the History." In this trial, Carola-Truth unsuccessfully demands that Mauro-Memory and Alonso-History reveal their truth. They eventually start a new Audiencia, without formalities, in which each of them voices their secrets. However, after the truth is revealed, nothing changes for the characters. In the final moments of the play, the characters come together around the pieces of a broken mural and joyfully talk about the next time they will perform the Audiencia as if it were a recurring game.[24]

La Audiencia de los confines places the unfinished work of mourning at the center of its plot. To elaborate further on this, I will focus on three aspects. First, I will discuss the meaning of the "eternal night" that the characters inhabit, which I interpret as a metaphor for unresolved mourning. Second, I will analyze the demand for justice portrayed in the play that unfolds both formally and informally through the Audiencia. Finally, I will explore how, despite the play's apparent goal, *La Audiencia de los confines* exposes how truth itself is insufficient to bring the work of mourning to closure.

La Audiencia de los confines opens with darkness and silence. Then, the three characters emerge, wandering in the nothingness. The stage direction insists, "Silence and quietness. Impenetrable darkness."[25] This atmosphere is broken by the ringing of a bell that allegedly announces the end of the eternal night.[26] Despite the initial enthusiasm, Alonso and Mauro rapidly return to their skepticism. "Aquí no amanece nunca. Aquí nunca va a amanecer," says Alonso.[27] Although toward the end of the play it is learned that all the characters are, in fact, dead, during the first half, readers, spectators, and characters only know that they inhabit a limbo, an out-of-joint space. In Mauro's words, they live in "este hediondo portal perdido en el tiempo, pudriéndonos, en una noche de dos décadas, de diez décadas, de cien décadas, de todas las décadas de la tierra."[28] Mauro's characterization of this space connects recent Salvadoran history with its time as a republic. The "two decades" probably refers to the almost twenty years that separate the play from the signing of the peace accords that ended the civil war, which represents just another dark episode in El Salvador's history. The play thus stages what Valentina Ripa calls "la larga noche centroamericana,"[29] a moment where all the atrocities that have taken place in El Salvador come together in an eternal, out-of-joint time and space.

The darkness that houses Carola, Mauro, and Alonso operates in a twofold way. First, it serves as a limbo that offers a promise of redemption. The characters' permanence in the eternal night is only alleviated (at least partially) by the promise of the dawn. The dawn to come works as a promise of justice and redemption that will put an end to the darkness in which they—and the whole country—have lived over the last two centuries. Believing in the possibility of the dawn gives the characters the strength to wait for the Audiencia to take place. This is the only possibility for finally leaving that space of indetermination and abandonment. At the same time, the darkness embodies the characters' unfinished work of mourning. In the middle of the dark, the only light they can see is a tenuous red glow on the horizon that only projects suffering and perpetual pain. In Carola's words, "¡El bombardeo de Vietnam, el bombardeo de Afganistán, el bombardeo de Irak, el bombardeo de Morazán! ¡Al suelo! ¡Al suelo! ¡Es la ofensiva final! Los niños corren, se desangran.[. . .] Las mujeres paren bajo el agua y atraviesan el río sin cortar el cordón que las une desde el vientre con sus hijos."[30] Darkness, the only reality accessible to the characters, becomes a perpetual site of lament, joining the characters to the world's eternal sorrow.

The presence—albeit satirical—of the Audiencia de los Confines represents an apparent demand for justice. Cerritos discusses this in the prologue, where she claims that five centuries after the creation of the colonial Supreme Court, "Central America continues living in the confines of the Earth. Historically confined to conditions of poverty, social injustice, and marginalization." El Salvador, she continues, has a pending "audiencia," "to find the lights of its own truth, and be able to assume, however difficult that may be, its own identity."[31] In other words, justice, embodied in the Audiencia de los Confines is seen as a vehicle to achieve a potential form of national identity in the postwar era. Following E. J. Westlake, it can be said that Cerritos, despite her critical approach to El Salvador's history, cannot wholly avoid some sort of "nationalistic cause," considering theater as a tool that "calls citizens together to agree upon the re-creation of the nation's culture and history."[32] Like many other playwrights worldwide, Cerritos conceives of theater as a "tool of cultural transformation aiming to bridge the post-traumatic gaps in the sociopolitical fabric of the respective nations."[33] While trying to achieve some form of national identity through justice and mourning might be problematic, I believe this is a failed project in Cerritos's dramaturgy. Despite her repeated attempts (as I will further discuss toward the end of this chapter), the *ensayos* do not deliver any form of identity. Perhaps contrary to Cerritos's intentions, they make apparent the impossibility of completing the task of mourning.

Emanuela Jossa identifies two types of "Audiencias" in this play, the "Audiencia de los confines," where the characters assume alternative identities, and the "Audiencia de los márgenes," where the characters voice their truth.[34] However, it is possible to identify a third moment of the Audiencia, which takes place before the first Audiencia. This moment could be called the Audiencia as a "promise of redemption." This is expressed in different moments during the first half of the play. Under trance, for example, Carola says, "Después de la noche más oscura vendrá por fin la luz de la mañana al tercer tañido de la campana.[. . .] La hora del juicio ha llegado y su luz disipará las sombras. La gran audiencia nos espera."[35] At this time, the Audiencia represents hope, especially for Carola, the major believer in the prophecy. In addition to Carola's anticipatory words, later on, some of the characters also express their hope that the Audiencia will repair all wrongdoing. When Carola yells in the middle of an unrelated game, "¡Cuando las mujeres encuentren a sus hijos perdidos bajo la tormenta y la balacera, y a los cuerpos putrefactos les nazcan flores!,"[36] her claims are followed by Mauro, who says, "¡Que se levanten las víctimas en pos del victimario! ¡Que los cuerpos se reúnan con sus cabezas!"[37] These statements make it apparent that at least two of the three characters in the play await some form of justice, and therefore they are eager to hear the bell.

However, when the Audiencia begins, we quickly realize that it is a mock trial that will leave the characters' aspirations unfulfilled. Carola, Mauro, and Alonso impersonate Truth, Memory, and History, respectively, entering the scene dancing, singing, and joking. The first interaction among the new characters anticipates the denouement of the play. Each of them introduces themselves, and right after Carola says she is "la Verdad," Alonso-History asks Mauro-Memory who she was:

ALONSO. (*A Mauro*). ¿Quién dice que es? [(To Mauro). Who does she say she is?]
MAURO. No sé. [I don't know.]
ALONSO. ¿No escuchaste? [Didn't you hear?]
MAURO. Sí. [Yes.]
ALONSO. ¿No entendiste? [Didn't you understand?]
MAURO. Sí. [Yes.]
ALONSO. ¿Entonces cómo es que no sabes quién dijo que es? [So, how is it that you don't know who she said she was?]
MAURO. Es que ya lo olvidé. [I already forgot.]
ALONSO. ¡¿Lo olvidaste?! ¡Pero si tú eres La Memoria! [You forgot?! But you are The Memory!]
MAURO. Sí, pero soy una memoria de muy corto plazo . . . [Yes, but I am a very short-term memory . . .][38]

The trial proceeds with several jokes and misunderstandings. Carola-Truth tries, unsuccessfully, to obtain a confession from Memory and History. Carola, as the judge of the trial, ultimately declares, "Se les condena a pena de muerte por engaño doloso con premeditación, alevosía y ventaja sobre la Humanidad y futuras generaciones."[39] After saying this, Carola removes the clown nose Mauro put on her, and the Audiencia concludes. Despite the redemption it promised, the Audiencia ends without any positive outcome for the characters. Their eternal wait has apparently been in vain. "¿Y ahora qué se supone que pasa?" asks Alonso when they return to their original roles.[40]

After this, the third and last part of the play begins—what Jossa calls the "Audiencia de los márgenes." In this Audiencia, the characters finally confront the reality of what happened with them. Carola claims that the truth is the only way to escape the eternal night. Nonetheless, Alonso expresses his unwillingness to remember the past, interrogating both Mauro and Carola, "¿Acaso hay algo fuera de estos pilares? ¿Alguien nos espera?"[41] Later, Carola reflects, "Quizás por eso somos así, porque no recordamos nada . . . Por tener en la cabeza una falla tectónica . . . siempre cayendo y olvidando y volviendo a levantar (*Pausa*). Yo sí quiero saber lo que hice y lo que fue de mí."[42] Unlike the first Audiencia, Carola, Mauro, and Alonso now face it as themselves. This time, it is clear that Carola and Mauro want to face the truth, while Alonso rejects it. Finally, Carola and Mauro remember and speak about their fatal end, forcing Alonso to do the same not as part of a process of punishing but as a part of a process of healing: "La verdad dicen que cura. Deberías probar," says Mauro.[43] Reluctantly, Alonso finally acknowledges his participation in state terrorism: "creo que fui yo quien quemó a los niños en el monte y el mismo que se escondió por miedo mientras ardía la carpa . . . y quien puso la granada que acabó con la vida de la muchacha que se atravesó corriendo a la farmacia."[44] Despite uttering the truth and revealing that he was responsible for Carola's death, Alonso's words do not transform the characters' reality. Thus, the new Audiencia fails once again, suggesting that neither justice nor closure is accessible to the characters in their eternal wait.

The above can be used to discuss the role of truth in the play and its failure as a mechanism to bring the work of mourning to closure. Although the Audiencia repeatedly fails to achieve any transformation for the characters, it is undeniable that the notion of truth lies at the core of each trial. In the first Audiencia, "the Truth," impersonated by Carola, is presented as the judge who brings memory and history to trial. In the end, however, Carola-Truth's efforts to make them accountable for the atrocities of the past prove unsuccessful. Toward the end of the play, the characters ultimately manage to speak about their previous lives. Nonetheless, they realize that speaking

FIGURE 19 *La Audiencia de los confines*, Teatro Nacional de El Salvador, San Salvador, October 11, 2014. Photo by René Figueroa.

about what happened and what they did does not free them from the eternal night. In the end, the play portrays the insufficiency of truth by itself as a liberating device.[45]

In postwar El Salvador, everyone knows at least part of the truth about state terrorism and political violence. It is known that the army committed the majority of human rights violations. It is also known that the FMLN is responsible for numerous crimes. Anyone can access the *De la locura a la esperanza* report and read about dozens of well-documented crimes. In postwar El Salvador, the problem is not the truth itself but rather what has been done (and not done) with it. Unfortunately, the three decades that separate us from the signing of the peace accords reveal that justice (in all forms and expectations) has been considerably absent in the aftermath of the civil war.[46] Thus, *La Audiencia de los confines* is a play that embodies the demand for justice at all levels, aiming finally to achieve some form of accountability. Sadly, as the play portrays, neither the legal justice system, which represents the legacy of colonial power, nor the informal truth-telling experience fully satisfies the mourners. Notwithstanding their disappointment, the characters are not dominated by resignation. Despite the failures of the trials, they express their will to keep working and to continue having as many Audiencias as necessary to finally escape from the eternal night of mourning they cannot stop inhabiting.

To close this section, it is important to mention that Cerritos's *La Audiencia de los confines* directly references a namesake piece published by Guatemalan Nobel laureate Miguel Ángel Asturias in 1957. Asturias's play portrays the political and religious struggles that took place in mid-sixteenth-century Spanish America with the approval of the "New Laws" that aimed to end the encomienda system and prevent Indigenous peoples from becoming slaves at the hands of the Europeans. The play eulogizes Fray Bartolomé de Las Casas and portrays him as the savior of the Indigenous peoples, as someone willing to put his own life in jeopardy to protect his dearest "pobres desnudos." While the two plays have little in common at first sight, their opposite approach to issues of justice must be addressed. In Asturias's play, the Audiencia de los confines works as the uttermost manifestation of justice in Spanish America, ultimately saving Las Casas and the Indigenous population from the greed and violence of the Spanish conquistadors. In Cerritos's play, the Audiencia is a failed institution that does not serve the purpose of those seeking its aid. The Audiencia represents the collapse of the judiciary system, which, from its origins in the mid-sixteenth century to the present day, has never been able to truly grasp and satisfy the claims for justice that have been voiced in this territory.

To Mourn and to Be Mourned: *Bandada de pájaros. Segundo ensayo sobre la memoria*

In 2016, Jorgelina Cerritos published *Bandada de pájaros. Segundo ensayo sobre la memoria*. The play was staged in the Teatro Luis Poma for the first time in El Salvador in 2017. *Bandada de pájaros* is articulated through two main characters, Mujer Alta/Engracia and Mujer Pequeña/Susana. A third character, El Hombre Uniformado, performs several secondary masculine roles (el Profe, Raymundo, Gonzalo, and Toño). Unlike *La Audiencia*, which despite its harrowing topic is filled with jokes and mockery, *Bandada de pájaros* is presented as a tragedy from the beginning. This is the story of two sisters who inhabit "la nada," an out-of-joint time that resembles the eternal night of *La Audiencia*. On the one hand, Engracia wants to remember and learn what happened to her and her loved ones. Susana, on the other hand, chooses silence. Throughout their conversations, they revisit the past, and thus the audience learns about (and the characters remember) their lives. When the civil war started, they lived in a small town with their father, Toño. Some people in the village joined the guerrillas, such as Susana's boyfriend, Gonzalo, and el Profe, the town's teacher. During that time, Engracia was dating a soldier named Raymundo, a violent man who ultimately murdered the two sisters, their father, Gonzalo, and el Profe. Subsequently, we learn that the two women are dead, and their bodies have been disposed of in an unknown location without a burial. *Bandada de pájaros* interweaves three different times and spaces. The first takes place when the women were alive and used their real names, Engracia and Susana. The second is the present time of the story, which takes place on a cliff in the nothingness and in which the two women are only called Mujer Alta and Mujer Pequeña. Finally, in the third dimension, the women are also called Mujer Alta and Mujer Pequeña, but they are portrayed as old ladies. All these space-times overlap and may confuse the reader and spectators but ultimately nourish the play's final revelation.

Unlike *La Audiencia*, where the work of mourning is at times concealed behind the characters' jokes and games, *Bandada de pájaros* exposes the task of mourning from the beginning. The play opens with Engracia's cry, lamenting her own tears, "Me gustaría que no lloraras . . . Me gustaría que no hubieras llorado nunca . . . Me gustaría que las mujeres no lloráramos. Que no lloráramos nunca. Si yo pudiera me secaría las lágrimas. Aunque las lágrimas no se miren, siempre estamos llorando."[47] The opening words not only insert the play rapidly into the dynamics of the work of mourning but they also suggest that this is an involuntary but inevitable process in which the characters are compelled to participate.

Bandada de pájaros is a captivating play that portrays and connects the "two ends" of the work of mourning. On the one hand, it presents the lament of those who have lost their loved ones violently because of the Salvadoran internal conflict. On the other hand (and this is one of the play's novelties), the same characters demand to have their own deaths mourned. The perpetual circle in which the characters live portrays the inescapable situation in which thousands of people live in postwar Central America. The overwhelming grief that can be observed in this play unfolds against the background of metaphoric mourning for lost youth and innocence, which appear figuratively as wings.[48]

In particular, I would like to stress the partition of this play into two moments, which allows the expressions of the two forms of mourning mentioned above. In the first part, we observe what I call the mourning-for-others moment. This is what readers/spectators encounter during the first three-quarters of the play, where the sisters debate whether they should try to remember and where they cry for the death of their loved ones, especially their father, Toño, and Susana's boyfriend, Gonzalo. A second significant moment in the play occurs toward the end, when it is learned that the sisters have been assassinated and their bodies dumped in unknown locations. At this time, they begin a desperate cry to be found and mourned, what might be called the moment of self-mourning.

The mourning-for-others is expressed in the play in at least two different forms. The first manifestation of grief occurs in the play's initial part, which opens with the two sisters drinking alcohol next to a fire. The alcohol triggers memories, the first manifestation of their grieving. Mujer Pequeña says, "El olor a alcohol me recuerda a la mamá Toña frotándose las manos para sobarse las piernas," and remembers her funeral: "Todos lloraban y ella tan tiesa y callada. Todos lloraban. Todos menos yo."[49] Mujer Alta, on the other hand, also remembers her past, but with evident pity: "El olor a alcohol me recuerda a Raymundo bailando conmigo en las fiestas del pueblo.[. . .] Del otro agosto cuando borracho me escupía la cara y por no dejarlo que me tocara me pegaba."[50] After these initial manifestations of grief, the two sisters move on to the more delicate topic of their father's death. Here we find one of the first arguments between the two sisters:

MUJER ALTA. Ese día en la tienda . . . [That day in the store . . .]
MUJER PEQUEÑA. No quiero saber. [I don't want to know.]
MUJER ALTA. Mi papá no estaba ahí. [My father wasn't there.]
MUJER PEQUEÑA. No quiero saber. [I don't want to know.]
MUJER ALTA. No podemos seguir así . . . como si nada. [We can't continue like this . . . as if nothing.]
MUJER PEQUEÑA. Yo sí. [I can.]
MUJER ALTA. La nada no es nada. Es mejor saber. [The nothingness is not nothing. It's better to know.]
MUJER PEQUEÑA. La nada es la muerte. [The nothingness is death.]
MUJER ALTA. La muerte es la muerte, es parte de la vida, no es la nada. La muerte es natural, no la nada. [Death is death, it's a part

of life, it's not the nothingness. Death is natural, the nothingness is not.]

MUJER PEQUEÑA. Yo así estoy bien. Ni vida ni muerte. No quiero saber. [I'm fine like this. Neither life nor death. I don't want to know.][51]

The above dialogue reminds us of the discussion between Carola, Mauro, and Alonso that was previously observed in *La Audiencia*. However, what is different in this case is that the women are not responsible for anyone's death. On the contrary, they are victims of state terrorism, although they have decided to face their mourning differently. Mujer Alta is determined to learn the truth and end the limbo they inhabit, while Mujer Pequeña resists expressing her pain. This dialogue is an excellent example of how the struggle over mourning not only confronts people on divergent ideological fronts but also those who share a common tragic experience. The battle of mourning transcends any preexisting category imposed by social, political, cultural, or religious perspectives.

The obscure conversation that takes place during the above act is clarified in the following scene, which introduces spectators to the two women when they were alive and in their youth. Among other things, it is learned that their father was an illiterate mailman and that Susana was dating Gonzalo, a young man who joined the guerrillas, while Engracia was courted by a violent and abusive soldier named Raymundo. In the context of the civil war, Raymundo uses his authority to take revenge on Engracia and her family for not requiting his love. Because of Raymundo's intervention, Toño (the women's father), Casio (the town's teacher), and Gonzalo (Susana's boyfriend) are violently killed by the army. Toño and Casio are decapitated, and their heads are placed onto a stick. As the audience learns toward the end of the play, Gonzalo's head was introduced into Engracia's belly to simulate that she was pregnant with Gonzalo's baby. Once we learn about the tragic fate of Engracia and Susana's family, we better understand their sorrow. The war and Raymundo's jealousy have destroyed everything they loved, and it is precisely that pain, and how to deal with it, that divides them while they are in the nothingness. However, while the two female characters disagree about how to undertake their mourning for their loved ones, toward the end of the play, a new sadness emerges, the pain of their own death.

The closing scene of the play reveals the ultimate truth about its protagonists. Engracia and Susana, now dead as Mujer Alta and Mujer Pequeña, are standing on a cliff. They continue the conversation about the deadly morning when their father and the teacher were killed. But now Mujer Alta/Engracia reveals her truth against her sister's will:

> MUJER ALTA. Ese día en la tienda . . . [That day in the store . . .]
> MUJER PEQUEÑA. No quiero saber. [I don't want to know.]
> MUJER ALTA. Mi papá no estaba ahí. [My father wasn't there.]
> MUJER PEQUEÑA. No quiero saber. [I don't want to know.]
> MUJER ALTA. Yo morí. [I died.][52]

While not entirely unforeseen, the revelation of Engracia's death introduces a new perspective: the ghost's view. Engracia informs her sister that she has been looking after her in the realm of the living and that despite the town's gossip, she never slept with Gonzalo. To Engracia's surprise, Mujer Pequeña tells her that she already knows this because the now-deceased Mama Tola told her so. Curiously, although both sisters are dead, the play makes apparent that they are not "in the death" (*en la muerte*) surrounded by their loved ones but that they are in the "nothingness," an undetermined place and time. The reason why they have not been able to reach a definite resting place is because of their mourningless status.

The mutual realization of the sisters' death is only the beginning of their horrendous end. "Where are you?" Engracia asks her sister, who, after some hesitation, responds, "regada entre cuerpos amontonados [. . .] me sacaron los ojos para que tampoco viera a Gonzalo. [. . .] Estoy regada en una zanja, sobre mí hay otros cuerpos, ropa engusanada, un montón de pelo revuelto de otros cuerpos . . . hay dedos, orejas, bocas de niños asustados, hay un par de testículos."[53] After the gruesome description provided by Susana, Mujer Alta informs her sister about her fate. I am, she says, "En una quebrada . . . con la cabeza de Gonzalo en las entrañas."[54] The reader/spectator learns in that moment that not only had the two sisters been executed by the army but that they were also abandoned in an unknown location, and their bodies were mutilated and humiliated by their killers. Before this unsettling situation, both sisters redirect their will to mourn toward themselves, begging to be grieved. Susana verbalizes this desire more explicitly, "Yo quiero la muerte,

Engracia . . . el sepulcro, la tumba, la lápida . . . aunque sea una cruz maltrecha en la carretera con una coronita de flores.[. . .] No quiero la nada."[55] Unfortunately for the two sisters, the possibilities of being found and mourned are remote because "no hay nadie que nos ande buscando."[56]

The presence of two unburied sisters in the play is a powerful statement regarding the unfinished work of mourning in postwar Central America. Unlike Antigone, the classic mourning figure in Western theater, Cerritos presents a scenario in which mourning is impossible not only because of the dehumanization of the other, or their "unburiable" character (using Butler's words), but also because there is no one left to mourn them, no living community to engage in the communal act of grieving. This is the impossible mourning produced by the countless scorched earth operations. Paraphrasing Freud, the lost object and the self are indivisible in this situation not because of an irreversible attachment but because they were always the same being, thus canceling any possibility of conducting the task of mourning. Given the impossibility of receiving a proper burial, *Bandada de pájaros* offers a way out for its characters: the two sisters grow wings, a symbol of the dead characters in the play, and fly toward San Ignacio de la Frontera accompanied by Gonzalo, leaving behind the nothingness in which their killers left them (fig. 20).[57]

The ending of *Bandada de pájaros* opens two scenarios: one that works within the literary realm, and one that connects the audience with the commonality of grieving. Owing to the impossibility of being mourned by the living, Cerritos allows the dead to grieve and bury Susana and Engracia. This act, in which the ghosts grieve the dead, which Derrida calls "the ruin or the absolute ashes,"[58] represents the unfortunate situation of thousands of people in Central America who died during the civil wars. Beyond the tragic slaughter of thousands of unarmed civilians, scorched earth operations eliminated the possibility of mourning for the victims by destroying the roots of their affective communities. The end of the play makes the audience participate in the act of grieving through Susana and Engracia flying with their wings. However, it is clear that this possibility only works in the literary and theatrical realm and not in the tangible reality within El Salvador. Therefore, Cerritos's play can be interpreted as an ethical invitation to mourn together. To use Derrida's words, this serves to "exorcise the ghosts," not to get rid of them, but to welcome them "out of a concern for *justice*."[59] In this regard, unlike *La Audiencia*, where the claims for justice are unsuccessfully taken

FIGURE 20 *Bandada de pájaros,* Teatro Luis Poma, San Salvador, September 21, 2017. Photo by René Figueroa.

to a (mock) court, *Bandada de pájaros* is an invitation to communal grief between the characters and the audience without the participation of third parties. The play is, in other words, a call to take part in the battle of mourning, a struggle in which only the living can participate.

The Impossible Truth: *13703. El misterio de las utopías*

On August 12, 2017, the third and final *ensayo sobre la memoria,* titled *13703. El misterio de las utopías,* made its debut in the National Theater of El Salvador. This play introduces new elements into the trilogy. For example, it is the only play where most of the characters are alive and react to recent actual events that have taken place in El Salvador, establishing some historical markers within the story. The main event portrayed in the play is the discovery of a secret army document in 2013 containing the names, photographs, and information regarding "enemies" of the state, called the *Libro*

Amarillo. A second event is NASA's 2015 naming of a new asteroid in honor of Monseñor Romero, the 13703Romero. According to Cerritos, the finding of the *Libro Amarillo* represented the starting point of the final piece of the trilogy. When she and Los del Quinto Piso learned about the new asteroid, they considered it the "point of arrival" of the play and also of the trilogy.[60] Another noticeable difference between this play and those examined previously is the number of characters. While *La Audiencia de los confines* and *Bandada de pájaros* only have three characters each, *13703. El misterio de las utopías* has seven.[61] The temporalities and locations are also considerably more blurred in the final play. From the beginning, the audience learns that there is no linearity to the story and that time and space overlap, generating a chaotic situation in which voices and temporalities clash against one another.

Despite the intricate paths and circumstances presented in the play, one can identify some clear situations and stories within *El misterio de las utopías*. First, there is a story of two siblings, "El Hermano" and "La Hermana." The brother lives in the United States as a university professor, and the sister is a schoolteacher in El Salvador. The play begins with the brother's arrival, who brings news that the *Libro Amarillo* has been found. Within it, there is a picture of someone who resembles their brother, who presumably died during a bombing when they were kids. This triggers a search that leads the two siblings to a house where they will meet three women: Mariana (who is married to "el Gordo," a character who never appears and could be the missing brother), Julia, and Mercedes. While all of the above happens in the realm of the living, the play presents another scenario as a repeated memory, also portrayed as a dream, where the siblings evoke the day of the bombing when their brother disappeared or died. The phantasmagoric presence of this traumatic event functions in the play as a constant reminder of the siblings' loss and what motivates the story's development. Finally, the play also offers a parallel, alternate scenario in which Monseñor Romero is seen as a ghost next to an anonymous child (Niño), who could also be the dead brother.

In particular, I would like to examine three aspects of this play: first, the struggle over the work of mourning portrayed in the two families; second, the doubts and ambiguities presented in the play that prevent the characters from learning the truth; and third, the spectral presence of the dead.

The discussion regarding whether to remember and mourn is not new in Cerritos's oeuvre. However, the novelty here is that the struggle is not only introduced within one family or group of characters, as observed in *La Au-*

diencia and *Bandada de pájaros*, but in two. This suggests that mourning is an extensive, ongoing problem affecting most family structures in Salvadoran society. The first discussion over mourning is observed in the initial interaction between El Hermano and La Hermana. The brother, who just returned to El Salvador, informs her sister about the *Libro Amarillo*. He tells her of their alleged brother's picture in the book and how the army sought the people in that document during the civil war. The sister, however, expresses no interest in what her brother is saying. Eventually, it is learned that the sister's problem is not that she does not want her brother to be alive, or that she is not willing to discover what actually happened to him; the issue is that she has already mourned him: "Lo enterré en el patio, metí sus cosas en una cajita y lo sepulté en los recuerdos. Y ahora venís vos a obligarme a una exhumación que no quiero."[62] This is a compelling statement because, unlike all the characters that have been seen in the trilogy, one can observe here someone who seems to have conducted a successful work of mourning. Without a body or official recognition, the sister decided to undertake her own path, perform her own rituals, and bury her brother's belongings in the yard and her recollections of him deep in her memory. This explains why the appearance of the *Libro Amarillo* is so traumatic for her and why she refuses to learn any new information about her brother that would jeopardize the difficult and painful mourning she already undertook.

Nevertheless, despite her fears, the sister eventually gathers the courage to follow a clue to discover whether her brother is alive or not. She learns from a friend where the alleged brother lives, and they manage to visit his house with the excuse of being out-of-town visitors needing a place to sleep. That is when Mariana (el Gordo's wife) and Mercedes and Julia (twin sisters and Mariana's cousin) appear in the play. The meeting of the two families puts the multiple faces of the work of mourning on display. While the two siblings initially argue about whether to seek out the missing brother, halfway through the play they both agree that they must exhaust all possibilities in their search for him. However, the three women in the other family portray an ongoing discussion about the war and the losses it caused. It is clear that they all lost something in the internal conflict and that those losses are still present in their lives. Regardless, they approach the traumatic events very differently. Mercedes is the character who openly talks about the war and their experience. She shares that her father was a guerrilla killed by his comrades (something that resembles Roque Dalton's story), her mother was disappeared, and she and her twin sister grew up in Cuba. While Mercedes shares the story of their parents, her sister Julia remains indifferent. On the other hand, Mariana grew up in a conservative army family and therefore ignored the reality of the war until she became an adult. Nevertheless, the play makes clear that Mariana's father, a high-ranking officer, was responsible for assassinating her cousins' father, and it is also suggested that he tortured el Gordo, her husband. Although she is aware of the atrocities of the internal conflict, she represents the conservative view, claiming that the dead are "bajas" (casualties), and therefore things should be left as they are because the war ended a long time ago.

The counterpoint between the two families is worth noting not only because they embody a palpable example of the battle of mourning but also because one can observe some relevant features of this work. For example, Mariana's compulsive talking suggests that, despite representing the conservative perspective, many things that have yet to be clarified still affect her present life. She knows that silence, while convenient for herself and her family, will not solve her complex relationship with her husband, who was tortured during the war (presumably) by his future father-in-law. Although compelled to talk about her suffering and ignorance about political violence, Mariana struggles to listen and empathize with others. This is apparent when she refuses to see her cousin's point of view regarding her suffering due to the loss of their parents and when she insults her husband because of his silence regarding the torture he suffered. On the other hand, the two siblings present a relatively more peaceful picture. They somehow have already closed the mourning process for their brother and cautiously open themselves to the possibility of him being alive. What motivates them is not anger or a sense of revenge but a desire to clear the doubts provoked by the *Libro Amarillo*—as Derrida reminds us, "Nothing could be worse, for the work of mourning, than confusion or doubt."[63]

13703. El misterio de las utopías is arguably the most hopeless play within Cerritos's trilogy regarding the work of mourning. The story, motivated by the siblings' will to learn the truth about their deceased/missing brother, ultimately leads to a dead end where no answers are provided. In that regard, the play is a descent into doubt and confusion. When the play concludes, three main questions remain unanswered. Is the missing brother dead or alive? Is "el Gordo" and the missing brother the same person? Is the dead child (Niño) the brother? The play presents at least two contradictory situations as possible. Either the brother managed to survive, grew up without contacting his family ever again, joined the guerrillas, was tortured, and married Mariana, or the kid died in the bombing and is sharing a limbo with Monseñor Romero. Regardless of the path one takes, the brother's presence-absence is evident. The ambiguity makes him like a ghost regardless of whether he is a living character, absent from the play, or deceased.

Counterintuitively, after a tireless quest for answers, the characters seem to accept the veil shrouding the truth about the brother. In their final conversation, Mariana and La Hermana agree that "el Gordo" and the missing brother are probably two different people.[64] In the realm of the living, the characters have accepted carrying on with doubt and therefore assume the responsibility for their silence and their unfinished mourning. The limbo, on the other hand, does not offer any solution either. While at first Niño says some things that suggest he is the dead brother, at the end of his long, final speech, he cries, "no sé si soy un hombre con miedo, un niño perdido o una foto vieja en un libro amarillo . . . No tengo pasado, no tengo familia, ni madre, ni mujer, ni hijos . . . Tengo tan solo un nombre borrado y un rostro desconocido . . . ¿Dónde encontraré las respuestas para mí?"[65] Sadly, for him, the end of the play will not provide the answers he wishes to find. The ambiguities in the play stress the difficulties of apprehending truth in postconflict El Salvador and reaffirm the idea of mourning as an unattainable project.

One final aspect of this play that must be addressed is the phantasmagoric presence of the disappeared, especially through their visibility in the *Libro Amarillo*. This document, presumably created during the 1980s, was found by accident in 2013, and it compiles almost two thousand photographs as well as information about people considered to be terrorists by the Salvadoran army. On its first page, it reads, "Que lo usen. Sacar fotocopias de fotografías y ponerlo en boletinero para que conozcan a sus enemigos."[66] According to recent investigations, 43 percent of the people included in the book were victims of some type of political violence at the hands of the army.[67] Because of the amnesty law that was in effect until 2016, the *Libro Amarillo* has not served any concrete juridical purpose yet. Still, thousands await a time when this book will become a key piece of evidence in a future trial for crimes against humanity during the Salvadoran civil war. Nevertheless, the *Libro Amarillo* is not introduced in the story with any juridical or legal goal—another indication that Cerritos profoundly distrusts the judiciary system. Instead, its role in the plot is to conjure ghosts. Despite being the only play where all the main characters are alive, it has the most phantasmagoric manifestations, which make themselves present throughout the play, either as a memory, a photograph, or as phantasmal characters. The specters of the thousands of people whose photographs are included in the *Libro Amarillo*, the presence-absence of the missing brother whose fate is never revealed, and the ghosts of Monseñor Romero and Niño living in limbo take part in a performance in which the spectral presence cannot be avoided by the living characters or the audience. To stress the specters' visibility, directors often incorporate actual images that are projected onto a screen behind the characters when it has been staged. For example, in the play's debut, photographs from the murder of Monseñor Romero were used in the background (fig. 21).

Regarding the missing/dead brother's ghost, it is important to highlight that his phantasmagoric presence is multiplied. At least three appearances of the brother's ghost can be identified: first, as a memory or dream in the siblings' constant recollection of the bombing; second, as the alleged photograph of a political target; and finally, as the ghost of a kid who talks with Monseñor Romero. The brother's multiple presences contradict each other

FIGURE 21 *13703. El misterio de las utopías*, Teatro Nacional de El Salvador, August 12, 2017. Photo by René Figueroa.

and echo his numerous absences. As Ludmila da Silva Catela reminds us, the disappeared always implies at least a triple absence–the lack of a body, a moment of mourning, and a tomb.[68] For the two siblings, the existence of a photograph of someone who resembles their brother becomes a driving force in the play. It offers them an alternate reality they have ignored for years: that the brother did not die during the bombing but instead survived and lived to participate in guerrilla actions. Therefore, for the siblings, the *Libro Amarillo* does not work as proof of state terrorism but rather as proof of existence. The photograph of the brother is—allegedly—there, and paraphrasing Roland Barthes, he has—allegedly—"been there."[69] This possibility of existence is sufficient for them to undertake the search regardless of the outcome.

The myriad reactions to the ghosts observed in the play are an accurate portrayal of the different attitudes toward the work of mourning in post-conflict Central America. As it has been discussed, the play's focus is not the fate of the missing brother or a desperate call to bring to justice those responsible for the numerous crimes committed during the internal conflict. Instead, the play portrays the reactions of different people to loss. It is a picture of the struggle over the work of mourning, which takes place not only at the national level—as discussed in the previous chapter—but also within families and in the way those families relate to others. That is why the truth is never revealed and the brother is never presented in the play. He is a character whose sole purpose is to motivate the actions of others. He is the ghost that allegorically embodies the atrocities, pain, and doubts left by the war. Following this thread, the final words of the play, "Algo más habrá que hacer,"[70] uttered by La Hermana, can be understood as an invitation to continue the tireless work thousands of people have done over the last few decades. Willingly or not, this performance compels audiences to participate in the task of mourning.

A Failed Project?

To close this chapter, it is important to revisit the use of the word *ensayo* in these plays. This word has at least a twofold meaning as either an essay, closer to an argumentative work, or as a rehearsal in the theatrical context. While Cerritos has openly stated that the trilogy uses the term in the theatrical sense, meaning a rehearsal or practice, it can be argued that both definitions serve to characterize the plays' objectives. The trilogy puts forth a proposal in this trilogy, as Cerritos makes clear in the prologues. In the preface to the first play, she says that their goal as a theater company is to contribute to building a Salvadoran historical identity in the postwar era.[71] In the preface to *13703. El misterio de las utopías*, Cerritos claims that the main goal of the *ensayos* is to contribute to the reconstruction of memory in El Salvador from the point of view of the dramatic arts.[72] The latter means that similar to an argumentative essay, Cerritos and Los del Quinto Piso are trying to make a point regarding the civil war and its consequences. On the other hand, understanding this trilogy as a rehearsal or practice means that failing to attain these goals is a real possibility.

After carefully studying the trilogy, it is fair to claim that Cerritos and Los del Quinto Piso's project fails to meet their initial and declared goal of providing a tool of memory and contributing to the development of a Salvadoran historical identity. They do not offer a narrative of the war and its atrocities, and very little in the plays could be considered a significant element toward the building of a new Salvadoran identity. In this trilogy, it is hard to find a well-defined project that could gather different subjects under a common narrative, identity, or objective. Nevertheless, this does not mean that the plays do not substantially contribute to the postwar cultural and artistic scene and especially that they are not strongly committed to the victims of the war and their loved ones. Nor does it indicate that these plays should be discarded or overlooked. What I mean by this is that although Cerritos and Los del Quinto Piso's project sets out to build an identity and contribute to historical memory, it falls prey to the claws of the unfinished—perhaps impossible—work of mourning. In the trilogy, all characters, projects, and ideas ultimately reveal their hopelessness because of their environment's impunity, disrespect, and indifference. In this regard, the trilogy fails to articulate a narrative of the war and its violence capable of challenging the official narrative of the Salvadoran state. Regardless of how discouraging and unpromising these plays may be initially perceived, they assume their failure as a challenge, inviting the audience and themselves to persevere in the efforts to finally achieve justice, learn the truth, and build a committed and truthful historical memory. This invitation becomes a very concrete action, at least when the plays have been staged in El Salvador, for Los del

Quinto Piso often hold discussions and conversations about the play after presenting it. Cerritos claims that these exchanges have proven to be very effective in facilitating a space for conversing about the war and its losses, complementing the content of the plays.[73]

The trilogy, as a "failed project," exemplifies the productiveness of the unfinished work of mourning. Although the characters in the three plays fail to achieve their goals (they do not bring justice through the Audiencia, they cannot be found and mourned by their loved ones, and the truth about the fate of their loved ones is never revealed), their actions are presented as meaningful, even necessary. The trilogy does not focus on success, achievement, or overcoming. Instead, it is an ode to work, responsibility, and commitment, even when those actions prove unsuccessful over and over by the end of the plays. "Algo más habrá que hacer" are not only the closing words of the final play, but they are also the ultimate message of this trilogy.

The Specters of Monseñor Romero

It is not possible to close this chapter without dedicating some lines to the phantasmagoric presence of Monseñor Arnulfo Romero in Jorgelina Cerritos's trilogy. He, or rather his ghosts, are always present in these plays in a concatenated form. In Appelbaum's words, ghosts are "linked, one with the other, in repetition, linked repetition, or repetitive linkage."[74] Romero's words are used as epigraphs in all three plays, and his image is often projected when the plays are staged. Jossa argues that through all these mechanisms, his presence becomes the cohesive figure of the trilogy.[75] David Rocha, in the prologue to *13703. El misterio de las utopías*, goes even further and claims that although Romero does not emerge as a character until the last play, he is always present as a voice of truth and justice, becoming the omniscient narrator of the trilogy and the voice that "becomes a tropological suture that unites reality and theatrical fiction."[76] I think it is also possible to add that Monseñor Romero, assassinated under the orders of Major Roberto D'Aubuisson in 1980, becomes in this trilogy the specter of all specters. He is the symbol of all victims of state terrorism, the icon of all injustices that can never be fixed. "San Romero de América" is perhaps the most mourned person in El Salvador's history. His face, name, legacy, and memorabilia are everywhere in postwar El Salvador, from the International

Airport's name to the countless T-shirts featuring his face we can see in any Salvadoran city or village on any given day in addition to films, songs, and books made in his honor.

While in the first two plays, Romero's presence is limited to his words, either as an epigraph or as a quote in the characters' mouths, his ghostly presence in *13703. El misterio de los utopías*—which debuted the year of Romero's centennial—reveals more about Cerritos's intentions in conjuring his ghosts. In Monseñor Romero's first apparition, which ambiguously inhabits life and death, we see him as a human being who fears and questions his unavoidable reality.

> A veces tengo miedo. A veces lo tengo. A veces me pregunto por qué a mí este cáliz, y no quiero decir que lo alejen, pero tiemblo y sudo en el silencio. Jamás le he tenido tanto amor a la vida. Quiero un poco más de tiempo.[. . .] Yo no tengo vocación de mártir, no la tengo. ¿Será que había que ser prudente?[77]

His thoughts are rapidly crushed by the brutality of his assassination, which happens in both Romero's earthly life and the limbo. Monseñor talks to himself while Niño utters Romero's final words, "Que este cuerpo inmolado y esta Sangre Sacrificada por los hombres nos alimente . . . para dar conceptos de justicia y de paz a nuestro pueblo."[78] In the background, the sound of a car stopping and then a gunshot.

It should not go unnoticed that Monseñor Romero's *martirio* is the only assassination depicted in the entire trilogy. This becomes especially important when we consider that the three plays expose nothing but death. Also, Monseñor Romero is the only character in the trilogy that explicitly trespasses all possible realms. He is the ethical voice that, speaking from beyond, opens the plays, the human who fears his fatal destiny, the ghost that tries to bring calm to the living, the person who fears his encounter with God, and the living voice that claims "cease the repression!"[79] His spectral presence can be found everywhere throughout the entire trilogy.

It is also worth noting that Monseñor Romero is the only historical person mourned by these plays. In some regard, his presence-absence becomes an allegoric mourning for all the victims of state terrorism and political violence. Unlike the official, state-sponsored mourning of Handal and D'Aubuisson discussed in the previous chapter, grieving Monseñor Romero is one of the most extended, popular, and collective actions possible in postwar El Salvador. As José Napoleón Rodríguez's *Muerte en la consagración o la consagración de la muerte* claims in its opening lines, "Hoy la muerte ronda entre nosotros, nos persigue, Monseñor Romero."[80] Monseñor Romero's specters (always more than one) not only haunt Cerritos's work and Salvadoran dramaturgy but also hover over any possible demand of justice and reparation in postwar El Salvador. They are, Jorgelina Cerritos seems to claim, the specters of all specters.

CHAPTER 3

What to Do with the Dead?

The Specters of War in Claudia Hernández's De fronteras

The battle over mourning has found a privileged space of expression in literary works. Since the 1990s Central American fiction has extensively incorporated manifestations of grief, memory, and sorrow in relation to the civil wars of the late twentieth century.[1] Examples of this in the Salvadoran and Guatemalan letters are Rodrigo Rey Rosa's *El cojo bueno* (1996), *Que me maten si . . .* (1997), and *El material humano* (2009); Dante Liano's *El hombre de Montserrat* (1994); Héctor Tobar's *The Tattoed Soldier* (1998); Rafael Cuevas Molina's *300* (2010); Vanesa Núñez Handal's *Dios tenía miedo* (2011); Roger Lindo's *El perro en la niebla* (2008); Carol Zardetto's *Con pasión absoluta* (2005); Arnoldo Gálvez Suárez's *Puente adentro* (2015); Jorge Galán's *Noviembre* (2016); Víctor Muñoz's *La noche del 9 de febrero* (2014); Horacio Castellanos Moya's *La diabla en el espejo* (2000), *Insensatez* (2004), and *El sueño del retorno* (2013); Miguel Huezo Mixco's *La casa de Moravia* (2017); and Claudia Hernández's *Roza, tumba, quema* (2017), just to name a few. In its final three chapters, *Specters of War* will explore how contemporary fiction engages in the battle over mourning through the analysis of the work of Claudia Hernández, Mónica Albizúrez, and Eduardo Halfon. Since this chapter opens the study of postwar literature, I will comment on some relevant topics in the current discussion before proceeding to the analysis of Claudia Hernández's *De fronteras*.

Literary Criticism in Postwar Times

The signing of the peace accords in Central America produced a radical transformation in both the textual production and its interpretations. During the 1980s and early 1990s, testimonio was considered by many "the dominant form of narrative in Central America."[2] Testimonio aimed to represent the daily struggles of marginalized communities and the violence they suffered at the hands of the state, most commonly through a first-person narrator who, in some cases, sought to speak for a larger group. Testimonio, some scholars believed, was meant to replace traditional "high literature" in its political and transformative aspirations.[3] The boom of testimonio was intense and productive but short lived. Despite the tremendous interest it triggered among scholars and the general public, which resulted in the publication of major works such as Linda Craft's *Novels of Testimony and Resistance in Central America* (1997), testimonio lost momentum in the second half of the 1990s, as Georg Gugelberger acknowledged in the introduction to the 1996 edited volume *The Real Thing: Testimonial Discourses and Latin America.*[4] The decline of testimonio coincided with the emergence of the so-called postwar fiction, where authors such as Horacio Castellanos Moya, Rodrigo Rey Rosa, Estuardo Prado, Claudia Hernández, Javier Payeras, and Jacinta Escudos, to name just a few Salvadoran and Guatemalan writers, began to reshape Central American letters by breaking away from the "committed generation" that supported the revolutions through their actions and literary work.[5]

Arturo Arias, Beatriz Cortez, and Alexandra Ortiz Wallner were among the first scholars to produce overarching interpretations of postwar fiction based on the literary works produced between the 1990s and early 2000s. Arturo Arias claimed that postwar fiction had betrayed the political dreams and aspirations of the revolutions. This literature, he argued, evades the "ethical responsibility of elaborating the future starting from a critical problematization of the past."[6] Contemporary literature, according to Arias, is more interested in reaching transnational markets than in seeking a transformative political power. "Central American literary discourse has been disempowered politically while, paradoxically, being empowered as a commodity by globalizing trends," he claimed in his 2007 book *Taking Their Word.*[7] With significant nuances, Beatriz Cortez echoes some of Arias's claims regarding literature's depoliticization in *Estética del cinismo* (2010). She argues that in postwar times, fiction is moved by passion instead of reason or moral values. This results in what she calls an "aesthetic of cynicism," which is shaped by "the loss of faith in moral values and utopian social projects." Cortez claims that, as a consequence, the cynic project offers self-destruction as the only possible path, putting an end to people's political power and the utopian projects.[8] Alexandra Ortiz Wallner's book, *El arte de ficcionar* (2012), offers a different approach. She argues that postwar fiction is indeed politically committed to the work of memory, but in fulfilling that commitment it rejects national discourses and opens itself to transnational and transareal positions. For Ortiz Wallner, fiction and literary criticism are a form of engaging with the failures of history and historiography. In her words, "literary production has participated in this discussion as a means in which H/history has not been assumed as a finished and closed process, but instead, it is worked as a permanent crack that allows and fosters the associations, rearticulations, and fragments of historical tales."[9]

These readings influenced literary criticism tremendously in the 2010s. Nonetheless, it is fair to say that in the early 2020s, critics have departed from some of these positions, particularly Arias's and Cortez's.[10] In more recent criticism, there is a relative consensus that postwar fiction is, for the most part, engaged with its present and the legacy of the political violence, as it has been extensively demonstrated by the work of Magdalena Perkowska ("Una nación imposible," "Silencios que hieren"), Silvia López ("National Culture"), Nanci Buiza ("On Aesthetic Experience"), Werner Mackenbach ("Narrativas de la memoria"), Werner Mackenbach and Ortiz Wallner ("(De)formaciones"), Yansi Pérez ("Historias de metamorfosis," *Más allá del duelo*), Sergio Villalobos-Ruminott ("Literatura y destrucción," "La ficción de lo real"), and Jeffrey Browitt (*Cicatrices*), among others. Recent fiction has also expanded thematically and aesthetically in the first two decades of the twenty-first century. In Browitt's words, "Central American fiction now represents a virtual laboratory of fictional writing, daring in its subject matter and plots and nuanced in its fine-grained expression of both sociality and intimacy."[11] As a result, literary criticism is perhaps more diversified than ever, ranging from animal studies (Esch, "In the Company of Animals"; Buiza, "Trastornando") to migration (Padilla, *Changing Women, From Threatening Guerrillas*; Rodríguez, *Dividing the Isthmus*; Cárdenas, *Constituting Central American-Americans*), gender violence (Padilla, "Setting 'La Diable' Free"; Wieser, "Masculinidad"; Leandro Hernández, "La violencia"), and ecology (García, "Sin orquídeas ni agua"; Shea, "*Una mujer en la selva*"), just to mention some contemporary topics.

Despite the diverse approaches to contemporary fiction, neoliberalism is still one of the most studied themes within Central American literary studies. In his groundbreaking article, "After the Revolution" (2003), Misha Kokotovic argues that postconflict fiction "may express disillusionment with the socialist utopias of earlier decades, but that does not mean that they embrace the technocratic, neoliberal utopias of the 1990s."[12] On the contrary, he claims it is against neoliberalism that postconflict fiction expresses its political force and its desire for sovereignty. In "Nómadas, desempleados y suicidas" (2016), Christian Kroll-Bryce takes a step farther, proposing that it is neoliberalism (and the radical transformation of the sovereign power introduced by it), more than the recent civil wars, that should be taken into consideration when studying contemporary fiction. He claims Central American authors and intellectuals seem "more interested in thinking and exploring the present than in mourning the past and recent history."[13] While *Specters of War*'s hypothesis obviously disagrees with Kroll-Bryce's interpretation, the fact that neoliberalism plays a central role in postwar Central America is undeniable. In this regard, the battle over the work of mourning is not distant from the resistance to neoliberalism because it is in its name that impunity has been established as the status quo. As Browitt metaphorically claims, contemporary writers drag "the past like a dead corpse and confront an uncertain and precarious present as Central Americans attempt to find their niche within neoliberal globalization."[14]

This book contributes to literary criticism by approaching relatively less discussed texts (with the exception of Hernández's *De fronteras*) through a dynamic and productive understanding of the work of mourning that not only pays attention to multiple expressions of grief but also to the internal and external struggles around this process. Also, without losing sight of their literary and artistic essence, this research seeks ultimately to understand how these works dialogue with other narratives that coexist with them in the public sphere. I read postwar fiction as a form of critical interrogation of the narratives that led to the senseless, massive extermination of human beings and the possibilities and challenges left to the survivors. In my interpretation of Claudia Hernández, Mónica Albizúrez, and Eduardo Halfon, mourning is an ongoing struggle that does not offer any form of closure. The mourning process, however, does not exist only within the intimate domain; it also provides a collective sense in which people (and even animals) can participate and engage politically. My reading also demonstrates that these literary texts portray, although subtly at times, the multiple forces that try to prevent and sabotage the mourning process and how characters stand up to them.

Claudia Hernández's *De fronteras*

This chapter will pay close attention to a literary text that is a key element in the cultural productions regarding the work of mourning: Claudia Hernández's *De fronteras* (2007). Hernández is one of the most fascinating writers in postconflict Central America. Her work has been widely read and critically discussed among specialized readers and literary critics despite publishing her books with independent publishers in El Salvador, Guatemala, Colombia, Chile, and the United States. Between 2001 and 2013, she published five books of short stories: *Otras ciudades* (2001), *Mediodía de fronteras* (2002, republished in 2007 as *De fronteras,* the version I will discuss here), *Olvida uno* (2005), *La canción del mar* (2007), and *Causas naturales* (2013). She rapidly acquired international recognition, winning different awards (like the Anna Seghers Prize in 2004) and becoming one of the *maestras* of the Latin American short story. In 2017 Hernández began a new stage in her literary career with the publication of *Roza, tumba, quema,* her first novel, which was followed by *El verbo J* (2019) and *Tomar tu mano* (2021).[15]

De fronteras contains sixteen stories, most of which engage with death, loss, and grief.[16] One of the curiosities of this book is that even though it is replete with death and violence, the stories often overlook the actions that led to the decease of the characters. In most cases, the dead in *De fronteras* have already passed away before the beginning of the story, and the narration focuses on what happens next, on the actions that are triggered by these deaths.[17] In other words, death is not the end in Hernández's fiction but rather the starting point of her literature, which makes of the work of mourning one of the book's central elements.

My analysis of Claudia Hernández's *De fronteras* is guided by two hypotheses. First, I read this book as a manifestation of clashing forces regarding the work of mourning. In the different stories I will discuss here, we will observe how the work of mourning takes place against—or at least before—some figure or circumstance that aims to prevent (or terminate as soon as possible) the characters' grieving process. Consequently, the characters' mourning often remains unfinished. My second hypothesis is that in this scenario the characters embody an ethical attitude toward the dead and a drive to mourn, engaging in the work of mourning to the limit of their possibilities. To explore these hypotheses, I will focus on two main topics: first, on the emergence of a "community of mourners" that acknowledges the dead as "one of us" and therefore struggles to mourn them, and second, on the presence of mutilated bodies as symbols of loss and the possibilities they offer in the mourning process.

This reading discusses some previous criticism on Hernández's book. In *Más allá del duelo*, Yansi Pérez reads *De fronteras* as part of what she considers a Latin American tradition of expressing mourning through parody, "laughing at and with the specters." She claims that Hernández's stories "metamorphosize" the work of mourning through irony, the absurd, and sarcasm.[18] Yes, indeed, all those elements are present in the stories, but I do not think that mourning acts exclusively through them. As we will see, the experience of loss in the stories takes place also in very serious contexts. A second major issue in criticism of Hernández is whether (and if so, how) we can read *De fronteras* in relationship to the civil war traumatic experience and the postwar era. One of the most intriguing elements in *De fronteras* is the absolute lack of references to places, countries, or historical events.[19] Notwithstanding that, many critics read this book as directly connected with the Salvadoran civil war and the postconflict period. Misha Kokotovic, for example, claims that despite the book's "silences" regarding the civil war experience, Hernández's fiction remains rooted in the postwar Central American reality.[20] He also proposes that by making the "evasion visible," the book exposes "the unacknowledged costs of El Salvador's pacification and calls into question the project of national reconciliation without accountability for the crimes committed during the war."[21] Kokotovic is not alone in this interpretation. There is a tendency in literary criticism of Hernández to read her work as directly related to issues of trauma and neoliberalism in El Salvador or Central America, a way in which I have also read Hernández's literature elsewhere.[22]

This chapter aims to offer an intermediate approach (or perhaps an "inverse" one) to Hernández's book. While I will not lose sight of the civil war traumatic experience and the postwar era (this is a book about postconflict Central America at the end of the day), I am not trying to read El Salvador's reality within its pages, at least not directly. I do not aim to find figures that resemble civil war combatants or civilian victims, nor do I propose an allegoric interpretation of the stories. The reading I offer here is closer to Jeffrey Browitt's analysis of *De fronteras*, particularly in his goal of reading the book not from a sociological, historical, or political point of view but from a more philosophical or ethical perspective.[23] The above does not mean reading *De fronteras* naively as a "depoliticized" book. However, I think we should pay attention to the content of the stories first. The way they portray characters who mourn, the causes and the outcome of that process, and the motives that aim to block and cancel the mourning process, to name a few aspects. From there, as I will do in the conclusion to this chapter, we can discuss how these elements can contribute to a better understanding of postwar El Salvador, particularly regarding the work of mourning.

The Dead Is One of Us: The Community of Mourners

One of the key elements in the battle of mourning in postwar Central America is building a mourning community that acknowledges the dead as a member of a collective. Yet what is unique about Hernández's fiction is that the community that mourns the dead transcends its habitual representations, even taking the existence of said community into ethical dilemmas that could dissolve it. In other words, we observe in this book a drive to establish communities of mourners before the death of others. However, those communities are unstable, even questionable, yet they reappear over and over throughout the book as a constant drive to mourn. To explore this, I will take a closer look at two of the stories that better address this issue, "Hechos de un buen ciudadano" (parts 1 and 2) and "Carretera sin buey."

"Hechos de un buen ciudadano (Parte I)," the book's second story, begins with the discovery of a woman's corpse inside the protagonist-narrator's kitchen. Within the context of the disturbing discovery with which the story opens, the narrator's reaction is no less strange. He puts an ad in the newspaper describing the woman (saying that her name could be Lívida) and waits for a phone call from the family. The protagonist receives several phone calls from people who are looking for their missing relatives, but none of them knew the woman he found in his kitchen. Finally, after accepting that his method will not succeed, he calls back a man who previously reached out to him in search of a male body and gives her to him, so that he can place the woman in a sealed coffin to pass it off to his family as their dead relative. The story could have ended there; instead, the sixth story in *De fronteras*, "Hechos de un buen ciudadano (Parte II)," carries on the narrative. In the second part, the narrator receives several phone calls from people who also have found corpses in their houses and who seek help with this situation. The protagonist kindly invites all of them to his house and teaches them how to preserve and maintain the bodies in the best condition. The people then post ads in the newspapers describing the cadavers, hoping to have them reunited with their loved ones. After a few days, many of them successfully find the relatives of the dead, but seven bodies remain unclaimed. The narrator then reveals what he did with Lívida and everyone agrees to do the same if no one calls them soon. In the meantime, the narrator keeps the bodies in his house. Once everyone is gone, the narrator chops and cooks the corpses. Then, he takes the stew to the city's suburbs and feeds the starving homeless who live there. When the authorities find out about his charitable act (unaware of the real origin of the food), they decide to award him in a public ceremony for being an exemplary good citizen.

"Hechos de un buen ciudadano" accepts the constant appearance of unidentified cadavers throughout the city as a normal part of life. The problem is not who killed them nor how nor why. This is not a *novela policial,* and it is evident that the murderers will remain unpunished. The main issue in the story is what are the people going to do with the cadavers, placing the question of what is to be done with the dead at the core of the narration.

In this scenario of violence and impunity, the characters assume the responsibility of offering hospitality to the corpses and facilitating the task of mourning for others. Paraphrasing Derrida, they welcome the dead in their homes even without knowing their names. They let them arrive without asking or expecting any reciprocity.[24] In the world presented by Hernández, these little but powerful actions are the only ones available to the characters. It is because of this that all the people in the story make several efforts to find the relatives of the dead so that these corpses can be identified and buried. But they do not limit their efforts to just placing an ad and waiting. They also take the time to preserve the bodies—with "baños con bálsamo y sal de cocina"[25]—so they can be in the best shape possible when their families finally claim them. Although the latter could be read as a practical matter to prevent the smell of putrefaction and the hygienic problems related to it, I argue that preserving the corpses can be read as a metaphoric action that seeks to preserve the dead in the public sphere, thus avoiding the disappearance to which their killers tried to condemn them.[26]

The responsibility toward others reveals an ethical moment in which the communal dimension of the work of mourning emerges. This story proposes that every corpse has relatives and loved ones, and on top of this, that all of them—cadavers, their loved ones, and the main (living) characters—are part of the same community. Because of this, all the relationships and interactions that we find in the story are shaped by horizontality and mutual recognition. A good example of this is the naming of the anonymous dead body by the narrator, "tenía cara de llamarse Lívida."[27] By doing so, he confers a human status to the woman, something that was taken away by her assassins. By giving her a name, even if it is not her real one, the narrator reincorporates the woman into the community, he gives her a "face" (in the Levinasian sense). By the same token we should read the vocabulary that is constantly used in the narrative to express the belonging of the bodies, "Busco *dueño* de cadaver" (my emphasis); "comencé a recibir llamadas de gente que deseaba saber con urgencia cómo había yo solucionado el problema de tener un cadáver *ajeno* en casa" (my emphasis).[28] Although the use of these words may suggest a view of death as a private issue, especially in the context of neoliberal societies, I believe that this vocabulary takes us to a space in which violent death is understood as a transversal phenomenon that equally affects every member of the community. As a consequence, everybody has "their own dead ones," even if they ignore where they are, and therefore every community member engaged in the work of mourning shares a deep sense of responsibility toward other people's dead and deaths.

In this context, it is worth asking, What is the unifying thread that makes the building of a sense of community in this story possible? Unlike, for example, the cases studied in the previous chapters, there seems to be no element that connects the characters and the corpses. I propose that one of the fundamental components that gives shape to and sustains the community in the story (and in the book as a whole) is the shared condition of the precarity of the characters' lives.[29] Judith Butler argues that though precariousness is coextensive with birth itself, the precarious condition reveals that "the possibility of being sustained relies fundamentally on social and political conditions, and not only on a postulated internal drive to live."[30] Thus, precarity "designates that politically induced condition in which certain populations suffer from failing social and economic networks of support and become differentially exposed to injury, violence, and death."[31] In this sense, what invades the daily life of the characters in "Hechos de un buen ciudadano" is not only the brutal and inescapable violence that produces massive deaths (may that be from a war, gang violence, or any other party responsible for mass murdering the citizens) but also the precarity of their lives. It is this condition that enables them to build and support a sense of community within the story, one that does not hesitate to exhaust all possibilities to make sure that others have the right to mourn their loved ones. These efforts, nevertheless, will ultimately prove to be only partially successful, forcing the characters to face new decisions that will lead them to controversial actions.

Despite the efforts conducted by the protagonist-narrator and the other people who found dead bodies in their houses, some cadavers fail to be reunited with their relatives. Notwithstanding, this does not stop the characters from acting in favor of their community of precarious lives. In the first part of the story, we see an exchange (or a "substitution" if we want to use Freud's words) that, on the one hand, condemns Lívida's relatives to ignore her fate, but on the other hand, allows the relatives of a missing man to conduct funeral rites. On top of this, Lívida's body, even though not in her name, also receives a mourning rite and a burial. The result of this substitution is ambiguous and therefore only partially facilitates the work of mourning by unblocking the grieving process of the family that sought their missing relative.

The second part also ends with a substitution, albeit a much more macabre one. When the narrator decides to cook the bodies of the unknown and unclaimed bodies and feed the city's poor, he once again denies the dead's families any possibility of mourning them. This action is often read in a very negative light. Sophie Esch argues that the "utilitarianism of all these actions exposes the perversion and inhumanity of the so-called good citizen's civility."[32] In a similar reading, Hilda Gairaud Ruiz proposes that the narrator's house works like a cemetery/party house, where people gather to celebrate and laugh. Once the party is over, he cleans up the mess, which includes cooking the cadavers to then feed the poor without any consideration for the dead.[33] Kokotovic argues that the protagonist "depoliticizes the crime by minimizing public awareness or discussion of it, treating it instead as a simple matter to be resolved in a private exchange."[34] Against this trend, I think we can read the end of the story in a (relatively) more positive light, or at least in a less condemnatory fashion. In part, Yansi Pérez's interpretation goes in this direction. She reads the protagonist's controversial actions under the ethics of the hospitality taken to an absurd extreme (but still ethical), turning the ones who have received hospitality into a "gift" for those "who lack a house, to whom no one has given hospitality."[35] We cannot overlook that the narrator's actions, while counterproductive for some, are oriented toward his fellow citizens, whom the protagonist recognizes as people in need. The marginalized people—who are not only marked by poverty and deprivation but also by the precarity of their lives—are, therefore, acknowledged as part of the community.[36] In this regard, I agree with Browitt when he argues that through the process of endo-cannibalism, "the dead are incorporated into the community for the eternity."[37] This makes the narrator's actions highly symbolic; in the face of the impossibility of justice toward the anonymous corpses and the impossible mourning, the protagonist extracts from this situation a certain benefit for his precarious community. That is the only thing he can do to live a more ethical and just life in his horrific reality.

There are, of course, no right or wrong answers here. However, through the lens with which I read *De fronteras*, the questionable, even cynical actions of the protagonist, those that make him an "exemplary good citizen" under the eyes of the authorities—which means the eyes of those most likely responsible for the violence inflicted to the citizens—hold within them an ethical commitment to others. This commitment is first expressed through the honest concern and caring for the dead, and then, before the impossibility of reconnecting the corpses with their relatives, it becomes a bizarre—yet efficient—way of aiding those he considers part of the community of precarious lives. The dead are, ultimately, the ones who feed those who will soon be dead as well.

* * *

"Carretera sin buey" is another good example of how the characters in Hernández's stories express their responsibility toward the dead. This story presents a new compelling twist because the departed is not a human being but an animal. In "Carretera sin buey," two persons (who narrate in the plural "we") stop in the middle of the highway when they think they have seen an ox next to the road. When they approach it, they realize that the alleged animal is in actuality a person pretending to be an ox. The man tells them that he accidentally killed an ox and he is trying to replace it by becoming the ox himself. The two people sympathize with him and give him some suggestions, including self-castration, before leaving the scene.

I would like to emphasize the commonality that the story creates between humans' and animals' lives. The man who has killed the ox acknowledges that the lost life was worthy of living, and he accepts his responsibility toward the deceased animal.[38] In this case, the man who has killed the ox, unlike the people who have killed the persons in "Hechos de un buen ciudadano," recognizes the dead ox as one of them. Here, the traditional distinction and hierarchy between animal and person is blurred to propose a scenario in which both human and animal lives deserve to be grieved, and the person responsible for the ox's death will do everything in his power to replace the lost life.

Pérez proposes that the attempt to substitute the ox represents a "literalization of mourning which pretends to attain at a literal level what mourning proposes at a more metaphorical and symbolic level: the total restitution of a loss."[39] While it is true that the man who tries to substitute himself for the ox aims to become the lost object, the story suggests that the substitution, akin to "Hechos de un buen ciudadano," will fail. The protagonist has been trying for too long to overcome his loss without success: "Lo había intentado más de diez veces. Había levantado su duelo y regresado a casa; pero, a diario, cuando pasaba por ese camino, sentía la falta del buey."[40] Replacing the ox at whatever cost is a desperate move to mourn it. One that can even cost him his life. Unfortunately for him, becoming the ox is presented as an impossible task. The end of the story clearly suggests that the man will never become the ox regardless of how much he tries. Even in Hernández's strange and absurd world, substitutions never fulfill the void left by losses.

With considerable nuances, both "Hechos de un buen ciudadano" and "Carretera sin buey" are oriented toward a similar goal: acknowledging the lives of the other as one that deserves to be mourned and doing everything possible to facilitate said work. This is not a natural or given process and, quite the contrary, implies an active, creative, and constructive process. In Hernández's stories, the participation in the foundation of new realities and imaginaries is not limited, especially not to humankind. As Browitt claims, "the construction of reality is the work of both human and non-human actors, all of whom have agency in that construction."[41] In a similar fashion, Emmanuela Jossa proposes that Hernández's characters are forced to invent "other modes of being in the collective, beyond homologation, beyond the definition."[42] What lies behind the stories discussed here is the possibility of imagining a community, particularly a mourning community that exceeds the preconceived limits of humanity. In other words, in the mourning process portrayed in Hernández's fiction, everyone who does not identify with the oppressive forces is welcomed to participate (even if someone is responsible for the death of the other, like the man who killed the ox). That is the way in which the stories fight back against dehumanization and violence.

The characters include the other, value their lives, and do everything in their power to grieve them when the time comes.[43] Unfortunately, as both stories portray, the work of mourning is presented as an impossible task. This, however, does not discourage the participants to continue their tireless process of valuing life and grieving the death of those whose precarity did not allow them to keep breathing. The real issues are the questions, Who counts? Who can be mourned? Whose life is worth grieving? The response, Hernández's book seems to say, is all of them.

The Mutilated Body

The losses that flood Hernández's book take many forms. In addition to the appearance of cadavers discussed in the previous section, another common thread is the presence of mutilated bodies. The first story of *De fronteras*, "Molestias de tener un rinoceronte," is a perfect example. This is the story of a man who wanders in a quiet and peaceful city with a missing arm and a small rhinoceros next to him. The story disregards how or when he lost his limb or why he is (apparently) in a different city than the one he was born in. We only know that the rhinoceros appeared and began to follow him when he lost his arm. When he walks the streets, people approach him and ask him about the little animal, to which he only says that the rhinoceros is not his. After several attempts to get rid of the animal, he takes the rhinoceros to a remote area to abandon it. When he walks away from it, however, he begins to miss its steps echoing. Fortunately for him, the rhinoceros rapidly comes back, and since that day, the protagonist accepts the little animal in his life as his eternal companion.

This story has received considerable critical attention, most of which tries to connect it to the violence of the civil war and postwar times. Catalina Rincón-Chavarro, for example, claims that violence is portrayed as a result, not as an action, which contextualizes the story in the postwar era.[44] Esch suggests that the missing arm might refer to "a possible war trauma, as it is a wound often inflicted by firearms and landmines.[. . .] The story can be read as dealing with an ex-combatant."[45] Despite the numerous readings that propose that the story relates to the civil wars in Central America and their aftermath, there is nothing in the story that allows a clear connection to those events. As Browitt claims, there are "hints that a violent event may have occurred,"[46] but that is all the information we have.

A figure who wanders an undetermined place, who goes and returns without a beginning or an end, and whose main purpose seems to be making what is absent visible, reminds us of what Jacques Derrida calls the specter. The narrator, like the specter, is "a question of repetition: a specter is always a *revenant*. One cannot control its comings and goings because it *begins by coming back*."[47] With its reappearances, the specter can turn the gaze to what we cannot see, at first sight, allowing the "visibility of the invisible."[48] This is precisely what the narrator manages to do in the story. His only activity seems to be to walk around the city and converse with the people who greet him because of the rhinoceros. Through his constant, repetitive, and endless wander, he allows the inhabitants of that "peaceful and beautiful" city to see what is not there, his missing arm.

The lack of remarkable actions in the story enables us to focus on its main element, the acceptance of the rhinoceros's presence and therefore the absence of the arm. At first, the narrator makes clear that he does not fully accept either the little animal or the visibility of his missing arm: "[T]olero las miradas de la gente que lo ve [the rhinoceros], *me mira, mira el brazo que me falta*" (my emphasis).[49] Something similar is expressed when he recounts his efforts to get rid of the animal: "[E]l rinoceronte no es mío—les aseguro mientras me aseguro de que estén viéndolo a él y *no a mi brazo que no está*" (my emphasis).[50] The narrator's recurrent concern regarding whether people notice his missing arm suggests that he is still in the process of grieving its loss. Nevertheless, by accepting the rhinoceros's presence in his life, following this reading, the narrator assumes his responsibility as the one who must make visible what is not there anymore—even against his initial disposition. Accepting, in other words, his role as a specter. Thus, the narrator inscribes himself as the permanent reminder of a traumatic past that seems to be ignored by those who surround him.

It is also worth mentioning that the affect expressed by the narrator to the rhinoceros takes place precisely through the missing arm: "Lo acaricio al llegar a casa *con los dedos que no tengo* y le permito dormir bajo mi sombra" (my emphasis).[51] By caressing the animal with his absent fingers and cuddling it under his shadow, the narrator not only reaffirms his spectral character, one that cannot physically interact with others, but also demonstrates that his connection with the rhinoceros only takes place through the intangible and the absent.

The rhinoceros has been interpreted in numerous ways. Esch posits that it represents "the emergence of hope."[52] Kokotovic claims that toward the end of the story, the rhinoceros's role is making the people perceive the missing arm, drawing them "to the question of the violence responsible for its loss."[53] For Ana Patricia Rodríguez, the rhinoceros "signifies the magnified spectacle of living trauma in everyday contexts."[54] While all the above are indeed valid and well-supported interpretations, I think it is also necessary to think about the rhinoceros in a more unstable way. Jacques Derrida's early writings offer an interesting perspective: understanding the rhinoceros as a *supplément.* For Derrida, the supplement works as a relationship between at least two gestures. One of them is conceived as the original whereas the other, the supplement, comes to complete a seeming incompleteness of the former (speech and writing being the supplemental relationship furthest discussed in *Of Grammatology*). Derrida proposes that this is problematic because it means accepting that there is something naturally incomplete that can only be fully understood once the supplement appears. "The supplement, which seems to be added as a plenitude to a plenitude, is equally that which compensates for a lack."[55] The supplement is dangerous, Derrida warns, because we are at constant risk of overlooking the power relationship between the gestures, and even more, that the supplement overpowers the supplemented and pretends to be the original. "The sign, the image, the representation, which come to supplement the absent presence are the illusions that sidetrack us."[56]

In the story, we can read the rhinoceros as a supplement since its role in the story is to supplement what is apparently incomplete—the narrator. He refers to his "incompleteness" several times in the story: "Sonreí al ver que le era yo agradable y que él [the rhinoceros] me seguía a mí, que no tengo brazo, en vez de a cualquiera de *los que están completos*" (my emphasis); "temo que alguien lo acepte y él no oponga resistencia y me deje, y se vaya, y ya no tenga yo pasos enanos alrededor de mis pies de *hombre incompleto*" (my emphasis).[57] Since the rhinoceros appeared at the exact moment that the narrator lost his arm, it is possible to say that the rhinoceros comes to fill the narrator's incompleteness, and that is the description he repeatedly presents. Nevertheless, I think we should be more cautious before accepting the narrator's "incompleteness"—which is, indeed, one of the risks of the supplement. Is the narrator really incomplete? Is having a missing arm enough to consider the narrator an "incomplete" man? I do not have an answer for these questions, but I think it is important to formulate them since the perception of the little animal as what completes the man is potentially dangerous because it might eventually turn the gaze away from the absent arm altogether. This means that the rhinoceros could become the only visible consequence of the trauma that resulted in the loss of the narrator's limb. This is also potentially dangerous for the work of mourning because even though, as Esch argues, the end of the story proposes a scenario where the protagonist seems to accept his trauma and, therefore, is able to move on to a more stable situation,[58] the reiterative presence of the man and his rhinoceros, and the gazes they attract, are not free of the possibility of one day overlooking the lost object that is right in front of them.

The possibility of the rhinoceros becoming a supplement must raise awareness about some of the dangers faced by the work of mourning in postwar Central America, mainly, the risk that one day we stop seeing the absent, the disappeared, or the dead because of the images that aim to remember (or substitute) said loss without justice or the acknowledgment of the value of the lost lives. Following this logic, "Molestias de tener un rinoceronte" could be read as a warning, one that is carefully located on the threshold before diving into the book. Hernández's story seems to claim "be aware of the rhinoceros!"—do not let them deceive you. The pain is still there, and so are the specters that wonder around the book, over and over.

* * *

"Abuelo" and "Manual del hijo muerto" are two other stories in *De fronteras* that also portray dismembered bodies and that allow us to get a glimpse into how Hernández portrays the work of mourning in her short stories. "Abuelo" is narrated by a young man who misses his grandfather tremendously, who passed away three months ago. One day, the narrator goes to the cemetery to unearth the body. In the middle of the digging, the cemetery's undertaker sees him and offers to help with the condition that the young man will return the body a few days later. The narrator takes the body home and displays him in a family meeting. Everyone is so thankful for the narrator's actions that, instead of returning the body as he promised, he decides to saw it into pieces so that every family member can keep a part of the grandfather's corpse. Everyone agrees to bring their piece to every family meeting so the grandfather will be complete and present with them.

There are at least three points that must be noted regarding this story. First, it is clear that the family is going through an unfinished mourning process even though everything suggests that the grandfather died of natural causes and that he was properly buried without major complications. The above is particularly relevant because this story defies the extended reading of the book as a portrayal of the aftermath of political violence and state terrorism. What "Abuelo" proposes is that mourning could be a failed process even under the most "ideal" circumstances. It has been three months since the grandfather's death, and the narrator cannot get used to his absence: "aún no podía acostumbrarme a su ausencia, [. . .] al silencio de las madrugadas sin sus pies tropezándose con los muebles de la casa a oscuras ni a los almuerzos sin sus historias obsesivas. No podía. Lo había intentado—de verdad—pero no conseguía habituarme a estar sin él."[59] What is left for the other characters in the book if this family struggles to mourn someone who apparently died peacefully and at old age? The solution, not less extravagant than what we have seen in the other stories, is the restitution of the grandfather's presence through his cadaver or, at least, part of it. This substitution, akin to the ones we have seen in previous cases, is partially effective. The family is aware that the corpse is a substitution for the lost grandfather. That is why the narrator easily accepts the dismemberment of the body so that everyone can take a piece with them. In this regard, the grandfather's corpse, a metaphor in itself, becomes a synecdoche in which just a limb of his cadaver is enough to replace and substitute his absence, and thus facilitate the work of mourning for his relatives.

A second aspect that must not be overlooked is the apparent incorruptibility of the grandfather's body. Three months after his death, the story suggests that the body has not decomposed. It is in good shape to be easily recognizable, sited in a chair, sawed, and brought to future events without fearing its decay. This unique situation must be read against other stories in *De fronteras* where the bodies show signs of putrefaction. One of them is "Hechos de un buen ciudadano," where the characters must treat the corpses with different techniques to avoid decomposition until they can be found and mourned. Even with these procedures, after one week, Lívida's body shows signs of fetidness.[60] In "Fauna de alcantarilla," a group of neighbors assassinates a family that lives in the sewer system because they are hunting and eating their pets. After a few days, the smell of the dead bodies spread through the neighborhood.[61] If we compare these stories, we observe that the preservation of the corpses is linked to the work of mourning. In both "Hechos de un buen ciudadano" and "Fauna de alcantarilla," the victims of assassination, who also happen to struggle to be mourned, are susceptible to decomposition, to their erasure from the face of the earth. That is exactly what the characters in "Hechos de un buen ciudadano" try to prevent. In "Abuelo," on the other hand, the apparent peaceful death of the grandfather, in addition to the mourning rituals conducted in his honor, seem to facilitate the eternal preservation of his body. Mourning, in these stories, does not only affect the psychology of the characters but also the materiality of the cadavers.

One final noteworthy aspect of this story is when the narrator decides not to keep his word to the undertaker. This could be easily overlooked, but one of the main features of Hernández's characters is their high honorability and ethics. The narrator is well aware of what he is doing, and because of that he reflects in the closing lines of the story, "Acepté su tributo, satisfecho de haber decidido lo correcto para mi familia y no para el sepulturero ni para mi honor, que a fin de cuentas vale menos que tener al abuelo de vuelta en casa."[62] Not honoring his word is an acceptable price to pay to soothe his family and his own work of mourning. As we have seen throughout the book, every effort to facilitate this process is valid, even contradicting Hernández's character's frequent ethical imperative.

"Manual del hijo muerto" is the story that closes the book. After confronting readers with astonishing and gruesome scenarios, Hernández ends *De fronteras* with an aseptic story that resembles Julio Cortázar's *instrucciones.* The story pretends to be page 23 of a manual called *Manual del hijo muerto.* In this section, the text explains what to do when a son is found in pieces. The story begins with apparent sympathy toward the reader, who is obviously in pain, "Causa especial emoción reconstruir el cuerpo del niño (24–25 años) que salió completo de la casa hace dos o seis días. Por tal razón, se recomienda tener a mano una caja de pañuelos desechables."[63] Then, it suggests that the reader verify the pieces they received truly belong to their son before putting all the pieces together and dressing him, because "**NO SE ACEPTAN DEVOLUCIONES**" (in bold and capitalized in the original). The manual emphasizes that knowing the circumstances around the death is unnecessary, and it recommends covering hands and feet to avoid speculations regarding his suffering before his passing. Once the body is fully reassembled, the instructions conclude by saying "Muéstrelo a familiares y amigos. Reparta fotografías de cuando vivía. Llore cada vez que alguien mencione su nombre."[64]

"Manual del hijo muerto" has been read as the description of a murder or as a metaphor for a society too numb to mourn.[65] Against this reading, I claim that this is one of the few stories that does not present us with a cadaver, nor should it be read metaphorically. Unlike the other stories discussed here, no one has truly died in this one. I read "Manual del hijo muerto" as the straightforward voice of power, one that orders the people under its control not to mourn, or at least not publicly.[66] Despite its apparent intentions of providing consolation to the families who have lost a son, the manual embodies what has been the official attitude of the postwar Central American administrations regarding the work of mourning, one that demands the return of mourning to the private, apolitical sphere. Similarly to the official grief studied in chapter one, "Manual del hijo muerto" portrays mourning as an aseptic, systematized, and undifferentiated process. In the closing story of *De fronteras*, we encounter the voice of those who claim for the end of mourning. It is the ultimate mandate to regulate and normalize grief and therefore to inscribe it within the logic of the power. This is the subterranean demand that traverses the book and the one to which the characters act in relation. However, as the book demonstrates, the official endeavors to regulate the work of mourning constantly fail before the tireless capacity of the mourners to acknowledge the "other" as a life that deserves to be lived and grieved, and therefore that resists giving up their fight for the right to mourn. In other words, *De fronteras* profoundly embodies what I have called here the battle over the work of mourning.

The Specters of War in Claudia Hernández's *De fronteras*

The most common and predominant activity in *De fronteras* is to grieve the dead. Mourning is expressed in multifarious ways throughout the book. Some stories present the point of view of someone who lost something (like an arm), others explore the perspective of the people who encounter death and violence without being directly affected by it, and some narrate the story from the point of view of the killers who regret their actions. The above portrays the multiple faces of grief. Regardless of the different approaches to the same issue, it is possible to identify some common threads in many of these stories.

One of the first elements that stands out is the discussion regarding who deserves to be grieved. Stories like "Hechos de un buen ciudadano" and "Carretera sin buey" embody an ethical attitude in which the characters seem to acknowledge the importance of the lost lives, recognizing them as members of their community even if they belong to a different species. Another common thread in these stories is the presence of mutilated bodies. Limbs perform different roles in the book. In "Molestias de tener un rinoceronte," for example, they may engage with past traumatic events and their visibility in the present. In "Abuelo," a limb represents a catalyst in the work of mourning for the grieving family.

What all these stories have in common is the drive to mourn. I see in their action the will of conducting the work of mourning against the imperative to not do so—which we explicitly observe in "Manual del hijo muerto." The inclusion of all these perspectives regarding the work of mourning is one of the book's biggest successes. Through them, we can witness a literary world in which the question of what to do with the dead reappears repeatedly, and the characters must make a decision of whether or not to engage in the grieving process of others; in other words, whether or not to participate in the battle of mourning.

An interesting feature of all these stories is that the actions, despite how violent and bizarre they are, take place before the undaunted gaze of the state or the authorities. The latter, as many critics claim, could be read as a manifestation of the neoliberal policies implemented in the region in the postwar era, in which the state denies its responsibility for the well-being and safety of its citizens (a task they have historically neglected). The above results in the free market as the ultimate regulator of people's lives (and deaths), and an extended interaction between private parties in which all characters acknowledge that no one but their fellow citizens can provide any help in case of necessity. In Ortiz Wallner's words, "when no space offers protection, shelter nor security, the attitudes that predominate in the characters are pragmatism and impulsivity, perhaps the will to find ways to live together with the dead and violence, to survive them or to surrender to them."[67] On the very few occasions that the stories refer to the state, they always do it with distrust, to make its detachment clear in the situations the characters are facing (which does not mean it did not cause them). An example of this is the attitude of the authorities in "Hechos de un buen ciudadano," who call the narrator to make sure he is taking good care of the body to avoid any health hazards for the population, and who inform him that if something happens, he will be held responsible. Another example of the state's apparent disinterest (and perhaps its complicity) regarding the death and the pain of its citizens is overt in "Manual del hijo muerto," the placement of which at the end of the book helps us to better understand the context in which the stories we have just examined take place, one in which the state seems to be very interested in fast-forwarding the mourning process regardless of the circumstances that led to the death of its citizens.

One element that cannot be overlooked in Hernández's *De fronteras* is the aesthetic connection between language and mourning. In the short stories that make up this book, readers observe a radical rejection of the mimesis and referentiality that defined most of the literature of the revolutionary period. In this regard, Hernández's literature is part of what has been considered post-testimonial literature since "it breaks away with the representative-symbolic-mythical character of testimonio."[68] In Hernández's fiction, the said and unsaid are equally important. An expression like "busco dueño de cadaver" bears witness to the overwhelming presence of death in the characters' world, but it also demonstrates their inability to communicate freely with others. As Walter Benjamin states, in mourning, there is always a tendency to silence.[69] But we might take this even further. As Alberto Moreiras suggests, mourning is an operation that resists the mimetic operation because it recognizes in it the place of the law, and mourning should work as a process of disappropriation.[70] When Central American letters, and especially Claudia Hernández's fiction, assume mourning as the mourning of the mimesis, they do not only engage with the unspeakable losses provoked by the civil wars but also with the duty of resisting the reappropriation of literature for some of the political forces and discourses that triggered the massive extermination of human beings in the region.

De fronteras is a collection that brings the struggle over mourning to its core, which makes it a significant participant in the battle of mourning in postwar Central America. The book, as a whole, portrays not only different attitudes regarding the work of mourning but also represents, at times obliquely, the difficulties of conducting said work because of the circumstances that surround the characters. In many ways, the book translates the struggle faced by millions of people in postconflict Central America, whose grief and responsibility toward the dead, the missing, and the displaced is often seen with distrust and suspicion. Like Cerritos's plays and some of the memorials studied in the first chapter, Hernández's literature is an act of defiance toward the imperative to overlook the atrocities around us, past and present. Against the official voice of oblivion and presentism we find in political discourses and places like the Monument to Reconciliation or the Reconciliation Park, Hernández's *De fronteras* invites us to mourn. Be that a nonhuman animal, a relative, or a stranger. In Hernández's universe, all of them deserve the right to be grieved.

The question of whether (or how much) we can link *De fronteras* to the Salvadoran (or Central American) reality remains open. I think that is the elephant (or the rhinoceros) in the room. While I refrain from proposing what I consider to be forced connections between the short stories and El Salvador's recent past, I do believe that the civil war and the postwar era are present, at least spectrally, in the book. The specter, as Derrida argues, is the "*frequency* of a certain visibility. But the visibility of the invisible."[71] However, how much of that visibility is connected with our own desire of finding something that will tell us anything about, or explain, the postwar reality? The specter is also, Derrida continues, "what one imagines, what one thinks one sees and which one projects—on an imaginary screen where there is nothing to see."[72] Why are so many of us, literary critics and the general public, fascinated by *De fronteras*? Perhaps, we feel observed by the book, haunted by it, as if the book were telling us something important that we are compelled to interpret or understand. Those, I believe, are the specters of the war in Claudia Hernández's *De fronteras*.

CHAPTER 4

Somos la masa silenciosa

Archival Work and the Work of Mourning in Mónica Albizúrez's Ita

> Yo no soy víctima, ni mi familia tampoco. No somos tampoco victimarios. Somos la masa silenciosa.
>
> —MÓNICA ALBIZÚREZ GIL, *ITA*

The 2005 serendipitous finding of the Archivo Histórico de la Policía Nacional (AHPN) was a major breakthrough in the search for truth and justice in postwar Guatemala. The AHPN is undoubtedly the most extensive witness and repository of Guatemala's atrocities. Usually scarce and incomplete, official documentation about state terrorism is a solid pillar in many cases against former dictators and high-ranking officials in Latin America. In this regard, Guatemala is an exceptional case. No other country has found an archive as robust as the AHPN for documenting human rights violations (it is estimated that the archive hosts nearly eighty million documents).[1] Sadly, perhaps no other country has wasted the opportunity of enacting change regarding transitional justice despite having abundant information at hand.[2]

What makes the AHPN so unique is not only its exceptionality in Latin American history (an archive of the national police's surveillance documents during almost one hundred years, including the internal conflict) but also how the archive rapidly became the site of multiple reflections. In the years following its finding, numerous creative and scholarly works explored the multiple faces of the AHPN. In 2009, Rodrigo Rey Rosa published what is arguably the most emblematic novel about the AHPN, *El material humano*. The novel is a thriller that narrates autofictional Rey Rosa's incursions into the National Police Archive. While at first he is allowed to read some documents before the outburst of political violence, his access is suddenly revoked, and he begins to receive death threats. In 2010 Rafael Cuevas Molina won the Certamen Una Palabra in Costa Rica with his novel *300*, published the following year, which also revolves around the AHPN. Its title, *300*, evokes the code used by the police to indicate that someone has been assassinated. Cuevas Molina's polyphonic novel seeks to portray the nuances and complexities of postwar Guatemalan society through the first-person narration of different characters, ranging from former archive staff to *mareros*, political exiles, and elites. All of them, at some point, comment on the AHPN and the civil war, expressing, for the most part, a profound disinterest in what happened to the hundreds of thousands of dead and disappeared left by the armed conflict. The AHPN has also been studied and explored outside the literary realm. In 2009, German documentary filmmaker Uli Stelzner released *La isla: Archivos de una tragedia*, which aims to combine the narration of the victims with the life and work of the archivist serving at the AHPN in its early years. In 2014, Canadian historian Kristen Weld published *Paper Cadavers: The Archives of Dictatorship in Guatemala*, arguably the most important and influential scholarly publication on this matter to date.[3]

This chapter analyzes the role of archives—particularly the AHPN—in the work of mourning through a reading of Mónica Albizúrez's debut novel *Ita* (2018). Unlike Rey Rosa's and Cuevas Molina's books, *Ita* is a novel about the archive that is not set in the archive or its surroundings. Instead, Albizúrez places the AHPN at the center of the story even though it only dedicates a limited number of pages to it.

Ita is part of a corpus of Central American novels in which the story is narrated from the point of view of a ladino/a or a white person who grew up in an upper-class family during the civil wars and whose relatives were not assassinated, disappeared, or tortured by the army or the guerrillas.[4] While it could be easy to dismiss these narratives' relevance for examining the work of mourning because of the narrators' privileged position, I contend they are not only great literary works but also offer an insight into mourning from a wider perspective, one in which a broad part of society can participate and is invited to take part in shared grief.[5] Following Magdalena Perkowska, *Ita* and other similar novels "reveal that the violence of a war (or a dictatorship) can hurt and disintegrate at different levels and with diverse intensities, hit where no one expects it, poison bodies and spirits that seemed protected, producing physical and affective pain."[6] These works of literature demonstrate that the battle of mourning is fought on several fronts, even within the privileged groups that, consciously or not, supported or turned a blind eye to the political violence of the internal conflicts.

The National Police Archive and the Work of Mourning

In 1881 Guatemalan president Justo Rufino Barrios created the first regulated police in the country. In 1900 dictator Manuel Estrada Cabrera established the Secret Police as a sub-department within the police institution. Once the state had been able to secure its presence and position throughout most of the country, José María Orellana signed Presidential Decree 901 in 1925, creating the National Police and, more importantly for this chapter, the Servicio de Identificación, commonly known as "el Gabinete de Identificación." This would be the first office to systematically produce and organize data about individuals with a criminal history.[7]

Brutality and criminality were not unprecedented during the first decades of the National Police, but it was not until 1954, following the CIA-sponsored coup that installed Castillo Armas in power, that the National Police would actively engage in state terrorism. Castillo Armas's government relied on the generous support of the United States, which included assisting in police training and operations and also in educating them about the best practices to keep a record of insurgency actions in the country. In Weld's words, "U.S. aid impacted both the *form* of the police (and military) archives—their comprehensiveness, storage and organization methods, and materials used—and their *content*.[. . .] The United States led the restructuring of the PN from 1954 until the shutdown of its global police aid program in 1974.[. . .] U.S. assistance in matters archival cannot be separated from U.S. assistance in matters more broadly counterinsurgent."[8] The AHPN continued operations until 1997, when, following the signing of the peace accords, it terminated them, leaving behind millions of documents in deleterious environmental conditions.

After the end of the internal armed conflict, government forces emphatically denied the existence of any archive or records of state terrorism. President Álvaro Arzú successfully impeded the UN Truth Commission from accessing public records about military and police actions. The official version faltered in 1999 when four U.S.-based human rights organizations published a military document produced in the mid-1980s, and smuggled out of the military archive, containing information about 183 people and their "subversive activities." This document, commonly referred to as "Diario militar," was the first public proof of the existence of official records regarding political persecution during the internal conflict.[9] The government's lies regarding the nonexistence of an archive of political persecution and repression were fully debunked after the 2005 finding of the AHPN.

In the months following the discovery, the Human Rights Procuratorate was responsible for securing and handling the documents. Most of the work was conducted by volunteer staff from diverse human rights organizations. In January 2006, thanks to the funds channeled by international cooperation through the United Nations Development Programme (UNPD), the Proyecto de Recuperación del Archivo Histórico de la Policía Nacional launched the most challenging and important archival initiative in Guatemala's history.[10] Another significant milestone happened in 2011, when the AHPN signed an agreement with the University of Texas, Austin, to exchange technology and resources and, perhaps most importantly, to begin the laborious task of digitalizing the files.[11]

Since the archive's finding, the arduous and rigorous archival work conducted at the AHPN by dozens of volunteers and professional archivists has focused on establishing the truth about the thousands of Guatemalans who were victims of state terrorism. One significant feature of the Proyecto is that, especially in the early years, a considerable number of the volunteer and professional staff were relatives of the dead and disappeared during the internal conflict. They saw the opportunity of working at the archive not only as a necessary task toward justice but also as a personal quest for truth. The archive's staff has thereby actively participated in the work of mourning of numerous citizens, themselves included, who have been grieving their loved ones for decades.[12] Nevertheless, as Weld says, the best archives can do is resurrect a "paper cadaver." They are not citizens; they do not replace the dead. The archival work does not bring them back to life. The archive is a "testament to the repression suffered by thousands of people" and a "thin and tragic representation of a once-full life."[13] The archival work conducted at the AHPN is an exercise in conjuring ghosts, work oriented, at least, to provide some solace in the truth that the archive can deliver for the mourning citizens.

The archival work conducted at the AHPN contributes tremendously to the work of mourning as a tool for truth seeking. Through the reading of Albizúrez's *Ita*, this chapter explores how the AHPN can have an impact beyond the people immediately involved with it and the people whose loved ones' fate is hidden within those millions of documents. In my interpretation of the novel, the AHPN, like other major sites of memory, can bring people together beyond the immediate affective ties, even contributing to communal mourning where victims, bystanders, and members of the conservative sectors can come together and grieve.

The *Masa Silenciosa* Also Cries: Mónica Albizúrez's *Ita*

Ita tells the story of Inés (called Ita by her friends and family). She is a lawyer in her forties who lives a relatively quiet and comfortable life in Guatemala City. She is married to Juan José, also a lawyer, and they have a successful law firm together. Two unrelated events spark tremors in Ita's tranquil life. The first is the reencounter with Sebastián, the son of Delfina—the maid who used to work at her house when she was a child. The second event is the diagnosis of fibromyalgia, a condition that causes severe pain all over the body. These events trigger a chain of actions that will take Ita on a journey to her childhood traumas and to the Guatemalan internal conflict through an exploration of physical and psychological archives.

In particular, I am interested in four elements elaborated in the novel: (1) Ita's trauma, (2) Sebastián's role as a guide into Guatemala's historical inequalities, (3) how archival work becomes a crucial tool for the work of mourning, and (4) Ita's attitude regarding others' work of mourning. Even though all these themes overlap throughout *Ita*'s pages, I will isolate and discuss them separately to build an argument that will explain how even narratives told from a privileged point of view can actively engage in an ethical work of mourning in postwar Guatemala.

Disease and Trauma

Ita could serve as an example of what has recently been called "pathography" or "autopathography," namely, an autobiographical narrative of illness or disability that can be expressed either as fictional or nonfictional narratives. These texts, as G. Thomas Couser clarifies, are also often written by privileged women.[14] This is indeed the case here. *Ita* tells the story of an upper-class woman who, from one day to the next, is diagnosed with fibromyalgia and details the struggles and changes the disease introduces in her life. However, unlike the usual pathography narratives, which following Anne Hunsaker Hawkins often fall under three categories—the testimonial, the anger-driven narrative, and the narrative that advocates for alternative treatment[15]—the disease narrative serves here as a starting point that will not only take the reader through the narrator's personal journey but also to the connection between the narrator's own story and Guatemala's recent history. More importantly, it will take the reader from Ita's struggles to overcome her traumas to her engaging with a communal dimension of mourning in postwar times.

In the novel's second chapter, Ita's disease, fibromyalgia, is introduced without previous indication. The novel does not explain the circumstances and symptoms that led Ita to undergo medical examinations. Instead, the event that turns her life upside down is omitted, and the novel focuses on what happens following the daunting diagnosis. After learning about her disease, Ita wishes to know more about it and turns to the internet. Thus she learns that recent research claims that her condition "estaría ligada a algún padecimiento psicológico, abuso en la niñez, por ejemplo, imposibilidad de expresar un trauma, otro caso."[16] Her head spins around possible causes, but in the end, "Sólo se delinea tenuemente la ida de mamá."[17] Andrea, Ita's mother, abandoned her and her family in 1981, and her daughters have no news of their mother for months. Consequently, and this is the second part of her trauma, her father becomes a solitary and bitter man who barely communicates with his daughters. At some point, Ita remembers her childhood: "Estaba sola. La madre ausente. El padre encallado en el silencio."[18] The absence of Andrea introduces a fracture in Ita's psychology. In the present of the novel, almost thirty years after her mother's disappearance, Ita is unable to forgive her. They have little communication, only talking and seeing each other on special occasions.

Ita's traumatic experience can be grasped without excessive theorization. The novel makes clear in numerous passages that her mother's abandonment produced a psychological fracture in her.[19] She is unable to talk about it, she cannot communicate readily with her mother, and most of the references to her mother are metaphorical or lateral. While Ita, in a reasoned reflection, understands that her mother's abandonment is not that atrocious since others have lived more terrible episodes,[20] she overtly uses a trauma vocabulary to refer to Andrea. Ita calls her mother "el territorio vedado" and stresses that for so long she carried a weight that "no pude nombrar."[21] When remembering her visits to the therapist in her adolescence, Ita even names her mother's absence as a *duelo*.[22] In a compelling passage, Ita and her sister, Fabiola, recall how none of them has painful childhood memories. The condition for this is nothing else than the mother's symbolic burial: "La condición para esta memoria es un lugar oscuro, en donde imaginamos la sepultura. La de mamá, me refiero. Ambas sacamos la tierra con mucha dificultad hasta quedar un hoyo suficiente para depositar el cuerpo. Allí lo metimos. Pero como fuimos torpes e improvisamos, hay momentos en que la tierra afloja y sale una mano o se oye una palabra. Son las llamadas obligadas de navidad que hace Fabiola. Son mis conversaciones entrecortadas y diluidas en lo nimio. Son las pesadillas que nunca nos contamos."[23] This passage combines symbolic and factual elements that throw light on Ita's troubled grieving process. The mother becomes a living dead, haunting the two sisters despite their constant attempts to make her specter disappear. The mother's crypt will finally be opened once Ita learns about her condition and begins the archival work that facilitates the mourning process. Nevertheless, as I will further elaborate, the novel is not oriented toward overcoming her particular sorrow. Instead, what will begin as a personal search for the truth about her mother will result in an ethical operation oriented toward building a community of mourners that is broader than Ita's losses.

Sebastián and the Journey into Guatemala's Violence

After learning about her condition, Ita decides to explore the source of her suffering and the circumstances around it. Since this pain is still active, she avoids questioning her mother directly and reconnects with Sebastián instead. Sebastián is Ita's absolute reverse. He is a Maya artist, from a poor family, and politically active. Ita is a ladina, from a wealthy family, politically conservative, and a lawyer. After encountering Sebastián at her mother's birthday party, she obtains his phone number and sets a meeting. Sebastián's role in the novel is to accompany Ita in her examination of the past, allowing her to see what she could not realize was happening when she was a child. By approaching Sebastián, following Jossa, Ita "begins to question the borders, and her emotions reorient the affects, dislocating the margins of the normed space."[24] As an artist, Sebastián is interested in exploring what lies inside the homes. It is there, he claims, that truth resides: "Uno no puede conocer este país por las afueras. Uno tiene que irse bien adentro. Si lo sé yo, hijo de la de adentro."[25] Sebastián leads Ita into an interior journey through his research on the intimacy of homes. He invites her to dive into her family home and look at it otherwise, through the eyes of others.

Even though the novel is not linear, the events in the second chapter are profoundly connected to the situations narrated in the first. There, Ita revisits her family home and remembers her father's violence toward Delfina and Sebastián. When Delfina began working with them, Sebastián was prohibited from being inside the house. Thus, the boy's childhood unfolded in a small room in Ita's family's home backyard. When he was three and began to explore, "Delfina lo amarró a la pata de la cama con un lazo, de longitud suficiente para que pudiera moverse en aquella circunscripción."[26] Three years later, Juan Batres, Ita's father, fires and evicts Delfina and Sebastián from the house after the boy breaks the grandmother's special dishes.[27] Perkowska highlights that removing Delfina and Sebastián from the house will become a second significant loss for Ita, since Delfina partially filled the void left by the mother.[28] These reminiscences anticipate some elements that will emerge in the following pages, namely, Ita's family racism, her emotional debt to Delfina, and Ita's unawareness of the violence that was taking place while she enjoyed her childhood and adolescence.

In parallel to these recollections, Ita undertakes a journey away from her zone of comfort and privilege and into the "other" Guatemala, that of Indigenous and politically active people. The first displacement takes place when Delfina dies of a heart attack. Ita and Fabiola travel to Santa Catarina Palopó, a village located on the shore of Lake Atitlán. They acknowledge that attending Delfina's wake and funeral is an overdue expression of gratitude, one that arrives too late.[29] As most of the attendees belong to the Maya Kaqchikel community, Ita feels out of place and can hardly communicate and engage with the people participating in the funeral. Despite these feelings, Ita makes an unexpected but meaningful decision when they are about to return to the city: she wants to stay. While Ita claims to be in too much bodily pain to undertake the journey, which is true, she also wishes to stay in that part of the country surrounded by a community that she has systematically ignored and despised her whole life. Ita finds solace in the village and, more importantly, in Sebastián's care. What had all her life been a distant space now offers her, for the first time following her diagnosis, a moment of tranquility.

A second major moment occurs when Ita attends a political rally at the San Carlos University. Manuela, Sebastián's girlfriend, is one of the speakers. She is a law student who has been politically active for years, focusing on serving the Indigenous population. Manuela speaks passionately about the Native communities and how the Guatemalan state has plundered and destroyed national resources to fulfill the demand of international markets. Even though the two women will not get along because of their romantic interest in the same man, Ita is impressed by Manuela's words during the speech. For her, this is a learning experience where she repeatedly uses the word *aprendo* (I learn).[30] On her way out, Ita sees some banners demanding the respect of the Maya people's rights and against the colonial power of the "white man." The whole experience rattles Ita's pillars, "los significados de esa noche me rebasan. El lenguaje me deja atrás."[31] She experiences lasting consequences from attending the rally. She wakes up the following day in severe pain after having a nightmare about her father's funeral in which she emphasizes that he was a white man, not a Maya, highlighting his—and therefore her—privileged position in society and their responsibility in the historical violence against the Indigenous population.

Sebastián guides Ita into spaces and sites of resistance she has never visited despite inhabiting the same country. Thanks to this companion, she is able to transcend the invisible frontiers of her privileged life. Nonetheless, the novel does not follow any patronizing narrative, and Sebastián is portrayed as a character who lives with his own ghosts and resentments, especially toward Ita's family for the reasons expressed above. It is important to highlight here that Sebastián serves the purpose of offering Ita a window into a reality she never saw before despite being right in front of her. A good example of how Ita's attitude toward the "other" (in particular the Maya population) changes thanks to Sebastián is observed when she reflects on his activism: "Hace veinte años, hubiera sido mi silencio asustado, no mentira, mi propia voz denunciante: indio resentido comunista guerrillero. Hace diez: yo no soy racista pero allí están estancados desde siglos. Y hoy, cuando leo *somos los hijos de las analfabetas, poder indígena popular, los mayas también somos el pueblo*, me lacera el filo del vidrio quebrado y la caricia de Delfina."[32] Thanks to this initial stimulus, Ita will undertake the central actions of the novel, the archival work that will lead her to the path of mourning.

Archival Work and the Work of Mourning

Ita is a novel about the archive. Not only about the AHPN or similar repositories of documents but also about the dynamic and transformative political functions of physical and psychological archives. *Ita* is relevant in the context of the battle over mourning because it portrays how the struggle over the archive is strongly connected to the fight for the right to grieve publicly. The struggles about the archive have been identified by Albizúrez herself elsewhere, where she argues that the archives "erosionan los límites de una institucionalidad endeble sobre la cual se construye la memoria colectiva, y a la vez, ponen al descubierto un conjunto de fuerzas en disputa."[33] A similar claim has been made by Kristen Weld, who emphasizes the "archival wars" in postwar Guatemala, where the archives "were not just technologies of rule; they were sites of battle between rulers and ruled."[34] *Ita* allows us to take a step further and consider not only the role of archives with tremendous relevance in contemporary Guatemala, such as the AHPN, but also the complexities, aporias, and impossibilities of archival work itself alongside its social and political implications regarding the work of mourning.

The word *archivo* is mentioned on the novel's first page, in a section with no title and in which the reader encounters Ita for the first time. She is in her childhood and running around the family home (in retrospect, it is clear that her mother has recently left the house and that she is in sorrow). Ita enters her mother's library and is confronted with what Derrida calls "archival fever," the mutual drive to destroy and conserve the archive.[35] This passage from the novel is lengthy but relevant:

> La casa la siento vacía. La mayoría de los habitantes simulamos dormir, tal vez alguno rompió la conciencia con esa mañana. Desde mi cama quiero correr y saltar lejos. Cierro los párpados y los aprieto fuertemente. Voy a bajar hasta el fondo. A ese momento cuando la escuché comparar su cabeza con un *archivo* saqueado. Sin entender muy bien, corrí despavorida a su biblioteca y empecé a tirar libros, a derramar una témpera, a escribir mi nombre en el suelo. *Tuve el impulso de quemar alguna página*, pero la llama no sería el saqueo sino la destrucción. Tomé el libro en el que ella estaba trabajando, lo abrí hasta que oí un sonido de hueso roto. Por un segundo creí que podía entrar al cerebro, ese de corredores gelatinosos por donde una sombra deambula en busca de la fuga.[. . .] Se interrumpe el silencio de aquella casa de Mariscal, que quisiera ver *derrumbada, en ruinas*. Como debí sentirme con diez años cumplidos. Como estaba la ciudad entera [my emphasis].[36]

The first page of the novel anticipates the book's central questions. Ita's desire to descend "to the bottom" in search of her mother's truth clashes with her fears of what she will find there. She understands that digging into the past, conducting the archival work, and opening the mother's crypt will inevitably force her to face the pain she has battled for so long to leave behind. The debate between the urge to know the truth, face the pain, and mourn, on the one hand, and pretend that nothing happened and continue with her life as she has done during her adult life, on the other, centers the battle of mourning, and therefore the struggle over the archive at the core of the novel.

The archival work is expressed in at least two ways in the novel. First, we observe Ita's research in her family documents, the National Police Archive, and the National Library. Second, there is the sealed archive of her mother's and Ita's psyches. As mentioned above, Ita's sorrow for her mother's abandonment is still ongoing in the present of the novel. Her mother is a forbidden archive she cannot access. Therefore, instead of confronting and demanding the truth from her, Ita takes an oblique path and investigates the public archives. The archival fever manifests itself once again in the novel, since Ita's task is "never to rest, interminably, from searching for the archive right where it slips away. It is to run after the archive, even if there's too much of it."[37] This frantic search will ultimately lead her to issue a call for responsibility and transit the path of mourning.

Ita's archival work begins with the family archive. At one point, she remembers a document she found when organizing her father's papers after he passed.[38] The document is a police report about the finding of an unidentified cadaver at "La granja," the family's recreational house, in September 1981. At the scene, the police arrested Rosendo López, the watchman. With that information, Ita goes to the AHPN hoping to find anything about her mother. She suspects that the murder of the anonymous man and her mother's escape might be connected. As Magdalena Perkowska proposes, the murder opens an abyss of intelligibility and produces a rupture in the family narration.[39] For the first time, Ita thinks that her mother's actions might be far more complex than she imagined in her youth, "Algo me dice que aquella salida de la casa y la renuncia a su vida de artista tienen que ver con la Historia."[40]

When asked by the AHPN's archivist whether she was herself a victim or was there for "administrative affairs," Ita does not hesitate to say the latter. She then reflects, "yo no soy víctima ni mi familia tampoco. No somos tampoco victimarios. Somos la masa silenciosa. Los que hemos trabajado en horarios puntuales. Los que algo supimos de una violencia que se llamó conflicto armado. Los que estuvimos del lado del orden. Los que fundamos la normalidad anormal."[41] I will elaborate on the latter in the next section, but for now it is important to note Ita's initial attitude toward her family's role during the internal conflict. As a member of a privileged family, Ita believes that the civil war had nothing to do with her. Her family supported the army, and she never questioned that position. The civil war was other people's problem. Inadvertently, by visiting the AHPN, Ita has put in motion the machinery that will take her into the path of mourning. She is unaware of what she truly seeks with all her efforts, but the process seems more important than the finish line. "Y en efecto, salgo de allí con la calma de quien puede recorrer un largo trecho sin interés en llegar a ningún punto exacto. Solo recorrerlo es suficiente,"[42] thinks Ita when leaving the AHPN.

Two months later, she returns to the archive and receives a dossier with documents regarding the murder. She learns the name of the victim, Rolando Cajas Sagastume, and also that her father went to the police station to release Rosendo and to inform them that subversives had occupied the house without their knowledge. What is most striking for her is that she had never heard that story. The findings at the National Police Archive trigger more research, this time at the National Library, where Ita discovers that Rolando was a student of her mother's. In this instant, two seemingly unrelated events, the Guatemalan civil war and her mother's disappearance, appear to be connected. Perhaps, even without knowing, she is also a victim, and an indirect one at least, of the political violence.

The archival work conducted by Ita gives her the courage to finally face her mother and to metaphorically confront her childhood trauma. During the inauguration of Sebastián's exhibition, Ita confronts Andrea about Rolando: "Y con eso de la muerte, mamá, ¿qué querés decir? ¿Esa experiencia la tenés tú? ¿De Rolando Cajas te viene esa cercanía? ¿Viste el cadáver? ¿Lo velaste? ¿Fuiste a su entierro? ¿Tú quién eras allí, mamá?"[43] Andrea, to Ita's surprise, does not avoid the conversation and opens up herself for the first time. Ita's mother says she did not attend the funeral or give her condolences or see the body—in other words, she did not participate in Rolando's mourning rites. After all her archival work, Ita has been able to penetrate the impossible archive: "La puerta de un último archivo se vino abajo. El archivo de los afectos de mi madre."[44] Through the mother's confession, readers learn that Rolando, like thousands of young people in the 1980s, participated in guerrilla or "subversive" activities. Andrea allowed Rolando and his friends to use La Granja without anyone else knowing. Eventually, they were discovered, and Rolando was killed. The assassination submerges Andrea in a mournful silence. She does not dare to tell the truth to Teresa, Rolando's sister, and fearing for her life, she decides to escape and resigns from her job at the university and abandons her family without pronouncing a word.

Andrea's confession, nevertheless, is partial, and some things remain unsaid. Most importantly, Ita understands that her mother was probably having an affair with Rolando. Ita is aware of her mother's silence, but she also understands that Andrea has closed that episode of her life and has no intentions of reopening it: "ella vive una clausura de por vida y es muy tarde para salir."[45] Andrea embodies the conscious closing of an unresolved mourning, one that accepts living in silence, attempting to leave the pain behind, and avoiding the conjuring of the specters. In many ways, Ita's reaction to her loss—at least before the beginning of the novel—is not so different from her mother's. Nevertheless, thanks to the archival work she has conducted, she is capable of breaking with the family tradition of silence. She is determined to learn the truth and work in the name of mourning, in the name of her own sorrow, but also her mother's and Rolando's family's.

Thanks to her archival work, Ita understands that her biggest trauma in life, which could be the cause of her present health condition, is also a consequence of the armed conflict that she and part of her family chose to ignore. Also, she acknowledges that she holds the truth about the fate of one direct victim of state terrorism and assumes her responsibility toward him and his relatives. She embodies the heir's responsibility, which inevitably implies "involvement in action, doing, a *praxis*, a *decision* that exceeds simple conscience or simple theoretical understanding."[46] To end her search and, to some extent, her grieving, Ita decides to collect all the materials regarding Rolando's assassination and leave them in Teresa's mailbox without daring to meet her personally. With this action, which aims to bring closure or at least truth to Rolando's grieving sister, Ita hopes to alleviate, albeit partially, Teresa's (and perhaps her own) sorrow. The novel's final action demonstrates that for Ita the work of mourning, far from being a private, individual act, can only be carried out with some level of collectivity. Helping (or at least believing she is helping) Teresa overcome her grief is the final element that allows her to initiate a healing process regarding her childhood trauma. With different degrees, Ita understands that both Teresa and she are in grief because of the political violence carried out by the internal conflict. And therefore, only a collaboration—partial, insufficient, or ineffective—can allow her to activate the work of mourning.

The documents (the archive) left by Ita in Teresa's mailbox embody what Derrida calls the *messianic* condition of the archive. The moment in which the archive "no longer has any relation to the record of what is, to the record of the presence of what is or will have been *actually* present" to become a "performative to come."[47] From that moment on, the archive, no longer in Ita's hands, can only exist as a demand and hope, pushed forward to another one (Teresa), who might or might not embrace the work presented before her. The reader ignores whether Rolando's sister will receive, read, and understand the documents left by Ita. Even though there is a letter with Teresa's name in the mailbox, enough evidence for Ita that Teresa lives there, she might have moved to a different house, another city, or even another country. She might have died. Neither the reader nor Ita will ever know whether those documents reached their addressee and whether they were interpreted as the protagonist anticipated. Also, nothing in the novel suggests that Ita left an explanatory letter. The documents, extracted directly from multiple archives, are expected to speak for themselves. As in many other cases, whether the will to know meets the truth that might facilitate the work of mourning remains a secret. What matters here is not whether Ita's action ultimately alleviates Teresa's pain. Instead, I am more interested in the gesture of working in favor of mourning. Conducting archival work in all its dimensions and spreading the findings may not bring peace, but it does, at least, further truth. That community-oriented gesture is the one we must emphasize in Albizúrez's novel even if it fails or if it remains an eternal secret. Whether the archival work, like the work of mourning, ultimately succeeds in bringing peace, truth, and justice to the mourners once again remains to be seen in the future to come.

Toward a Communal Mourning

The novel's first page, quoted above, where the protagonist is in her mother's library, confronts the reader with Ita's crucial decision regarding the archive: Should she let it burn (or even burn it herself), bury the past, and until her final days embrace the silence regarding the atrocities of the civil war? Should she, like her family, disregard the mourners' pain? Ita's ambivalent relationship to these matters makes them stand out in the development of the novel. In my reading, the archival work conducted by Ita—and all her reflections about it—ultimately facilitates a shift in her perception and attitude toward the mourning of others, which is one of the most significant aspects of the novel.

The novel portrays a radical move from utter disinterest in others' sorrow to embracing communal mourning as a political disposition oriented toward justice. To better understand Ita's shifting attitude toward the work of mourning, we must focus on the first part of the novel, where indifference toward other people's pain is instilled in her, primarily by her father and her paternal grandparents. They express complete disregard for the country's inequalities, the demands for social justice, and the lives of the poor. The best example of their apathy occurs after the deadly earthquake of 1976, which heavily affected Ita's maternal grandparents but whose consequences were mainly ignored by her father and her upper-class circle, who considered the tragedy to be others.' A few months after the earthquake, members of her paternal family "entonarían emocionados la canción del anuncio del 'Pollo Campero,' que llamaba a levantarse a Guatemala. Los treinta mil muertos *no les pertenecían*" (my emphasis).[48] As a child and adolescent, Ita expresses compassion for others and their feelings, but in her transition to adult life, right before entering law school, she understands that to succeed in her privileged world, she must leave all emotional considerations behind: "Así debía iniciar mi vida fuera de aquella casa, terminada por fin mi infancia y mi juventud, con la fuerza suficiente para cerrar el corazón. *No mirar a los muertos*" (my emphasis).[49] As a result, she accepts the family narrative that expulses the disadvantaged outside of the frame of humanity, becoming part of the *nosotros*, the silent mass that supported the "order" offered by the army and that only heard the political violence from afar.

Ita's individualism and disregard toward the suffering of others gradually changes thanks to the archival work discussed in the previous section. This work will also have repercussions in her personal life, especially when she divorces Juan José and gets a job at an NGO that provides assistance to women victims of gender violence. The trial against Guatemalan dictator Efraín Ríos Montt begins shortly after this abrupt rupture in her way of life, which moves something inside of her. She attends the trials and, for the first time, sees and feels the suffering of the victims of the internal conflict. While listening to the testimonies of the victims and survivors, Ita reflects, "Palabras que explotan del dolor guardado. La angustia que sale de altos y silencios, de respiraciones para retomar el impulso, de llantos suaves que traicionan la entereza, de lágrimas que se aspiran para seguir contando."[50] The confrontation with one of the most dramatic forms of pain experienced in Guatemala shakes Ita in all aspects. It is not coincidental that shortly after the trial, Ita decides to collect the documents and search for Rolando's sister. That is, in her words, the way of "closing the wound."[51] She initiates her healing process by helping the direct victims of the internal conflict and acknowledging their right to grieve, which is also her mother's sorrow.

Interestingly, like in many other fictional works, the novel does not emphasize the resolution of Ita's grief. By the end of the text, it is evident that even though she learns and partially understands why her mother abandoned her, she does not fully forgive her. Ita's final words regarding her mother make clear that the relationship has improved but is not fully restored: "mantenemos un contacto medio y por ello sincero."[52] The novel's openness regarding Ita's ongoing grief should be read similarly to what I have discussed earlier in the context of Claudia Hernández's literature. The novel's main thrust is not the resolution of the impossible mourning but rather the activation of that process in a context that seeks to prevent it from happening.

The novel's epilogue reinforces the communal dimension that Albizúrez has been developing throughout the book. In it, all the characters (Andrea, Juan José, Sebastián, and Fabiola) come together to participate in the national public demonstrations against corrupt Guatemalan president Otto Pérez Molina that took place on August 27, 2015. Along with hundreds of thousands of people participating in the event, Ita perceives the voices of the "absent ones," such as Manuela (who was assassinated) and many others, demonstrating that the specters are indispensable in any meaningful political action and demand for democracy.[53] The final paragraph condenses the strength of the political community, one that can only exist through mutual recognition and the mutual acknowledgment of their worthy life:

> Allí estamos nosotros. Lo que alguien nombró patria. Lo que alguien dijo casa. La patria es una plaza. Allí dejaremos fluir el miedo acumulado, la ira acumulada, la ignorancia acumulada. De allí saldremos por rumbos distintos y también opuestos. Nadie hable de unidad. Nadie hable de permanencia. Alguien diga salida. Alguien pronuncie límite. *Alguien grite inicio, en este país de profundas heridas* [my emphasis].[54]

The novel's epilogue is perhaps too conciliatory, as Jossa suggests,[55] or even naive, considering that little changed in the country after Pérez Molina's resignation. The call for communal mourning nevertheless stands out in the book's final sentence with its acknowledgment of the lost lives and the attempt to establish ties with those who were invisible to the protagonist at the beginning of the novel. In this regard, *Ita*'s final lines echo the closing of Jorgelina Cerritos's final play, "Algo más habrá que hacer." Even though Ita has not fully overcome her traumas, she ultimately understands the indispensable role of collective mourning in any process of social transformation. But this comprehension is not given. It is the direct result of sorrow and work, especially archival work, which allows Ita to transit the path of mourning and connect with others' pain.

Conclusion

Ita is a novel that invites us to reconsider the role of archives in postauthoritarian societies. Unlike the extended understanding of the archive as a site of power invested with the force of law, the novel offers a window into the political and sensible dimension of the archive from the point of view of ordinary citizens. In particular, the novel emphasizes the role of the Archivo Histórico de la Policía Nacional as a catalyst for the work of mourning in postconflict Guatemala. The AHPN defies the traditional understanding of the archive because, since its finding and transformation in 2005, its foundational role in identifying and persecuting deviants, criminals, and political enemies has been turned against itself. Now, the Archive's sole purpose is to tell its secrets, always balancing between its self-destruction and its preservation for the sake of mourning and justice. Aside from any theoretical consideration, the archival work conducted at the AHPN has contributed substantially to the grieving process of thousands of families in Guatemala who had been seeking the truth about their dead and disappeared relatives. Perhaps, one day, that information could help in a judicial cause that will result in justice being served for the atrocities committed during the internal conflict.

One of the novel's most noteworthy elements is the connection between the archival work, the work of mourning, and the development of a collective sense of mourning, particularly from Ita's point of view. Perhaps more importantly, the novel elaborates on these connections in ways that avoid making unethical claims and without trying to appropriate or embody the voice of the direct victims of the internal armed conflict. In *Ita*, the privileged position of the narrator allows readers to grasp two major ideas. First, that even without noticing it, privileged groups were also affected by state terrorism, although indirectly and in a much lesser degree. In Ita's particular case, the civil war and her mother's involvement with young activists and guerrillas resulted in the collapse of her family structure, a wound she had not been able to overcome for thirty years. Second, Ita understands that the path of mourning cannot be transited individually, and the only way to launch the process is to connect and work toward the suffering of others, even when they have no affective ties and do not know each other.

The novel's end leaves many matters unresolved. Did Teresa read and understand the documents left by Ita? If so, Did those documents provide her any solace? Will Ita ever pardon her mother? Will Ita and Sebastián be together again? The lack of resolution is neither problematic nor entirely surprising in the novel. Following the thread of this book, mourning seems to be constantly embodied as an ongoing matter that rejects any form of closure, as I discussed previously regarding Cerritos's theater and Hernández's fiction. While not knowing what happened with Teresa might be questionable for some, I believe it aligns well with the novel's overall perspective. *Ita* does not try to assume the voice of the direct victims of the war, and Teresa is definitely one of them. Whatever she decides to do with the files, if she finds them, it will be up to her. Also, the power of the sealed envelope containing the truth about Rolando's assassination does not reside in its actual use but rather in its promise, its hope.

Ita's actions invite us to reconsider the emancipatory and disruptive possibilities of the archive. Unlike the passive and depoliticized understanding of the archives as mere document holders, or the Foucauldian conception of the archive as an expression of power that controls "what can be said" and the operations around them,[56] *Ita* might be read as movement toward *anarchivism*, a disruption of the discursive and sensorial regimes of the archive. The archive, claims Andrés Maximiliano Tello, functions as a social machine, one that operates "in the hierarchic organization of the records of social production [. . .] starting from an articulation of different bodies, practices, techniques, and enunciative functions in a given time."[57] The archive therefore organizes the sensorial and discursive regimes, and it is there that the archive meets the police (in Jacques Rancière's terms): "the police determine a sensorial regime in the social body that is intimately articulated with the disposition of the records that operate the social machine of the archive. Therefore [. . .] the police order holds an unarguable reciprocity with the archive, because *the police law* [ordenamiento de la policía] *is always supported by the police record* [ficha policial]."[58] Against the social order of the archive, particularly the National Police Archive, the inception of which is inseparable from the strengthening of the Guatemalan state and its repressive and controlling institutions, Ita uses the AHPN in disruptive terms. By conducting archival work, the protagonist seeks to break the sensorial and visual regimes of the elites. Where her family and friends see "un indio," "un guerrillero," "un resentido," she now sees a Maya community that has suffered segregation, racism, and violence. Against her family's indifference toward the poor and the victims of state terrorism, she manages to feel the pain of others. Ita's anarchivist movements aim to demolish "the social control expressed and delimitated in the archives."[59]

The first two decades of the twenty-first century have demonstrated that postwar Guatemala may very well offer powerful examples of ethical community engagement, of the disruption of sensible regimes, and even of hope. The existence of the National Police Archive and the numerous reflections created around it are great examples of the force of mourning. As this book argues, mourning must be understood as an intensity that can traverse the social fabric, even reaching sectors of society that have been immune to the sorrow of others, growing and expanding exponentially. Therein lies its power. By confining mourning to the victims and their relatives, we cancel the possibility of ethical empathy, support, and even political actions from those who once may have disregarded the atrocities of the civil wars. As *Ita* demonstrates, there is an invisible force inherent in archival work that can contribute to forging ethical connections between different layers of society. The archives hold one of the keys to a more just Guatemalan society.

CHAPTER 5

Eduardo Halfon

A Global Struggle for Mourning

> Yo era muy niño entonces, en Guatemala. Pero recuerdo perfectamente que le pregunté a mi padre qué estaban haciendo esas personas tumbadas sobre un viejo colchón. Él me observó hacia abajo, alterado, sus ojos un poco más abiertos de lo normal.[. . .] Su respuesta me llegó en un hilo susurrado, frío, cauteloso, bien dirigido y hermosamente entonado para que sólo yo lo percibiera: "Están de luto."
>
> —EDUARDO HALFON, "LUTO"

Perhaps no other Central American author has reflected and written more about the work of mourning than Guatemalan Eduardo Halfon. Born in 1971, he has penned over fifteen books, mostly novels and short stories. Halfon has had an unusual literary career. At the age of ten, he and his family fled the violence of the internal conflict and relocated to the United States, where he attended college and graduated with an engineering degree. Halfon returned to Guatemala to work for his father's company in his mid-twenties. Feeling unsatisfied with his life, he eventually took literature classes at Rafael Landívar University, becoming a university professor some years later. In 2003, at the age of thirty-two, he began his literary career with the publication of two books, *Esto no es una pipa, Saturno* and *De cabo roto*, and has continued publishing uninterruptedly to the present. In the early twenty-first century, Halfon is among the most read, translated, and discussed Central American authors and one of the most global Latin American writers.[1]

Reading Eduardo Halfon's oeuvre is a detective task. Erica Durante and Maude Havenne use the term *matryoshka* to refer to his literary work. They argue that in each new book, Halfon uses his previous writing as an endogenous force, making each text something "inseparable from the global archaeology of the oeuvre."[2] This can manifest itself in multiple ways. For example, many of his stories have been published and republished in different formats and venues over the years. In some cases, these actions seem to respond merely to editorial decisions (the books where some stories were originally published did not circulate widely, which is certainly the case with Halfon's first books). Some of the stories published in his first book of short stories, *Siete minutos de desasosiego* (2007), for instance, were later included in *Clases de Hebreo* (2008)—such as "Clases de hebreo" and "Llanta pache." Also, the stories "Corazón no moleste," "El poder de la euforia," and "Polvo," which became widely known after being included in *Mañana nunca lo hablamos* (2011), were originally published in the 2009 book *Clases de dibujo*. In 2017 Halfon published a compilatory volume titled *Clases de chapín* that included all the stories previously published in *Clases de hebreo* and *Clases de dibujo* along with other stories originally included in *Siete minutos de desasosiego*. Another common practice is the inclusion of previously published short stories in his latest novels. For example, *Monasterio* (2014) contains three previous stories with minor modifications: "Fumata blanca" (originally included in *El boxeador polaco* [2008]), "Luto" (published in *Clases de hebreo* [2008]), and "Los ocasos" (published in the journal *Letras Libres* in 2011). In *Canción* (2021), Halfon includes, with variations, "El ultimo café turco" and "La señora del gabán rojo," both originally published in *Mañana nunca lo hablamos* (2011). The short story "Oh gueto mi amor," published in *Signor Hofman* (2015), was later issued as an illustrated book in 2018 with artwork by Spanish illustrator David de las Heras. On top of this, some short stories became the starting point for novels. *Monasterio*, for example, expands "Fumata blanca," and *La pirueta* further develops "Epístrofe."

There are two major lines of interpretation in literary criticism of Eduardo Halfon's work. First, scholars have read his fiction as an exemplary case of what Marianne Hirsch has called "postmemory," meaning that Halfon's literature embodies the intergenerational trauma from both the Guatemalan internal conflict and the Shoah.[3] The connection with the civil war would be the result of growing up in Guatemala in the 1970s. However, since he left the country at the age of ten, he would not be old enough to develop his own traumas regarding the armed conflict. His relationship with the Shoah is the result of having numerous family members assassinated by the Nazis. This trauma would be transmitted to him primarily by his maternal grandfather, a survivor who was imprisoned in Auschwitz, among other extermination camps.[4] A second line of analysis is reading his work through the lens of the Jewish tradition, putting Halfon next to other Latin American authors of Jewish descent (such as Argentinean Sergio Chejfec or Chilean Cynthia Rimsky). Jewishness indeed plays an important role in his fiction, and many characters are Jews or of Jewish descent.[5] Magdalena Perkowska has noted that these two themes are not only predominant in criticism of Halfon's work but are also directly connected with the translation and circulation of his books in metropolitan languages and markets because of their relevance in "post-Holocaust Europe and in the United States."[6] Ultimately, Halfon's literature has been often labeled as "autofictional," and therefore, his biography and interviews are frequently included in the study of his work.[7]

Eduardo Halfon's literature is a continuous portrayal of loss, absences, silence, and grief, which are expressed in multifold ways throughout his novels and short stories. The present chapter maps and discusses some of the expressions of mourning in Halfon's fiction by tracing their development throughout different publications. This chapter's goal is to offer an overarching analysis of Halfon's oeuvre—from *Esto no es una pipa, Saturno* (2003) to *Un hijo cualquiera* (2022)—identifying the predominant themes and sources of grief in it. I will focus on two main leitmotifs. First, the troubled relationship between father and son. Halfon's fiction expresses a constant rejection of the father, who is often portrayed as a lost object whose presence is mostly spectral. The symbolic loss of the father is represented in multiple forms, from his (literary) death to representations of him as a diminished figure. The death (or weakening) of the paternal figure serves in Halfon's fiction as a mechanism to resist, and eventually break, the law of the father, which establishes among other things, the prohibition to mourn. The second section explores Halfon's storytelling of traumatic issues. In particular, this part discusses the veracity, ambiguities, and inconsistencies of the story of the Polish boxer and how the Guatemalan internal conflict is portrayed in Halfon's literature.

Based on some of the characteristics of Halfon's fiction, such as the similarities and the homonymy of the narrators and the author, the frequent references to the same events and characters, and the inclusion of some stories in later novels, I have decided to treat his oeuvre as one major literary project in which arguments can be drawn from multiple books. In this regard, I follow Matías Barchino, who conceived Halfon's fiction as a nonlinear "hiperrelato" that comes together through certain nucleus and narrative catharsis.[8] Thus, while this chapter focuses on selected novels and short stories, it will always return to the major lines of analysis proposed here, making connections with other texts when pertinent.

The interpretation advanced here seeks an alternative approach to existing criticism for a variety of reasons. First, my analysis emerges from a reading of Eduardo Halfon's oeuvre that seeks to understand the roots of the work of mourning in his fiction without a preconceived notion or tradition—with the exception of considering him a Guatemalan author who portrays multiple expressions of grief in the postwar era. This panoramic reading reveals some issues often overlooked by previous scholarship. First, readings of his work through the lens of postmemory often erase the narrator's losses, as if mourning in his fiction was exclusively related to his family and not to his own traumas. The reading proposed here also dialogues with the "Jewish interpretations." Halfon can easily be grouped in as a Latin American–Jewish author based on his ancestry (all four grandparents were Jews who migrated to Guatemala) and the observance of the traditions by his family. In some cases, however, reading his work through the lens of Judaism has led to dubious interpretations, such as equating the "struggles" and the "exile" of Halfon's privileged family with the victims of the ethnocide that took place in Guatemala during the internal conflict.[9] Also, the Jewish readings of Halfon's fiction pay close attention to the story of the maternal grandfather, who survived imprisonment in Auschwitz. Nonetheless, two major aspects are often overlooked. First, the beautiful story of survival that the grandfather tells his grandson in "El boxeador polaco" is put into question in "Discurso de Póvoa," the following story within *El boxeador polaco*.[10] Second, the narrator is affectively connected to the grandfather, being the only family member—with the exception of the mother—whom he always remembers and mentions with love, care, and affection. In other words, the connection to the grandfather and his horrific experience is not necessarily religious or identitarian but rather emotional and affectionate, especially in the context where the narrator has a difficult relationship with his father.

Eduardo Halfon's fiction offers an entirely different insight into the battle over the work of mourning in postwar Central America. Unlike the radical deterritorialization we find in Claudia Hernández's book or the more historical narration Mónica Albizúrez presents in *Ita*, Halfon introduces his readers to a complex web of grief that expands into transgenerational and transnational scenarios. Mourning predominantly exists in his literature in relation to other forms of pain and loss. In this regard, the traumatic experience of the Guatemalan internal conflict is never too far from the symbolic loss of his father or the silence of his Polish grandfather about his imprisonment in Auschwitz. Halfon's literature offers a reflection about the work of mourning that, in the end, demands a global understanding of mourning, one that can only exist by rebelling against the prohibition to grieve (embodied in what I call here "the law of the father") and by challenging the Western hierarchy of pain.

The Father, the Specter

One of Halfon's most recurrent themes is the constant friction between the narrator and his father. An examination of his oeuvre rapidly reveals that the father is a character often portrayed as authoritarian and dominant, and in many of his apparitions, he is yelling at or in the presence of his family.[11] Despite being alive in most of Halfon's fiction, the paternal figure is often mentioned in absentia. Readers see him through his traces, such as the presents and food he sends when the narrator is at the hospital in "Muerte de un cácher," or as the irresponsive addressee of the narrator's words in *Saturno*. The father is the eternal revenant in Halfon's fiction. It is a character that rarely performs meaningful actions or interacts with others in his literature, but still, he constantly looms over the narrator's conscience as a spectral reminder of his existence and dominance.

This section explores the troubled father-son relationship through an arc that goes from the death of the father (literarily and symbolically)—and the subsequent rejection of the father's law—to the reappearance of the paternal figure in Halfon's most recent books. Interestingly, at the time of writing (2023), his first (*Esto no es una pipa, Saturno*) and last book (*Un hijo cualquiera*) seem to open and close that circle.[12]

Killing the Father

Esto no es una pipa, Saturno (2003) is not only Eduardo Halfon's first book but also a key to interpreting his fiction. This book—almost ignored by critics, perhaps because there are no references to the Guatemalan civil war or the Holocaust—is compounded of two novellas (or long short stories) connected by the topic of suicide. *Esto no es una pipa* tells the story of the death of French-Guatemalan painter Carlos Valenti, who killed himself in Paris in 1912, through a polyphonic text that immerses the reader into the European art world of the early twentieth century. In *Saturno*, we find for the first time the narrator we will later identify as Halfon's homonymous autofictional narrator, although that voice will remain anonymous in this book.

Saturno introduces the hatred that the narrator feels for his father, which is anticipated by the title.[13] The story is narrated by an unnamed voice that intertwines stories of artists, writers, and intellectuals who committed suicide (Alejandra Pizarnik, Andrés Caicedo, Ernest Hemingway, and Sylvia Plath, among others, many of whom had a troubled relationship with their fathers) with paternal memories of violence, disappointment, and coldness. The first lines of the story introduce the narrator's need for his father and the indifference and disdain of the latter:

> Sus cartas, padre, me llegaban un par de veces cada año. Yo estaba lejos en la universidad; pero usted estaba aún más lejos, de mí. Al inicio, ingenuo, yo abría el sobre con una emoción contenida. Y siempre, sin falta, hallaba un papel doblado en tres. Un solo papel con el membrete de su empresa. Mal doblado, por prisa, supongo. Buscando sus palabras, padre, necesitándolas, lo desdoblaba con ansia. Y como una hoja seca hamaqueándose en la brisa, lento, el cheque caía hacia el suelo. Lo dejaba allí, casi olvidado a la par de mis pies, pues lo que realmente me interesaba no era su dinero, padre, sino sus palabras. Y en medio del papel, escrito en tinta negra, encontraba yo siempre lo mismo: su nombre. Nada más. Sólo su nombre firmado con prisa. Una palabra. Sólo una palabra. El padre es un nombre.[14]

Halfon's literature opens with a desperate cry for affection from the father but one that immediately expresses the necessity to repress it through "una emoción contenida." Instead, he only receives the father's name on a poorly folded piece of paper. The father enters Halfon's fiction as an unnamed phantasmagorical figure, but it is clear that this is not the first time. This letter reminds the narrator of all the previous correspondence and anticipates the letters to come. The father is, and will recurrently be in Halfon's fiction, a returning spectral figure, one that self-identifies as the father, who signs as the father, who imposes the law of the father, but always from afar, from an anonymous name inked in a piece of paper.

Within *Saturno*'s chaotic narration, it is possible to distinguish that, while not the only one, a major reason behind the distant father-son relationship is the narrator's literary inclinations: "Le parecía a usted ridículo que su hijo pretendiese ganarse la vida escribiendo. Se avergonzaba usted de mi vocación. A sus amigos les solía mentir.[. . .] Te presento a mi hijo, el ingeniero. Otras veces, yo era un abogado.[. . .] Yo, padre, le daba pena. Lo humillaba. Ante sus ojos, yo era un fracaso y, por lo tanto, como padre, usted también era un fracaso."[15] From the first lines of the novella, it is clear that the distance between father and son was already pronounced before the son became a writer. Nevertheless, this decision seems to be the last nail in the coffin. *Saturno*'s narrator cries that his father never cared about his literary work and never bothered to read anything written by him. Had he done so, the father would have learned that "mi escritura era toda sobre usted; todo lo que allí hice, padre, fue llorar lo que no pude llorar sobre su pecho."[16] Literature, for Halfon's narrator, is a form of crying. He wishes his father to hold him and let him cry, but he crashes against not only the father's indifference and unavailability but also with what I call here the law of the father.

The father in Halfon's fiction is much more than a male parent. He is the embodiment of authority, the one that imposes and administers the law. This is, in part, what the closing sentence of the novella's first paragraph quoted above anticipates: "the father is a name." These words resonate with Jacques Lacan's concept of "the Name-of-the-Father," which is precisely the imposition of the symbolic father's law.[17] While inviting, we should resist the temptation of reading Halfon's fiction from a purely psychoanalytical point of view, mostly because Freud's and Lacan's understanding of the "name of the father" connects with the Oedipus complex and the prohibition of the son from sleeping with his mother. I do not think that is the case here. Still, the notion of the law of the father is relevant because it represents an imposition that the narrator will try to break away from in his entire oeuvre. The father's law is visible in quotidian things, such as the father's power to assign the seats in a restaurant ("No podíamos sentarnos sin su consentimiento. Usted imponía el orden, señalando con su índice extendido el puesto de cada persona. Usted mandaba. Más que un padre, usted era un tirano"),[18] to major aspects of the narrator's life, like indoctrination into Judaism and the prohibition to mourn.

Saturno openly exposes the role of the father as the embodiment of authority and the law, which will become a central topic during the first decade of Halfon's fiction. At one point, the narrator remembers when he shared his concerns about his identity with his father. The narrator, who presumably lives in the United States, does not feel Latino or European or U.S. American, and "Aún menos judío." The father's reaction is aligned with the authoritarian attitude I have exemplified above: "Al sólo mencionar no sentirme judío, usted, echado, su mirada siempre en otro sitio, se enfureció. [. . .] De niño, usted me obligó a actuar judío, a seguir las tradiciones. Así es, me decía, *esa es la ley*. Pero la verdad es que *usted era la ley, padre. Yo vivía bajo su Ley*" (my emphasis).[19] In the novella, and in Halfon's fiction in general, the father *is* the law, and everyone in the household is subject to that rule.[20] But this is a law without justice. It is pure force, a law that justifies itself only in its application, in its *enforcement*.[21]

Saturno's end presents a scene that has not been repeated so far in Halfon's fiction (as of 2023): the death of the father. Without anticipation, the narrator says "Ni si quiera me habló antes de irse, padre.[. . .] Usted se murió sin despedirse, padre."[22] In the next four paragraphs, the finale of the novella, the narrator continues expressing his resentment toward the now-dead father, confronting him about his silence and indifference in both life and death. Interestingly, the narrator emphasizes that he followed the father's law even after his death, participating in the eight days of mourning mandated by Judaism, but without meaning it and without crying, "Ocho día actué ante un público hebreo, ocho día sonreí, padre, del asco. Pero jamás lloré. Ni una lágrima. Eso me lo enseñó usted."[23] Three ideas must be noted about this important passage. First, the law of the father becomes spectral since it is capable of surviving the death of the father himself. In Óscar Cabezas's words, "the spectral law is metaphysical, it is an abstract law that structures the immaterial conditions of domination as *a priori*."[24] Put differently, the spectral law of the father is embedded in the narrator's psychology through a series of procedures that guarantee its survival even beyond the father's death. Perhaps the main mechanism through which this law will be instilled in the narrator is the indoctrination into Judaism, which the father used as a facade to impose his law. Second, the lines quoted above communicate a key element in the reading offered here: the prohibition to mourn. "Pero jamás lloré. Ni una lágrima. Eso me lo enseñó usted" is the father's mandate not only against the act of crying but against grieving itself. As we will see in the following pages, it is precisely about this aspect of the father's law that Halfon's narrator will rebel throughout his entire oeuvre. Third, it must be noted that while the father imposes the prohibition against mourning, he orders at the same time that Jewish funerary rites must be strictly followed.

There is no contradiction here. For the father, mourning belongs to the realm of law, and therefore, its duration (eight days) and rituals ought to be followed. On the contrary, what the father rejects is the power of mourning as a free, emancipatory process. He opposed what Halfon embraces, a work of mourning that exists out of joint, without timelines, without appropriations, without foreseeable end.

The father's death, however, does not erase the narrator's resentment toward him since he felt already abandoned: "Usted me abandonó, padre, no el día de su muerte, sino el día de mi nacimiento. Usted murió cuando yo nací. Yo entré al mundo un huérfano, padre."[25] These lines, in part, anticipate the spectral status of the father in Halfon's following books and clarify his spectral presence in *Saturno*. He will no longer die in fiction because, for the narrator, he was already a ghostly revenant in the first place.

What makes the death of the father in this book particularly compelling is that the father of Eduardo Halfon was alive at the time of writing it. For an author who is accustomed to making his readers glance into his personal life, introducing the father's death when he was still living must not be taken lightly. In *Saturno*, the father dies of natural causes (a heart attack), but it can be interpreted as an act of murder by the transcendent narrator of Halfon's fiction. The Guatemalan author comments on this in an interview, where he says "*Saturno* fue la muerte definitiva del Eduardo Halfon ingeniero, del Eduardo Halfon primogénito, del Eduardo Halfon hijo obediente, el que llevaba toda una vida portándose bien y haciendo y estudiando lo que le decían. De pronto salgo con esta cosa irreverente, subida de tono, en la cual *mato a mi padre*, cuando en realidad mi padre vive" (my emphasis).[26] The death of the father in *Saturno* is a symbolic act of assassination. It is a way of rejecting the violent, abusive, and unaffectionate father and, perhaps more importantly, his law. The murder of the father that opens Halfon's literary career is the only possible solution for the narrator's desperate situation. He either kills the father or commits suicide—like all the other writers and intellectuals he names in the book. But he wants to live and be born again, beyond the father's law, and the paternal figure's death is the only way to break free from it.

In *Saturno*, the murdering/death of the father does not lead to his idealization nor to the son's identification with the deceased father (Freud's interpretation of the murdering of the father in *Totem and Taboo*). Instead, by getting rid of the paternal figure, Halfon opens the possibility of mourning, which is prohibited under the law of the father. The father's death and breaking away from his law allows the narrator to connect and empathize with others, to mourn others. If the law of the father is the negation of mourning because crying is not allowed under his mandate, escaping the father's law means embracing the mourner's position in a context where grieving is not permitted, assuming thus a role in the battle of mourning.

By unlocking the work of mourning through the death of the father, Halfon's literature begins to transit the path of grief. Notwithstanding, mourning the father becomes inevitable despite how much the narrator hated and resented him. The father's ghost exits just to reenter his fiction as the revenant. This is the mourning that traverses his fiction but at the same time liberates him from the law, tradition, and forced identity.

The Reappearance of the Grieving Father

The first decade of Halfon's fiction mostly deals with the symbolic loss of the father. While the death of the father will not be portrayed again in the following books, criticism and diminishing of the paternal figure will be a staple in his work. Readers will find this in stories such as "Clases de hebreo" (included in *Siete minutos de desasogiego*) and more consistently in *Mañana nunca lo hablamos* (2011), which offers perhaps one of the most interesting insights into the troubled father-son relationship in Halfon's fiction, a book I will discuss later in this chapter. It is also worth mentioning that the father is completely absent in the short stories collection *Signor Hoffman* (2015), with the exception of a reference in a dream.[27] Curiously, after spending multiple books trying to vanish the father from his literature—and finally achieving the task in *Signor Hoffman*—Halfon conjures the father's specter in the novel *Duelo* (2017), portraying him in a completely different light.

Duelo offers a more sympathetic vision of the father, which is comprehensible since the novel tells the story of the death of the father's brother, Salomón, who died at an early age while living by himself in a clinic in New York. Through the retelling of multiple deaths in the family, in addition to many other deaths not related to the narrator, like the children who drown in a lake and the violence of the civil war, Halfon slowly and cautiously reapproaches his father and reintroduces him into the fiction.

Although *Duelo* includes common situations of the father's authority and disinterest, such as the father talking to his son without lifting his eyes from the newspaper or yelling at him "just with the gaze,"[28] readers can identify new behavioral patterns, at least within the father's limited possibilities. For example, in the middle of a family discussion, the narrator interprets the father's silence as a form of protecting him and his brother from something "sinister."[29] The representation of the father changes dramatically within Halfon's literary universe when, toward the end of the novel, the father extensively speaks to his son without admonition or aggressiveness. This situation follows a fight between an adolescent Eduardo and his little brother, where the latter ends up with a fractured foot. The narrator, expecting a heavy reprimand from his father, is surprised not to hear his father yelling at him. Instead, the father sits on the bed next to him and narrates the death of his brother Salomón. The father speaks uninterruptedly for over three pages, his speech interwoven with numerous "me dijo" (he told me) by the narrator, who reproduces the father's speech. The final words of the father portray the silent but still hurtful mourning for his dead brother: "Y me dijo mi papá que eso era lo último que él sabía de su hermano.[. . .] No sabía de qué enfermedad había muerto, ni en qué año había muerto. Ni siquiera sabía, me dijo, el nombre del cementerio judío en Nueva York donde estaba enterrado. Pero al menos sí conocía, me dijo, por esa vieja foto que yo aún tenía en mis manos, por esa foto de él en la nieve, el rostro de su hermano."[30] In *Duelo*, the father reemerges as a mourning figure. He cries not only about the death of his brother but also for the lack of knowledge regarding his corpse and his last moments. This is a great example of the father's experience of trauma, where, following Cathy Caruth, "knowing and not knowing are entangled [. . .] in the stories associated with it."[31] This novel is a turning point in Halfon's fiction regarding the father. It is noteworthy that the father, the figure that prohibits mourning to others, especially to his son, now returns as a griever himself, seemingly the only form in which Halfon accepts to conjure his presence. It must also be noticed that the reappearance of the father occurs now under the narrator's terms. Unlike, for example, the controlling and dominating paternal figure Halfon presents in "Mañana nunca lo hablamos" and "Clases de hebreo," who speaks to his son through a direct speech, in *Duelo* it is the narrator who filters and reproduces the father's narrative, limiting, at least symbolically, his power.

The portrayal of the father in a more positive light continues in *Canción* (2021), a novel dedicated to the paternal family. Here we read about the distress produced by the kidnapping of Halfon's paternal grandfather—the Lebanese one—in 1967. In addition, the novel refers to the death of the grandfather years later and the grief that his passing produced for the narrator's father. Eduardo is in his first year in college when he receives a call from his father informing him about the passing of the Lebanese grandfather. His father, Halfon recalls, "Respiraba rápido, como si le faltara oxígeno, o como haciendo un esfuerzo por no soltarse en llanto, o como si estuviera prohibido llorar la muerte de un padre."[32] Mourning, as explained above, is prohibited under the law of the father. Therefore, it is meaningful that the father, despite his usual resistance to cry and express emotions, in the end grieves the death of both his father and his brother. The father's mourning allows for a better connection, or at least a better understanding, between father and son, which only seems to be possible once the paternal figure has opened up to the possibility of mourning.

Un hijo cualquiera (2022), a book about Eduardo Halfon's own paternity, could be considered the end of the cycle in the diatribe against the father. The opening story, "Un pequeño corte," offers a somewhat troubling story in which the narrator decides to circumcise his newborn son. At that moment, he imposes his newly founded law over his son, who is now no longer "un hijo cualquiera" and becomes "his own." He, as the father of that boy, imposes his will over his son's body. In a passage with profound psychoanalytic potentiality, Halfon claims, "Había pronunciado mi primer mandato como padre. Y entendí, de una manera categórica o mística, que el pene de mi hijo, a partir de ese momento, ya no era suyo."[33] While the first story anticipates a near-Freudian scheme where the narrator becomes the father, the following stories portray a harmonious, caring, loving, and affective relationship between Halfon and his son over the first three years of his life. The narrator understands that, in part, his son represents a path of healing for him, a way of recovering from that "little cut" that introduced him to the law of his father.

The birth of his first son, and the possibility of breaking the cycle of imposing the father's law over him, ultimately allows a relative closure with the father. This is portrayed at the end of the volume, where readers find the story "El baile de la marea," first published in *Mañana nunca lo hablamos*, but now called simply "La marea." In this tale, the narrator remembers when his father told him, while walking by the shore of the sea, that many years ago, he drowned and died near there. Fortunately, the father was rescued and resuscitated by a U.S. soldier. The narration does not only serve as a cautionary tale to make the narrator aware of the risks of the sea but it also triggers some questions in him about who his father would be had he died that day. The story is reproduced almost identically, mostly with small stylistic variations. But one modification is powerful while imperceptible: replacing "papá" with "padre." In *Mañana nunca lo hablamos,* this story represents the protectiveness of the father when the narrator is a little boy.[34] Therefore, referring to him as "papá," an affectionate word commonly used by children, positions the narration from that point of view. In *Un hijo cualquiera,* however, the story that closes the book is told from the narrator's point of view as an adult, as a father himself. Thus, the retelling of the story inverts its original meaning. In *Mañana nunca lo hablamos,* it represents the point of departure of the anticipated distance between father and son that will end with the utter diminishing of the former. In Halfon's most recent book, the same story represents a point of arrival for the narrator, who understands that that is the paternal role he must reproduce. If he is going to become the father of *his* son, not "any" father of "any" son, he must assume the protective role his father showed him once. Whether Halfon becomes his father is yet to be seen. Nevertheless, what is relatively clear in his most recent books, is that the narrator has somehow closed the wound of the father. He has grieved him, exorcised him, and allowed him to return, provided that he embraces the possibility of mourning.

Portraying the Shoah and the Guatemalan Civil War

In addition to the struggles with the father, Halfon also has an interest in exploring other forms of grieving that linger with him. In particular, two traumatic historical events are extensively present in his fiction: the Shoah and the Guatemalan civil war. The former comes from the maternal grandfather's survival story while imprisoned in Auschwitz and other extermination camps during the Second World War. The latter is the result of two experiences. His early life in Guatemala during the internal conflict, and the information available during the postwar era upon his return to the country. While Halfon uses different techniques to narrate and explore these catastrophes, his fiction embodies a constant desire to question, face, interrogate, and narrate trauma, often revealing the impossibility of articulating a tale of a traumatic past or having a transparent memory of it.

Was There Ever a Polish Boxer?

The story of the Polish boxer, mentioned in multiple books and told in detail in "El boxeador polaco," is one of the most powerful and well-known short stories in Halfon's oeuvre and, for many, the core of his fiction.[35] "El boxeador polaco" narrates the day Eduardo's maternal grandfather tells his grandson the true origin of the numbers he has tattooed on his arm. The grandfather was born and raised in Łódź, Poland. In 1939 he was arrested and taken to different extermination camps. In 1942, for unclear reasons, he was transported to Auschwitz. During his first night in the infamous Block Eleven, he meets a boxer from Łódź who tells him, in Polish, how to answer the questions he will be asked the following day. The grandfather follows the advice and saves his life. In shock after hearing the story, Eduardo enquires about the exact words the boxer told him, but the grandfather remains silent. The narrator then remembers that the grandfather has refused to speak his mother tongue for decades because, he claimed, the Poles betrayed them and handed them to the Nazis.

My goal is to pay attention to the contradictions and denials in the grandfather's story, reflecting on how these elements contribute to understanding how trauma is portrayed in Halfon's fiction. While "El boxeador polaco" has received much attention, the following story of the volume, "Discurso de Póvoa," tends to be overlooked. In this story, the narrator is invited to participate in a literary event with the topic "La literatura rasga la realidad" (Literature tears reality). After much hesitation, he decides to talk about his Polish grandfather's experience in the extermination camps. He recounts the story told above and the context in which the conversation took place (an arranged videotaped interview), and he explains some of the difficulties in turning the man's experience into a short story. Eventually, Halfon feels the story is ready and *con olor a tinta*: "Había logrado llevar la realidad a la literatura; había logrado, a través de la literatura, penetrar una realidad."[36] But then, one morning, he opened the newspaper and saw a picture with an interview of his grandfather where—to the narrator's shock—he explained that he survived Auschwitz thanks to his skills as a carpenter. Was there ever a Polish boxer?[37]

Julie Marchio, one of the few scholars who has reflected on this inconsistency, argues that Halfon, in the end, accepts the ambiguity of the grandfather's story and praises the uncertainty of it, understanding it as the "grey zone" experience of many Holocaust survivors.[38] It is curious, however, that despite questioning the existence of the Polish boxer right after telling the story, the providential meeting between the grandfather and the boxer has been mentioned and accepted without question in Halfon's following publications.[39] While Halfon's narrator will never cast doubt on the authenticity of the grandfather's story again, he has introduced subtle clues in the retelling of the story that raise suspicions: the grandfather's age at the moment of his detention, who arrested him, and who was with him. "El boxeador polaco" does not provide much information about the arrest itself, so there are no reasons to distrust the narrator of *Monasterio* when he says that the grandfather was sixteen when the Gestapo caught him in 1939 while playing dominoes with his girlfriend and some friends.[40] In "Oh gueto mi amor," included in *Signor Hoffman* (2015), however, the narrator declares that the Gestapo arrested the grandfather when he was nineteen. But the story ratifies that he was with his girlfriend, Mina (the first time she is mentioned by name), and some friends when it happened.[41] In *Duelo*, Eduardo claims that the grandfather was twenty years old and that he was playing dominoes with some friends and cousins (no girlfriend in the scene this time). He is also unclear whether the Germans or the Poles detained him.[42] I do not believe these inconsistencies are by chance or a *gazapo*. Instead, the dissimilar ages of the grandfather, who arrested him and who was with him at that moment, contribute to putting the story into question even within a literary universe that has opted to accept and incorporate the story of the Polish boxer.

To add a layer of complexity, it must be said that the Polish boxer is not the only story told by the grandfather that is put into question in Halfon's literature. For example, the grandfather only had one photograph of his family, taken shortly before the war. The origin of the picture, however, is uncertain. "A veces decía mi abuelo que había conseguido la foto a través de uno de sus tíos que salió de Polonia antes del 39. Otras veces decía que él mismo había logrado guardarla durante los seis años que pasó en campos."[43] The latter version is of course implausible because it would have been nearly impossible to keep the photo with him during all those years. In "Arena blanca, piedra negra," Halfon expands on the story of the grandfather's black ring, which he wore for decades as a sign of mourning for his lost relatives during the Shoah. In the late 1970s, two people robbed him on the streets of Guatemala City, but he managed to keep the ring. The story, however, often changed. "A veces nos decía que suplicó ante ellos hasta quedarse con su anillo. A veces nos decía que forcejeó con ellos hasta quedarse con su anillo. A veces nos decía que luchó contra ellos para quedarse con su anillo. La versión variaba dependiendo del paso de los años, o de su nostalgia o de su estado de ánimo."[44] The grandfather, the narrator states, understood that a story always grows, it changes its skin, and in sum, one story is always many stories.[45] These examples clarify that the tales told by the Polish grandfather cannot be fully trusted. He, like his grandson, was a fantastic storyteller. And both grandfather and grandson are more interested in the rhizomatic life of a story, in its variations and multiple existences rather than in its actuality. In other words, what matters here is the productivity of mourning and trauma to produce narrations even if they are inaccurate or lack transparency.

Halfon's literature accepts that the story of the Polish boxer may not be true. Nonetheless, it is the story produced and narrated by the grandfather regarding his imprisonment in Auschwitz, and as such, it should be accepted. The point is not whether the miraculous encounter between the grandfather and the boxer took place but rather that the meeting, that secret dialogue in Polish, is the grandfather's form of speaking about his experience in the Nazi extermination camps, an experience that is in part kept in secret through the grandfather's auto-imposed exile from the Polish language. Following this thread, the story of the Polish boxer seems to be an acceptable version of the events that prevents asking the question that never ought to be asked of a survivor: What did you do to survive? Perhaps, there is no more truth in the story of the Polish boxer than in the explanation the grandfather used to give about the numbers when his grandson was a child (when the grandfather used to say that it was his phone number and he tattooed it on his arm not to forget it). What matters is that Halfon acknowledges and portrays the grandfather as a man who lived in perpetual sorrow, who wore for over sixty years on his little right finger a black ring he acquired in New York to remember his dead family. A man who never spoke Polish again and who never set foot in his motherland after his exile. And as such, Halfon's only possibility is accepting the story of the boxer, not only because it is moving and "literarily powerful" but because it is the only narrative that the grandfather was able to produce; it is the legacy he chose to pass on to his heirs.[46]

El boxeador polaco is perhaps Halfon's ars poetica. In the first story, "Lejano," Halfon discusses with his students, following Ricardo Piglia, that any short story has two stories, the one that is told on the surface and a secret one. In "Discurso de Póvoa," Halfon argues that: "La literatura no es más que un buen truco [. . .] que hace a la realidad parecer entera, que crea la ilusión de que la realidad es una. O tal vez la literatura necesita construir una realidad destruyendo otra—algo que, de un modo muy intuitivo, ya sabía mi abuelo—es decir, destruyéndose a sí misma y luego construyéndose a partir de sus propios escombros."[47] Halfon's fiction acknowledges and accepts the impossibility of reproducing the traumatic past—not only the grandfather's, but everyone's. The act of storytelling is both creative and destructive but is still a necessary tool in post-traumatic scenarios. In this regard, Halfon's fiction has much in common with Hernández's and Albizúrez's. Approaching the past and its violence is an unavoidable command but one that seemingly becomes a constant failed action. Writing, concludes Halfon in the story that closes *El boxeador polaco,* is knowing that there is something important to tell about reality, "y que tenemos ese algo al alcance, allí nomás, muy cerca, en la punta de la lengua, y que no debemos olvidarlo. *Pero siempre, sin duda, lo olvidamos*" (my emphasis).[48]

Halfon's literature is a perfect example of how fiction can actively engage in the work of mourning without aiming to conclude this task. Truth and transparent narrations are not a goal in his literary work. Quite the contrary, decentering memory and casting doubts about its veracity is Halfon's way of drawing attention to the lack of trustworthiness of memory and the relevance of mourning as an ongoing work. This is precisely the lesson Eduardo learns toward the end of his trip to Poland, when Madame Maroszek gifts him three books that tell how life was in Poland's ghettos and in the extermination camps. He realizes that what matters "no era dónde escribimos nuestra historia, sino escribirla. Narrarla. Dar testimonio. Poner en palabras nuestra vida entera. Aunque tengamos que escribirla en papeles sueltos o en papeles robados."[49] To write and tell the stories over and over, even if, as the Polish boxer's story suggests, they might not be true.

The Internal Armed Conflict

As many other writers of his generation, Eduardo Halfon has a keen interest in the Guatemalan civil war. Like Mónica Albizúrez, he understands the ethical dilemma of approaching a traumatic event that he was not directly involved in or victimized by. From a panoramic perspective, it is possible to say that Halfon develops two approaches to the Guatemalan internal armed conflict. His first approach, exemplified in *Mañana nunca lo hablamos,* is lateral, where the narrator recalls his childhood in Guatemala in the late 1970s and early 1980s. This first method emphasizes the questioning of the narratives of the dominant powers, particularly the army and the father's position. In Halfon's most recent work, like *Canción* and *Un hijo cualquiera,* Halfon has tackled the violence of the civil war not only from an adult's point of view but also from a more emotionally detached perspective, privileging a more effective communication of the facts.

* * *

The ten short stories in *Mañana nunca lo hablamos* are told by an adult narrator who remembers his childhood in Guatemala in the late 1970s and the early 1980s. Following Jeffrey Browitt, the volume interweaves two major tensions. First, the experimentation of events as a child that cannot be named but which are "retroactively assigned a named emotion by the adult narrator," and second, the awareness of his privileged situation "against the backdrop of the war."[50] While the stories in the book have often been read through the lens of "postmemory," meaning that the narrator inherits trauma from the previous generation, my goal here is to focus on how trauma is experienced and portrayed by the narrator even if that traumatic experience is not remotely close to the atrocities of the civil war. Trauma, as Boris Cyrulnik claims, is not mediated by the monstrosity of a certain occurrence but rather by the surprise that said event generates in the observer/victim.[51] The narrator's return to the traumatic events of his childhood as an adult embodies the delayed experience of trauma as understood by Cathy Caruth, one that seeks to apprehend what remained unknown at the moment of happening. In her words, "a rethinking of reference is aimed not at eliminating history but at resituating it in or understanding, that is, at precisely permitting *history* to arise where *immediate understanding* may not."[52] Following these ideas, I will read Halfon's *Mañana nunca lo hablamos* as a return to the foundational trauma of the narrator. While this book overlaps in some aspects with the symbolic death of the father discussed earlier, the focus this time will be on the racism of the father and his silence regarding the atrocities of the civil war and the inequalities in Guatemala.

The civil war in *Mañana nunca lo hablamos* is constantly mentioned through metaphors, synecdoche, or lateral references. For the adult narrator that remembers his childhood, the war still signifies an event he cannot shape with words. For example, when the narrator is at the hospital in

"Muerte de un cácher," he comments on the normality of seeing soldiers in a hospital in the 1970s. In "Mañana nunca lo hablamos," the narrator says, referring to 1981, that "Eran días de disparos." The most direct reference to the civil war is included in "Corazón, no moleste," when the narrator evokes, in the context of the disappearance of Anderson, an employee of his father, that "Era el inicio de los ochenta en Guatemala, y no era extraño que las personas desaparecieran. Había aumentado la violencia—especialmente en la capital—entre el gobierno militar y los grupos guerrilleros. Y yo lo vivía todo como un niño sobreprotegido."[53] The internal conflict is the background of the narrator's childhood, but this background gets closer and closer throughout the book until it enters his life in the final and most important story, "Mañana nunca lo hablamos."

"Mañana nunca lo hablamos" begins with the narrator, nine years old at the time, leaving school on a bus following a violent combat between the army and the guerrillas that ended with a safe house destroyed and fourteen guerrillas dead. That was the last straw for the narrator's family, and the father decides to relocate them to the United States. The following day, the narrator visits the house of his friend Oscar and reads in the newspaper about the bombing. There, the narrator makes the shocking discovery that both guerrillas and soldiers look equally Indigenous to him, which contradicts the idea that *all* guerrillas were "Indians" imposed by his father. By the end of the story, the narrator asks his father about the common ethnicity of both combatant groups, but the father remains silent and promises to speak about it the following day, which never happens.

There are many relevant elements in this story, but I am particularly interested in the fracture of the narrator's psychology, which will lead him to expose the contradictions and lies of his father, disarticulating his authority and pushing him into silence. The story's breaking point is the moment when the narrator reads the newspaper at Oscar's house and sees the photographs of the dead guerrillas next to the soldiers: "Me quedé mirando los rostros de los militares, tan morenos y tan indígenas como el rostro del guerrillero de la guitarra y el televisor. No entendí. ¿Los militares también eran indígenas? ¿No era todo indígena un guerrillero? ¿Quién era, entonces, un guerrillero?"[54] This is the first moment of a truly traumatic surprise, something that did not happen during the fight between the soldiers and guerrillas or when he saw the dead body of a woman on their way out of the school, and not even when he was told that his family would relocate to the United

States.[55] The surprise of identifying a fissure within the paternal discourse awakens in him an "ethnic awareness," which will be expressed through the sudden visibility of the ethnicity of the people around him, whom he has always seen through the unfiltered lens of infancy.

The most remarkable example of the narrator's ethnic awareness is his final piano lesson with Otto. During the session, the narrator looks carefully at Otto and realizes that his face resembles the faces of the soldiers and the guerrillas. Otto appears to be an Indigenous person.[56] When the lesson is over, Otto stands up and presents his hand to the boy, who, after some hesitation, reflects, "tardé un poco en comprender que quería que yo también me pusiera de pie y estirara la mía, que quería despedirse de mí, no como profesor y alumno, no como adulto y niño, *no como indígena y blanco*, sino *como lo harían dos hombres*" (my emphasis).[57] The beauty of this passage lies in the ethical and communitarian connection the narrator perceives in the apparently meaningless act of shaking hands. He acknowledges the ethnic differences between them for the first time, but that does not prevent the boy from seeing the humanity and value in the other. A simple action but one that becomes an act of defiance once the father's inconsistencies and racism are revealed.

Before commenting on the story's final scene, it is important to note that throughout the entire book, the narrator has been confronted with his privileged position in society. This happens as early as in the second story, "Polvo," when the narrator is taken by his uncle Benny to assist the victims of the 1976 earthquake, where he sees dead people and their loved ones grieving them. In "Quieto a la orilla del lago," Rolando, the gardener at the narrator's house, shares with him how life was when he was a kid living in poverty. In "Corazón no moleste," the narrator cannot hide the shocking impression of seeing a girl with no hands.[58] If he sees himself and his piano teachers as equal despite their ethnic differences, why cannot the father do the same? Does the father not see the inequalities in Guatemala? Why cannot the father feel the pain of others? As discussed earlier, the father is a figure that resists mourning at all costs. He refuses to consider the Indigenous population and the poor as his equal even if that means depriving them of their humanity and (albeit tacitly) supporting their extermination.

The father's racism and inconsistencies are ultimately challenged in the memorable dialogue that closes *Mañana nunca lo hablamos*:

—Papi . . .

—¿Mmm?

—¿Qué es un guerrillero?

[. . .]

—¿Un guerrillero?

—Ajá.

—Pues los guerrilleros son los culpables de todo este lío.

—¿Qué lío?

—Todo este lío—susurró firme—el lío frente a su colegio, en la fábrica, en las calles, en todo el maldito país.

—¿Los guerrilleros son indios?

[. . .]

—Claro—me dijo—su mirada hacia la ventana.

—Pero ¿también los soldados son indios?

Mi papá suspiró, pareció enojarse en la semioscuridad.

—Ay, amor, éstas no son horas para hablar de eso.[. . .] Mejor duérmase y lo hablamos mañana.[59]

The location of this dialogue at the end of the book only contributes to the demolishing of the father not only for being a racist but also because of his lack of empathy. Throughout the story—and the volume—the narrator has slowly seen and identified the Indigenous people in his life. Therefore, equating "Indians" with guerrillas is absurd, something even a nine-year-old kid can notice because Indigenous people surround the family in their daily life at all times. The father's discourse is a defense of the elite's vision of the national community, which is perceived as at risk, and therefore he accepts the elimination of the Indigenous communities as a form of defending Guatemalan identity, culture, and traditions. Under the father's logic, the "Indians" are responsible for ruining the tranquility of honest citizens like him.

It is worth mentioning that "Mañana nunca lo hablamos" does not bring to the fore the history of oppression of the Indigenous peoples nor the genocide taking place against them at the time. As a boy, he does his best in this situation: asking questions of the figure of authority. And here the second surprise of trauma takes place, one that can only be processed belatedly in the present of the narration: the father supports the army. He always did, and when put against the wall by his son, he chooses silence, as the final sentence of the story makes clear: "Pronto llegó mañana y mañana nunca lo hablamos."[60] That silence extends to the present of the narration, informing the reader that the interrupted dialogue had no closure.

Silence, interruptions, and lateral expressions of violence clearly mark Halfon's first approach to the Guatemalan civil war. Nevertheless, they are powerful enough to break the narrator's psychology and make him realize that his world has become a lost place. The narrator loses much more than his house, friends, and toys in the book. He loses his innocence and the protective bubble that kept him apart from seeing Guatemala's inequalities and violence. Halfon's writing, as Perkowska puts it, becomes a symbolic answer to that infantile question that astutely understands one of the "painful contradictions of Guatemalan history."[61] And perhaps more importantly, he loses his father again.

* * *

Compared to the exquisiteness of *Mañana nunca lo hablamos*, the recounting of the war in Halfon's most recent books may have less literary appeal. Nonetheless, now that he is a widely known author whose books circulate around the world in many metropolitan languages, it should be valued as a form of communicating some of the horrendous deeds that took place during the internal conflict. Eduardo Halfon has openly commented on some of the risks of narrating the Guatemalan civil war. In a 2015 article published in *The Guardian*, titled "Better Not to Say Too Much" (translated as "Mejor no andar hablando demasiado" and included in the 2018 book of chronicles *Biblioteca bizarra*), Halfon expresses the fears of a Guatemalan writer. "If anyone dared to speak out, they either disappeared into exile or disappeared literally. This fear is still prevalent, woven deep into the subconscious of the Guatemalan people, who over time have been taught to be silent. To not speak out. To not say or write words that might kill you."[62] Topics such as the Indigenous genocide, extreme racism, violence against women, and rampant corruption are topics that just cannot be easily narrated by Guatemalan authors and journalists, says Halfon. Perhaps because of this, his recent books take up the challenge of openly addressing the civil war even if that means doing it at the price of not engaging emotionally.

Halfon's first work of fiction to directly explore the civil war is *Canción*. In this novel, the narrator talks through a historical account of the inequalities in Guatemala: the CIA-sponsored coup against Juan Jacobo Árbenz, the United Fruit Company, the origin of the guerrilla movement, the kidnapping of multiple people by the revolutionaries, and the atrocities committed by the army during the war, among other aspects. While the thirty-five-day kidnapping of his paternal grandfather by a group of guerrillas is the book's central point, the story overlaps with the invitation to participate in a conference for Lebanese writers in Japan, where, toward the end, he is challenged about his Lebanese authenticity.

In *Canción*, Halfon expresses sympathy for the guerrilla's cause despite the kidnapping of his grandfather (upon his return, the grandfather would inform the family that he was treated well and respectfully, and the narrator clarifies that he was not robbed even though he was carrying a large sum of cash and wearing a three-carat ring). In addition to the informative historical account of Guatemala's inequalities and the war disseminated throughout the novel, *Canción* narrates a massacre conducted by the army in San Juan Acul. In front of the Lebanese writers, Halfon tells the story of Azzari, a Guatemalan rancher who used to live in the Ixil region (one of the most affected by the war). One day, the soldiers in the nearby military quarter discover Azzari was collaborating with the guerrillas. He was warned by some villagers and fled. The day following his escape, the army entered the village and murdered eighteen people.

Unlike, for example, the story of the Polish boxer, there is no room here for questioning the narration. Halfon, both the author and the narrator, is well aware of what it means to cast doubts on the atrocities committed during the civil war. Perhaps because of that, he decides to tell the story in the most disengaged form possible, letting the events speak for themselves. A long quote is necessary to understand the style of the narration:

> Luego los militares colocaron a los dieciocho hombres desnudos y magullados frente a una fosa común y, con el resto del pueblo observando, con amigos y familiares como único público, empezaron a asesinarlos.

> Un solo balazo en la cabeza. De uno en uno. Los dieciocho fueron cayendo en aquel hoyo negro en la tierra hasta llenarlo de brazos y piernas de hombre. Pero varios seguían vivos, aullando en el fondo, y entonces uno de los soldados brincó hacia abajo y les ensartó su machete en el cuello. La masacre había concluido. No era aún mediodía.[63]

This passage lacks many of Halfon's literary marks. He does not provide unrelated information. This event does not remind him of something else, there are virtually no adjectives, and there are no references to alternative scenarios (he imagines some situations regarding Azzari, the man who tells him about the massacre, but never about the killing itself). No "what if," either or, or thoughts. Just the facts. The only evident literary resource is the use of the synecdoche "brazos y piernas de hombre" to refer to the cadavers. He does not even bother to explain the relationship between the story and Lebanon, which bothers some people at the convention.[64] He just narrates it, only marking the silences made by Azzari when he told Halfon the story.[65]

A similar form of narrating the horrors of the civil war can be found in "Beni," a chilling story within *Un hijo cualquiera*. Once again, the narrator uses the experience of a third person to access the political violence—a technique that resembles Albizúrez's. In this case, it is Beni, a Kaibil (a bloody military elite group responsible for some of the most horrific crimes of the war) that is unclearly associated with the narrator's family.[66] Beni takes the young Eduardo, presumably nineteen or twenty years old in the late 1980s, to a military barrack to register and obtain his military card through a bribe. The narrator interweaves the visit to the military quarters with the history of the Kaibiles, including the infamous Dos Erres massacre, which occurred in December 1982.

"Beni" is built in crescendo. The more the readers learn about the Kaibiles, the more the narrator's anguish grows for being in a military quarrel in the late years of the civil war. At first, we see the vague answer of the father the first time the narrator asks him about the Kaibiles (which may have forced the father to explain why he has a professional relationship with one), but then the story rapidly moves forward to inform the readers about their strict and ruthless training, including killing a dog after taking care of it for two months. The speaker then narrates the massacre of Dos Erres, which is presented in two parts, interrupted by the narrator's anxiety once everybody leaves the quarrel at night, and he has not spoken to anyone about his situation yet. Unlike the massacre told in Canción, the story does not cite any third party, and as a result, the narration seems even more neutral, without hesitations or silences:

> Un bebé de tres meses fue lanzado vivo a un pozo seco. Era mediodía. Los cincuenta y ocho kaibiles se dirigieron entonces a dos iglesias y sacaron a todos los niños y los colocaron en fila.[. . .] Los mayores recibían un golpe en el cráneo con una almádana o un tiro en la frente y luego eran arrojados al pozo. A los más pequeños bastaba sujetarlos de los pies y golpearlos contra un muro o contra el tronco de un árbol y luego botarlos al pozo. Las niñas y las mujeres, antes de caer muertas o medio muertas en el pozo, fueron violadas.[67]

Halfon decides to narrate the massacre of Dos Erres in a forensic fashion. Like in the previous case, there are no subjective adjectives, no speculation, and, most importantly, no doubts regarding the veracity of the events. Not even the smallest literary figures enter this account. The narration produced by Halfon could be part of the truth commission report or the work of a serious journalist or scholar.

In postwar Guatemala, where the atrocities of the civil war are often relativized and put into question not only by the elites and the army but also by common citizens, producing the less literary (and more literal) narration possible of the events embodies in itself a strong commitment toward justice, memory, and survivors' grief. The price for this, however, is the narrator's emotional detachment. He lets the facts speak for themselves without openly criticizing or condemning them. The voice of the story transmits the horrendous deeds in the most transparent way possible, letting them affect the reader with the least subjective mediation possible. Whether the reader will be moved and embrace the pain produced by these stories, is entirely up to them.

By putting together these two forms of narrating the traumatic events of the civil war, it is clear that Halfon makes not only an aesthetical decision but also an ethical one. In the stories included in *Mañana nunca lo hablamos,* Halfon feels free to experiment with oblique references to the armed conflict, focusing on the narrator's psychological fracture and unresolved traumas. Nonetheless, when he decides to confront the war's most brutal and senseless events, he develops a narrative closer to the ones we find in historical memory projects than to the ongoing work of mourning. The decision is indeed ethical. On the one hand, he feels compelled to talk, relying on the safety of his privileged position as an internationally acclaimed writer and winner of Guatemala's National Prize of Literature. But to do so, he must present these facts unambiguously, as free as possible of any literary intervention.

The Sum of All Mourning

Eduardo Halfon is a writer fascinated by the work of mourning. He expressed his attraction for this theme early in his career in a short story called "Luto," included in the 2008 book *Clases de hebreo* (and later incorporated into the novel *Monasterio*). In this story, the narrator remembers the first time his father took him to a wake. He is shocked and fascinated at the same time by the ritualistic performance of the Jewish mourning, including people wearing ragged shirts and dirty clothes, next to candles and food. The word *luto* is introduced into the narrator's vocabulary through his father, who paradoxically will become one of the lost objects in his fiction and who instills the prohibition against it: "le pregunté a mi papa qué estaban haciendo esas personas tumbadas sobre un viejo colchón.[. . .] Su respuesta me llegó en un hilo susurrado, frío, cauteloso, bien dirigido y hermosamente entonado para que sólo yo lo percibiera: 'Están de luto.'"[68] "I'm lucky," says the narrator, because one does not always remember the first time one listened to a new word. "Así escuché yo la palabra luto. Así conocí la palabra luto. Así conocí el luto judío. Así es el luto judío. Dan ganas de morirse un poco."[69] It is thought provoking that this brief story puts together some of the main topics discussed in this chapter. Mourning, from then on, will be intimately connected to the father, which in Halfon's fiction represents the law and authority. In this tale Halfon also envisions that death is not the end, foreseeing the possibility of action from the afterlife: "estaba absolutamente seguro de que, mientras tres veces rezaban, bien escondido abajo de alguna de esas sábanas blancas, se revoloteaba y sacudía, riéndose, el fantasma del muerto."[70] From his early literary work, Halfon understands that the dead can return, even laugh, and that the most fascinating thing about the work of mourning is the work itself.

The sources of mourning are multiple in Halfon's literature, from the symbolic loss of the father to the imprisonment of the maternal grandfather in Nazi extermination camps to the political violence of the Guatemalan civil war, among others. While the presence of these multiple forms of suffering and loss is compelling in itself, more interesting is the multiple forms in which his fiction handles them. The loss of the father, for example, is in part due to the father's incapacity for grieving, and therefore he is only conjured once he has accepted being open to the possibility of mourning without rules. The story of surviving the Holocaust is questioned but in the end always accepted as the grandfather's truth (in other words, what is questioned is the story, not the experience itself). Representations of the civil war also vary over time, from oblique approaches to the more direct, nearly forensic descriptions of crimes against humanity. The several expressions of grief portrayed in Halfon's fiction reveal the dynamic and ever-changing forms of mourning. Unlike the perception of mourning as a paralyzing force, mourning becomes a driving force that expands into multiple directions and at times introduces new forms of grieving even when returning to the same losses. Halfon's fiction is a great example of the productive power of mourning, and more notoriously, one that adapts to the changes outside the literary realm, like the booming circulation and translation of his work.

Halfon's literature is not only global, cosmopolitan, and multi-identitarian, as many critics have argued, but it is also a site in which multiple expressions of mourning come together and, at times, clash with other forces that seek to prevent and cancel them, like the narrator's father. Halfon's fiction demonstrates that the battles over the work of mourning take place at a planetary scale: in the attitude of some Poles when Halfon visits Łódź, in the disregard for human rights violations in Guatemala, in the lack of empathy portrayed by many characters (such as the journalist in the Lebanese writers' conference), and in the silence that links Halfon's Polish grandfather with Aiko's grandfather, who survived the atomic bomb in Hiroshima and whose kimono embedded into his skin as a perpetual reminder, to name a few. One of the reasons to close this book with a chapter dedicated to Halfon's literature is to put the grief provoked by the Central American civil wars on a global scale. In his work, one form of suffering embodies all past and future sorrow, which ultimately calls for communal solidarity and empathy toward the grievers. Halfon, perhaps like no other Central American writer, embodies the ultimate call for a universal community of mourners.

Halfon's literature opposes the extended tradition (especially in Western societies) of the hierarchization of sorrow and its subsequent unequal valorization of life to create a literary realm where all losses deserve to be equally grieved.[71] While his fiction often sheds light on major traumatic events, like the Shoah and the Guatemalan internal conflict, it also takes the time to include more personal losses, most importantly the father, but also the death of anonymous people, such as the numerous children who drown in the lake whose stories are told in *Duelo*, or the silent grief of the family who lost a member (presumably during the war) in "Han vuelto las aves" (*Signor Hoffman*). The equality between the Guatemalan internal conflict and other world atrocities in Halfon's fiction is oriented toward a world ethic that finds in the history of suffering more than simple commercial value in the literary markets. It is a form of revisiting the unclosed wounds of the past, resisting forgiveness and forced reconciliation as a compulsory acceleration of mourning without justice. Halfon's fiction is a defense of the right to mourn.

Conclusion

Whither Mourning?

> La guerra "caliente" en Guatemala terminó en 1996, pero a partir de ese momento el mal no hizo sino ponerse saco y perfumarse para esconder el olor a sangre y a heces.
>
> —FÉLIX ALVARADO, *ENSAYOS DESDE UN ESTADO PERVERSO*

Who has the right to mourn? Who can call themselves a mourner? Who can dare to speak in the name of the dead? Who can speak when the survivors are not allowed to speak? Who can mourn when there is no one left to mourn? These are some of the questions I have explored in this book. Unfortunately, these interrogations are not merely rhetorical. They are relevant beyond the literary, historical, and theoretical debates, directly affecting survivors and mourners and the possibilities of justice in postwar Central America. Mourning, as this book demonstrates, is not restricted to individual, intimate expressions; it is an open battle in the public sphere.

Studying the struggle over the work of mourning matters precisely because there are numerous forces in postconflict Central America that have been pushing for decades to either cancel or apprehend and resignify the grieving process of the internal conflicts' victims and their loved ones. A paradigmatic example of the latter can be found in the public debate that took place in Guatemala during the failed trial against Efraín Ríos Montt. On April 16, 2013, a group of prominent Guatemalans, including former vice presidents, ex-guerrilla leaders, and economists, published a paid ad in *Prensa Libre* titled "Traicionar la paz y dividir a Guatemala" (Betraying Peace and Dividing Guatemala).[1] Those signing this piece expressed in it their opposition to the trial against the former dictator, arguing that amnesty was fundamental to achieve peace in the postconflict era and declaring that the accusation of genocide threatened to destabilize Guatemalan society. In a highly problematic statement, the authors claim "La acusación de genocidio es una fabricación jurídica que *no corresponde con el anhelo de los deudos de las víctimas de dignificar a sus seres queridos, de finalizar el luto inconcluso y de hacer justicia*" (my emphasis).[2] This ad sparked a national debate and was rejected by numerous voices.[3] The most polemic thing about this ad, however, is not the opposition to the trial against Ríos Montt but rather the delicate (and unethical, I should add) claim of speaking in the name of the mourners. The statements in this declaration are openly contradictory (even though no one expects intellectual sophistication from Guatemala's elite). On the one hand, they acknowledge that the survivors and loved ones of the dead of the war live in an ongoing mourning. The authors also express that they seek justice and dignity for the victims of the internal struggle. Nevertheless, conducting a trial against someone who is responsible for the death of thousands of people during the internal conflict is not what mourners desire. If the mourners do not want a trial for (at least some of) the crimes committed during the war, what is it that they wish? The signatories do not answer that basic question. The only thing that matters for them is the fear (or was that a threat?) that prosecuting civil war crimes will cause political and social instability. What is particularly concerning about ads and public declarations like "Traicionar la paz" is that they exceed the singularity of the immediate context in which they are produced. They are part of a systemic (and systematic) abuse of power that has successfully impeded any form of justice, memory, mourning, and real reparation for the hundreds of thousands of victims of the Central American conflicts.

The ambiguous message of "Traicionar la paz" perfectly exemplifies the politics of memory and reparations in the postwar era. On the one hand, the pain of the survivors and relatives is acknowledged on certain occasions, but on the other, any means of easing their suffering is completely off the table. This is, in part, what happens with the very few state-sponsored programs created to recompensate the victims financially. For example, the National Program of Indemnification (Programa Nacional de Resarcimiento), created in 2003 to compensate victims of the Guatemalan civil war, has only offered a modest economic reparation (between US$1,600 and US$3,600 dollars, depending on the crime) to less than 20 percent of the victims (or their relatives) and ignored a significant part of the claims for sexual violence. The PNR's budget and reach depend exclusively on the president's position regarding the civil war. The program experienced a peak in compensations during Álvaro Colom's administration (2008–12), reaching over nine thousand victims in his first year in office. Along with the benefits, Colom's government also sent survivors official letters with apologies on behalf of the state. The number of beneficiaries drastically decreased during General Otto Pérez Molina's administration (2012–15), averaging less than one thousand per year, and this trend has been maintained ever since.[4] In 2016 the PNR temporarily interrupted its operations when Jimmy Morales's administration closed several regional offices and did not renew the contract of hundreds of employees.[5] On the other hand, accepting money from the Guatemalan state has multiple consequences for the victims and their relatives, like a sense of settling, family disputes, and even a tacit understanding that they do not deserve any other form of justice or reparation.[6]

In 2013 Salvadoran president Mauricio Funes created the Program of Reparations to the Victims of Grave Violations of Human Rights Committed During the Internal Armed Conflict (Programa de reparaciones a las víctimas de graves violaciones a los derechos humanos occuridas en el contexto del conflicto armado interno), which produced the first official record of victims of the civil war. As of 2018 less than five thousand people had been included in this database.[7] In 2016 President Sánchez Cerén announced the Transference Program, which was expected to pay between US$15 and US$50 monthly to some survivors of the war depending on the availability of funds.[8] According to the research conducted by the Institute of Human Rights, the payment of these "symbolic"—not to say offensive—sums is often delayed, sometimes by up to six months, and has excluded numerous victims.[9] In 2019 Nayib Bukele closed various public offices, such as the Secretary of Social Inclusion, responsible for the payment to the victims. The compensations were frozen for over a year until the Secretary of Local Development assumed this responsibility without giving much clarity on how the process would continue.[10] In June 2022 the Legislative Assembly approved a specific law to compensate *only* the victims of the massacre of El Mozote, following (with a ten-year delay) the sentence of the Inter-American Court of Human Rights.[11]

Postwar Central America sadly proves Enzo Traverso's chilling statement, "[T]he remembrance of the victims seems unable to coexist with the recollection of their hopes, of their struggles, of their conquests and their defeats."[12] Presidents may ask for forgiveness (like Colom in Guatemala and Funes in El Salvador), governments may agree to build a memorial (as Bukele has for El Mozote), politicians may participate in acts that seek to remember and honor the victims of the civil wars (like Rivas Zamora, the mayor of San Salvador, who attended the inauguration of the Monument to Memory and Truth). But, as experience has demonstrated over the last three decades, none of the above means that the reasons why hundreds of thousands of people lost their lives have been appropriately addressed. In simple words, acknowledging and apologizing for the senseless massacre of Dos Erres means nothing if the state does not apologize and make amends to the civilian population for the systematic extermination of villages (most of which were inhabited by Indigenous communities) to steal their land and transfer them to private hands.[13] What is the purpose of building a memorial in El Mozote if Bukele repeatedly claims that the war was a lie? The former does not amount to embracing civil war discourses of popular struggle but rather acknowledging that all the atrocities that took place in Central America happened for a reason. They were not a mistake. They were not because of temporary "locura," as the truth commission report for El Salvador suggests in its title, or under the "senseless logic of the war," as CACIF claimed during the trial against Ríos Montt.[14] The horrors of the civil wars were the result of a well-elaborated agenda with clear goals in mind, and for the most part, those objectives were fulfilled.

Many scholars have rightfully claimed that a politic of "forgiveness" has been imposed in postwar Central America.[15] The term *forgiveness*, nonetheless, deserves further discussion. The notion of "forgiveness" has been in vogue over the last few decades, and many scholars have used the term "age of apology" to refer to the wave of apologies offered worldwide since the 1990s.[16] Nonetheless, these apologies often take place against a background of impunity supported by our neoliberal present (and presentism). In Peter Banki's words, "forgiveness functions today as an ethico-political currency that can be bought and sold in the globalized marketplace."[17] According to Zoodsma and Schaafsma, by 2019, the Guatemalan state had apologized seven times for crimes committed during the civil war, while El Salvador had done so six times.[18] The most delicate aspect of "forgiveness" in postwar Central America is that it rarely involves the victims and their loved ones. Heads of state have offered apologies without any real implications, and powerful people—politicians, former guerrilla leaders, high-profile businesspeople—have told the victims that they have to forgive (and hopefully forget) the crimes and atrocities of the wars. This posture was translated in a very concrete way in the amnesty laws that were passed shortly after the peace accords in both countries.

The postwar Central American governments have applied what Derrida calls the King's "right of reprieve," the right to clemency, which he considers the only "inscription of forgiveness in the law."[19] The most questionable aspect of this is that the state is not the victim in the crimes against humanity but rather the perpetrator (under no circumstance, says Derrida, following Kant, should the sovereign grant clemency for a "crime committed where he is not the one intended").[20] Therefore, what we have witnessed in recent decades is the criminals who forgive themselves—even if they have to give an empty apology in public every now and then—exercising thus the absolute sovereign power regained in the aftermath of the internal conflicts. The instrumentalization of forgiveness as a mechanism of impunity and as an exercise of power in postconflict Central America must always be singled out and rejected. Forgiveness, returning to Derrida, "is not, *it should not be*, normal, normative, normalizing. It *should* remain exceptional and extraordinary, in the face of the impossible: as if it interrupted the ordinary course of historical temporality."[21] Forgiveness, like the work of mourning, is an experience of the impossible. If ever given or overcome, it will not be mediated by the perpetrators, their accomplices, or anyone invested in erasing the memory, the experience, and the suffering of the victims of the armed conflicts.

Expressions of Mourning Beyond This Book

Specters of War seeks to offer a panoramic perspective on how fiction, theater, and sites of memory engage with the work of mourning in postconflict El Salvador and Guatemala. Of course, as in any research project (at least one that hopes to be finished one day), I had to carefully choose what to include and what to leave out. Although many expressions were overlooked, such as testimonios and poetry, I would like to briefly comment on the absence of Indigenous voices in this book, with the exception of the Casa de la Memoria Kaji Tulam discussed in chapter one. The Indigenous peoples that inhabit Guatemala were the most affected groups in the internal conflict. These communities have had a particularly difficult grieving process, frequently combined with other urgent challenges such as mining and the construction of hydroelectric dams in their ancestral land, as has been documented by numerous anthropologists, journalists, historians, literary and cultural critics, and filmmakers.[22] Nevertheless, not speaking any Indigenous language and not having spent enough time with Indigenous communities automatically disqualifies me from an ethical reflection on their mourning process, which I have only followed through secondary sources.

However, even though I am familiar with some Indigenous literature published in Spanish by Humberto Ak'abal, Luis de Lión, and Víctor Montejo, among others, I have not identified civil war violence as a predominant topic in this fiction.[23] My preliminary impression is in part confirmed by Arturo Arias's expert opinion on this matter; he claims that contemporary "Indigenous literatures are for the most part, a rediscovery of learning as spirituality and nurture.[. . .] Contemporary Indigenous writers are reconfiguring them, rediscovering those lost footprints that nevertheless remain and haunt them in dreams."[24] Many Indigenous communities not only experienced the civil war in uniquely harrowing ways, often unknown and unimaginable to their non-Indigenous counterparts, but also many of them signify violence and the ethnocide differently than mestizo/ladino communities, often connecting the recent civil war with the five centuries of European colonization, as Casa de la Memoria Kaji Tulam perfectly exemplifies. Also, as Arias points out, we are presently witnessing the process of constituting a "Maya textual archive," which is in itself "a counter-discursive strategy of the first order for the re-articulation of an alternative social imaginary [. . .] and a promise of peoples' abilities to rearticulate their knowledges within the limits of the Eurocentric world."[25] I look forward to learning more about how Indigenous communities conduct the work of mourning in Guatemala.

Had I had unlimited time to finish this book, I would have included at least a few chapters on contemporary Central American cinema. I will not discuss them here extensively, but a brief comment should be made regarding some recent films. In the twenty-first century, many documentaries and movies that address the civil wars have been released, and a great deal of them engage with the unfinished work of mourning.

Salvadoran Marcela Zamora has produced some of the most important documentaries of the postwar era, and she is one of the filmmakers most committed to exploring and showcasing the multiple expressions of the work of mourning. In 2011 she released the harrowing film *María en tierra de nadie*, which follows doña María Inés (from Sensuntepeque, El Salvador) in her desperate search for her daughter, Sandra, who disappeared while traveling to the United States. Also in 2011, Zamora collaborated with the digital newspaper *El Faro* and launched the short documentary film *Las masacres de El Mozote*. It is worth mentioning that this film was released one year before President Funes issued an apology for the massacre, which was still denied by many at the time. Marcela Zamora's documentary *Las aradas: Masacre en seis actos* (2014) is a powerful telling of the massacre of Las aradas (also known as El Sumpul Massacre), where the Salvadoran army, supported by Honduran soldiers, murdered hundreds of people in May 1980 (estimations range from three hundred to six hundred). The film explores the massacre by giving voice to the survivors, who recount the experiences that brought them to the area, and how they managed to survive the killing—most of them by crossing the Sumpul River into Honduras. In parallel, Zamora exhibits the apathy of the Salvadoran state toward the victims of the massacre, most notoriously by showing how President Funes avoided his responsibility to release military records. The final section of the film, titled "Los que no están" (The absent ones), shows the survivors naming some of the people who died at the hands of the army, making evident the pain that their absence still provokes in them. *El cuarto de los huesos* (2015) explores the Forensic Anthropology office of El Salvador, which houses countless bones and human remains, from the civil war to the victims of gang violence and dead migrants. *Los ofendidos* (2016) uses the information provided by *El Libro Amarillo* (where the name of Zamora's father, tortured during the internal conflict, was included) to tackle some of the torture methods employed by the army during the civil war, presenting locations and testimonies of both perpetrators and victims. Zamora's cinematic works contribute tremendously to the work of mourning by telling multiple stories of death and suffering and also by connecting them to present-day issues.

La batalla del volcán (2018), directed by Julio López Fernández, offers some interesting counterpoints regarding the work of mourning. This documentary tells the stories behind "la ofensiva hasta el tope," FMLN's final attempt to take control of the country in November 1989. The director places the narrative of the documentary in the hands of the combatants, bringing together former guerrillas and members of the state forces. *La batalla del volcán* portrays amicable relationships between ex-combatants, who offer relatively emotionless narrations of how they killed other people during the offensive.[26] In line with what I discussed in chapter one, mourning is not a central issue in this film. During the first half, spectators can see a former soldier commenting on the death of a child, saying, "la guerra es así," and a former guerrilla leader talking about how the casualties on the guerrilla side were "insignificant" compared to their enemy's.

In the middle of the documentary, however, a window is opened to present expressions of grief. For nearly ten minutes, we can see a combination of archival and new footage in which civilians, guerrillas, and soldiers grieve the dead. One of the most powerful moments occurs when a former member of the National Police, el Barón, remembers how he connected emotionally with two dead guerrilla women through their belongings. For reasons that the film does not explain, he took a small bloodstained notebook (with handwritten poems) from a dead guerrilla and a backpack with over twenty bullet holes from another one and kept them until the end of the war. As part of his own healing process, he took the backpack and notebook to a remote place one day, threw the backpack, cut the poems into little pieces, and let the wind take them. Crying, he says how that meaningful act "burnt his spirit" because even though he was not the one who had killed the two women, he felt their losses as his own, *propias*. This moment is compelling and powerful because he portrays a double grieving process. First, he is heartbroken for the dead guerrillas, with whom he connected after reading the poems and holding onto the backpack. But at the same time he demonstrates how he is still haunted in the present by the violence of the civil war ("the war shatters you," he says), often having nightmares and being incapable of talking about what he experienced. For many, whether former state forces may qualify as victims of the civil war is still up for debate. It is well known that the army forcibly recruited thousands of people, including children, but it is also true that the army was responsible for the overwhelming majority of the crimes committed during the internal conflict. What matters here is the very peculiar gesture of a former police officer acknowledging the humanity of his enemy, allowing himself to grieve the death of two guerrilla fighters (he never met in life) killed by his fellow police officers.

After this "parenthesis," the documentary goes back to the narrative of reconciliation that predominates in the film. *La batalla del volcán* concludes with the words of Herald, a former member of the BIRI Atlacatl Battalion:

> Ese es el valor que hay que rescatar para nuestros jóvenes, para las nuevas generaciones. De que si nosotros que peleamos en la guerra *hemos sido capaces de enterrar esos muertos*, de enterrar esos odios que alguna vez pudimos tener, y vernos ahora como hermanos [*sic*]. [. . .] En la guerra *sólo existe una hermandad, y es la hermandad de los que estuvimos en las trincheras.* No importa en qué lado militaste.

> El sufrimiento que ellos vivieron en esas trincheras es el mismo que nosotros vivimos en nuestras trincheras. Es por eso que los combatientes rápido hicimos el cambio de actitud y hemos podido reencontrarnos. En cambio, los que no pelearon son los que nos mantienen en esa eterna confrontación [my emphasis].[27]

The closing remarks of the film, similarly to what happens in the Museo de Historia Militar, blatantly overlook the death of the civilians and the pain of their loved ones. The only relevant actors in the postwar era, according to their criteria, are the former combatants. Following these words, we see the former soldiers and guerrillas leaving the scene, talking and laughing. The documentary closes with a dedication to the three thousand people who died during the offensive who are mostly ignored during the film. *La batalla del volcán* embodies very well some of the features of the work of mourning discussed in this book. We see how the efforts to present a conciliatory and definitive version of the events are interrupted by the unspeakable memories and pain of both the combatants and the civilian victims. This documentary demonstrates one of the premises of this book: if given a chance, many people would choose to grieve.

Jayro Bustamante's *La llorona* (2019) is a great example of how fictional films have also explored issues of mourning and justice in the postwar era. Bustamante's movie is the embodiment of the spectrality of the war, where the ghosts return to demand justice. In *La llorona*, former dictator Enrique Monteverde (based on Efraín Ríos Montt) is acquitted by the Guatemalan justice and returns home. In the following days, a mysterious Indigenous woman, played by María Mercedez Coroy, shows up to assist with the house chores following the mass resignation of servants at Monteverde's house. In the end, although it is anticipated, the audience learns that the woman is a ghost. She died during the civil war at the hands of the army, and now, given the impossibility of obtaining justice in the obscure and corrupt Guatemalan legal system, she has returned from the afterlife to take revenge and murder the genocider. Bustamante reinterprets the myth of "La llorona" (the crying woman), who cries after murdering her own children to punish her husband and then commits suicide; his adaptation showcases the power and the demands for justice embedded in the act of crying.[28]

There is an uncountable number of expressions of bereavement in postwar Central America. The films mentioned here are just some examples of contemporary audiovisual productions that engage in the battle of mourning (of course, they are not the only ones).[29] The struggles over the work of mourning permeate multiple cultural productions from both professional and amateur creators (from Carlos Cañas's painting *El sumpul* to the community-painted mural created in Arcatao, Chalatenango; fig. 22), and sometimes take place at a very intimate level. As this book has demonstrated, expressions of grief exist even where there have been numerous attempts to conceal them.

Whither Mourning?

In a well-known statement, Warren Buffett (CEO of multinational holding company Berkshire Hathaway) said to Ben Stein that "There's class warfare [. . .] but it's my class, the rich class, that's making war, and we're winning."[30] I am afraid a similar perspective may apply to postwar El Salvador and Guatemala. If there is a battle over the work of mourning, this is not because peo-

FIGURE 22 Mural painted by Pedro, Manuel Leiva, Melvin, Ovidio, Marvin, Chepe, and David portraying the El Sumpul Massacre (1980), Arcatao, El Salvador. Photo by Javiera Escobar Yametti.

ple do not want to grieve their dead but rather because there are powerful forces heavily invested in impeding them from doing so. And they might be winning. The price of "pacification" in Central America was none other than impunity and forced oblivion. Since the signing of the peace accords, the elites, political parties, armies, and guerrillas put their efforts into "turning the page." They seized every opportunity and grabbed any inch of political power that was available at the time. It has already been said that the Central American elites, in the end, benefited the most from the end of the wars and rapidly took back control of the economy through the neoliberal reforms introduced by postwar administrations. At the same time, an unprecedented (although insufficient, corrupt, and fragile) democratic system has been in place for over three decades.[31] The elites and the political parties were happy. Why bother thinking about the price of "peace"?

Mourning in Central America only seems to proliferate. Like in the play *Los ausentes*, mentioned in chapter two, the sorrow provoked by the recent internal conflicts is multiplied in the present by new losses, such as the thousands of assassinations that take place each year at the hands of criminal organizations; the death and destruction provoked by natural disasters; the social and economic conditions that have forced millions of people to flee their home countries and (at least attempt to) relocate elsewhere, particularly in the United States; and the most recent disappearance and death of thousands of alleged gang members by Bukele's regime of exception (the so-called terrorist).[32] This is a particularity of the Central American experience. Unlike what happened in the Southern Cone, where the end of dictatorships led to relative social stability—and by this, I do not mean the absence of social and political manifestations, which are the norm in places like Argentina, but rather a significant decrease in violent deaths and state terrorism—the aftermath of the civil wars in countries like El Salvador and Guatemala was equally violent and deadly for the citizens. Thus, it has become commonplace to say that the political violence turned into deadly criminal violence and that the wars have continued "by other means."[33] Therefore, multiple questions arise. How do we grieve when a son or daughter disappears somewhere along the path to the United States and their body is never found? How do we express sorrow for a relative taken by Salvadoran forces, accused of terrorism, and killed during their illegal imprisonment? How do we overcome the multiple losses provoked by forced migration and, sometimes, deportation?

One of the most problematic facets about the battle over the work of mourning in postwar Central America is its unpredictability. One simply does not know where the path of mourning will take those grieving, and that is a reality that everyone who participates in (or desires to accompany) the mourning process must accept. But not knowing the outcome beforehand does not make this process powerless. In the work of mourning, in loss itself, there is a "transformative effect," as Butler claims.[34] The commitment to the work of mourning, even before its impossibility, is what Derrida calls the experience of messianicity without messianism. Thousands of people embrace an unfinishable work of mourning because despite the continuous failures of this process, they see the event of justice as a "promise and an injunction that call for commitment without delay." This messianicity (that should not be confused with any form of utopian thought, especially a revolutionary one in its traditional sense) is a force that demands the reexamination of the present and the interruption of the "ordinary course of things, time and history."[35] Pausing, or at least slowing down the rearrangement of forces and discourses in the postwar era is one of the most important challenges for those who have accepted the task of mourning the losses caused by the recent internal armed conflicts. Resist, through any means possible, the codification of the dead in the national and regional continuum of violence that willingly sacrifices all the cadavers of the past—and ignores their specters—to defend and justify the powers of the present.

In a similar vein, there is in the unfinished work of mourning a certain demand for a democracy to come (as the end of *Ita* suggests), one that can exist beyond the suffrage, the political parties, and the notions of political representation. And most definitely, one in which corruption and coercion are not the norm. A democracy that does not reinforce teleologies or embrace identity but rather one that begins by "breaking with their naturalness or their homogeneity, with their alleged place of origin."[36] The years that separate us from the signing of the peace accords have demonstrated that democracy, at least for the political parties and Central American elites, only seems possible if the living "allow" the dead to rest regardless of how they died, who killed them, or where they are. Democracy, many seem to claim, can only exist in the realm of impunity. Nonetheless, the literature, theater, and some of the museums and memorials studied here demonstrate that there is a strong will to act politically in the present outside the rigid vocabulary of the state and the political parties. They claim for another form of political action and participation, one that does not exclude the specters, one in which the democratic promise may exist without the sacrifice of lives, without enmity or exclusions.

So, whither mourning? It is hard not to be downhearted when losses and indifference grow exponentially. Nevertheless, the materials studied here, particularly the ones committed to the grieving process of the victims, convey a more hopeful message. Not because they express optimism that one day justice and reparations for the atrocities of the wars will be achieved but because they have chosen their inheritance. Against the imperative to rapidly mourn the dead, turn the page, and focus on the future, many writers, artists, intellectuals, and ordinary citizens have decided to embrace melancholy not as a pathology but rather as an ethical commitment. In Derrida's words, melancholy "must never resign itself to introjection. It must rise up against what Freud says of it with such assurance, as if to confirm the norm of normality. The 'norm' is nothing other than the good conscience of amnesia. [. . .] Forgetting begins there. Melancholy is therefore *necessary*."[37] At least for now, the work of mourning ought to remain an experience of the impossible. It must resist its apprehension by the state and its apparatus. It must fight back any attempt to inscribe it into the neoliberal reason. Perhaps it should remain spectral for the time to come.

NOTES

Introduction

1. While homicides, kidnapping, and disappearance were some of the most visible crimes that took place during the internal conflicts, many other nefarious actions were carried out by the army, the governments, religious institutions, and/or the guerrillas, including but not limited to rape, torture, and child trafficking.

2. Connerton, *The Spirit of Mourning*, 26.

3. In this aspect I follow Nelly Richard, who claims that the prefix "post" does not belong to the simple order of chronology. Instead, it designates "un salto epistemológico que ayuda a reconceptualizar ciertos nudos teóricos de las matrices de origen del discurso de la modernidad (en la filosofía, la historia, la cultura), desocultando lo que había quedado reprimido o silenciado por sus dogmas y cánones" (Richard, *Crítica y política*, 31–32). I have further elaborated on the catastrophic character of the civil wars in Sarmiento, "Comunidad y catástrofe." Among some literary critics, there is a debate regarding the use of the term *postwar*. Alexandra Ortiz Wallner ("Narrativas centroamericanas de posguerra") criticizes its use by literary scholars because of its historical weight. Beatriz Cortez (*Estética del cinismo*) however, uses the term *posguerra* to refer to a sensibility and an aesthetic.

4. Examples of different mourning rituals are abundant. Embalming cadavers is one of the most common funeral practices in the United States but is almost nonexistent in Latin American societies. Many communities in Tibet and surrounding areas practice "sky burials," while the traditional Indian rite includes the cremation of the body in an open space. The practice of cremation is becoming more common in Latin America (despite the opposition of the Catholic Church), but it often takes place in private and enclosed places not accessible to relatives. Mourning practices are not only multiple, they are also in constant mutation. For example, until the first half of the twentieth century, the "velorios de angelitos" where a common practice in Latin America after the death of an infant. In the twenty-first century, that practice is almost extinct.

5. A historical reading of *Antigone* and how it relates to debates of public mourning can be found in Honig, "Antigone's Laments."

6. See Valtierra, "Las plañideras."

7. Cann, *Virtual Afterlives*, 6.

8. Renan, "What Is a Nation?," 19.

9. Ahmed, *The Cultural Politics of Emotion*, 19.

10. Déotte, *Catástrofe y olvido*, 29.

11. Benjamin, "Theses on the Philosophy of History," 256.

12. A curious example of the present-day use of mourning as a concealed political tool is what seems to be a recurrent struggle between the British government and FIFA. Each November, British citizens wear a poppy to remember and honor the soldiers that died in the world wars. In November 2011, England was scheduled to play a friendly game against Spain and requested permission to wear a poppy on their jerseys. FIFA denied the request based on the rule that no political symbol can be worn during a football game. The United Kingdom's prime minister, members of the royal family, and the media viscerally attacked FIFA's decision, claiming that wearing a poppy (therefore, remembering the British soldiers that died during the wars) was not a political statement. An interesting analysis of this case can be found in Fox, "Poppy Politics." In 2016, Scotland, England, Wales, and Northern Ireland defied FIFA and wore poppies on their jerseys during the November eleventh matches for the World Cup qualifiers. FIFA punished all associations with a combined fine of US$100,000 (Ramsay, "FIFA Fines British National Teams").

13. It should be noted that the twenty-first century has also witnessed a revival in mourning-like narratives from conservative and white supremacist groups, among others, especially before what many of them consider the near death of their narratives as a consequence of global events such as migration, gender diversity, and environmental awareness. In the introduction to *The Cultural Politics of Emotion*, Sara Ahmed comments on the rhetoric of the British National Front, a neofascist British organization. She argues that "the nation becomes the object of love precisely by associating the proximity with others with loss, injury and theft [. . .]. The Presence of non-white others is even associated by the British National Front with death: 'Britain is Dying: How long are you just going to watch?' To become the 'you' addressed by the narrative is to feel rage against those who threaten not only to take the 'benefits' of the nation away, but also to destroy 'the nation,' which would signal the end of life itself" (Ahmed, *The Cultural Politics of Emotion*, 12).

14. See McElya, *The Politics of Mourning: Death and Honor in Arlington National Cemetery*; Délano Alonso and Nienass, "Deaths, Visibility, and Responsibility"; Stelian Rusu, "Politics of Mourning"; Brown, *The Politics of Mourning in Early China*; J. Martínez, *Haunting Without Ghosts*; Ribas-Casasayas and Petersen, "Theories of the Ghost"; and Avelar, *The Untimely Present*.

15. Agamben, *Stanzas*, 3–18.

16. For a history of the concept of mourning, see Eng and Kazanjian, "Introduction." A thorough discussion about mourning and melancholia, particularly in Benjamin and Freud, can be found in Ferber, *Philosophy and Melancholy*. Agamben offers a complex and overarching discussion of some of the main figures in the mourning and melancholia discussion—from Aristotle to Freud—in *Stanzas*.

17. Freud, "Mourning and Melancholia," 243.

18. Derrida, *Specters of Marx*, 121.

19. Freud, "Mourning and Melancholia," 245.

20. Freud, 246.

21. Freud, *The Ego and the Id*, 36.

22. Abraham and Torok, *The Wolf Man's Magic Word*, 19.

23. In addition to the mentioned works, other major publications on mourning are Freud's *Totem and Taboo*, Nicolas Abraham and Maria Torok's *The Shell and the Kernel*, Jean Allouch's *Érotique du deuil a temps de la mort sèche*, and Laurence A. Rickels's *Aberrations of Mourning*, among others.

24. Butler, *The Psychic*, 188. While narcissistic for Freud, Butler does notice that in Freud's definition of mourning, the social is always present (*The Psychic*, 185), and they will return to this in *Frames of War* and *Precarious Life*.

25. While I will use the term *mourning* extensively throughout the book, I will often replace it with near terms such as *grief* and *sorrow* for stylistic reasons. Some authors have distinguished between "grief" and "mourning," understanding the former as an emotional condition and as an internal process and the latter as an external manifestation of grief. For a clinical distinction of the terms see Shear, "Grief and Mourning." A philosophical approach to this difference can be found in Cholbi (*Grief*, 44).

26. Derrida, *Specters of Marx*, 9.

27. Appelbaum, *Jacques Derrida's Ghost*, 32.

28. Derrida elaborates extensively on the violent origins of the law in "Force of Law," where he engages with Walter Benjamin's "Critique of Violence." There he states, among other things, that "Since the origin of authority, the founding or grounding, the positioning of the law cannot by definition rest on anything but themselves, they are themselves a violence without ground" (Derrida, "Force of Law," 242).

29. Derrida, *Points . . .*, 321.

30. Derrida, like other authors I cite here, uses the term *melancholy* to avoid the pathological significance of Freud's concept of "melancholia." Both, in the end, refer to an unfinished work of mourning, but "melancholia" is too loaded with psychoanalytic meaning. I will also use *melancholy* in this book to refer to the nonpathological ongoing work of mourning.

31. Freud, "On Transience."

32. Derrida, *Specters of Marx*, 121.

33. Derrida, 220.

34. Derrida, xviii.

35. For example, Jean-Luc Nancy claims that the community, which is always a community of *others*, "is revealed in the death of the other," emphasizing that a community "is the presentation to its members of their mortal truth" (Nancy, *The Inoperative Community*, 15). The presence of melancholy in communitarian though has been explored by Roberto Esposito in *Terms of the Political*, particularly in chapter 2, "Melancholy and Community."

36. Butler, *Precarious Life*, 22.

37. Butler, 23.

38. Butler, *Frames of War*, 14.

39. Butler, *Precarious Life*, 21–22.

40. Derrida, *The Gift of Death*, 9.

41. Derrida, *The Work of Mourning*, 144.

42. Michael Naas synthetizes very well the ongoing ambiguities of the work of mourning in Derrida's reflection: "mourning always negotiates between the infidelity of not mourning insofar as we leave the dead outside us, leave them to their alterity with no attempt to recognize, identify, remember, and incorporate them, and the infidelity of not mourning insofar as we have identified too much, understood too much, taken in and comprehend an alterity or remains that cannot and should not become part of us or our history, then mourning remains between these two 'there shall be no mournings.'[. . .] Mourning must always endure the aporias of knowing and not knowing, of identifying and not being able to identify, of getting at what cannot and can never be identified" (Naas, *Derrida from Now On*, 184).

43. See Cortez, *Estética del cinismo*; Sanford, *Buried Secrets*; Hatcher, *The Power of Memory*; Weld, *Paper Cadavers*; Pérez, *Más allá del duelo*; Ching, *Stories of Civil War*; Nelson, *Reckoning, Who Counts?*; and Portillo, Gaborit, and Cruz, *Psicología social en la posguerra*.

44. The interconnection between mourning and memory is present, among others, in the work of Marchio ("Memoria, duelo y olvido"), Roque Baldovinos ("Duelo y memoria"), and Cortez ("Memorias del desencanto"). It is important to clarify that there is nothing wrong with studying both terms in closeness, but clearly distinguishing them is essential for the purposes of this book.

45. The discussion over memory expands into multiple disciplines, including historiography, literary criticism, sociology, philosophy, psychology, and the interdisciplinary field of "memory studies." See Ricoeur, *Memory, History, Forgetting*; LaCapra, *History and Memory*; Huyssen, *Twilight Memories*, *Present Past*; Confino, *Foundational Pasts*, "Collective Memory"; Connerton, *How Societies Remember*; Halbwachs, *On Collective Memory*; and Jelin, *Los trabajos de la memoria*, *La lucha por el pasado*.

46. In Pierre Nora's words, "memory not as a remembrance but as the overall structure of the past within the present" (Nora, "From *Lieux de mémoire*," xxiv).

47. Nora, "Between Memory and History," 8.

48. In his monumental *Memory, History, Forgetting*, Paul Ricoeur argues that memory defines itself, at least initially, "as a struggle against forgetting," and that the duty of memory "is proclaimed in the form of an exhortation not to forget" (413). Similarly, Mabel Moraña argues that memory's primary function is "la del resguardo de lo perdido que constantemente amenaza con disolverse en el olvido, o con domesticarse como discurso histórico, o con anquilosarse en la privacidad de lo doméstico, en los rituales secretos de los deudos y en la conciencia de los victimarios" (Moraña, "Maldita memoria," 28).

49. Huyssen, *Twilight Memories*, 7.

50. In Murphy's words, *testimonio* and memory (or "memory mapping"), "respond to similar sociopolitical contexts and engage with memory narratives when the state, as a collectivity, completely fails to acknowledge an experience" (Murphy, *Mapping Memory*, 48).

51. See Burgos-Debray, *Me llamo Rigoberta Menchú*; Stoll, *Rigoberta Menchú*; Arias, *The Rigoberta Menchú Controversy*.

52. Mackenbach and Marchio, "Presentación," 7.

53. Avelar, *The Untimely Present*, 20.

54. Avelar, *The Letter of Violence*, 47.

55. For this book's purpose, the distinction between mourning and memory is fundamental. However, it is important to acknowledge that despite following different—and often coexisting—paths, memory and mourning are a duty assumed by the survivors and the heirs in the name of the victims of the political violence. The works of memory and mourning, in the end, are driven by a demand for justice—"there can be no ethics or responsibility without them," rightfully claims Michael Naas (*Derrida from Now On*, 233).

56. Jelin, *Los trabajos de la memoria*, 49.

57. Mackenbach, "Narrativas de le memoria."

58. A paradigmatic example of the battles over memory within Latin American studies is Steve Stern's trilogy on postdictatorship Chile, *The Memory Box of Pinochet's Chile*, which identifies the existence of four "emblematic memories" regarding Pinochet's dictatorship.

59. Sprenkels, "El trabajo de la memoria," 43.

60. Ching, *Stories of Civil War*. Other texts that study the battle over memory in postwar Central America are Hatcher, *The Power*; Ortiz Wallner, "Las batallas de la memoria"; Cal Montoya, "La historia y su uso público"; Zardetto, "Arte y posguerra"; Grinberg Pla, "Oralidad, imagen, acción"; Rey Tristán, Martín Álvarez, and Juárez Ávila, "Las limitaciones de la paz."

61. Arias, "Post-identidades"; Beatriz Cortez, "Memorias del desencanto"; Ricardo Roque Baldovinos, "Duelo y memoria."

62. Arias, "Post-identidades," 122.

63. Arias, 130.

64. Cortez, "Memorias del desencanto," 279.

65. Butler, *Precarious Life*, 30.

66. Pérez, *Más allá del duelo*, ix–x.

67. This can be found in different statements throughout the book. In the chapter about Claudia Hernández, for example, Pérez claims that Hernández's short stories "allow us to imagine another exercise of memory, where mourning alternates with irony, humor, and parody" (Pérez, *Más allá del duelo*, 96).

68. Pérez is also particularly concerned about the tremendous influence of previous scholarship on postdictatorship Southern Cone in the study of postconflict Central America, particularly the extensive discussion triggered by Idelber Avelar's and Elizabeth Jelin's influential books among Central Americanists. Of course, I agree

with Pérez that we should not lose sight of the historical particularities of the Central American revolutions and their aftermaths, for there are significant differences between the revolutions in the isthmus and the dictatorships in the Southern Cone. Still, we cannot ignore the fact that the pioneer research regarding issues of memory and mourning in Latin America began around the traumatic experiences of Chile, Argentina, and Uruguay. Therefore, it is understandable that some of these previous reflections will be incorporated and adapted in studies on Central America. In the same vein, my ultimate objective is that the reflection we develop of the Central American experience can also influence the work on other regions. This has already been noticed, for example, by Michael J. Lazzara and Fernando A. Blanco. In the introduction to *Los futuros de la memoria en América Latina* (10), they highlight that one of the novelties brought forward by Central Americanists is the robust reflection regarding the "gray zones," where the border between victims and perpetrators becomes blurry.

69. Roque Baldovinos, "Duelo y memoria," 172.

70. Christine J. Wade explains in *Captured Peace* how Salvadoran elites rapidly recovered their central position in the postwar era, controlling not only the private sector but also successfully supporting the ARENA party, which remained in power almost twenty years after the end of the war. See also Lungo Rodríguez, "Castillos de ARENA." In Guatemala, the Coordinating Committee of Agricultural, Commercial, Industrial, and Financial Associations (CACIF) has held enormous political power since its creation in 1957. One of its particularities, as Aaron Schneider claims, is their ability to prevent the creation of new elites within the country (*State-Building and Tax Regimes*, 175). They openly supported the army during the internal conflict, opposed peace negotiations, and benefited from the privatization and the neoliberal turn following the peace accords. CACIF also has publicly spoken against persecution for human rights violations. In 2013, days after the sentencing of General Ríos Montt for genocide, CACIF requested the annulment of the sentence because they claimed that there was no genocide in the country ("CACIF pide"). One week later, the trial was nulled.

71. Villalobos-Ruminott, *Soberanías en suspenso*, 27.

72. Žižek, *Violence*, 7.

73. Avelar, *The Untimely Present*, 211.

74. Derrida, *Specters of Marx*, 112.

75. My reading of mourning as a tool for critical thinking does not, obviously, extend to all cultural works produced in postwar times. Some novels, for example, embrace melancholy as a nostalgic cry for the "good old days" of the revolution. Magdalena Perkowska identifies this tendency, for example, in some novels by Salvadoran author Miguel Huezo Mixco. In her words, "Si propongo analizar las ficciones de Huezo Mixco como melancólicas, es porque creo que hay un objeto perdido que sus protagonistas no logran desplazar o introyectar [. . .]. La añoranza implícita por un tiempo pasado mejor, el que cobija esa virilidad guerrillera, hace que estos relatos exuden nostalgia" (Perkowska, "Del militarismo," 134). Salvadoran

writer Carmen González Huguet's *El rostro en el espejo* is a good example of a conciliatory vision of mourning, where the presence of ghosts leads to forgiveness and stability.

76. Nichanian, "Mourning and Reconciliation," 192.

77. Derrida and Stiegler, *Echographies of Television*, 120.

78. Derrida understands the "spectral oath" as the promise of fidelity toward the nonliving. "There would be no urgent demand for justice, or for responsibility, without this spectral oath" (Derrida and Stiegler, *Echographies of Television*, 124).

79. Ching, *Stories of Civil War*, 256.

80. Cortez, "Memorias del desencanto," 277–78.

81. Examples of major publications in history and the social sciences about Guatemala are Sanford, *Buried Secrets*; Nelson, *Reckoning, Who Counts?*; Vrana, *The City Belongs to You*; Weld, *Paper Cadavers*; and McAlister and Nelson, *War by Other Means*. On El Salvador, I must highlight Binford, *The El Mozote Massacre: Anthropology and Human Rights*; Hernández Rivas, "Cartografía de la memoria"; Wade, *Captured Peace*; Moodie, *El Salvador in the Aftermath*; Lauria-Santiago and Binford, *Landscapes of Struggle*; López Bernal, *Memoria*; Rey Tristán and Cagiao Vila, *Conflicto, memoria y pasadas traumáticos*; and Sprenkels, *After Insurgency*.

82. For example, Cortez, *Estética del cinismo*; Ortiz Wallner, *El arte de ficcionar*; Aparicio, *Post-Conflict Central American Literature*; Arias, *Taking Their Word*; Rodríguez, *Dividing the Isthmus*; Chaves Alfaro, *Los sujetos culturales*; Escamilla, *El protagonista*; Craft, *Novels of Testimony*; and Caso, *Practicing Memory*.

83. Rodríguez, *Dividing the Isthmus*, 2.

84. Grieving during the Central American civil wars was in itself an act of defiance that put the lives of many people in jeopardy. In *The City Belongs to You*, Heather Vrana narrates the fatal end of Robin Mayro García Dávila and Aníbal Leonel Caballeros, who disappeared on their way to attend a clandestine funeral for three members of the Ejército Guerrillero de los Pobres (EGP) and whose bodies were later found with signs of torture (Vrana, *The City Belongs to You*, 200–5).

85. Derrida, *The Work of Mourning*, 142.

Chapter 1

1. Rosenzweig and Thalen, *Presence of the Past*.

2. Steinberg and Taylor, "Public Memory," 450.

3. "Álvaro Arzú pide perdón"; "Guatemala pidió perdón." Although I will use the term *internal armed conflict* repeatedly during this book, it is important to note that the concept, while widely accepted and used by scholars and Guatemalans, it is not entirely free of discussion. Julieta Rostica argues that the "thesis" of the internal armed conflict "invisibilizes and naturalizes social factors and consensus that not only guaranteed the genocide but also symbolically commit it every day" (Rostica, "Naturalization of Peace," 199). In other words, the narrative of the internal armed conflict may rapidly reduce the political violence to the confrontation between the army and the guerrilla (the "dual violence" interpretation), excluding the social and

cultural conditions that have contributed to the historical oppression of the Indigenous population, which ultimately facilitated the genocide.

4. Martínez and Gómez, *Las reparaciones*.

5. A well-documented analysis of Ríos Montt's regime can be found in Garrard-Burnett, *Terror in the Land*.

6. See Falla, *Massacres in the Jungle*.

7. See Bosdriesz and Wirken, "An Imperfect Success"; Burt, "From Heaven to Hell," "The Justice We Deserve"; Casaús, "El juicio."

8. The "no hubo genocidio" claim appeared as a counterslogan to "sí hubo genocidio," the decision reached during the trial against Efraín Ríos Montt in 2013. Otto Pérez Molina, Guatemalan president at the time, also proclaimed after the sentence that in Guatemala "no hubo genocidio" ("Otto Pérez Molina asegura"). Film director Pamela Yates portrays how frequent this vision is in her documentary *500 Years*. In the context of the Ríos Montt's trial, three unidentified ladinos are questioned about the genocide, and all of them declared that "there was no genocide." During the 2015 protests, which ended with the resignation of Pérez Molina and his vice president Roxana Baldetti, the claim "sí hubo genocidio" and the online campaign #síhubogenocidio gained momentum. For more about "sí hubo genocidio," see Stuesse et al., "Sí hubo genocidio." For more about "no hubo genocidio," see Falla, "En Guatemala," and F. Martínez, "Francisco García Gudiel."

9. Valencia Caravantes, "Funes pide perdón."

10. "Justice Prevailed."

11. Nelson, *Who Counts?*, 104.

12. A thorough discussion regarding the removal of Confederate memorials can be found in Cox, *No Common Ground*. On the removal of statues of Columbus, see Pfosi, "Protesters Tear Down Christopher Columbus Statues"; Capps, "Why There Are Still 149 Statues"; Brito, "Dozens of Christopher Columbus Statues." For an in-depth discussion of the transformation of Chile's "Plaza Baquedano" into "Plaza de la Dignidad" during the 2019 protests, see Paredes, "La 'Plaza de la Dignidad' como escenario de protesta."

13. Sherlock, "The Reformation of Memory," 31.

14. Sherlock, 40.

15. Nora, *Pierre Nora en* Les lieux de mémoire, 20.

16. Jacobson, *Place and Belonging*, 128.

17. Jacobson, 103.

18. Lopes and Murriello, "El movimiento de los museos," 203.

19. See Vega y Ortega Báez, "La vida pública del Museo Nacional de México."

20. See "Museo Nacional de Historia Natural."

21. For more about the Salvadoran Museo Nacional, see Morán, "Breve reflexión."

22. Guatemala was an exception in this trend. As Marta Casaús Arzú demonstrates, the Guatemalan governments of the nineteenth century were not particularly concerned about creating a national museum to build a "Guatemalan identity," and therefore the building of public museums did not happen until the first half of the

twentieth century with the refoundation of the Museo Nacional de Arqueología y Etnología in 1931 and the creation of the Museo Nacional de Historia Natural in 1950 (Casaús Arzú, "Museo nacional y museos privados en Guatemala").

23. Cuenin, "La conmemoración del centenario," 70.

24. A detailed analysis of the memorialization, modernization, and construction of public buildings in San Salvador can be found in Salamanca, "Lugares sagrados." For a detailed analysis of sculptures and state formation in El Salvador, see Salamanca, *El Salvador*, 79–95. For more about the invention of traditions and national heroes, see López Bernal, "Inventando tradiciones."

25. For more on the building of the heroic figure of Morazán, see Lacaze, "Acercamiento al proceso de heroización."

26. Young, "The Counter-Monument," 270.

27. See Rabinbach, "From Explosion to Erosion"; Getso, "Revisiting Holocaust Memorialization"; Margry and Sánchez-Carretero, *Grassroots Memorials*; Williams, *Memorial Museums*.

28. Sodaro, *Exhibiting Atrocities*, 13.

29. Till, *The New Berlin*, 10.

30. Loewen, *Lies Across America*, 17.

31. Zegers, "Sitios de memoria en Chile."

32. *Espacios de la memoria*, 5.

33. Cann, *Virtual Afterlives*, 13.

34. Doss, *The Emotional Life*, 19.

35. Murphy, *Mapping Memory*, 114.

36. Murphy, 20.

37. Winter, *Sites of Memory, Sites of Mourning*, 98.

38. Steinberg and Taylor, "Public Memory," 459.

39. "Dalai Lama Changes."

40. In March 2023 I took the tour to Guatemala's National Palace. The tour stopped at the Patio de la Paz, and the guide provided technical information regarding the flame and Manos de la Paz, a sculpture located in the middle of the quad. Despite spending some time in that specific spot, the guide does not include any single information regarding the civil war that would explain why those memorials were created in the first place.

41. One of the first reports connecting the Palacio with political crimes was the 1981 International Amnesty report "Guatemala: A Government Program of Political Murder." The authors claim that "Amnesty International has not been able to confirm the allegations by some Guatemalans that the agency holds prisoners inside the Presidential Guard annex—but that the agency exists and that it serves as the centre of the Guatemalan Government's program of 'disappearance' and political murder seem, on the evidence, difficult to dispute" (Amnesty International, *Guatemala*, 9).

42. For more on the role of the Catholic Church in postwar Guatemala, see Steinberg and Taylor, "Public Memory"; and Salamanca Villamizar, "Los lugares de la memoria."

43. By this, I mean a memorial museum of national implications. In both Guatemala and El Salvador there are local museums and sites of memory that engage mostly at the regional level. For example, in 1999 the Museo Comunitario Rabinal Achi' (Community Museum Rabinal Achi'), in Baja Verapaz (Guatemala), was inaugurated to preserve the memory of the people who were assassinated by the army during the war and to support the community in its legal battles against the state (Museo Rabinal; Arias, "El pasado maya y el poder ladino"). In September 2019, amid the political crisis in Nicaragua, the Asociación Madres Abril (AMA) opened a memory museum at the Universidad Centroamericana de Nicaragua called Ama y no Olvida, Museo de la Memoria contra la Impunidad (https://www.museodelamemorianicaragua.org/). The museum's goal was to stress the human rights violations committed by Daniel Ortega's regime rather than memorializing the victims of the Contras War during the 1980s. The museum closed in December of the same year, but it became a virtual museum with an itinerant exhibition. The museum has traveled to Costa Rica, France, and Spain among other countries. See Medrano, "Inauguran el Museo"; Cruz, "Museo de la Memoria"; "Museo de la Memoria contra la impunidad será llevado a Costa Rica"; and Rappaccioli, "AMA y No Olvida." In June 2023, Honduran president Xiomara Castro inaugurated the Museo de la Memoria y la Reconciliación in Tegucigalpa. This museum seeks to officially reject the coup d'état that overthrew President Zelaya in 2009 and work in favor of the memory of those who lost their lives as a consequence of state repression in the aftermath of the military insurrection ("Presidenta hondureña").

44. During my second visit to Casa de la Memoria, in July 2019, the site was temporarily closed to the public because of a power outage that, surprisingly, did not affect any other building in the neighborhood.

45. For example, the Memory Museum in Chile mainly addresses the events that took place from the 1960s to the 1990s.

46. Casa de la Memoria's plaques and infographics are only in Spanish. All translations are mine.

47. Connerton, *Spirit of Mourning*, 15.

48. Weld, *Paper Cadavers*, 33.

49. Weld, 254.

50. For an in-depth analysis of the AHPN murals, see Bentley, "In and Out," 96–102.

51. Murphy, *Mapping Memory*, 19.

52. The virtuality of the memory route is much more concrete than it sounds. With the support of foreign agencies, civil society organizations created *Memoria Virtual Guatemala* (https://www.memoriavirtualguatemala.org/), a digital project that contributes to the labor of memory in contemporary Guatemala. They have created a fascinating project called "Mapeo de la Memoria" (Memory Mapping) that compiles sites of memory throughout the country despite how small they are. With that information, *Memoria Virtual* has created "Routes of Memory" in Gua-

temala City and San Cristóbal Verapaz. All the sites mentioned here are included in these routes.

53. McLoughlin, "Introduction," ix.

54. Archival work was indeed a form of the labor of mourning for many volunteers who joined the AHPN in the early years. As Weld comments, many volunteers had relatives who died or disappeared during the war, so working at the archive was a personal issue. Through archival work, volunteers were not only aiding in the arduous work of learning the truth about victims of political violence but also accomplishing a form of bringing "*their* dead back to life" (Weld, *Paper Cadavers*, 159). I will further discuss the role of the AHPN in the work of mourning in chapter 4.

55. See Hernández Mayén, "Asociación Amigos"; Orozco and Cumes, "Ministro Degenhart"; and "Archivo Histórico."

56. I visited Guatemala's Museum of Military History in March 2023. The room dedicated to the internal conflict was closed, but a room exclusively dedicated to the Kaibiles is at the center of the exhibition. In it, visitors can see Kaibiles' photographs, symbols, and military standards without any mention of the numerous atrocities they carried out during the civil war.

57. La comisión de la verdad para El Salvador, *De la locura a la esperanza*, 197.

58. Hernández Rivas, "Cartografía de la memoria," 4.

59. DeLugan, *Reimagining National Belonging*, 44.

60. See DeLugan for an insightful analysis of the rebuilding of national identity in postwar El Salvador. She particularly analyzes the role museums and sites of memory play in these endeavors in chapters 2 and 5.

61. Salamanca, *El Salvador*, 106.

62. This memorial is still a powerful site for the FMLN. On January 16, 2020, before Nayib Bukele's decision to not hold any official ceremony to celebrate the twenty-eighth anniversary of the peace accords, the FMLN held a public event at the Cristo de la Paz to commemorate the event ("El silencio del gobierno").

63. While this chapter explores constructed sites, it is important to mention that the memorialization process in postconflict El Salvador does not solely take place through the building or preservation of physical locations. For instance, numerous natural sites are important places of memory for different communities and individuals. An emotional example of this can be found in Tatiana Huezo's documentary *El lugar más pequeño* (2011), where a group of people return to Cinquera, a village destroyed by the army during the war. There, they connect through certain natural places with their memory and Cinquera's tragic story. Another example is the memorial park built as homage to the victims of the Sumpul River massacre (which took place on May 14, 1980). On May 14, 2020, for the fortieth anniversary of the tragedy, the community inaugurated a memorial that consisted of several "árboles de fuego" (firetrees), which bloom red in May, that remember the "martyrdom" of their loved ones. See Asociación Sumpul, https://www.asociacionsumpul.org/.

64. Sprenkels, "Roberto D'Aubuisson vs Schafik Handal," 24.

65. "Salvadorans Observing 3 Days"; "Hace 27 años."

66. While many of his followers claim that there is no evidence of D'Aubuisson's involvement in Monseñor Romero's assassination, his responsibility has been established numerous times. See Dada, "How We Killed."

67. Arauz, "La frustrada condecoración."

68. See Labrador, "Primer concejo," "Quijano defiende"; "Nombrar calles"; "D'Aubuisson: No Street Will Carry Your Name!" In my March 2023 trip to San Salvador, I noticed that the plaques I mention here were removed, although the memorial remains. I have not been able to find proper information about it, but everything suggests that it is related to Bukele's orders.

69. López Bernal, "Schafik Jorge Handal," 95.

70. López Bernal, 99, 110–17.

71. Alarcón and Binford, "Revisiting the El Mozote Massacre," 518.

72. "Route of Peace," *Infoguía El Salvador*, https://infoguiaelsalvador.com/ruta-de-paz/?lang=en.

73. See Hernández Rivas, "Cartografía de la memoria," 230–69; Sierra Becerra, "Historical Memory"; DeLugan, *Reimagining National Belonging*, 117–21; Pérez, *Más allá del duelo*, 155–68; Hernández Juárez, "Contra el caos de la desmemoria."

74. In recent years, civil society organizations have undertaken several projects to develop a "historical memory" in the small village of Arcatao. This region was dramatically affected during the first years of the civil war, including the infamous "Masacre del Sumpul" in 1980 and the "Guinda de Mayo" in 1982. The political violence forced many of the survivors to flee, especially to neighboring Honduras, and the area was not repopulated until the last years of the war. Today, the village has developed different projects to educate the people about their history. The Museo de la Memoria Histórica de Arcatao informs locals and visitors about the civil war, communal organization, and the horrific massacres that took place during the armed conflict. The community has also been conducting compelling ceremonies to mourn their slaughtered loved ones. For more about the memorialization practices, see *Museo de la Memoria Histórica de Arcatao* and Von Vogt, "Oraciones incompletas." For a history of Arcatao and the Chalatenango region during the armed conflict, see Lara Martínez, *Memoria histórica*, and Hernández Rivas, "Cartografía de la memoria," 96–118.

75. Ching, *Stories of Civil War*, 204.

76. "Museum of the Revolution."

77. Binford, *The El Mozote Massacre: Human Rights and Global Implications*, 192.

78. The guerrilla took advantage of Monterrosa's desire of capturing Radio Venceremos, the rebel radio station controlled by Comandante Santiago. When the guerrilla learned about Monterrosa's visit to Morazán in 1984, they placed a bomb inside the radio equipment and left it to be found by the army. Monterrosa fell into the trap. He captured the radio and took it with him into his helicopter. Once in the air, the guerrilla detonated the bomb killing all occupants.

79. Peterson and Peterson, "Martyrdom," 537.

80. Sobrino, "De una teología solo," 35.

81. Information provided by the tour guide during my March 2023 visit. See also "Visita su tumba en Morazán"; Genaro and Gato, *Dos pueblos*, 102.

82. Pérez, "El poder," 67.

83. Salamanca, "40 Years."

84. Avelar, *The Untimely Present*, 210.

85. "Decreto No. 65," 22.

86. Tejada, "Ráfagas de historia."

87. In 2012, after asking for forgiveness for the massacre at El Mozote, FMLN president Mauricio Funes spent $20,000 to create a commission to assess whether the army might continue paying homage to Monterrosa and other human rights violators. Ultimately, the commission concluded that the army could continue honoring them (J. Alvarado, "$20 mil gastó gobierno de Funes").

88. Picardo Joao, *El humor social y politico*, 83.

89. Nayib Bukele (@nayibbukele), "Se ordena a la @FUERZARMADASV retirar de inmediato el nombre del Coronel Domingo Monterrosa, del Cuartel de la Tercera Brigada de Infantería, en San Miguel." Twitter, June 1, 2019, 8:58 pm, https://twitter.com/nayibbukele/status/1134987672563408897. Without losing sight of his authoritarian administration, Bukele has been the first postwar Salvadoran president to acknowledge that, although some people should not be forgotten, this does not mean they should be commemorated.

90. Taum, *The Mourner's Song*, 20. Taum uses these words to refer to the presence of the "Moving Wall," a mobile Vietnam war memorial, at Norwich University, a U.S. private military college.

91. Guzmán Orellana and Mendia Azkue, *Mujeres con memoria*, 82.

92. For further details about the memorial and its construction process, see Hernández Rivas, "Cartografía de la memoria," 218–22; Mendia and Guzmán, "Tejiendo," 52–55.

93. Hernández Rivas, "Cartografía de la memoria," 223.

94. In one of the testimonies collected by Mendia Azkue and Guzmán Orellana, a person spoke about how this site became the only place where their family can visit their deceased father: "Cuando mataron a mi papá lo enterramos [registramos] con otro nombre. Después, cuando empezamos a trabajar en exhumaciones, hicimos su exhumación para legalizar su condición de fallecido, pero no encontramos absolutamente nada de él. Entonces lo único que tenemos ahora es el monumento" (Guzmán Orellana and Mendia Azkue, *Mujeres con memoria*, 85).

95. Individual donations started at US$4, which allowed the "sponsorship" of one name in the memorial. For US$600, it was possible to donate an entire plaque with the name of one hundred and fifty people ("Monumento a la Memoria y la Verdad El Salvador").

96. Hernández Rivas, "Cartografía de la memoria," 199.

97. Flores, "Un monumento."

98. Guzmán Orellana and Mendia Azkue, "Tejiendo," 55.

99. "Familiares de víctimas."

100. Binford, *The El Mozote Massacre: Human Rights and Global Implications*, 84.

101. Binford, 18.

102. Binford, 28.

103. Rauda Zablah, "El estado." For more details about the massacre, see Binford, *The El Mozote Massacre: Human Rights and Global Implications*, 15–33; Danner, *The Massacre at El Mozote*, 62–84; La comisión de la verdad para El Salvador, *De la Locura a la Esperanza*, 118–25; Zamora, *Las masacres*; Ana Patricia Rodríguez offers a compelling analysis of cultural works regarding the massacre of El Mozote in "Mozote Homeland."

104. On December 24, 1981, Comandante Santiago broadcasted the news about the massacre through Radio Venceremos. On January 26, 1982, the *New York Times* published Raymond Bonner's "With Salvador's Rebels in Combat Zone." On January 27, the *Washington Post* published Alma Guillermoprieto's "Salvadorans Peasant Describes Mass Killing." For an in-depth study of El Mozote Massacre coverage, see Danner, *Massacre at El Mozote*, 85–109, and Cantrell, "Killing US Softly."

105. Quoted in Danner, *The Massacre at El Mozote*, 89.

106. Argentine Forensic Anthropology Team, *Annual Report 1992*.

107. The statement can be seen in the video "Fragmento del Discurso de Funes," posted on YouTube by El Faro, October 28, 2013.

108. Corte Interamericana de Derechos Humanos "Caso Masacres."

109. "Resolución de la Corte Interamericana," 2–3.

110. See Rauda Zablah, "Exsoldados"; "El Salvador General Admits Army Carried out El Mozote Massacre"; "Declaran crimen de lesa humanidad la masacre de El Mozote." For further discussion regarding the Inter-American Court sentence and its implementation, see Guardado, "*El Mozote nunca más*." In 2022 judge Mirtala Portillo de la Cruz was appointed to reopen the investigation for the massacre. In December 2023, in a highly controversial decision, she ordered the arrest of the leaders of the 1993 National Assembly, accusing them of *encubrimiento* for approving the amnesty law. What make this order problematic is that she targeted the leadership of the Assembly, regardless of whether they voted in favor of the law or not. Noteworthy is the case of Rubén Zamora Rivas, a former political prisoner who voted against the amnesty and still received a provisional order of arrest. In March 2024 judge Portillo agreed to revoke her decision of prosecuting him. See Rauda Zablah, "La nueva jueza de El Mozote"; "Jueza Portillo contamina el caso El Mozote"; and Pineda, "Jueza retrocede."

111. Binford, *The El Mozote Massacre: Human Rights and Global Implications*, 190.

112. Alarcón and Binford, "Revisiting the El Mozote Massacre," 519.

113. I am heavily relying on Binford, *The El Mozote Massacre: Human Rights and Global Implications*, and Alarcón and Binford, "Revisiting the El Mozote Massacre," for the dates. Unfortunately, there is no information on site about when each section of the memorial was built. In August 2019, when I interviewed doña Delfina, the memorial's chief guide about the timeline of the building of the memorial, she told me dates that were not entirely accurate.

114. A compelling testimony of exile in Honduran refugee camps and the return to northern Morazán can be found in Romero de Thoma, *Verónica decide vivir*. Also, see Cagan's photo essay in Cagan, "Salvadoran Refugees."

115. Alarcón and Binford, "Revisiting the El Mozote Massacre," 520.

116. Bernardi, "Whispers at El Mozote," 251.

117. Alarcón and Binford, "Revisiting the El Mozote Massacre," 520.

118. Bernardi, "Whispers at El Mozote," 251–52.

119. I will not deal with the veracity of the memorial's narration. As Alarcón and Binford point out, "there exists no standard narrative," and "the historical facts about the massacre itself are never exactly the same, not even with the same guide" (Alarcón and Binford, "Revisiting the El Mozote Massacre," 522). A good example of the above takes place in the "Garden of Reflections," where visitors are often told that the army threw children in the air and impaled them with their bayonets. Nevertheless, as Alarcón and Binford clarify, "this story is decidedly apocryphal, sustained by no evidence, whether written, oral or forensic." (523). They conclude, "Some guides may hope that adding copious amounts of blood and gore to the oral rendition of the events will compensate for the lack of graphic depictions of the massacre in the mural images and encourage visitors' donations" (523).

120. López Bernal, "El FMLN," 55.

121. Barrera, "Las luchadoras."

122. Alarcón and Binford exemplify the religious dispute in the chapel's murals. They argue the murals confront the "inward-looking spiritualist theology of Father Juan José del Cid and the outward-looking, more politicized Liberation Theology of Father Rogelio Poncelee. According to one interview, Father Juan José has taken the position that the Church of the Three Kings belong to the Catholic Church, and that as head of the parish, he possesses the authority to destroy the murals if he wishes. He thinks that the 'Mural of the Light' depicts pagan religious ideas by identifying God with the image of the sun." Alarcón and Binford, "Revisiting the El Mozote Massacre," 524.

123. Bernardi, "Whispers at El Mozote," 250.

124. "Gobierno salvadoreño estrena documental."

125. https://www.facebook.com/watch/live/?ref=search&v=754601514734104.

126. Benítez, "Nayib Bukele."

127. Lovo, "Preocupa desinfomación"; Portillo, "Exigen que DOM."

128. Boquín and Espinoza, "El Mozote"; Arévalo, "En El Mozote piden justicia."

129. Binford, *The El Mozote Massacre: Human Rights and Global Implications*, 269.

130. Derrida, *Specters of Marx*, 9.

131. Some families had to wait until 2018 to finally receive their relatives' remains ("Gesto por la masacre"). In a very dramatic case, the remains of the victims of the cave in Cerro Ortiz were exhumed in 2019. The government promised to return the bodies in no more than six months. Nevertheless, the remains were not returned for three years, disturbing the families' grieving process (González Díaz, "El Mozote"). Other bodies are still waiting to be found.

132. Alarcón and Binford, “Revisiting the El Mozote Massacre,” 527.

133. Alarcón and Binford quote a local interviewee who speaks of Martin Luther King and Ghandi as “a brown-skinned evangelical man and the guy who sits (. . . *un moreno evangélico y el señor que se sienta*)” (527).

134. Ruta de Paz. https://rutadepaz.com/circuito-memorias-y-paisajes/.

135. For a fragment of the inauguration ceremony, including Sánchez Cerén’s speech, see “Monumento a la reconciliación, un símbolo para profundizar la paz en El Salvador.”

136. For all these claims, among others, see “Desde ‘Mater Civis’ hasta ‘La Michi.’” For a selection of memes created to mock the monument, see “¿Monumento a la reconciliación o monumento a la burla?”

137. Hatcher, “Victims and Violence,” 10.

138. Maciel, “Recordando desde enero o mayo,” 6.

139. As Hatcher notices, most of the people depicted in the mural “tell a story of resistance to repression,” and with the exception of Abelardo Torres, member of Cristiani’s government’s peace negotiation team, “there are no conservatives among these [. . .] figures” (Hatcher, “Victims and Violence,” 8). The latter reinforces the idea that this monument aimed to support the FMLN’s existence as the alleged continuators of previous figures who fought oppression in different times during Salvadoran history.

140. “Bukele ordena.”

141. Hompanera, “FOTOS.”

142. Funes, “Este espacio.”

143. Menéndez, “El cine al aire libre.”

144. Hatcher, “Victims and Violence,” 2.

145. Velásquez Estrada, “Grassroots Peacemaking,” 82.

146. In addition to the actions described above, it is relevant to mention that in April 2022, Bukele’s government seized two houses that belonged to ARENA and a bronze statue of Roberto D’Aubuisson. This occurred in the context of an investigation against ARENA for appropriating funds sent by Taiwan to aid in the reconstruction after the 2001 earthquake (Velásquez, “Escultura del mayor”; “Estatua del mayor”). While these actions happened in the context of a police investigation, they also affected ARENA’s memorialization of its founder.

147. Winter, *Sites of Memory, Sites of Mourning*, 98.

148. The Monumento a la Constitución was inaugurated on October 12, 1990 (“‘La Chulona’ vuelve a su sitio”). Nevertheless, the Ministry of Tourism’s website says that the monument was inaugurated in 1991 (“Monument to Constitution”). The municipality of San Salvador, on the other hand, says that the monument was built in 1992 (“Monumento a la constitución”). Citizens’ unawareness of the history of the memorial is well portrayed in different videos posted on YouTube by Salvadorans whose goal is showing the city to tourists and “hermanos lejanos.” See “Monumento a la constitución (chulona)” and “La Chulona #Salvadoreña.” For more on the feminist protest, see Machuca, “Exigen a Fiscalía, Policía y al Estado justicia.” In a 2019

interview, Rubén Martínez, the creator of "la Chulona," expresses his joy about the resignification of the place. In his words, "estoy contento de haberla hecho y además, todo el mundo está contento porque se la han tomado 'las dignas.' Cada uno es dueño de la escultura" ("Entrevista: Reconocimiento a un artista salvadoreño").

Chapter 2

1. Ridgeway, *The Origin of Tragedy*, 38.
2. Cole, *The Absent One*, 165, 9.
3. González Betancur, "Antígona y el teatro latinoamericano," 81.
4. de la Puente, "Memorias performativas," 90.
5. For more on issues of memory in contemporary Latin American theater, see Bixler, "Signs of Absence"; de la Puente, "Memorias performativas"; Solano, "El teatro documental"; Camelo and Jiménez Quenguan, "Teatro para la memoria."
6. Taylor, "Trauma and Performance," 1674.
7. Jossa, "Re-presentar la memoria," 104.
8. Taylor, "Trauma and Performance," 1676.
9. Murphy, *Mapping Memory*, 14.
10. The school opened under the direction of Spanish actor Gerardo de Nieva, who traveled to El Salvador during a tour with his theater company and decided to stay. The school, says David Rocha, dynamized the dramatic arts in El Salvador, and its alumni actively participated in radio theater (*Convergencias*, 68).
11. López Bernal, "Identidad nacional," 41.
12. Roque Baldovinos, *La rebelión*, 31.
13. Rocha, *Convergencias*, 69.
14. Córdova, *Hippies de barranco*, 49.
15. Salomón, "Theater in El Salvador," 175. For further details about the Bachillerato en Artes, see Rocha, *Convergencias*, 71–87; Córdova, *Hippies de barranco*, chap. 2; and Roque Baldovinos, *La rebelión*, chap. 3.
16. Salomón and Córdova, *Teatro*, 47.
17. Salomón, "Theater in El Salvador," 179.
18. Despite its importance in the history of El Salvador's theater, *San Salvador después del eclipse* was not well received by some critics. In his analysis of the 1994 Festival Centroamericano de Teatro, which took place in Honduras, Robert E. King argues that this play, along with *El día que me quieras*, "fueron propuestas poco rigurosas, más bien convencionales, de poca búsqueda, apoyadas, en la mayoría de los casos, en diálogos dramáticos o el chiste fácil" (were proposals of little rigor, rather conventional, of little exploration, supported, in most cases, in dramatic dialogues or easy jokes). King, "Reporte teatral," 154.
19. This play, as Evelyn Galindo suggests, establishes a dialogue with Álvaro Menen Desleal's *Luz negra*, mentioned above, and Samuel Beckett's *Waiting for Godot* ("Santa María").
20. Jorgelina Cerritos, personal interview with the author, September 29, 2021.
21. Cerritos, *13703. El misterio de las utopías*, 21.

22. Cerritos, "Así iniciaron."

23. Cerritos, *La Audiencia de los confines,* 10.

24. The play makes clear that they are talking about Fernando Llort's mural, which was created and placed in San Salvador cathedral to commemorate the fifth anniversary of the peace accords. However, this mural was destroyed by the Catholic Church in 2011. For further information about the mural's destruction, see Labrador, "¿Por qué la iglesia?"

25. Cerritos, *La Audiencia de los confines,* 11.

26. It is important to note that although the darkness is explicit in the text, this is not always translated onto the stage. In Candray's version, staged in El Salvador in 2014, the stage was always illuminated. When the play was staged in Costa Rica in 2019 by La Hebra, under the direction of John Sánchez, it began with a dark atmosphere, and the stage was illuminated with the ring of the bells.

27. "It never dawns here. It is never going to dawn here." Cerritos, *La Audiencia de los confines,* 18.

28. "this stinky portal lost in time, rotting, in a night of two decades, of ten decades, of a hundred decades, of all the decades of the Earth." Cerritos, 32.

29. Ripa, "Esperando el amanecer," 74.

30. "The bombing of Vietnam, the bombing of Afghanistan, the bombing of Iraq, the bombing of Morazán! Down! Down! It's the final offensive! The children run, they bleed out.[. . .] The women give birth underwater and cross the river without cutting the cord that tethers them to their children." Cerritos, *La Audiencia de los confines,* 38.

31. Cerritos, 9.

32. Westlake, *Our Land,* 24.

33. Romanska, Introduction, 6.

34. Jossa, "De la 'Audiencia de los confines.'"

35. "After the darkest night, the morning light will finally come during the third ring of the bell . . . The hour of judgment has arrived, and its light will dissipate the shadows. The great audience awaits us." Cerritos, *La Audiencia de los confines,* 16.

36. "When the women find their lost children under the storm and the shooting, and flowers will be born out of the putrefied bodies!" Cerritos, 28.

37. "May the victims rise in the pursuit of the murderers! May the bodies be reunited with their heads!" Cerritos, 29.

38. Cerritos, 43.

39. "You are sentenced to the death penalty for malicious and premeditated deception, and for taking advantage of Humanity and the future generations." Cerritos, 53.

40. "And now what's supposed to happen?" Cerritos, 56.

41. "Is there something outside these pillars? Is there someone waiting for us?" Cerritos, 58.

42. "Perhaps that's why we are this way, because we don't remember anything . . . Because we have a tectonic fault in the head . . . we are always falling and forgetting

and getting back up. (*Pause.*) I do want to know what I did and what became of me." Cerritos, 61.

43. "They say that the truth heals. You should try it." Cerritos, 79.

44. "I think I was the one who burned the children on the hill and hid out of fear while the tent was burning . . . and the one who threw the grenade that ended the life of the girl who was running toward the pharmacy." Cerritos, 79–80.

45. Jossa interprets the distressing end of the play as a result of Alonso's refusal to participate in some form of justice and truth telling. For her, Alonso's words are "una aproximación mal lograda a la verdad" (Jossa, "De la 'Audiencia de los confines,'" 94) that does not facilitate a transformative process. I claim, however, that the problem here is not a more or less precise version of the truth. Instead, the play portrays how truth, by itself, does not satisfy the mourners.

46. Edelberto Torres-Rivas's reflection on Guatemala also fits the Salvadoran case very well: "el desafío a la convivencia en el interior de la sociedad nacional, ya no es que la verdad del crimen se desconozca, sino que sabiéndolo, no se castigue" (Torres-Rivas, "La justicia, la verdad," 13).

47. "I wish you didn't cry . . . I wish you had never cried . . . I wish us women didn't cry. That we never cry. If I could, I would dry my tears. Even if tears can't be seen, we are always crying." Cerritos, *Bandada de pájaros*, 14. As Lucía Leandro Hernández suggests, Engracia's lament is not only a result of the atrocities of the civil war but also of gender and patriarchal violence, as the play will further elaborate (Leandro Hernández, "Una lectura," 47).

48. Cerritos comments on this in the book's prologue. She explains that the "bandada de pájaros" represents her memories of childhood, when kids used to be able to play without worrying about violence. When the bombing, the shootings, and the decapitations began, "A la bandada de niños y niñas se nos acabaron los juegos" (The games were over for us, the flock of boys and girls) (Cerritos, *Bandada de pájaros*, 9). Throughout the play, the use of different space-times becomes a constant reminder of the losses provoked by the war.

49. "The smell of alcohol reminds me of mamá Toña rubbing her hands to rub her legs." "Everyone was crying and she was so stiff and quiet. Everyone was crying. Everyone except me." Cerritos, 19.

50. "The smell of alcohol reminds me of Raymundo dancing with me at the village party.[. . .] Last August, when drunk he spat in my face and hit me because I didn't let him touch me." Cerritos, 19.

51. Cerritos, 27–28.

52. Cerritos, 70–71.

53. "Lying between piled up bodies [. . .] they took out my eyes so that I couldn't see Gonzalo.[. . .] I am lying in a ditch, over me there are other bodies, wormy clothing, a lot of tangled hair of other bodies. . . . There are fingers, ears, mouths of frightened children, there is a pair of testicles." Cerritos, 79.

54. "In a creek [. . .] with Gonzalo's head in my entrails." Cerritos, 79.

55. "I want death, Engracia. . . . The tomb, the grave, the headstone. . . . Even if it's a damaged cross in the road, with a crown of flowers.[. . .] I don't want the nothingness." Cerritos, 80.

56. "There is no one looking for us." Cerritos, 81.

57. San Ignacio de la frontera is a fictional town. However, according to Cerritos, its name comes from San Ignacio, Chalatenango. This town is located near the Sumpul River, which witnessed countless atrocities during the civil war. Jorgelina Cerritos, personal interview with the author, September 29, 2021.

58. Derrida, *Specters of Marx*, 220.

59. Derrida, 220.

60. Cerritos, *13703. El misterio de las utopías*, 22.

61. Strictly speaking, *Bandada de pájaros* has seven characters, but the play was created so that all male characters were performed by the same actor, whose initial identity is El Hombre Uniformado. The description of this character makes evident that he is all the other characters at once, assuming their voices when the play needs it.

62. "I buried him in the yard, I put his things in a small box and I buried him in my memories. And now you come to force me into an exhumation that I don't want." Cerritos, *13703. El misterio de las utopías*, 49.

63. Derrida, *Specters of Marx*, 9.

64. Cerritos, *13703. El misterio de las utopías*, 111.

65. "I don't know if I am a fearful man, a lost child, or an old picture in a yellow book . . . I don't have a past, I don't have a family, neither a mother, a wife nor any children . . . I only have an erased name and an unknown face . . . Where will I find my answers?" Cerritos, 121.

66. "Let them use it. Make copies of the photographs and put them on bulletin boards so they know who their enemies are."

67. "El Libro Amarillo."

68. Quoted in Larralde Armas, *Relatar con luz*, 97.

69. Barthes, *Camera Lucida*, 77.

70. "Something else must be done." Cerritos, *13703. El misterio de las utopías*, 122.

71. Cerritos, *La Audiencia*, 9–10.

72. Cerritos, *13703. El misterio de las utopías*, 21.

73. Jorgelina Cerritos, personal interview with the author, September 29, 2021.

74. Appelbaum, *Jacques Derrida's Ghost*, 35.

75. Jossa, "'¿Y qué pruebas tenemos ahora?,'" 461.

76. Cerritos, *13703. El misterio de las utopías*, 15.

77. "At times, I'm afraid. At times I'm. At times I ask myself why is this chalice for me, and I don't want to say that they push it away, but I tremble and sweat in silence. I have never had so much love for life. I want a little more time.[. . .] I don't have a martyr's vocation, I don't have it. Should I have been more prudent?" Cerritos, 52.

78. "May this immolated body and this Blood Sacrificed by men feed us . . . to give concepts of justice and peace to our people." Cerritos, 53.

79. Cerritos, 90.

80. "Today death surrounds us, Monseñor Romero haunts us." Rodríguez, *Muerte en la consagración*, 9.

Chapter 3

1. This does not mean that expressions of mourning were not present in the fiction written before the signing of the peace accords. Examples of this are Horacio Castellanos Moya's *La diaspora* (1989) and Marco Antonio Flores's *Los compañeros* (1976). However, the 1990s was the decade when these kinds of works grew exponentially.

2. Beverly and Zimmerman, *Literature and Politics*, 172.

3. For more on testimonio, see Beverly and Zimmerman, *Literature and Politics*; Beverly, "The Margin at the Center"; Yúdice, "Testimonio and Postmodernism"; and Moreiras, "The Aura of Testimonio."

4. Gugelberger states: "Obviously the euphoric 'moment' of the testimonio has passed, and it is now time to assess in a more self- and metacritical spirit its reception by the critical and academic disciplines." Gugelberger, "Introduction," 1.

5. Some writers often associated with the *generación comprometida* are Manlio Argueta, Ítalo López Vallecillos, Roque Dalton, José Roberto Cea, Otto René Castillo, and Luis de Lión. For more on this group of authors, see Alvarenga, "La generación comprometida."

6. Arias, "Post-identidades," 123.

7. Arias, *Taking Their Word*, 25.

8. Cortez, *Estética del cinismo*, 31, 131.

9. Ortiz Wallner, *El arte de ficcionar*, 65.

10. Magdalena Perkowska offers an elaborated discussion of Cortez's and Arias's arguments in "La infamia de las historias." She argues that while Arias's argument regarding the depoliticization of postwar fiction is correct within his corpus of study, the corpus itself is not representative of the majority of works published in the postwar era (2). Regarding Cortez's proposal, Perkowska makes the important distinction between a character's cynicism and literature's cynicism. The distinction, claims Perkowska, is unclear in Cortez's book, but they should not be confused (6). Postwar authors, claims Perkowska, successfully navigate this paradox and are able to establish the difference between the infamy of the actions presented and the writers' point of view about them (17). Cortez's "aesthetic of cynicism" hypothesis has also been discussed by Kroll-Bryce ("Nómadas, desempleados y suicidas") and Moreiras ("The Question of Cynicism"). Ortiz Wallner's idea of nomadism and transnationalism is aligned with the reading proposed by Ana Patricia Rodríguez in *Dividing the Isthmus* (2009). However, the work of Silvia López ("National Culture") and Yvette Aparicio (*Post-Conflict Central American Literature*) offers the opposite interpretation, proposing that contemporary fiction seeks a "return" to the national.

11. Browitt, *Contemporary Central American Fiction*, 2.

12. Kokotovic, "After the Revolution," 24.

13. Kroll-Bryce, "Nómadas, desempleados y suicidas," 624.

14. Browitt, *Contemporary Central American Fiction*, 3.

15. In 2016, the short story "La han despedido de nuevo," originally included in *Olvida uno*, was translated by Aarón Lacayo and published as a bilingual novella by Sangría Editora, an independent publisher based in New York City. Because of this, some critics and secondary sources claim that *La han despedido de nuevo/They Have Fired Her Again* is Hernández's first novel, but that is not the case.

16. *Mediodía de fronteras* originally contained eighteen stories. "Trueque," "De estampa," and "Obsequio" were removed in the second edition, and "Un demonio de segunda mano" was added.

17. Only two assassinations and one suicide take place in the book. In "Lázaro, el buitre," a man kills a vulture who, he believes, wishes to eat his daughter. In "Fauna de alcantarilla," a community decides to murder a family who lives in the sewer system because they eat their pets. It is worth noting that in the first case the animal is being humanized, and in the latter, the family has been animalized. Nevertheless, in the end of both stories, the characters regret having committed those assassinations. In "Mediodía de fronteras," a woman commits suicide in front of a dog in the restroom of a border between two unnamed countries.

18. Pérez, *Más allá del duelo*, 105, 111.

19. Sophie Esch offers an illustrative summary of the little markers that could connect the stories with Central America. She claims that "only one story employs *voseo*, while another has a vague reference to the tropics and to houses with 'muros gruesos y rejas.' Both the *voseo* and gated communities are common in Central America but are not exclusive to the region" (Esch, "In the Company of Animals" 572).

20. Kokotovic, "Telling Evasions," 54.

21. Kokotovic, 55.

22. See Perkowska, "Los archivos del malestar"; Buiza, "On Aesthetic Experience"; Rincón-Chavarro, "De violencia"; Caamaño, "Parodia"; Kokotovic, "Telling Evasions"; Aparicio, *Post-Conflict Central American Literature*; Ortiz Wallner, "Claudia Hernández." I have also offered a reading of Hernández's fiction in relation with civil war trauma and neoliberalism in "¿Qué hacer con los muertos?," "Frecuencias de lo (in)visible," and "Trabajo, etnicidades y figuraciones de la pobreza." There are alternative interpretations, of course. Sophie Esch, for example, argues that the book can also be read as unrelated to postwar Central American societies, favoring a "universalistic" reading of *De fronteras*, especially since the book avoids "any geographical or linguistic hints connecting it to the isthmus" (Esch, *Modernity at Gunpoint*, 234). In this line, reading her work from animal studies and posthumanism perspectives have also become a trend. See Vázquez Enríquez, "Companion Species"; Esch, "In the Company of Animals"; and Buiza, "Trastornando."

23. Browitt, *Contemporary Central American Fiction*, 110.

24. Derrida, *Of Hospitality*, 25.

25. C. Hernández, *De fronteras*, 19.

26. In her interpretation of the story, Aparicio emphasizes the "practicality" of the narrator's actions (*Post-Conflict Central American Literature*, 47–48). They are

indeed very practical (although it would have been more practical to call the authorities or dispose the bodies outside of their houses), but I also claim that they are meaningful and oriented to his community. My reading also goes against Caamaño's interpretation, who suggests that the narrator could also be an assassin because of his suspicious knowledge on how to preserve a dead body ("Parodia," 247).

27. "Her face suggests that her name is Lívida." C. Hernández, *De fronteras*, 17.

28. "I search for the *owner* of a cadaver"; "I started to receive calls from people that urgently wanted to know how I had solved the problem of having *someone else's* cadaver at home." C. Hernández, 17, 39.

29. Precarity is one of the main threads in Hernández's fiction. I have further elaborated about this in Sarmiento, "Claudia Hernández y la escritura de la precariedad."

30. Butler, *Frames of War*, 21.

31. Butler, 25.

32. Esch, "In the Company of Animals," 579.

33. Gairaud Ruiz, "Rutas de Muerte," 207.

34. Kokotovic, "Telling Evasions," 60.

35. Pérez, *Más allá del duelo*, 112.

36. Aparicio claims that a form of *patria* emerges with the cannibalization of the bodies (*Post-Conflict Central American Literature*, 49). I do not believe this community goes in that direction, but I agree with her in the communal gesture of supplying the needs of others who are neglected by official institutions.

37. Browitt, *Contemporary Central American Fiction*, 117.

38. Browitt and Esch are some of the critics who have identified this point. Browitt claims that one of the most overlooked aspects of the story is "the connection of the ox to the man or the community" (*Contemporary Central American Fiction*, 117) and that the most significant element of the story is "the desire to make reparations, the empathy displayed by the man" (119). Esch argues that the story "advocates healing through a particular form of restitution" that invites us to ask "what it would mean to truly accept the guilt of having taken the life of another being" ("In the Company of Animals," 588).

39. Pérez, "Memory and Mourning," n.p.

40. "He had tried it more than ten times. He had ended his grief and returned home; but daily when he passed by that road, he felt the absence of the ox." C. Hernández, *De fronteras*, 24.

41. Browitt, *Contemporary Central American Fiction*, 119.

42. Jossa, "Cuerpos y espacios," 14.

43. Although I will not discuss the story here, another great example of interspecies mourning in Hernández's *De fronteras* can be found in "Mediodía de fronteras." In this story, a stray dog enters a women's bathroom in an unnamed border station and finds a woman who has cut her tongue and is preparing to commit suicide. Yajaira Padilla offers a reading of this story that goes in the same direction of what I have argued here. She posits that the dog, disregarding the fact that the woman be-

longs to a different species, “respect the woman’s choice regarding her motives [. . .] but also mourns her death, crying and refusing to leave her side” (Padilla, *Changing Woman*, 90).

44. Rincón-Chavarro, “De violencia.”

45. Esch, *Modernity at Gunpoint*, 176.

46. Browitt, *Contemporary Central American Fiction*, 111.

47. Derrida, *Specters of Marx*, 11.

48. Derrida, 6.

49. “I tolerate the stares of the people that see him [the rhinoceros], then watch me, *then look at the arm I am lacking*.” C. Hernández, *De fronteras*, 12–13.

50. “The rhinoceros is not mine—I assure them while I make sure they are looking at him and *not at my arm that is not there*.” C. Hernández, 11.

51. “I caress it when I arrive home *with the fingers I don’t have* and I allow it to sleep under my shadow.” C. Hernández, 13.

52. Esch, *Modernity at Gunpoint*, 177.

53. Kokotovic, “Telling Evasions,” 59.

54. Rodríguez, *Dividing the Isthmus*, 227.

55. Derrida, “Freud and the Scene of Writing,” 212.

56. Derrida, *Of Grammatology*, 154.

57. “I smiled when I saw that it liked me and that it [the rhinoceros] followed me, even though I have no arm, instead of any of *those who are complete*”; “I fear that someone accepts it and it won’t oppose resistance and leaves me, and goes away, and I won’t have dwarf steps around my feet of an *incomplete man*.” C. Hernández, *De fronteras*, 12, 13.

58. Esch, *Modernity at Gunpoint*, 177.

59. “I couldn’t get used to his absence, [. . .] to the silence of the early mornings without his feet tripping over the furniture of the dark house nor to the lunches without his obsessive tales. I couldn’t. I had tried—for real—but I couldn’t get used to being without him.” C. Hernández, *De fronteras*, 57.

60. C. Hernández, 19.

61. C. Hernández, 64.

62. “I accepted their tribute, with the satisfaction that I had decided to do what was correct for my family and not for the undertaker, nor my honor, that in the end worth less than to have my grandfather back home.” C. Hernández, 59.

63. “It is very emotional to reconstruct the body of a boy (24–25 years of age) that left home complete two or six days ago. For this reason, it is recommended to have a box of disposable tissues at hand.” C. Hernández, 107.

64. “**NO RETURNS ACCEPTED**”; “Show him to family and friends. Distribute photographs of when he was alive. Cry every time someone mentions his name.” C. Hernández, 107, 109.

65. Pérez argues that this story portrays “una ética anestesiante.” She claims that “La sociedad de consumo tiene solución para todo, y si se siguen con atención y esmero las instrucciones sobre cómo rearmar al hijo muerto, se le quitará el patetismo

al proceso del duelo y se hará algo productivo con la pérdida" (*Más allá del duelo*, 113). Esch argues that the story does not present a perpetrator or a weapon, "only a mutilated cadaver and a numb society that has forgotten how to grieve" (*Modernity at Gunpoint*, 174).

66. While I disagree with the overall interpretation of the story offered by Kokotovic, I do agree with him when he claims that the narrator of the story can be identified with the voice of the state, or any organization affiliated with it. Kokotovic, "Telling Evasions," 64.

67. Ortiz Wallner, "Claudia Hernández," 7.

68. Ortiz Wallner, *El arte de ficcionar*, 79.

69. Benjamin, *The Origin of German Tragic Drama*, 224.

70. Moreiras, *Tercer espacio*, 168–69.

71. Derrida, *Specters of Marx*, 125.

72, Derrida, 125.

Chapter 4

1. Lovell, "The Archive that Never Was," 204.

2. While rare, the AHPN is not the only archive of military criminal activities found in Latin America. In 1992 Martín Almada and José Agustín Fernández discovered the so-called Archivos del terror. The near four hundred thousand documents recorded crimes committed by Paraguayan dictator Alfredo Stroessner (1954–89) and Operation Condor's criminal activities. See Boccia Paz, González, and Palau Aguilar, *Es mi informe*.

3. Although these are perhaps the most notorious works produced regarding the AHPN, they are not the only ones. In 2011, documentary filmmaker Patricia Yates used the materials found at the AHPN in her film *Granito: How to Nail a Dictator* (2011). In November 2009, Guatemalan visual artist Daniel Hernández Salazar installed his "Ángel de Guatemala" in a temporary exhibition at the AHPN ("El Ángel Global"). For a discussion regarding these materials and their relationship with the AHPN, see Albizúrez Gil, "Arquitecturas de control."

4. As Jelena Mihailovic rightly identifies, there are some parallels between *Ita* and, for example, Vanessa Núñez's *Dios tenía miedo* (Mihailovic, *Memoria, trauma y crimen*, 32). We should also include in this corpus the literature of Guatemalan author Eduardo Halfon, whose work I will discuss in the following chapter.

5. I therefore disagree with Cortez when she argues that the predominance of ladino voices in postwar fiction may lead to indifference toward the direct victims of the civil wars, particularly the Indigenous population in Guatemala (Cortez, "Memorias del desencanto"). On the contrary, I read *Ita* as a novel that proposes an ethical approach to the victims in the postwar era despite their indifference during the internal conflict.

6. Perkowska, "Silencios que hieren," 451.

7. *Del silencio a la memoria*, 50–52.

8. Weld, *Paper Cadavers*, 93.

9. Weld, 63–67; Doyle, "The Guatemalan Police Archives"; Lovell, "The Archive that Never Was," 206–7. In May 2021, Guatemalan judge Miguel Ángel Galvez ordered the arrest of a number of military officers in connection with the crimes described in the "Diario militar." The trial and sentence are still pending (Santos Cid, "Guatemala juzgará a nueve militares"; Burt and Estrada, "Juez en Guatemala").

10. Weld, *Paper Cadavers*, 29–42; "Silenciando la memoria."

11. University of Texas Library, https://ahpn.lib.utexas.edu/about_ahpn.

12. Uli Stelzner's documentary *La isla* offers many examples of how the archival work conducted at the AHPN permitted the staff to perform their own work of mourning. Weld also offers different examples in *Paper Cadavers*. For example, she interviews a staff worker she identifies as "Esteban." In his interpretation, writes Weld, "the reencounter with the companion via the documents could provide both relief and vindication: relief in the sense of offering a release valve, and vindication (*reivindicación*) in the sense of reassigning agency, subjectivity, and identity to the dead. The police archives brought these workers' dead to life" (166).

13. Weld, *Paper Cadavers*, 19.

14. Couser, *Recovering Bodies*, 4; "Autopathography," 164.

15. Hawkins, *Reconstructing Illness*, 4.

16. "would be linked to some psychological suffering, childhood abuse, for example, impossibility of expressing trauma, for instance." Albizúrez Gil, *Ita*, 39.

17. "Only mom going away delineates [on her mind]." Albizúrez Gil, 39.

18. "I was by myself. The absent mother. The father in absolute silence." Albizúrez Gil, 14.

19. Literary critics also agree on this. See Mihailovic, "Memoria, trauma y crimen"; Perkowska, "Silencios que hieren"; "La foto."

20. Albizúrez Gil, *Ita*, 39.

21. Albizúrez Gil, 17, 14.

22. Albizúrez Gil, 54.

23. "The condition for this memory is a dark place where we imagined the tomb. My mom's, I mean. We both dig the land with great difficulty until there was a whole big enough to place the body. There we placed it. But because we were not careful and we improvised, sometimes the earth loosens and one hand comes out or a word is heard. They are the mandatory phone calls that Fabiola makes for Christmas. They are my choppy conversations with her diluted into trivialities. They are the nightmares we never tell each other." Albizúrez Gil, 105.

24. Jossa, "Espacio."

25. "One cannot get to know this country only from the outside. One has to go deep inside. I know this well, I'm the son of the woman inside." Albizúrez Gil, *Ita*, 51–52.

26. "Delfina tied him to the bed's leg with a lasso, long enough so he could move within that circumscription." Albizúrez Gil, 20.

27. Albizúrez Gil, 24.

28. Perkowska, "Silencios que hieren" 445.

29. Albizúrez Gil, *Ita*, 62.

30. Albizúrez Gil, 108–9.

31. "that night's meanings overwhelm me. The language left me behind." Albizúrez Gil, 110.

32. "Twenty years ago, it would have been my frightened silence, I'm lying, my own denouncing voice: resentful communist guerrilla Indian. Ten years ago: I'm not racist but they have been at a standstill for centuries. And today, when I read, *we are the sons and daughters of the illiterate women, Indigenous popular power, we the Maya are also the people*, the sharp edge of the shattered glass and Delfina's caress cut me." Albizúrez Gil, 68.

33. "erode the limits of a weak institutionality on which collective memory is built, and also, they expose a set of forces in dispute." Albizúrez Gil, "Arquitecturas de control."

34. Weld, *Paper Cadavers*, 52.

35. Derrida, "Archive Fever," 19.

36. "The house feels empty. Most of its inhabitants pretend to sleep, perhaps someone broke the conscience with that morning. From my bed I want to run and jump very far. I close my eyelids and press them strongly. I'm going to descend to the bottom. To that moment when I heard her comparing her head with a sacked *archive*. Without understanding very well, I ran terrified to her library and began to throw books, to spill tempera, to write my name on the floor. *I had the impulse to burn some pages*, but the flame would not be the sacking but the destruction. I grabbed the book she had been working on, I opened it until I heard the sound of a breaking bone. For a second, I thought I could enter the brain, that one of gelatinous corridors where a shadow in search of an escape wanders. [. . .] Silence is interrupted in that house of Mariscal, that I wish to see *demolished, in ruins*. As I should have felt when I just turned ten years old. Like the whole city was." Albizúrez Gil, *Ita*, 11.

37. Derrida, "Archive Fever," 57.

38. It is important to say that the novel is not entirely clear about this situation. It is valid to say that she found the document many years ago, kept it safe, and came back to it in the present of the narration (this is how I read the chain of events). Yet it is equally valid to claim that she found the document while searching through her father's old records—the way Mihailovic reads it ("Memoria, trauma y crimen," 37).

39. Perkowska, "La foto," 40.

40. "Something tells me that her leaving the house and quitting her life as an artist has everything to do with the History." Albizúrez Gil, *Ita*, 78.

41. "I am not a victim and neither is my family. We are not perpetrators either. We are the silent mass. The ones that worked punctually. The ones that knew something about the violence called armed conflict. The ones that supported the order. The ones that founded the abnormal normality." Albizúrez Gil, 79.

42. "And indeed, I leave that place with the calm of someone who can run for a long while with no interest in reaching an exact point. Just going through is enough." Albizúrez Gil, 84.

43. "And what do you mean with that thing about death, mom? Do you have that experience? That closeness comes from Rolando Cajas? Did you grieve him? Did you go to his funeral? Who were you there, mom?" Albizúrez Gil, 150.

44. "The door of the last archive fell. The archive of my mother's affects." Albizúrez Gil, 150.

45. "she lives a closure for life and it's too late to leave it." Albizúrez Gil, 168.

46. Derrida, *The Gift of Death*, 25.

47. Derrida, "Archive Fever," 47.

48. "they will sing excitedly Pollo Campero's jingle, which called Guatemala to stand up. The thirty thousand dead *did not belong to them*." Albizúrez Gil, *Ita*, 27. After the earthquake, Guatemalan fried chicken fast-food chain Pollo Campero released the song "Cantemos a Guatemala," which invited everyone to join and work together in favor of the Guatemalan nation. This kind of advertisement continues to the present. In Ioulia Fenton's words, instead of "promoting systemic change of structural issues that contribute to poverty, crime, and violence, the ads promote personal change inside each Guatemalan" (Fenton, *Changing Chicken in Guatemala*, 9).

49. "That's how I must begin my life outside of that house, having finished my infancy and youth, with enough strength to close the heart. *Not looking at the dead*." Albizúrez Gil, *Ita*, 35–36.

50. "Words that explode because of the hidden pain. The anguish that flows from pauses and silences, from breathings to retake the impulse, from soft crying that betrays the strength, breathing in the tears to keep telling." Albizúrez Gil, 164.

51. Albizúrez Gil, 171.

52. "we keep a moderate contact and therefore a sincere one." Albizúrez Gil, 181.

53. Albizúrez Gil, 182.

54. "Here we are. Those that someone called the fatherland. Those that someone said house. The fatherland is a square. There we will let flow the accumulated fear, the accumulated rage, the accumulated ignorance. We will leave that place by different and opposed routes. Do not speak of unity. Do not speak of permanence. Someone says exit. Someone utters limit. *Someone yell begin in this country of profound wounds*." Albizúrez Gil, 182.

55. Jossa, "Mónica Albizúrez, *Ita*," 424.

56. Foucault, *Archaeology of Knowledge*, 129; *Foucault Live*, 66.

57. Tello, *Anarchivismo*, 62. Tello also adds that "la máquina del archivo es social porque a través de su funcionamiento se definen justamente los parámetros en que las actividades colectivas se desarrollan, en ella se disponen los registros que buscan reglamentar los comportamientos humanos, las actas y los actos, los dichos y los hechos" (63).

58. Tello, 272.

59. Tello, 267.

Chapter 5

1. In 2014 Alexandra Ortiz Wallner already considered Halfon the "most universal of the young Guatemalan writers" ("Una escritura," 35).

2. Durante and Havenne, "La obra en 'matryoshka,'" 270.

3. "Postmemory" is a concept elaborated by Marianne Hirsch in her influential book *The Generation of Postmemory* (2012). This notion refers to the "generation after," the one that did not experience traumatic events firsthand but rather "remembers" them through individual and collective narratives.

4. The "postmemory" reading has been developed, among others, by Marchio, "(Pos)Memoria(s)"; Laorden Albendea, "Lidiar con el pasado familiar"; and Constales, "Postmemoria y autoficción."

5. Examples of this reading can be found in Pridgeon, "Silences," "Jewish Guatemalan Fiction"; Gartenberg, "Inheriting Ghosts"; Fiorani, *Habitar la distancia*; and Kobyłeka-Piwońska, "Perturbar el orden de los sentidos."

6. Perkowska also highlights how these translations, especially to English, are often not the same as the Spanish originals but a rearrangement of other materials ("When Does Central American Literature Become Global," 91).

7. Ortiz Wallner says that "El recurso de la autoficción en la literatura de este autor—como una forma de escritura del yo—confunde, borra y trasciende los límites entre realidad y ficción en una puesta en escena lúdica en donde las figuras del autor, narrador y personaje (en este caso la duplicación del Eduardo Halfon extraliterario en el mundo intraliterario: Eduardo, señor Halfon, Eduardito o Dudú) son uno que nunca parece o puede ser el mismo." (The resource of autofiction in the literature of this author—like a form of writing of the self—confuses, erases, and transcends the limits between reality and fiction in a ludic staging in which the image of the author, narrator, and character [in this case the duplication of extraliterary Eduardo Halfon in the interliterary world: Eduardo, Mr. Halfon, Eduardito, or Dudú] are one that never seem or can to be the same) (Ortiz Wallner, "Una escritura," 36–37). For more on autofiction in Halfon's literature, see Barchino "Los cuentos de Eduardo Halfon," and Constales, "Postmemoria y autoficción." While I am not against the use of interviews to understand his work—this chapter cites some interviews—this practice has contributed to the excessive equivalence between Halfon's literary work and his life. Halfon, the author, openly despises the term: "el término autoficción me molesta, me parece nefasto. O, como mínimo, redundante. Toda literatura es autobiográfica. Toda. Emilio Renzi de Ricardo Piglia lo es de alguna manera. Y toda escritura es ficción." (The term autofiction bothers me, it seems appalling. Or at least redundant. All literature is autobiographical. All. Ricardo Piglia's Emilio Renzi it is in some way. And all writing is fiction) Larrea, "Eduardo Halfon."

8. Barchino argues that some stories "permiten una lectura más amplia a modo de retablo en la que se pueden detectar vasos comunicantes o marcas hipertextuales que pueden actuar bien como núcleos comunes bien como elementos secundarios que configuran una narración más compleja, aportando una nueva lectura más amplia a la colección" (allow for a broader reading as an altarpiece in which one can detect communicating vessels or hypertextual marks that can act as a common nuclei as well as secondary elements that configure a more complex narration, contributing a new wider reading to the collection) (Barchino, "Los cuentos de Eduardo Halfon," 5).

9. Stephanie Pridgeon suggests that Halfon's family displacement to the United States embodies the political condition of the exile of the Jewish people. She argues that the narrator's family is depicted as "not participating in the country's politics" (Pridgeon, "Silences" 102) and that the family is a sort of indirect victim of the political violence. She claims that the father's silence regarding the common ethnicity of guerrillas and soldiers is the result of his "ignorance [. . .] surrounding ethnic categories in Guatemala, since 'indio' is an imprecise term." (103). I strongly disagree with this reading because it is evident that the father is a supporter of the army and the government, and he is perfectly aware of the racial and ethnic differences in Guatemala. The father is a racist, despite descending from a historically oppressed ethnic group. Jeffrey Browitt phrases this problematic situation very well: "One is struck by the irony of a middle-class family with a background of racial-religious persecution (the Jewish grandfather), perpetuating the structural racism against Indigenous Guatemalans, the same Indigenous Guatemalans who populate the army that protects those selfsame middle-classes, the same Indigenous Guatemalans who lived that other genocide" (Browitt, *Contemporary Central American Fiction*, 88).

10. A good example of how the ambiguous veracity of the grandfather's story is ignored can be found in Gartenberg's "Inheriting Ghosts in Latin American Jewish Literature." After proposing an interesting interpretation of the story, the author cites a passage from "Discurso de Póvoa" without mentioning that the story refutes the powerful narration of the encounter between the grandfather and the boxer (133).

11. The father's shouts and mistreatments are present in almost every book. In *Saturno*, the narrator recalls, "El silencio sólo se rompía con sus gritos. ¿Recuerda usted esos gritos?" (The silence was only broken by your screams. Do you remember those screams?) (*Esto* 118). "Mi papá nos volvió a gritar algo con fuerza, su tono casi mitológico" (My father yelled something at us again with force. His tone almost mythological) remembers the narrator in "La señora del gabán rojo" (*Mañana* 73). The father's reaction to the news of his daughter's wedding follows the same pattern: "Mi papa agarró el teléfono, gritó un rato, intentó disuadirla otro rato" (My dad grabbed the phone, yelled for a while, he tried to dissuade her for another while) (*Monasterio* 14). Sometimes, the father's yelling is even silent: "él me gritó con sólo la mirada y entonces mejor me quedé callado" (He yelled at me only with his gaze, and so I remained silent), remembers the narrator in *Duelo* (49). The father's disregard for his son is also a constant element. In *Saturno*, the narrator cries, "yo debía hacerle una pregunta dos veces, por lo menos dos veces, antes de recibir una respuesta" (I had to ask a question twice. At least twice, before receiving an answer) (*Esto*, 112), an attitude we observe directly in memorable scenes like the father-son dialogue in "Mañana nunca lo hablamos" that I will analyze later in this chapter.

12. *Tarántula*, Halfon's latest novel, appeared in June 2024, when this book was already in the prepress process.

13. Saturn (Cronus in Greek mythology) is the mythic Roman god who ate his sons and daughters to prevent them from overthrowing him. When Ops, his wife, discovers that she is pregnant with Jupiter, she tricked Saturn and hid her son. When

Jupiter grows up, he confronts his father and forces him to vomit his other children, who then fight and defeat Saturn together.

14. "Your letters, father, arrived a couple of times per year. I was away in college, but you were even farther, from me. In the beginning, naively, I opened the envelope with suppressed emotion. And always, without fail, I found a piece of paper folded into three parts. One piece of paper with the letterhead of your company. Poorly folded, the hurry, I guess. Looking for your words, father, needing them, I unfolded it with a rush. And like a dry leaf hammocking in the breeze, slowly, the check fell to the ground. I left it there, almost forgotten, next to my feet, because what truly interested me, father, wasn't your money but your words. And in the middle of that piece of paper, written in black ink, I always found the same: your name. Only your name signed in a hurry. One word. Just one word. The father is a name." Halfon, *Esto*, 105.

15. "You considered it ridiculous that your son pretended to make a living by writing. You were ashamed of my vocation. You used to lie to your friends [. . .] This is my son, the engineer. Other times, I was a lawyer [. . .] I, father, produced pity in you. I humiliated you. Before your eyes, I was a failure and, therefore, as a father, you were also a failure." Halfon, *Esto*, 121–22. In "Garibaldi" (included in *Siete minutos de desasosiego*), we find the same theme, albeit less confrontational. This time, the son invites his father to see a bull run with the money he has earned as a writer to demonstrate to his father that he can make a living as such.

16. "all my writing was about you; everything I did there, father, was crying what I couldn't cry on your chest." Halfon, *Esto*, 128.

17. Lacan distinguishes the Symbolic, the Imaginary, and the Real father. The symbolic function is the one I am referring to here, particularly when Lacan claims that "It is in *the name of the father* that we must recognize the basis of the symbolic function which, since the dawn of historical time, has identified his person with the figure of the law" (Lacan, *Écrits*, 230).

18. "we couldn't have a seat without your consent. You imposed the order, pointing at everyone's place with your extended finger. You mandated. More than a father, you were a tyrant." Halfon, *Mañana*, 108.

19. "Only by mentioning that I didn't feel Jewish, you, leaning back, your sight always elsewhere, got furious. [. . .] When I was a child, you forced me to act Jewish, to follow the traditions. That's it, you used to tell me, that is the law. But the truth is that *you were the law, father. I lived under your Law*." Halfon, *Esto*, 126–27.

20. The mother is also victim of the father's authority. In "Mañana nunca lo hablamos," for example, the father reprimands the mother for telling the kids that they will only move to the United States "por un tiempito," and then she looks down and sighs (Halfon, *Mañana*, 121).

21. In Derrida's words, "law is always an authorized force, a force that justifies itself or is justified in applying itself, even if this justification may be judged from elsewhere to be unjust or unjustifiable" (Derrida, "Force of Law," 233).

22. "You did not even talk to me before leaving, father. [. . .] You died without saying good-bye, father." Halfon, *Esto*, 134.

23. "Eight days I acted in front of a Hebrew audience, I smiled for eight days, father, of disgust. But I never cried. Not even a tear. That's what you taught me." Halfon, 135.

24. Cabezas, *Postsoberanía*, 158.

25. "You abandoned me, father, not the day of your death but the day of my birth. You died when I was born. I entered the world an orphan, father." Halfon, *Esto*, 136.

26 "*Saturno* was the definitive death of engineer Eduardo Halfon, of firstborn Eduardo Halfan, of obedient son Eduardo Halfon, the one who spent all his life doing and studying what everyone told him. Suddenly I come up with this irreverent, risqué thing, in which *I kill my father*, when in reality, my father lives." Riehn, "La vidas ficcionales."

27. This is one of the very few books where the father is not mentioned directly. Another example is *Elocuencias de un tartamudo*, which is understandable because the book compiles other people's stories.

28. Halfon, *Duelo*, 24, 49.

29. Halfon, 69–70.

30. "And my dad told me that that was the last thing he knew about his brother. [. . .] He didn't know the cause of death, nor the year in which he died. He didn't even know, he told me, the name of the Jewish cemetery in New York in which he was buried. But at least he did know, he told me, thanks to that old photo that I was holding in my hands, thanks to that photograph of him in the snow, his brother's face." Halfon, 100.

31. Caruth, *Unclaimed Experience*, 4.

32. "He was breathing rapidly, like if he was running out of oxygen, or like making an effort not to cry profusely, or like it was forbidden for him to cry the death of a father." Halfon, *Canción*, 82.

33. "I had pronounced my first command as a father. And I understood, in a categorical or mystical way, that my son's penis, from that moment on, was no longer his." Halfon, *Un hijo cualquiera*, 14.

34. Perkowska "Infancia e historia," 605.

35. Durante and Havenne claim that *El boxeador polaco* is the central book in Halfon's works because it creates a true literary cycle ("La obra en 'matryoshka,'" 266). Fiorani offers a similar interpretation when he speaks of the "Polish question" as the "unavoidable" referent in Halfon's autofiction (*Habitar la distancia*, 119). Campisi argues that at the core of Halfon's oeuvre "lies his grandfather's experience at Auschwitz" ("Dislocation," 118). Ewa Kobyłecka-Piwońska posits that "la herencia de la Shoá cose con un hilo invisible casi toda su obra [Halfon's], cuyo punto central, una especie de signo-estrella alrededor de la cual gravitan otros signos, es el recuerdo del número tatuado en el brazo del abuelo" (The heritage of the Shoah sews with an invisible thread nearly all his [Halfon's] work, whose central point, a kind of star-sign which other signs gravitate around, it is the memory of the number tattooed on the grandfather's arms) ("Perturbar el orden de los sentidos," 369). It is evident that the story of the grandfather is a central piece in the literary universe created by Eduardo Halfon.

However, this story is somehow the rhinoceros in his fiction (to use the image I have previously discussed in chapter three). The powerful story of the Polish grandfather has taken attention away from other compelling elements within his fiction, such as the struggles with the father I discussed previously. What is more curious for me is the fact that many critics, perhaps under the moral position of never questioning the victim, have overlooked the possible lack of veracity of the story. This is the central point of my analysis.

36. "I had managed to bring reality to literature; I had managed, through literature, to penetrate reality." Halfon, *El boxeador*, 102.

37. I want to thank Magdalena Perkowska for bringing to my attention that there was a real person whose story resembles the Polish boxer in Halfon's story. His name was Tadeusz Pietrzykowski, and he was born in Warsaw, Poland, in 1917. He was a Polish Catholic boxer who participated in the resistance against the Germans. He was arrested in 1940 after the defeat of the Polish troops and sent to Auschwitz. At the extermination camp, he participated in dozens of boxing fights, which allowed him to survive for years. In 1943, he was transferred to Neuengamme, where he continued boxing until the camp was liberated in 1945. His story was told in the 1962 film *The Boxer and Death* directed by Peter Solan. In 2020, Polish director Maciej Barczewski released *Mistrz* (translated as *The Champion*), also based on his story. In 2021, Tadeusz Pietrzykowski's daughter, Eleonora Szafran, published her father's story in the book *Mistrz* (Jakubek, "'Champion of Auschwitz'").

38. Marchio, "(Pos)Memoria(s)," 34.

39. Accepting a story that has been previously debunked is becoming a trend in Halfon's fiction. The most recent example of this can be found in "El lago," included in *Un hijo cualquiera*. Toward the end of the story, the narrator returns to the drowning of his uncle Salomón, even though the true story of his death was discovered in *Duelo*, published five years earlier.

40. Halfon, *Monasterio*, 107.

41. Halfon, *Signor Hoffman*, 118.

42. Halfon, *Duelo*, 39.

43. "My grandpa sometimes said that he obtained the photo through one of his uncles who fled Poland before 1939. In other occasions, he said that he managed to keep it through the six years he spent in the camps." Halfon, 45–46.

44. "Sometimes he told us that he begged for it to the thieves until he kept the ring. Sometimes he told us that he wrestled with them until he kept his ring. Sometimes he told us that he fought against them to keep his ring. The version varied depending on the passing of time, or his nostalgia, or his mood." Halfon, *Signor*, 94.

45. Halfon, 94.

46. Halfon, *El boxeador*, 101. I disagree with Fiorani on this point, who argues that the strength of the grandfather's story lies in its verisimilitude and veracity (*Habitar la distancia*, 117).

47. "Literature is nothing more than a good trick [. . .] that makes reality seem whole, that creates an illusion that reality is one, or perhaps that literature needs to

construct a reality by destroying another one–something that, in a very intuitive way, my grandfather knew–namely, destroying itself and then constructing itself from its own rubble." Halfon, *El boxeador*, 102–3.

48. "And that we have that something within reach, right there, very close, on the tip of the tongue, and that we shouldn't forget it. *But always, without a doubt, we forget it*." Halfon, 104.

49. "it was not where we wrote our history, but to write it. To narrate it. To give testimony. To put our entire life into words. Even though we have to write it on loose papers or on stolen papers." Halfon, *Signor Hoffman*, 143.

50. Browitt, *Contemporary Central American Fiction*, 77.

51. Cyrulnik, *The Whispering of Ghosts*, 4.

52. Caruth, *Unclaimed Experience*, 11.

53. "It was the beginning of the eighties in Guatemala, and it wasn't strange that people disappeared. Violence had increased—especially in the capital—between the military government and the guerrilla groups. And I lived all that like an overprotected child." Halfon, *Mañana*, 106.

54. "I kept looking at the soldier's faces, as brown and as Indigenous as the face of the guerrilla with the guitar and the television. I didn't understand. Were the soldiers also Indigenous? Wasn't every Indigenous person a guerrilla? Then, who was a guerrilla?" Halfon, *Mañana*, 125.

55. Some critics have argued that the real trauma in the story is the experience of exile (Perdu). This reading is, in great part, supported by Halfon's nonfictional text "La memoria infantil," published in 2011 in *Cuadernos Hispanoamericanos*. In this piece, he claims, "El día después de mi décimo cumpleaños, entonces, salimos huyendo con mis papás y hermanos hacia Estados Unidos, y yo me partí en dos. Mi lenguaje se partió en dos. Mi memoria se partió en dos. Un pedazo de mi memoria, el primero, el más diáfano y liviano, se quedó suspendido en la Guatemala de los años setenta. Desde aquí, desde cada página en blanco, lo sigo buscando" (The day after my tenth birthday we fled with my parents and brothers to the United States, and I split in two. My language was split in two. My memory was split in two. A piece of my memory, the first, the clearest and lightest, stayed suspended in the Guatemala of the seventies. From here, from every blank page, I keep looking for it) (Halfon, "La memoria infantil," 27). This passage has been quoted multiple times in numerous academic articles. Nevertheless, it is important to make the (obvious) distinction between Halfon's literature and his personal experience. While it is evident that the author Eduardo Halfon experienced a loss when he left Guatemala, there are no indications of that in the story "Mañana nunca lo hablamos." When the narrator hears that the family will move, he sees it as an adventure without entirely understanding the implications of leaving the country. The day following the news of their departure, he even feels disappointed for not finding everything ready to leave.

56. "Se me ocurrió que su rostro se parecía al rostro del guerrillero de la guitarra y el televisor y que también se parecía al rostro de los soldados, y después se me ocurrió que su rostro de alguna manera se parecía a cualquier rostro, a mi rostro"

(It occurred to me that his face resembled the face of the guerrilla with the guitar and the television, that also resembled the faces of the soldiers, and then it occurred to me that his face in some manner resembled any face, my face) (Halfon, *Mañana*, 134), reflects the narrator.

57. "it took me a little to understand that he wanted me to stand up as well and to extend my hand, he wanted to say goodbye to me, not as student and teacher, not as adult and child, not as an *Indigenous and a White person*, but *like two men would do*." Halfon, *Mañana*, 134.

58. Browitt makes an important point regarding this, arguing that the narrator does not offer a "didactic" approach to his privileges and wealth. Instead, the narration uses clues and brief comments to mark the distance between his family and the majority of Guatemala ("La *performance*," 90).

59. —Daddy . . .

—¿Mmm?

—What is a guerrilla?

[. . .]

—A guerrilla?

—Yeah.

—Well, the guerrillas are to blame for all this mess.

—What mess?

—All this mess—he said firmly—the mess in front of the school, in the factory, in the streets, all over the damned country.

—The guerrillas are Indians?

[. . .]

—Of course—he told me—he looked toward the window.

—But, aren't the soldiers also Indians?

My father sighed, he appeared to be getting annoyed in the semi-darkness.

—Oh, my love, this is not the time to be talking about that.[. . .] You better go to sleep, and we'll talk about it tomorrow.

Halfon, *Mañana*, 137–38.

60. "Soon tomorrow came, and tomorrow we never talked about it." Halfon, 138.

61. Perkowska, "Infancia e historia," 608.

62. Halfon, "Better Not to Say Too Much."

63. "The military then placed the eighteen naked and bruised men in front of a mass grave and, with the rest of the town watching, with friends and family as the only audience, began to murder them. A single bullet to the head. One by one. The eighteen were falling into that black hole in the ground until it was filled with the arms and legs of men. But various were still alive, howling in the background, and then one of the soldiers jumped down and skewered their necks with his machete. The massacre had concluded. It was not yet noon." Halfon, *Canción*, 104–5.

64. "un periodista con saco y corbata comentó solemne—sin verme—que no había entendido qué sentido tenía relatar ahí, en un congreso de libaneses, la historia

de un ganadero guatemalteco y su rebaño de vacas" (A journalist with a jacket and tie commented solemnly—without seeing me—that he had not understood the point of telling there, in a conference of Lebanese people, the story of a Guatemalan rancher and his herd of cows) (Halfon, *Canción*, 116). It must be noted that the journalist is more concerned about the lack of relationship between Guatemala and Lebanon than the occurrence of the massacre itself.

65. Halfon is narrating "La masacre de la comunidad de Acul," Illustrative Case 107 in Comisión para el Esclarecimiento Histórico (Guatemala), *Guatemala, memoria del silencio*. This massacre was conducted by the army and the Patrullas de Autodefensa Civil (PAC) on April 22, 1982, thanks to the information provided by an Ixil person.

66. "No recuerdo si Beni había sido empleado de mi abuelo libanés, o si había sido empleado de mi papá, o si no había sido empleado de mi abuelo libanés ni de mi papá y ellos sólo lo contrataban puntualmente para ayudar con trámites y gestiones oficiales" (I don't remember whether Beni had been an employee of my Lebanese grandfather or if he had been an employee of my father, or if he had not been an employee neither of my Lebanese grandfather nor of my father and they only hired him occasionally to help with paperwork and official handlings) (Halfon, *Un hijo cualquiera*, 81).

67. "A baby of three months old was thrown alive into a dry well. It was noon. The fifty-eight Kaibiles then went to two churches and took out all the children and lined them up.[. . .] The older ones received a blow to the skull with a sledgehammer or a shot to the forehead, and then they were thrown into the well. It sufficed to hold the little ones by the feet and hit them against a wall or against the trunk of a tree and then throw them into the well. Girls and women, before falling dead or half dead in the well, were raped." Halfon, 92–93.

68. "I asked my father what those people were doing lying on the old mattress. [. . .] His answer came to me in a cold, cautious, well directed, and beautifully intoned whisper so that only I could perceive it: 'They are in mourning.'" Halfon, *Clases*, 30.

69. "That is how I heard the word mourning. That is how I came to know the word mourning. That is how I learned about the Jewish mourning. That's how it is the Jewish mourning. It makes you want to die a little." Halfon, 32.

70. "I was absolutely sure that, while they were praying three times, well hidden under one of those sheets, the ghost of the dead man hovered and shook, laughing." Halfon, 32.

71. Butler expresses the inequalities of the worth of life very well in their book *Precarious Life*, "A hierarchy of grief could no doubt be enumerated [. . .] since we seldom, if ever, hear the names of the thousands of Palestinians who have died by the Israeli military with United States support, or any number of Afghan people, children and adults.[. . .] To what extend have Arab peoples, predominantly practitioners of Islam, fallen outside the 'human' as it has been naturalized in its 'Western' mold by the contemporary workings of humanism?" (32). The equation of all forms of horrors is also important in the twenty-first century because a certain hierarchization exists

even among well-intended scholars. Peter Banki offers a compelling example of self-awareness of this in *The Forgiveness to Come*, where he reflects, "One would perhaps today have to ask forgiveness for speaking about the Shoah, when apparently so much has already been thought, said, and seen; and so little of other genocides" (100). In a very compelling reflection, Ben Kiernan sheds light on the "wall of silence" regarding the Guatemalan ethnocide within the so-called Genocide Studies, demonstrating that the systematic killing of the Indigenous population in Guatemala is barely mentioned by "genocide scholars" ("Wall of Silence").

Conclusion

1. "Traicionar la paz y dividir a Guatemala." http://www.plazapublica.com.gt/sites/default/files/traicionar_la_paz_y_divdir_a_guatemala_0.pdf. This ad was signed by Luis Flores Asturias, Eduardo Stein Barillas, Gustavo Porras Castejón, Raquel Zelaya Rosales, Richard Aitkenhead Castillo, Adrián Zapata, Arabella Castro de Paiz, Rodolfo Mendoza Rosales, Marta Altolaguirre, Marco Tulio Sosa, Mariano Ventura Zamora, and José Alejandro Arévalo Alburez.

2. "the accusation of genocide is a juridic fabrication that does not respond to the *victims' wishes to dignify their loved ones, finish the work of mourning, and make justice*."

3. Examples of the responses generated by this ad are Menchú Tum, "La verdad"; Balsells, "La verdadera"; Marroquín, "Por lo menos"; Comisión Internacional Contra la Impunidad en Guatemala (CICIG), "Un llamado."

4. Martínez and Gómez, *Las reparaciones*.

5. Hernández and Corresponsales, "Gobierno no aclara cierre de oficinas del PNR."

6. Diane M. Nelson elaborates extensively on the consequences of accepting financial reparations for some Maya communities. First of all, "it requires giving testimony to the state, attached to your name, ID number, address, and phone. [. . .] It also gets you into scary uncontrollable databases" (Nelson, *Who Counts?*, 110). Among other problems, since only part of the victims have received financial reparations, some of those who have received the money feel guilty for it. Nelson also points out how reparations could work as a form of clientelism to buy votes, and more traumatically, it could make women feel like prostitutes for accepting money for being raped (110–14).

7. Tobar Serrano, "Aportaciones," 4.

8. "El Salvador indemniza."

9. Tobar Serrano, "Aportaciones," 3–4.

10. Arteaga, "Resarciendo Daños"; Tobar Serrano, 3.

11. "Asamblea aprueba." For more details about the reparation programs in El Salvador and Guatemala, see Gutiérrez, "Negar el pasado."

12. Traverso, *Left-Wing Melancholia*, 10.

13. As of 2023 many communities in Guatemala still fight to get their land back. See O. Hernández, "Acul y Tzalbal."

14. Quoted in Alvarado Valenzuela, "Análisis."

15. Sprenkels, "La guera"; Martínez and Gómez, *Las reparaciones*; Orellana Calderón, "Discurso oficial"; Chacón Serrano et al., "Abusos."

16. Zoodsma and Schaafsma have established that over two hundred official apologies have been made around the world in the first two decades of the twenty-first century, supporting the notion of an "age of apology" ("Examining the 'Age of Apology,'" 441).

17. Banki, *The Forgiveness to Come*, 50.

18. Zoodsma and Schaafsma, "Examining the 'Age of Apology,'" 441. For a detailed analysis and a comparative perspective of official apologies in El Salvador and Guatemala, see Hatcher, *The Power of Memory*, 189–212.

19. Derrida, "To Forgive," 32.

20. Derrida, 33.

21. Derrida, *On Cosmopolitanism*, 32.

22. Nelson, *Who Counts?*; Suffern, *Finding Oscar*; Wilkinson, *Silence on the Mountain*; Yates, *500 Years*, *Granito*; Arias, "The Ghosts"; Knowlton, "Q'eqchi' Mayas"; and Casaús Arzú, "La recuperación."

23. I am referring specifically to literary production. Víctor Montejo, for example, published *Testimony: Death of a Guatemalan Village* (1987), a text in the tradition of testimonio. Another valuable testimonial book is *Memorias rebeldes contra el olvido: Paasantzila Txumb'al Ti' Sortzeb'al K'u'l* (2008), compiled by Rosalina Hernández Alarcón, Andrea Carrillo Samayoa, Jacqueline Torres Urízar, Ana López Molina, and Ligia Z. Peláez Aldana.

24. Arias, "From Indigenous Literatures."

25. Arias, "Indigenous Women" 135. Postwar Indigenous narratives have been studied by scholars such as Arias ("Indigenous Women at War," *Taking Their Word*) and Chacón (*Indigenous Cosmolectics*, "El nacimiento").

26. The tone of the documentary is established in the first interaction between former guerrillas and soldiers. Herald, a veteran of the BIRI Atlacatl Battalion, enters a room where a group of former guerrillas is waiting for him. When they see him, one of them asks, "Where are you going to put the bombs?" and everyone laugh. This group will traverse San Salvador remembering, commenting on, and laughing about some situations that took place during the offensive.

27. "That is the value that we must rescue for the new generations. If we, who fought in the war, *were capable of burying those dead*, burying that hatred that once we held against each other, and see each other as brothers now [*sic*]. [. . .] In the war, *there is only one brotherhood, the brotherhood of those who were in the trenches*. It doesn't matter which side you were on. Their suffering was the same as we had in our trenches. That's why we, the combatants, rapidly changed our attitude and have been able to meet again. On the other hand, those who didn't fight are the ones who keep us in that eternal confrontation."

28. For an in-depth analysis of *La llorona*, see Cabello del Moral, "Tomar la casa"; and Albizúrez Gil, "El film."

29. I would also include in this list Tatiana Huezo's *El lugar más pequeño* (2011) and César Díaz's *Nuestras madres* (2019).

30. Stein, "In Class Warfare."

31. The Central American democracies live in perpetual siege. The 2024 election in El Salvador has established the base for a single political party (Nuevas Ideas) to control the Salvadoran state. The present situation in Guatemala is no more promising. After winning the election in August 2023, elected president Bernardo Arévalo's party was suspended, and his inauguration was in jeopardy, literally, until the very last minute. Despite the above, even authoritarian regimes, like Bukele's, still try to sustain themselves "democratically," even if that means violating the constitution.

32. Over sixty-five thousand people were detained in the first year of Bukele's state of exception. Once a person is detained, the relatives are not informed, and therefore the detainees' loved ones are forced to visit multiple prisons in search of answers (like during the civil war). At least 153 people died while in custody of the state without being convicted for their alleged crimes during the first year of this plan. See "Informe de Cristosal"; "El Salvador: A un año del régimen de excepción"; Labrador and Martínez, "Un año de régimen"; Rubio, "Tengo a mi hijo libre"; and Wolf, "El Salvador's State of Exception."

33. Violence, death, and criminality in postwar Central America have been studied by Moodie, *El Salvador in the Aftermath*; Levenson, *Adiós Niño*; and McAllister and Nelson, *War by Other Means*.

34. Butler, *Precarious Life*, 21.

35. Derrida, "Marx and Sons," 249.

36. Derrida, *The Politics of Friendship*, 105.

37. Derrida, *Sovereignties in Question*, 160.

WORKS CITED

Abraham, Nicolas, and Maria Torok. *The Shell and the Kernel: Renewals of Psychoanalysis*. Vol. 1. Translated and edited by Nicholas T. Rand. Chicago: University of Chicago Press, 1994.

Abraham, Nicolas, and Maria Torok. *The Wolf Man's Magic Word: A Cryptonymy*. Translated by Nicholas T. Rand. Minneapolis: University of Minnesota Press, 2005.

Agamben, Giorgio. *Stanzas: Word and the Phantasm in Western Culture*. Translated by Ronald L. Martínez. Minneapolis: University of Minnesota Press, 1993.

Ahmed, Sara. *The Cultural Politics of Emotion*. Edinburgh: Edinburgh University Press, 2004.

Alarcón Medina, Rafael, and Leigh Binford. "Revisiting the El Mozote Massacre: Memory and Politics in Postwar El Salvador." *Journal of Genocide Research* 14, no. 4 (2014): 513–33.

Albizúrez Gil, Mónica. "Arquitecturas de control: Espacio y memoria en la cultura guatemalteca." *Cahiers d'études romanes* 28 (2014). https://doi.org/10.4000/etudesromanes.4398.

Albizúrez Gil, Mónica. "El film *La llorona* de Jayro Bustamante: Memoria cultural y género en la justicia transicional guatemalteca." *Cuadernos del CILHA* no. 34 (2021). http://ref.scielo.org/dydjwc.

Albizúrez Gil, Mónica. *Ita*. Guatemala City: F&G, 2018.

Allouch, Jean. *Érotique du deuil a temps de la mort sèche*. Paris: Editions et publications de l'Ecole lacanienne, 1995.

Alvarado, Félix. *Ensayos desde un estado perverso*. Guatemala City: Catafixia Editorial, 2022.

Alvarado, Jimmy. "$20 mil gastó gobierno de Funes en informe que recomienda continuar el culto a Domingo Monterrosa." *El Faro*, January 12, 2015. https://elfaro.net/es/201501/noticias/16323/$20-mil-gast%C3%B3-gobierno-de-Funes-en-informe-que-recomienda-continuar-el-culto-a-Domingo-Monterrosa.htm.

Alvarado Valenzuela, Ana Cristina. "Análisis de los discursos negacionistas del genocidio en Guatemala." *Contenciosa: Revista sobre violencia política, represiones y resistencias en la historia iberoamericana*, no. 12 (2022). http://portal.amelica.org/ameli/journal/607/6073558007/html/#fn14.

Alvarenga, Luis. "La generación comprometida de El Salvador: Problemas de una denominación." *Istmo: Revista virtual de estudios literarios y culturales centroamericanos*, no. 21 (2010). http://istmo.denison.edu/n21/articulos/11.html.

Álvarez Solís, Ángel Octavio. *La república de la melancolía: Política y subjetividad en el barroco*. Buenos Aires: La Cebra, 2015.

"Álvaro Arzú pide perdón a Guatemala." *El Tiempo*, December 30, 1998. https://www.eltiempo.com/archivo/documento/MAM-809656.

Amnesty International. *Guatemala: A Government Program of Political Murder*. Amnesty International Report. New York: Amnesty International Publications, 1981.

Aparicio, Yvette. *Post-Conflict Central American Literature: Searching for Home and Longing to Belong*. Lewisburg, Pa.: Bucknell University Press, 2014.

Appelbaum, David. *Jacques Derrida's Ghost. A Conjuration*. Albany: State University of New York Press, 2009.

Arauz, Sergio. "La frustrada condecoración de D'Aubuisson." *El Faro*, February 19, 2007. https://web.archive.org/web/20070610012426/http://www.elfaro.net/secciones/Observatorio/20070219/observatorio4_20070219.asp.

"Archivo Histórico de la Policía Nacional es declarado Patrimonio Cultural de la Nación." *Diario de Centroamérica*, October 16, 2020. https://dca.gob.gt/noticias-guatemala-diario-centro-america/archivo-historico-de-la-policia-nacional-es-declarado-patrimonio-cultural-de-la-nacion/.

Arévalo, Karla. "En El Mozote piden justicia y reparación, antes que un CUBO." *Elsalvador.com*, December 11, 2021. https://www.elsalvador.com/noticias/nacional/masacre-el-mozote-salvador-familiares-de-victimas-piden-justicia-y-reparacion-antes-que-un-cubo/908712/2021/.

Argentine Forensic Anthropology Team. *Annual Report 1992*. https://eaaf.org/wp-content/uploads/2018/08/elsalvador_ar_1992.pdf.

Arias, Arturo. "El pasado maya y el poder ladino. Raza, herencia colonial y política." In *Los futuros de la memoria en América Latina: Sujetos, políticas y epistemologías en disputa*, edited by M. J. Lazzara and F. A. Blanco, 209–30. Raleigh: A Contracorriente, Department of Foreign Languages and Literatures, North Carolina State University, 2022.

Arias, Arturo. "From Indigenous Literatures to Native American and Indigenous Theorist: The Making of a Grassroots Decoloniality." *Latin American Research Review* 53, no. 3 (2018). https://www.cambridge.org/core/journals/latin-american-research-review/article/from-indigenous-literatures-to-native-american-and-indigenous-theorists-the-makings-of-a-grassroots-decoloniality/CCC4AD9BF98C4E6D4AB39EBCE0E7EECA#article.

Arias, Arturo. "The Ghosts of the Past, Human Dignity, and the Collective Need for Reparation." *Latin American and Caribbean Ethnic Studies* 5, no. 2 (2010): 207–18.

Arias, Arturo. "Indigenous Women at War: Discourses on Revolutionary Combat." *A contracorriente* 10, no. 3 (2013): 108–40.

Arias, Arturo. "Post-identidades post-nacionales: Duelo, trauma y melancolía en la constitución de las subjetividades centroamericanas de posguerra." In *Hacia una historia de las literaturas Centroamericanas III: (Per)Versiones de la modernidad. Literaturas, identidades y desplazamientos*, edited by Beatriz Cortez, Alexandra Ortiz Wallner, and Verónica Ríos, 121–39. Guatemala City: F&G, 2012.

Arias, Arturo, ed. *The Rigoberta Menchú Controversy*. Minneapolis: University of Minnesota Press, 2001.

Arias, Arturo. *Taking Their Word: Literature and the Signs of Central America*. Minneapolis: University of Minnesota Press, 2007.

Arteaga, Leonor. "Resarciendo daños en El Salvador: La experiencia de reparaciones a víctimas de la guerra." *Justicia en las Américas*, April 15, 2021. https://dplfblog.com/2021/04/15/resarciendo-danos-en-el-salvador-la-experiencia-de-reparaciones-a-victimas-de-la-guerra/#_ftn24.

"Asamblea aprueba ley que permitirá a sobrevivientes de la masacre El Mozote recibir compensación económica." *Asamblea Legislativa*, June 28, 2022. https://www.asamblea.gob.sv/node/12256.

Asturias, Miguel Ángel. *La audiencia de los confines: Crónica en tres andanzas*. Buenos Aires: Ariadna, 1957.

Avelar, Idelber. *The Untimely Present: Postdictatorial Latin American Fiction and the Task of Mourning*. Durham, N.C.: Duke University Press, 1999.

Avelar, Idelber. *The Letter of Violence: Essays on Narrative, Ethics, and Politics*. New York: Palgrave Macmillan, 2004.

Balsells, Edgar. "La verdadera traición a la paz." *La Hora*, April 17, 2013, 13.

Banki, Peter. *The Forgiveness to Come: The Holocaust and the Hyper-Ethical*. New York: Fordham University Press, 2018.

Barchino, Matías. "Los cuentos de Eduardo Halfon: Hiperrelato y autoficción." *Lejana: Revista crítica de narrativa breve*, no. 6 (2013). http://ojs.elte.hu/index.php/lejana/article/view/63/56.

Barczewski, Maciej, dir. *Mistrz*. Warsaw: Iron Films, Polski Instytut Sztuki Filmowej, Telewizja Polska, 2020.

Barrera, Ezequiel. "Las luchadoras de El Mozote." *La prensa gráfica*, September 3, 2018. https://www.laprensagrafica.com/elsalvador/Las-luchadoras-de-El-Mozote-20180902-0069.html.

Barthes, Roland. *Camera Lucida: Reflections on Photography*. Translated by Richard Howards. New York: Hill and Wang, 1981.

Benítez, Jorge. "Nayib Bukele en su visita a El Mozote: La guerra fue una farsa, como los acuerdos de paz." *La prensa gráfica*, December 17, 2021. https://www.laprensagrafica.com/elsalvador/Nayib-Bukele-en-su-visita-a-El-Mozote-La-guerra-y-los-Acuerdos-de-Paz-fueron-una-farsa-20201217-0067.html.

Benjamin, Walter. "Critique of Violence." In *Reflection: Essays, Aphorisms, Autobiographical Writings*, edited by Peter Demetz, translated by Edmund Jephcott, 277–300. New York: Schocken Books, 1978.

Benjamin, Walter. "Theses on the Philosophy of History." In *Illuminations*, edited by Hannah Arendt, translated by Harry Zohn, 253–64. New York: Schocken Books, 1969.

Benjamin, Walter. *The Origin of German Tragic Drama*, translated by John Osborne. New York: Verso, 1998.

Bennett, Tony. *The Birth of the Museum: History, Theory, Politics*. London: Routledge, 1995.

Bentley, Andrew. "In and Out of Peripheral Network City: Urban Spaces Written by Violence in Postwar Guatemala." 2019. PhD diss., Michigan State University.

Bernardi, Claudia. "Whispers at *El Mozote*." *Peace Review: A Journal of Social Science* 22, no. 3 (2010): 250–52.

Beverly, John. "The Margin at the Center: On *Testimonio*." *Modern Fiction Studies* 35, no. 1 (1989): 11–28.

Beverly, John, and Marc Zimmerman. *Literature and Politics in the Central American Revolutions*. Austin: University of Texas Press, 1990.

Binford, Leigh. *The El Mozote Massacre: Anthropology and Human Rights*. Tucson: University of Arizona Press, 1996.

Binford, Leigh. *The El Mozote Massacre: Human Rights and Global Implications*. Rev. and enl. ed. Tucson: University of Arizona Press, 2016.

Bixler, Jacqueline Eyring. "Signs of Absence in Pavlovsky's 'teatro de la memoria.'" *Latin American Theatre Review* 28, no. 1 (1994): 17–30.

Boccia Paz, Alfredo, Myriam Angélica González, and Rosa Palau Aguilar. *Es mi informe: Los archivos secretos de la policía de Stroessner*. Asunción: Centro de documentación y estudios, 1994.

Boquín, E., and Espinoza C. "El Mozote: Lugareños inconformes por cambios de Bukele." *La prensa gráfica*, December 11, 2021. https://www.laprensagrafica.com/elsalvador/El--Mozote-lugarenos-inconformes-por-cambios-de-Bukele-20211210-0077.html.

Bosdriesz, Hanna, and Sander Wirken. "An Imperfect Success: The Guatemalan Genocide Trial and the Struggle Against Impunity for International Crimes." *International Criminal Law Review* 14 (2014): 1067–94.

Brito, Christopher. "Dozens of Christopher Columbus Statues Have Been Removed Since June." *CBS News*, September 25, 2020. https://www.cbsnews.com/news/christopher-columbus-statue-removed-cities/.

Browitt, Jeffrey. *Contemporary Central American Fiction: Gender, Subjectivity, and Affect*. Portland, Ore.: Sussex Academic Press, 2018.

Browitt, Jeffrey. *Cicatrices: Central American Fiction in the 21st Century*. Brighton: Sussex Academic Press, 2019.

Browitt, Jeffrey. "La *performance* de la memoria en *Mañana nunca lo hablamos* de Eduardo Halfon." *Istmo: Revista virtual de estudios literarios y culturales centroamericanos*, no. 38 (2019): 85–97. http://istmo.denison.edu/n38/dossier/06.pdf.

Brown, Miranda. *The Politics of Mourning in Early China*. Albany: State University of New York Press, 2007.

Buiza, Nanci. "On Aesthetic Experience and Trauma in Postwar Central America: The Case of Horacio Castellanos Moya's *El asco* and Claudia Hernández's *De fronteras*." *Hispanófila* 184 (2018): 99–115.

Buiza, Nanci. "Trastornando la jerarquía humano-animal: La alienación de la sociedad en la obra de Claudia Hernández." *Istmo: Revista virtual de estudios literarios y culturales centroamericanos*, no. 34 (2017). http://istmo.denison.edu/n34/articulos/07_buiza_nanci_form.pdf.

"Bukele ordena demoler Monumento a la Reconciliación." *ContraPunto*, June 5, 2020. https://www.contrapunto.com.sv/bukele-ordena-demoler-monumento-a-la-reconciliacion/.

Burgos-Debray, Elizabeth. *Me llamo Rigoberta Menchú y así me nació la conciencia*. Havana: Casa de las Américas, 1983.

Burt, Jo-Marie. "From Heaven to Hell in Ten Days: The Genocide Trial in Guatemala." *Journal of Genocide Research* 18, no. 2/3 (2016): 143–69.

Burt, Jo-Marie. "The Justice We Deserve: War Crimes Prosecutions in Guatemala." *Latin American Research Review* 56, no. 1 (2021): 214–32.

Burt, Jo-Marie, and Paolo Estrada. "Juez en Guatemala amenazado tras ordenar juicio por caso 'Diario Militar' de años 80." *WOLA*, May 24, 2022, https://www.wola.org/es/analisis/juez-en-guatemala-amenazado-tras-ordenar-juicio-por-caso-diario-militar-de-anos-80/.

Bustamante, Jayro. *La llorona*. Guatemala City: La Casa de Producción, Les Films du Volcan, 2019.

Butler, Judith. *Frames of War: When is Life Grievable?* London: Verso, 2009.

Butler, Judith. *Precarious Life: The Powers of Mourning and Violence*. London: Verso, 2006.

Butler, Judith. *The Psychic Life of Power: Theories in Subjection*. Stanford, Calif.: Stanford University Press, 1997.

Caamaño Morúa, Virginia. "Parodia, simulación y canibalismo en 'Hechos de un buen ciudadano I' y 'Hechos de un buen ciudadano II' de Claudia Hernández." *Revista de filología y lingüística de la Universidad de Costa Rica* 42 (2016): 339–56.

Cabello del Moral, Pedro. "Tomar la casa: *Politics of haunting*, contra-archivo y resitencia indígena en *La llorona*, de Jayro Bustamante." *Revista ístmica*, no. 30 (2022): 65–89.

Cabezas, Óscar. *Postsoberanía: Literatura, política y trabajo*. Buenos Aires: La Cebra, 2013.

"CACIF pide anular fallo por genocidio contra Ríos Montt." *Prensa Libre*, May 12, 2013. https://www.prensalibre.com/guatemala/cacif-pide-anulacion-fallo-rios_mont_0_917908328-html/.

Cagan, Steve. "Salvadoran Refugees in the Camp at Colomoncagua, Honduras, 1980–1991." *ReVista: Harvard Review of Latin America* 15, no. 3 (2016): 54–59.

Cal Montoya, José Edgardo. "La historia y su uso público: Reflexiones desde Guatemala." *Bajo el volcán: Revista de posgrado de sociología*, no. 13 (2007): 161–73.

Camelo Gómez, Michael Steven, and Myriam Jiménez Quenguan. "Teatro para la memoria: Danzantes de pensamientos." *Revista Educación* 45, no. 1 (2021): https://doi.org/10.15517/revedu.v45i1.42261.

Campisi, Nicolás. "The Dislocation of Cosmopolitan Identities in Eduardo Halfon's *Monasterio*." *INTI: Revista de literatura hispánica y transatlántica*, no. 87/88 (2018): 113–24.

Cann, Candi. *Virtual Afterlives: Grieving the Dead in the Twenty-First Century*. Lexington: University Press of Kentucky, 2014.

Cantrell, Tania H. "Killing US Softly with Their Story: *New York Times* Coverage of the My Lai and El Mozote Military Massacres." *Global Media Journal* 6, no. 10 (2007). https://www.globalmediajournal.com/open-access/killing-us-softly-with-their-storynew-york-times-coverage-of-the-my-lai-and-el-mozote-military-massacres.php?aid=35185.

Capps, Kriston. "Why There Are Still 149 Statues of Christopher Columbus in the U.S.?" *Bloomberg*, October 9, 2021. https://www.bloomberg.com/news/articles/2021-10-09/how-many-statues-of-christopher-columbus-are-left.

Cárdenas, Maritza E. *Constituting Central American-Americans: Transnational Identities and the Politics of Dislocation*. New Brunswick, N.J.: Rutgers University Press, 2018.

Caruth, Cathy. *Unclaimed Experience: Trauma, Narrative, and History*. Baltimore: Johns Hopkins University Press, 1996.

Casaús Arzú, Marta Elena. "El juicio por genocidio contra el pueblo Maya Ixil: Del acuerdo a la recuperación de la memoria colectiva de los pueblos indígenas a raíz del conflicto armado en Guatemala (1979–2013)." *alter/nativas*, no. 5 (2015). https://alternativas.osu.edu/assets/files/Issue5/essays/casaus.pdf.

Casaús Arzú, Marta Elena. "La recuperación de la memoria histórica del pueblo Maya Ixil a raíz del juicio por genocidio contra el gral., Efraín Ríos Montt durante el conflicto armado en Guatemala, 1979–2013." In *El pensamiento y la lucha: Los pueblos indígenas en América Latina organización y discusiones con trascendencia*, edited by Pedro Canales Tapia, 17–40. Santiago: Ariadna, 2018.

Casaús Arzú, Marta Elena. "Museo nacional y museos privados en Guatemala: Patrimonio y patrimonialización; Un siglo de intentos y frustraciones." *Revista de Indias* 72, no. 254 (2012): 93–130.

Caso, Nicole. *Practicing Memory in Central American Literature*. New York: Palgrave Macmillan, 2010.

Castel, Harry. *Santa María de la espera*. San Salvador: Índole Editores, 2013.

Cerritos, Jorgelina. "Así iniciaron los ensayos sobre la memoria de Jorgelina Cerritos (Entrevista de 2014)." Interview by Miriam García. *Vanguardia El Salvador*, April 10, 2018. https://vanguardiasv.net/asi-iniciaron-los-ensayos-sobre-la-memoria-de-jorgelina-cerritos/2018/.

Cerritos, Jorgelina. *Bandada de pájaros. Segundo ensayo sobre la memoria*. San Salvador: Índole Editores, 2016.

Cerritos, Jorgelina. *La Audiencia de los confines. Primer ensayo sobre la memoria*. San Salvador: Índole Editores, 2014.

Cerritos, Jorgelina. *13703. El misterio de las utopías. Tercer ensayo sobre la memoria.* San Salvador: Índole Editores, 2017.

Chacón, Gloria. "El nacimiento de la novela indígena y el rechazo a la integración eurocéntrica." *Revista de crítica literaria latinoamericana,* no. 91 (2020): 39–58.

Chacón, Gloria. *Indigenous Cosmolectics: Kab'awil and the Making of Maya and Zapotec Literatures.* Chapel Hill: University of North Carolina Press, 2018.

Chacón Serrano, Fernando, Cristián Fabián, Jacqueline Escobar, Daniela Marroquín, Andrea Aparicio, and Flavio Menjívar. "Abusos de la memoria por el Gobierno salvadoreño y las prácticas de resistencia desde las nuevas generaciones." *Revista de Estudios Psicosociales Latinoamericanos* 4 (2021): 97–115.

Chaves Alfaro, Iris. *Los sujetos culturales en la nueva novela histórica de Centroamérica: Ficción, historia, identidad y escritura.* San José: Editorial Universidad Nacional, 2021.

Ching, Erik. *Stories of Civil War in El Salvador: A Battle over Memory.* Chapel Hill: University of North Carolina Press, 2016.

Cholbi, Michael. *Grief: A Philosophical Guide.* Princeton, N.J.: Princeton University Press, 2021.

Cole, Susan Letzler. *The Absent One: Mourning Ritual, Tragedy, and the Performance of Ambivalence.* University Park: Pennsylvania State University Press, 1985.

Comisión Internacional contra la Impunidad en Guatemala (CICIG). "Un llamado a la mesura." CICIG, April 18, 2013. https://www.cicig.org/history//index.php?mact=News,cntnt01,detail,0&cntnt01articleid=360&cntnt01returnid=67.

Comisión para el Esclarecimiento Histórico (Guatemala). *Guatemala, memoria del silencio.* Guatemala: Oficina de Servicios para Proyectos de las Naciones Unidas, 1999.

Confino, Alon. "Collective Memory and Cultural History: Problems of Method." *American Historical Review* 102, no. 5 (1997): 1386–1403.

Confino, Alon. *Foundational Pasts: The Holocaust as Historical Understanding.* Cambridge: Cambridge University Press, 2012.

Connerton, Paul. *How Societies Remember.* Cambridge: Cambridge University Press, 1989.

Connerton, Paul. *The Spirit of Mourning: History, Memory and the Body.* Cambridge: Cambridge University Press, 2012.

Constales, Sofie. "Posmemoria y autoficción en *Mañana nunca lo hablamos* de Eduardo Halfon y *Dios tenía miedo* de Vanessa Núñez Handal." Thesis, Universiteit Geint, 2015.

Córdova, Alejandro. *Hippies de barranco: Legado de Roberto Salomón al teatro salvadoreño.* San Salvador: Índole Editores, 2016.

Corte Interamericana de Derechos Humanos. "Caso Masacres de El Mozote y lugares aledaños vs. El Salvador." October 25, 2012. https://corteidh.or.cr/docs/casos/articulos/seriec_252_esp.pdf.

Cortez, Beatriz. *Estética del cinismo: Pasión y desencanto en la literatura centroamericana de posguerra.* Guatemala City: F&G, 2010.

Cortez, Beatriz. "Memorias del desencanto: El duelo postergado y la pérdida de la subjetividad heróica." In *Hacia una historia de las literaturas Centroamericanas III: (Per)Versiones de la modernidad. Literaturas, identidades y desplazamientos*, edited by Beatriz Cortez, Alexandra Ortiz Wallner, and Verónica Ríos, 259–80. Guatemala City: F&G, 2012.

Couser, G. Thomas, *Recovering Bodies: Illness, Disability, and Life Writing*. Madison: University of Wisconsin Press, 1997.

Couser, G. Thomas. "Autopathography: Women, Illness, and Life Writing." In *Women and Autobiography*, edited by Martine Watson Brownley and Allison B. Kimmich, 164–73. Wilmington, Del.: SR Books, 1999.

Cox, Karen L. *No Common Ground: Confederate Monuments and the Ongoing Fight for Racial Justice*. Chapel Hill: University of North Carolina Press, 2021.

Craft, Linda. *Novels of Testimony and Resistance from Central America*. Gainesville: University Press of Florida, 1997.

Cruz, Ana. "Museo de la Memoria contra la Impunidad cierra sus puertas tras más de dos meses de exhibición." *La prensa*, December 6, 2019. https://www.laprensa.com.ni/2019/12/06/nacionales/2618637-museo-de-la-memoria-contra-la-impunidad-cierra-sus-puertas-tras-mas-de-dos-meses-de-exhibicion.

Cuenin, Xavier. "La conmemoración del centenario del nacimiento de Morazán y las ambigüedades de la construcción nacional en Guatemala." *Anales de la Academia de Geografía e Historia de Guatemala* 87 (2012): 69–81.

Cuevas Molina, Rafael. *300*. San José: Editorial Universidad Nacional, 2011.

Cyrulnik, Boris. *The Whispering of Ghosts*. Translated by Susan Fairfield. New York: Other Press, 2003.

Danner, Mark. *The Massacre at El Mozote: A Parable of the Cold War*. New York: Vintage Book, 1994.

Da Silva Catela, Ludmila. *No habrá flores en la tumba del pasado: La experiencia de reconstrucción del mundo de los familiares de desaparecidos*. La Plata: Ediciones al margen, 2014.

"D'Aubuisson: No Street Will Carry Your Name!" *El Salvador Perspectives*, November 30, 2014. https://www.elsalvadorperspectives.com/2014/11/daubuisson-no-street-will-carry-your.html.

Dada, Carlos. "How We Killed Archbishop Romero." *El Faro*, March 25, 2010. https://elfaro.net/es/201003/noticias/1416/How-we-killed-Archbishop-Romero.htm.

"Declaran crimen de lesa humanidad la masacre de El Mozote." *La prensa gráfica*, December 15, 2018. https://www.laprensagrafica.com/elsalvador/Declaran-crimen-de-lesa-humanidad-la-masacre-El-Mozote-20181215-0216.html.

"Decreto No. 53." *Diario oficial*, September 2, 2016, 4–10.

"Decreto No. 65." *Diario oficial*, July 16, 1993, 22–23.

de la Puente, Maximiliano Ignacio. "Memorias performativas en el teatro político contemporáneo." *AURA: Revista de historia y teoría del arte* 3 (2015): 84–102.

Délano Alonso, Alexandra, and Benjamin Nienass. "Deaths, Visibility, and Responsibility: The Politics of Mourning at the US-Mexico Border." *Social Research: An International Quarterly* 83, no. 2 (2016): 421–51.

Del silencio a la memoria: Revelaciones del Archivo Histórico de la Policía Nacional. Guatemala City: Archivo Histórico de la Policía Nacional, 2011.

DeLugan, Robin Maria. *Reimagining National Belonging: Post-Civil War El Salvador in a Global Context.* Tucson: University of Arizona Press, 2012.

Déotte, Jean-Louis. *Catástrofe y olvido: Las ruinas, Europa, el Museo.* Translated by Justo Pastor Mellado. Santiago: Cuarto Propio, 1998.

Derrida, Jacques. "Archive Fever: A Freudian Impression." *Diacritics* 25, no. 2 (1995): 9–63.

Derrida, Jacques. *Cinders.* Translated by Ned Lukacher. Minneapolis: University of Minnesota Press, 2014.

Derrida, Jacques. "Force of Law." In *Acts of Religion,* edited by Gil Anidjar, 228–98. New York: Routledge, 2002.

Derrida, Jacques. "Freud and the Scene of Writing." In *Writing and Difference,* translated by Alan Bass, 196–231. Chicago: University of Chicago Press, 1978.

Derrida, Jacques. *The Gift of Death.* Translated by David Wills. Chicago: University of Chicago Press, 1995.

Derrida, Jacques. "Marx and Sons." In *Ghostly Demarcations: A Symposium on Jacques Derrida's* Specters of Marx, edited by Michael Sprinker, 213–69. 1999. Reprint, New York: Verso, 2008.

Derrida, Jacques. *Of Grammatology (Corrected Edition).* Translated by Gayatri Chakravorty Spivak. Baltimore: John Hopkins University Press, 1997.

Derrida, Jacques. *Of Hospitality: Anne Dufourmantelle Invites Jacques Derrida to Respond.* Translated by Rachel Bowlby. Stanford, Calif.: Stanford University Press, 2000.

Derrida, Jacques. *On Cosmopolitanism and Forgiveness.* Translated by Mark Dooley and Michael Hughes. London: Routledge, 2001.

Derrida, Jacques. *Points . . . : Interviews, 1974–1994.* Translated by Peggy Kamuf et al., edited by Elisabeth Weber. Stanford, Calif.: Stanford University Press, 1995.

Derrida, Jacques. *The Politics of Friendship.* Translated by George Collins. London: Verso, 2004.

Derrida, Jacques. *Sovereignties in Question: The Poetics of Paul Celan.* Edited by Thomas Dutoit and Outi Pasanen. New York: Fordham University Press, 2005.

Derrida, Jacques. *Specters of Marx: The State of the Debt, the Work of Mourning and the New International.* Translated by Peggy Kamuf. New York: Routledge, 2006.

Derrida, Jacques. "To Forgive: The Unforgivable and the Imprescriptible." In *Questioning God,* edited by John D. Caputo, Mark Dooley, and Michael J. Scanlon, 21–51. Bloomington: Indiana University Press, 2001.

Derrida, Jacques. *The Work of Mourning.* Edited by Pascale-Anne Brault and Michael Naas. Chicago: University of Chicago Press, 2001.

Derrida, Jacques, and Bernard Stiegler. *Echographies of Television: Filmed Interviews.* Translated by Jennifer Bajorek. Cambridge: Polity, 2002.

“Desde ‘Mater Civis’ hasta la ‘Michi,’ el monumento a la reconciliación que genera discordia.” *El Salvador Times*, January 2017. https://www.elsalvadortimes.com/articulo/sucesos/controversia-genera-monumento-reconciliacion-redes-sociales-apodan-muy-malas-maneras/20170114171154014981.html.

Díaz, César. *Nuestras madres*. Guatemala City: Need Productions, Perspective Films, Proximus, 2019.

Doss, Erika. *The Emotional Life of Contemporary Public Memorials: Towards a Theory of Temporary Memorials*. Amsterdam: Amsterdam University Press, 2008.

Doyle, Kate. “The Guatemalan Police Archives.” National Security Archive, National Security Archive Electronic Briefing Book no. 170. https://nsarchive2.gwu.edu//NSAEBB/NSAEBB170/index.htm.

Durante, Erica, and Maude Havenne. “La obra en ‘matryoshka’ de Eduardo Halfon: un proyecto literario global.” *Revista Iberoamericana* 37, no. 274 (2021): 265–87.

“El Libro Amarillo” [The yellow book]. Unfinished Sentences, September 28, 2014. https://unfinishedsentences.org/es/reports/yellow-book/.

“El Salvador: A un año del régimen de excepción, las autoridades cometen violaciones de derechos humanos de forma sistemática.” Amnistía Internacional, April 3 2023. https://www.es.amnesty.org/en-que-estamos/noticias/noticia/articulo/el-salvador-a-un-ano-del-regimen-de-excepcion-las-autoridades-cometen-violaciones-derechos-humanos-de-forma-sistematica/.

“El Salvador General Admits Army Carried Out El Mozote Massacre.” *Aljazeera*, January 25, 2020. https://www.aljazeera.com/news/2020/01/el-salvador-general-admits-army-carried-el-mozote-massacre-200125155053149.html.

“El Salvador indemniza a víctimas del conflicto armado.” TeleSur, August 31, 2016, https://www.telesurtv.net/news/El-Salvador-indemniza-a-victimas-del-conflicto-armado--20160831-0052.html.

“El silencio del gobierno opaca el 28 aniversario de fin de la guerra en El Salvador.” *Agencia EFE*, January 16, 2020. https://es-us.noticias.yahoo.com/persisten-deudas-v%C3%ADctimas-salvador-28-155045561.html.

Eng, David L., and David Kazanjian. “Introduction: Mourning Remains.” In *Loss: The Politics of Mourning*, edited by David L. Eng and David Kazanjian, 1–25. Berkeley: University of California Press, 2002.

“Entrevista: Reconocimiento a un artista salvadoreño. Rubén Martínez.” Posted on YouTube by Audiovisuales UCA, November 7, 2019. https://www.youtube.com/watch?v=INZT6MxsuR8.

Escamilla, José Luis. *El protagonista en la novela de posguerra centroamericana: Desterritorializado, híbrido y fragmentado*. San Salvador: Editorial Universidad Don Bosco, 2012.

Esch, Sophie. “In the Company of Animals: Otherness, Empathy, and Community in *De fronteras* by Claudia Hernández.” *Revista de Estudios Hispánicos* 51, no. 3 (2017): 571–93.

Esch, Sophie. *Modernity at Gunpoint: Firearms, Politics, and Culture in Mexico and Central America*. Pittsburgh: University of Pittsburgh Press, 2018.

Esch, Sophie, and Ignacio Sarmiento. "World Literature in a Minor Key: The Central American Shorty Story." In *Central American Literature as World Literature*, edited by Sophie Esch, 39–62. New York: Bloomsbury, 2023.

Espacios de la memoria en la Argentina. Buenos Aires: Ministerio de Justicia y Derechos Humanos de la Nación, 2015.

Esposito, Roberto. *Terms of the Political: Community, Immunity, Biopolitics*. Translated by Rhiannon Noel Welch. New York: Fordham University Press, 2013.

"Estatua del mayor Roberto d'Aubuisson está en posesión de la FGR." *Diario digital contrapunto*, April 25, 2022. https://www.contrapunto.com.sv/estatua-del-mayor-daubuisson-esta-en-posesion-de-la-fgr/.

Falla, Raúl. "En Guatemala, ¡No hubo genocidio!" *El Siglo*, May 28, 2018. https://elsiglo.com.gt/2018/05/28/en-guatemala-no-hubo-genocidio/.

Falla, Ricardo. *Massacres in the Jungle: Ixcán, Guatemala, 1975–1982*. Boulder, Colo.: Westview Press, 1994.

"Familiares de víctimas desaparecidas durante conflicto armado no pudieron enflorar en Monumento a la Memoria y la Verdad." *La prensa gráfica*, November 4, 2018. https://www.laprensagrafica.com/elsalvador/Familiares-de-victimas-desaparecidas-durante-conflicto-armado-no-pudieron-enflorar-en-Monumento-a-la-Memoria-y-la-Verdad-20181104-0024.html.

Fenton, Ioulia. *Changing Chicken in Guatemala: Relevance of Poultry to Income Generation, Food, Security, Health, and Nutrition*. N.p.: Tiny Beam Fund, 2020. https://www.issuelab.org/resources/36569/36569.pdf.

Ferber, Illit. *Philosophy and Melancholy: Benjamin's Early Reflections on Theater and Language*. Stanford, Calif.: Stanford University Press, 2013.

Fiorani, Flavio. *Habitar la distancia: Ficciones latinoamericanas sobre el judaísmo*. Rome: Nova Delphi, 2022.

Flores, Jenny. "Un monumento a las víctimas de la guerra." *Elsalvador.com*, December 7, 2003. Accessed May 28, 2020 (no longer posted). https://archivo.elsalvador.com/noticias/2003/12/07/nacional/nacio8.html.

Foucault, Michel. *The Archaeology of Knowledge and the Discourse on Language*. Translated by A. M. Sheridan Smith. New York: Pantheon Books, 1972.

Foucault, Michel. *Foucault Live (Interviews, 1961–1984)*. Edited by Silvère Lotringer. Translated by Lysa Hochroth and John Johnston. New York: Semiotext(e), 1996.

Fox, James. "Poppy Politics: Remembrance of Things Past." In *Cultural Heritage Ethics: Between Theory and Practice*, edited by Constantine Sandis, 21–30. Cambridge: Open Books, 2014.

"Fragmento del discurso de Funes pidiendo perdón por masacre en el Mozote." Posted to YouTube by El Faro, 28 October 2013. https://www.youtube.com/watch?v=uoIwALUNa1E&t=20s.

Freud, Sigmund. *The Ego and the Id*. Translated by Joan Riviere. London: Leonard and Virginia Woolf at the Hogarth Press and the Institute of Psycho-Analysis, 1927.

Freud, Sigmund. "Mourning and Melancholia." In *The Standard Edition of the Complete Psychological Works of Sigmund Freud*, vol. 14, translated by James Strachey, 243–58. London: Hogarth Press, 1957.

Freud, Sigmund. "On Transience." In *The Standard Edition of the Complete Psychological Works of Sigmund Freud*, vol. 14, translated by James Strachey, 305–7. London: Hogarth Press, 1957.

Freud, Sigmund. *Totem and Taboo: Some Points of Agreement Between the Mental Lives of Savages and Neurotics*. Translated and edited by James Strachey. New York: W. W. Norton, 1990.

Funes, Jonatan. "Este espacio no era visitado por nadie: Monumento a la reconciliación nacional es destruido." *Elsalvador.com*, January 3, 2024. https://www.elsalvador.com/fotogalerias/noticias-fotogalerias/monumentos-ministerio-de-obras-publicas-transparencia/1114292/2024/.

Gairaud Ruiz, Hilda. "Rutas de muerte en la narrativa de Claudia Hernández." *Revista de lenguas modernas*, no. 22 (2015): 203–15.

Galindo, Evelyn. "Santa María de la espera: El teatro de la memoria." *Meridiano 89 Oeste 89th Meridian West: El Blog de Evelyn Galindo*, January 20, 2015. http://postwarelsalvador.blogspot.com/2015/01/santa-maria-de-la-espera-el-teatro-de.html.

Galindo, Regina José. "La verdad." Posted on YouTube by Bea Gallardo, December 6, 2013. https://www.youtube.com/watch?v=aNMjcPVgXZM&t=2202s&ab_channel=BeaGallardo.

García, Claudia. "Sin orquídeas ni agua: Colapso ecológico, espacio privado y democracia en Centroamérica." *Lejana: Revista crítica de narrativa breve*, no. 6 (2013). https://edit.elte.hu/xmlui/bitstream/10831/33580/1/69-249-2-PB_.pdf.

Garrard-Burnett, Virginia. *Terror in the Land of the Holy Spirit: Guatemala Under General Efraín Ríos Montt, 1982–1983*. Oxford: Oxford University Press, 2011.

Gartenberg, Charlotte. "Inheriting Ghosts in Latin American Jewish Literature: Forging Stories and Selves out of Deathly Pasts in Sergio Chejfec and Eduardo Halfon." *Shofar: An Interdisciplinary Journal of Jewish Studies* 40, no. 1 (2021): 120–39.

Genaro, Javier, and Gato, comp. *Dos pueblos a los que amar, un mundo por el que luchar*. Grupo promotor de la memoria histórica de las y los internacionalistas. https://trabajadoresyrevolucion.files.wordpress.com/2013/10/urria-2013.pdf.

Getso, Robert. "Revisiting Holocaust Memorialization." *Peace Review: A Journal of Social Justice* 19, no. 2 (2007): 247–53.

"Gesto por la masacre de El Mozote en El Salvador." Posted to YouTube by DW Español, December 10, 2018. https://www.youtube.com/watch?v=gaMjYUEbKnE.

"Gobierno salvadoreño estrena documental 'El Mozote nunca Más.'" *El urbano*, December 9, 2017. https://elurbano.news/hemeroteca/gobierno-salvadoreno-estrena-documental-el-mozote-nunca-mas/.

González Díaz, Marcos. "El Mozote—'Al volver a enterrarlos, es como si volvieran a morir': la devolución de los restos de las víctimas de la mayor masacre del siglo

XX en América Latina." *BBC News Mundo*, December 19, 2022. https://www.bbc.com/mundo/noticias-america-latina-64009897.

González Betancur, Juan David. "Antígona y el teatro latinoamericano." *Calle 14* 4, no. 4 (2010): 72–85.

Grinberg Pla, Valeria. "Oralidad, imagen, acción: Intervenciones del cine documental en las batallas por la memoria del genocidio indígena en Guatemala." In *Guatemala nunca más-Niemals wieder: Desde el trauma de la guerra civil hacia la integración étnica, la democracia y la justica social*, edited by Roland Spiller, Werner Mackenbach, Elisabeth Rohr, Thomas Schreijäck, and Gerhard Strecker, 243–65. Guatemala City: F&G, 2015.

Guardado, Clara. "*El Mozote nunca más*: Debate sobre la contribución de los hallazgos forenses y el acceso a la justicia en El Salvador posconflicto." *Revista Realidad*, no. 153 (2019): 163–92.

"Guatemala pidió perdón por vieja masacre." *Univisión*, July 18, 2005. https://www.univision.com/noticias/noticias-de-latinoamerica/guatemala-pidio-perdon-por-vieja-masacre.

Gugelberger, Georg M. "Introduction: Institutionalization of Transgression; Testimonial Discourses and Beyond." In *The Real Thing: Testimonial Discourse and Latin America*, edited by Georg M. Gugelberger, 1–19. Durham, N.C.: Duke University Press, 1996.

Gutiérrez, Martha. "Negar el pasado: Reparaciones en Guatemala y El Salvador." *Colombia Internacional*, no. 97 (2019), 175–209.

Guzmán Orellana, Gloria, and Irantzu Mendia Azkue. *Mujeres con memoria: Activistas del movimiento de derechos humanos en El Salvador*. Bilbao: Universidad del País Vasco, Instituto de estudios sobre desarrollo y cooperación internacional, 2013.

Guzmán Orellana, Gloria, and Irantzu Mendia Azkue. "Tejiendo la memoria desde abajo: El Monumento a la Verdad y la Memoria de El Salvador." *Decisio*, no. 43/44 (2016): 51–56.

"Hace 27 años murió Roberto d'Aubuisson, fundador del partido ARENA." *Elsalvador.com*, February 20, 2019. https://historico.elsalvador.com/historico/569619/hace-27-anos-murio-roberto-daubuisson-fundador-del-partido-arena.html.

Halbwachs, Maurice. *On Collective Memory*. Translated by Lewis A. Coser. Chicago: University of Chicago Press, 1992.

Halfon, Eduardo. "Better Not to Say Too Much: Eduardo Halfon on Literature, Paranoia and Leaving Guatemala." *The Guardian*, November 4, 2015. https://www.theguardian.com/books/the-writing-life-around-the-world-by-electric-literature/2015/nov/04/better-not-say-too-much-eduardo-halfon-on-literature-paranoia-and-leaving-guatemala.

Halfon, Eduardo. *Biblioteca bizarra*. Zaragoza: Jekyll & Jill, 2018.

Halfon, Eduardo. *Canción*. Barcelona: Libros del Asteroide, 2021.

Halfon, Eduardo. *Clases de hebreo*. Logroño: AMG, 2008.

Halfon, Eduardo. *Duelo*. Barcelona: Libros del Asteroide, 2017.

Halfon, Eduardo. *El boxeador polaco*. Valencia: Pre-Textos, 2008.

Halfon, Eduardo. *Elocuencias de un tartamudo*. Valencia: Pre-Textos, 2012.

Halfon, Eduardo. *Esto no es una pipa, Saturno*. Guatemala City: Alfagura, 2003.

Halfon, Eduardo. "La memoria infantil." *Cuadernos Hispanoamericanos*, no. 731 (2011): 21–30.

Halfon, Eduardo. "Los ocasos." *Letras Libres*, February 28, 2011. https://letraslibres.com/revista-espana/los-ocasos/.

Halfon, Eduardo. *Mañana nunca lo hablamos*. Valencia: Pre-Textos, 2011.

Halfon, Eduardo. *Oh gueto mi amor*. Madrid: Páginas de espuma, 2018.

Halfon, Eduardo. *Siete minutos de desasosiego*. Bogotá: Panamericana, 2007.

Halfon, Eduardo. *Signor Hoffman*. Barcelona: Libros del Asteroide, 2015.

Halfon, Eduardo. *Un hijo cualquiera*. Barcelona: Libros del Asteroide, 2022.

Hatcher, Rachel. *The Power of Memory and Violence in Central America*. Cham, Switzerland: Palgrave Macmillan, 2018.

Hatcher, Rachel. "The Victims and Violence of Civil War: Presences and Absences in El Salvador's Monumental Narratives of Reconciliation." *de arte* 52, no. 2 (2019): 83–101.

Hawkins, Anne Hunsaker. *Reconstructing Illness: Studies in Pathography*. 2nd ed. West Lafayette, Ind.: Purdue University Press, 1999.

Hernández, Claudia. *Causas naturales*. Guatemala City: Punto de lectura, 2013.

Hernández, Claudia. *De fronteras*. Guatemala: Piedra santa, 2007.

Hernández, Claudia. *El verbo J*. Bogotá: Laguna Libros, 2019.

Hernández, Claudia. *La canción del mar*. San Salvador: La prensa gráfica, 2007.

Hernández, Claudia. *La han despedido de nuevo / She Has Been Fired Again*. New York: Sangría, 2016.

Hernández, Claudia. *Mediodía de fronteras*. San Salvador: Dirección de Publicaciones e Impresos, 2002.

Hernández, Claudia. *Olvida uno*. San Salvador, Índole Editores, 2005.

Hernández, Claudia. *Otras ciudades*. San Salvador: Alkimia Libros, 2001.

Hernández, Claudia. *Roza, tumba, quema*. Bogotá: Laguna Libros, 2017.

Hernández, Claudia. *Tomar tu mano*. Bogotá: Laguna Libros, 2021.

Hernández, Manuel, and Corresponsales. "Gobierno no aclara cierre de oficinas del PNR." *Prensa Libre*, April 2, 2016, https://www.prensalibre.com/guatemala/politica/gobierno-no-aclara-cierre-de-oficinas-del-pnr/.

Hernández, Oswaldo J. "Acul y Tzalbal, el despojo de los gobiernos militares." *Plaza Pública*, June 17, 2023. https://www.plazapublica.com.gt/content/acul-y-tzalbal-el-despojo-de-los-gobiernos-militares.

Hernández Alarcón, Rosalinda, Andrea Carrillo Samayoa, Jacqueline Torres Urízar, Ana López Molina, and Ligia Z. Peláez Aldana. *Memorias rebeldes contra el olvido: Paasantzila Txumb'al Ti' Sotzeb'al K'u'l*. Guatemala: AVANCSO, 2008.

Hernández Juárez, Saúl Iván. "Contra el caos de la desmemoria. Museo de la Palabra y la Imagen en El Salvador." *Anales del Museo de Antropología Dr. David J. Guzmán*, no. 57/58 (2017): 52–73.

Hernández Mayén, Manuel. "Asociación Amigos de la UNESCO alerta que Archivo de la Policía Nacional está en 'grave peligro.'" *Prensa Libre*, May 26, 2019. https://www.prensalibre.com/guatemala/justicia/unesco-alerta-que-el-archivo-historico-de-la-policia-nacional-esta-en-grave-peligro/?utm_source=modulosPL&utm_medium=linkinterno&utm_campaign=ux.

Hernández Mayén, Manuel. "PNUD deja el Archivo Histórico de la Policía Nacional en manos del Ministerio de Cultura." *Prensa Libre*, July 1, 2019. https://www.prensalibre.com/guatemala/comunitario/ministerio-de-cultura-se-hace-cargo-a-partir-de-hoy-del-archivo-historico-de-la-policia-nacional/.

Hernández Rivas, Annette. "Cartografía de la memoria: Actores, lugares y prácticas en El Salvador de posguerra (1992–2015)." PhD diss., Universidad Autónoma de Madrid, 2015.

Hernández Salazar, Daniel. "El Ángel Global." *Daniel Hernández-Salazar. Fotógrafo* June 24, 2010. http://danielhernandezsalazar.blogspot.com/2009/08/el-angel-en-el-archivo-historico-de-la.html?zx=b4f9911af33af1b.

Hirsch, Marianne. *The Generation of Postmemory: Writing and Visual Culture After the Holocaust*. New York: Columbia University Press, 2012.

Hompanera, Yessica. "FOTOS: Intento fallido del MOP para demoler Monumento a la Reconciliación." *Elsalvador.com*, December 30, 2021. https://www.elsalvador.com/fotogalerias/noticias-fotogalerias/monumento-reconciliacion-demolicion-fallida/913903/2021/?utm_source=twitter&utm_medium=noticias&utm_campaign=organico.

Honig, Bonnie. "Antigone's Laments, Creon's Grief: Mourning, Membership and the Politics of Exception." *Political Theory* 37, no. 1 (2009): 5–43.

Huezo, Tatiana, dir. *El lugar más pequeño*. Mexico City: Centro de Capacitación Cinematográfica/Foprocine production, 2011.

Huyssen, Andreas. *Present Pasts: Urban Palimpsests and the Politics of Memory*. Stanford, Calif.: Stanford University Press, 2003.

Huyssen, Andreas. *Twilight Memories: Marking Time in a Culture of Amnesia*. New York: Routledge, 1995.

"Informe de Cristosal revela torturas sistemáticas y 153 muertes de personas detenidas." YSUCA, 91.7 FM, May 29, 2023. https://ysuca.org.sv/2023/05/informe-de-cristosal-revela-torturas-sistematicas-y-153-muertes-de-personas-detenidas/?fbclid=IwAR3DC79pay0zg64pn1sBJGiKjZ9ajbccVkxar-XM6JcnNE2vwYc_SJYTSeg.

Jacobson, David. *Place and Belonging in America*. Baltimore: Johns Hopkins University Press, 2001.

Jakubek, Anna Maria. "'Champion of Auschwitz': New Book Tells the Story of a Boxer Who Brought Hope." *Times of Israel*, September 5, 2021. https://www.timesofisrael.com/champion-of-auschwitz-new-book-tells-story-of-boxer-who-brought-hope/.

Jelin, Elizabeth. *Los trabajos de la memoria*. Madrid: Siglo XXI, 2002.

Jelin, Elizabeth. *La lucha por el pasado: Cómo construimos la memoria social*. Buenos Aires: Siglo XXI, 2017.

Jossa, Emanuela. "Cuerpos y espacios en los cuentos de Claudia Hernández: Decepción y resistencia." *Centroamericana* 24, no. 1 (2014): 5–37.

Jossa, Emanuela. "De la 'Audiencia de los confines' a la 'Audiencia de los márgenes': El teatro de la memoria de Jorgelina Cerritos." *Centroamericana* 25, no. 1 (2015): 71–95.

Jossa, Emanuela. "Espacio y reorientación en *Ita* de Mónica Albizúrez." *Amerika: Mémoires, identités, territoires,* no. 20 (2020). https://journals.openedition.org/amerika/11796.

Jossa, Emanuela. "Mónica Albizúrez, *Ita.*" *Altre Modernità* 24 (2020): 421–24. https://riviste.unimi.it/index.php/AMonline/article/view/14533.

Jossa, Emanuela. "Re-presentar la memoria: Regina José Galindo, Claudia Hernández, Jorgelina Cerritos." *Istmo: Revista virtual de estudios literarios y culturales centroamericanos* 38 (2019): 98–112. http://istmo.denison.edu/n38/dossier/07.pdf.

Jossa, Emanuela. "'¿Y qué pruebas tenemos ahora?' El *Libro amarillo* y *13703. El misterio de las utopías,* tercer ensayo sobre la memoria de Jorgelina Cerritos." *Orillas* 8 (2019): 455–68.

"Jueza Portillo contamina el caso El Mozote con órdenes de captura fabricadas." *El Faro,* December 28, 2023. https://elfaro.net/es/202312/columnas/27190/jueza-portillo-contamina-el-caso-el-mozote-con-ordenes-de-captura-fabricadas.

"Justice Prevailed: Salvadoran Ex-colonel Gets 133 Years for Priest Slayings." *Reuters,* September 11, 2020. https://www.reuters.com/article/us-spain-el-salvador-massacre/justice-prevailed-salvadoran-ex-colonel-gets-133-years-for-priest-slayings-idUSKBN2621QP.

Kiernan, Ben. "Wall of Silence: The Field of Genocide Studies and the Guatemalan Genocide." In *Den dannede opprører,* edited by Nik Brandal and Dag Einar Thorsen, 169–98. Oslo: Omslag, Akademisk Publisering, 2016.

King, Robert E. "Reporte teatral centroamericano: ¿Qué hacemos? ¿Hacia dónde vamos?" *Latin American Theater Review* 29, no. 1 (1995): 153–58.

Knowlton, Autum. "Q'eqchi' Mayas and the Myth of 'Postconflict' Guatemala." *Latin American Perspectives* 44, no. 4 (2017): 139–51.

Kobyłeka-Piwońska, Ewa. "Perturbar el orden de los sentidos: Los viajes polacos de Eduardo Halfon." *Studia Neophilologica* 94, no. 3 (2021): 365–90.

Kokotovic, Misha. "After the Revolution: Central American Literature in the Age of Neoliberalism." *A contracorriente* 1, no. 1 (2003). https://acontracorriente.chass.ncsu.edu/index.php/acontracorriente/article/view/73/29.

Kokotovic, Misha. "Telling Evasions: Postwar El Salvador in the Short Fiction of Claudia Hernández." *A contracorriente* 11, no. 2 (2014): 53–75. https://acontracorriente.chass.ncsu.edu/index.php/acontracorriente/article/view/767/1342.

Kroll-Bryce, Christian. "Nómadas, desempleados y suicidas: Racionalidad neoliberal y subjetividades alternas en la literatura centroamericana de posguerra." *Revista de Estudios Hispánicos* 50 (2016): 605–27.

Labrador, Gabriel. "Por qué la iglesia pudo destruir el mosaico de la Catedral." *El Faro,* January 16, 2012. https://www.elfaro.net/es/201201/noticias/7196/Por-qu%C3%A9-la-Iglesia-pudo-destruir-el-mosaico-de-la-Catedral.htm.

Labrador, Gabriel. "Primer concejo plural capitalino se estrena borrando el nombre 'calle Roberto d'Aubuisson.'" *El Faro*, May 1, 2015. https://www.elfaro.net/es/201504/noticias/16927/Primer-concejo-plural-capitalino-se-estrena-borrando-el-nombre-calle-Roberto-d'Aubuisson.htm?st-full_text=all&tpl=11.

Labrador, Gabriel. "Quijano defiende homenaje a d'Aubuisson en víspera del 35 aniversario del asesinato de monseñor Romero." *El Faro*, November 27, 2014. https://www.elfaro.net/es/201411/noticias/16271/.

Labrador, Gabriel, and Óscar Martínez. "Un año de régimen de excepción: Se consolida un estado militar y policial." *El Faro*, March 26, 2023. https://elfaro.net/es/202303/el_salvador/26785/un-ano-de-regimen-de-excepcion-se-consolida-un-estado-militar-y-policial.

Lacan, Jacques. *Écrits*. Translated by Bruce Fink. New York: W. W. Norton, 2006.

LaCapra, Dominick. *History and Memory After Auschwitz*. Ithaca, N.Y.: Cornell University Press, 1998.

Lacaze, Catherine. "Acercamiento al proceso de heroización de Francisco Morazán en América Central (1848, 1892, 1942)." *Revista estudios* 26 (2013). https://revistas.ucr.ac.cr/index.php/estudios/article/view/8844/8326.

"La Chulona #Salvadoreña en #SanSalvador #ElSalvador—Parte final." Posted on *YouTube* by El Salvador Nation, May 24, 2017 (no longer posted). https://www.youtube.com/watch?v=w-PKCy2MA1o.

"'La chulona' vuelve a su sitio." *El Diario de Hoy*, October 5, 2004 (no longer posted). https://archivo.elsalvador.com/noticias/2004/10/05/metro/met8.asp.

La comisión de la verdad para El Salvador. *De la locura a la Esperanza: La guerra de 12 años en El Salvador*. Naciones Unidas, San Salvador/New York, 1992–1993. https://www.derechoshumanos.net/lesahumanidad/informes/elsalvador/informe-de-la-locura-a-la-esperanza.htm.

Laorden Albendea, María Teresa. "Lidiar con el pasado familiar: Posmemoria y trauma en *El boxeador polaco* de Eduardo Halfon." In *Tuércele el cuello al cisne: Las expresiones de la violencia en la literatura hispánica contemporánea*, edited by Cristóbal José Álvarez López, Juan Manuel Carmona Tierno, Ana Davis González, Sara González Ángel, María del Rosario Martínez Navarro, and Marta Rodríguez-Manzano, 589–99. Sevilla: Renacimiento, 2016.

Lara Martínez, Carlos Benjamín. *Memoria histórica del movimiento campesino de Chalatenango*. San Salvador: UCA Editores, 2018.

Larralde Armas, Florencia. *Relatar con luz: Usos de la fotografía del desaparecido*. La Plata: Edición de la Universidad de la Plata, 2016.

Larrea, Agustina. "Eduardo Halfon: 'El término autoficción me parece molesto.'" *El diario AR*, October 23, 2022. https://www.eldiarioar.com/cultura/eduardo-halfon-autoficcion-parece-nefasto_1_9629983.html.

Lauria-Santiago, Aldo, and Leigh Binford. *Landscapes of Struggle: Politics, Society, and Community in El Salvador*. Pittsburgh: University of Pittsburgh Press, 2004.

Lazzara, Michael J., and Fernando A. Blanco. Introduction to *Los futuros de la memoria en América Latina: Sujetos, políticas y epistemologías en disputa*, edited by Michael J. Lazzara and Fernando A. Blanco, 1–23. Raleigh: A Contracorriente, Department of Foreign Languages and Literatures, North Carolina State University, 2022.

Leandro Hernández, Lucía. "La violencia de género como detonante de lo sobrenatural: El rol de la víctima en 'Canícula' de Claudia Hernández y 'Yo, Cocodrilo' de Jacinta Escudos." *Istmo: Revista virtual de estudios literarios y culturales centroamericanos*, no. 38 (2019): 204–17, http://istmo.denison.edu/n38/dossier/13.html.

Leandro Hernández, Lucía. "Una lectura tanatopolítica de *Bandada de pájaros. Segundo ensayo sobre la memoria* de Jorgelina Cerritos." *Revista Ístmica* 28 (2021): 33–53.

Levenson, Deborah T. *Adiós Niño: The Gangs of Guatemala City and the Politics of Death*. Durham, N.C.: Duke University Press, 2013.

Loewen, James W. *Lies Across America: What Our Historic Sites Get Wrong*. New York: New Press, 1999.

Lopes, Maria Margaret, and Sandra Elena Murriello. "El movimiento de los museos en Latinoamérica a fines del siglo XIX: El caso del Museo de La Plata." *Asclepio* 57, no. 2 (2005): 203–22.

López, Silvia. "National Culture, Globalization and the Case of Post-War El Salvador." *Comparative Literature Studies* 41, no. 1 (2004): 80–100.

López Bernal, Carlos Gregorio. "El FMLN y las memorias de la guerra civil salvadoreña." *Revista de Historia*, no. 76 (2017): 47–71.

López Bernal, Carlos Gregorio. "Identidad nacional, historia e invención de tradiciones en El Salvador en la década de 1920." *Revista de Historia*, no. 45 (2002): 35–71.

López Bernal, Carlos Gregorio. "Inventando tradiciones y héroes nacionales: El Salvador (1858–1930)." *Revista de Historia Americana*, no. 127 (2000): 117–51.

López Bernal, Carlos Gregorio. *Memoria e historia en la posguerra: Schafik Jorge Handal y las izquierdas en El Salvador 1960–2019*. Mexico City: Universidad Nacional Autónoma de México, Centro de Investigaciones sobre América Latina y el Caribe, 2022.

López Bernal, Carlos Gregorio. "Schafik Jorge Handal: y la reconfiguración del Frente Farabundo Martí para la Liberación Nacional (1992–2014)." In *Sociedades en conflicto. Movimientos sociales y movimientos armados en América Latina*, edited by Roberto González Arana and Alejandro Schneider, 95–118. Buenos Aires: Universidad del Norte/CLACSO, 2016.

López Fernández, Julio, dir. *La batalla del volcán*. San Salvador: Argos Comunicaciones, Cine Murciélago, Trípode Audiovisual, 2018.

Lovell, George. "The Archive that Never Was: State Terror and Historical Memory in Guatemala." *Geographical Review* 103, no. 2 (2013): 199–209.

Lovo, Maynor. "Preocupa desinformación sobre obras que el DOM realizará en monumento a El Mozote." *La prensa gráfica*, March 6, 2022, https://www.laprensagrafica.com/elsalvador/Preocupa-desinformacion-sobre-obras-que-la-DOM-realizara-en-monumento-en-El-Mozote--20220306-0025.html.

Lungo Rodríguez, Irene. "Castillos de ARENA: Hegemonía y proyectos de derecha en El Salvador 1989–2004." MA thesis, Facultad Latinoamericana de Ciencias Sociales (FLACSO-México), 2008.

Machuca, Evelyn. "Exigen a Fiscalía, Policía y al Estado justicia por feminicidios." *La Prensa Gráfica*, April 29, 2018. https://www.laprensagrafica.com/elsalvador/Exigen-a-Fiscalia-Policia-y-al-Estado-justicia-por-feminicidios-20180428-0065.html.

Maciel, Eduardo. "Recordando desde enero o mayo: Memoria y olvido en El Salvador a partir del estudio estético de dos monumentos de la posguerra." *Realidad: Revista de ciencias sociales y humanidades* 156 (2020): 5–33.

Mackenbach, Werner. "Narrativas de le memoria en Centroamérica: Entre política, historia y ficción." In *Hacia una historia de las literaturas Centroamericanas III: (Per)Versiones de la modernidad. Literaturas, identidades y desplazamientos*, edited by Beatriz Cortez, Alexandra Ortiz Wallner, and Verónica Ríos Quesada, 231–57. Guatemala City: F&G, 2012.

Mackenbach, Werner, and Julie Marchio. "Presentación." Foreword to "Recordar el pasado para imaginar otro futuro: Artes y políticas de la memoria en Centroamérica." Special issue, *Revista de Historia* 36 (2019): 7–12.

Mackenbach, Werner, and Alexandra Ortiz Wallner. "(De)formaciones: Violencia y narrativa en Centroamérica." *Iberoamericana: América Latina—España—Portugal*, no. 32 (2008): 81–97.

Marchio, Julie. "Memoria, duelo y olvido en *Con pasión absoluta* de Carol Zardetto: Una tensión entre ética y estética." In *Guatemala: Nunca Más; Desde el trauma de la Guerra civil hacia la integración étnica, la democracia y la justicia social*, edited by Roland Spiller, 211–41. Guatemala City: F&G, 2015.

Marchio, Julie. "(Pos)Memoria(s) de la diáspora judía en Centroamérica: ¿De un trauma a otro?" *Revista de Historia*, no. 36 (2019): 25–40.

Margry, Jan Peter, and Cristina Sánchez-Carretero, eds. *Grassroots Memorials: The Politics of Memorializing Traumatic Death*. New York: Berghahn Books, 2011.

Marroquín, Oscar Clemente. "Por lo menos se acepta que hubo excesos." *La Hora*, April 17, 2013, 12.

Martínez, Denis, and Luisa Gómez. *Las reparaciones para víctimas del conflicto armado en Guatemala: Una promesa por cumplir*. Belfast: Reparations, Responsibility & Victimhood in Transitional Societies, 2021. https://reparations.qub.ac.uk/assets/uploads/Guatemalan-Report-ESP-LR-1.pdf.

Martínez, Francisco. "Francisco García Gudiel: No hubo genocidio, se cometieron excesos." *Prensa Libre*, September 28, 2018. https://www.prensalibre.com/guatemala/justicia/no-hubo-genocidio-se-cometieron-excesos/.

Martínez, Juliana. *Haunting Without Ghosts: Spectral Realism in Colombian Literature, Film, and Art*. Austin: University of Texas Press, 2020.

McAllister, Carlota, and Diane M. Nelson, eds. *War by Other Means: Aftermath in Post-Genocide Guatemala*. Durham, N.C.: Duke University Press, 2013.

McElya, Micki. *The Politics of Mourning: Death and Honor in Arlington National Cemetery*. Cambridge, Mass.: Harvard University Press, 2016.

McIvor, David. *Mourning in America: Race and the Politics of Loss*. Ithaca, N.Y.: Cornell University Press, 2016.

McLoughlin, Kate. "Introduction: Memory, Mourning, Landscape." In *Memory, Mourning, Landscape*, edited by Elizabeth Anderson, Avril Maddrell, Kate McLoughlin, and Alana Vincent, ix–xiv. Amsterdam: Rodopi, 2010.

Medrano, Mario. "Inauguran el Museo de la Memoria contra la Impunidad 'AMA y No Olvida' en Managua." *CNN en Español*, September 30, 2019. https://cnnespanol.cnn.com/2019/09/30/alerta-nicaragua-inauguran-museo-de-la-memoria-contra-la-impunidad-ama-y-no-olvida/.

Menchú Tum, Rigoberta. "La verdad no traiciona ni divide." *Latin America in Movement*, April 16, 2013. https://www.alainet.org/en/node/75436?language=es.

Menen Desleal, Álvaro. *Luz negra*. 1967. San Salvador: Dirección de Publicaciones e Impresos, 2018.

Menéndez, Nicolle. "El cine al aire libre en nuevo parque de San Salvador inicia con éxito." *Diario El Salvador*, February 25, 2024. https://diarioelsalvador.com/el-cine-al-aire-libre-en-nuevo-parque-de-san-salvador-inicia-con-exito/468065/.

Mihailovic, Jelena. "Memoria, trauma y crimen en la novela *Ita* de Mónica Albizúrez Gil." *Istmo: Revista virtual de estudios literarios y culturales centroamericanos*, no. 41, (2020): 30–48.

"Monumento a la constitución." *Alcaldía de San Salvador* (blog), April 30, 2009. https://alcaldiass.wordpress.com/2009/04/30/monumento-a-la-constitucion/.

"Monumento a la constitución (chulona) san salvador El Salvador." Posted on YouTube by Conociendo El Salvador 503, October 14, 2017. https://www.youtube.com/watch?v=z2-SE7pnjFA.

"Monumento a la Memoria y la Verdad El Salvador." *Fundación cultura de paz*. N.d. https://ods.ceipaz.org/wp-content/uploads/2014/11/7Monumento-a-la-Memoria-y-la-Verdad.pdf.

"Monumento a la reconciliación, un símbolo para profundizar la paz en El Salvador." Posted on YouTube by Prensa Latina, January 24, 2017. Accessed April 13, 2020 (no longer posted). https://www.youtube.com/watch?v=AmpaboEcgV4.

"¿Monumento a la reconciliación o monumento a la burla?" *Última Hora*, January 16, 2017. https://ultimahora.sv/monumento-a-la-reconciliacion-o-monumento-de-la-burla/.

"Monument to Constitution." *Ministerio de Turismo, Gobierno de El Salvador*. Accessed June 6, 2020 (no longer posted). https://www.mitur.gob.sv/en/travel/monumento-a-la-constitucion-2/.

Moodie, Ellen. *El Salvador in the Aftermath of Peace: Crime, Uncertainty, and the Transition to Democracy*. Philadelphia: University of Pennsylvania Press, 2010.

Montejo, Víctor. *Testimony: Death of a Guatemalan Village*. Willimantic, Conn.: Curbstone Press, 1987.

Morán, Liuba. "Breve reflexión a partir de la elaboración del guión curatorial sobre el surgimiento del primer museo de El Salvador." *Anales del Museo de Antropología Dr. David J. Guzmán*, no. 57/58 (2017): 74–93.

Morales, Frieda. "La flama de la paz." *MuniGuate*. Accessed January 10, 2020 (no longer posted). https://cultura.muniguate.com/index.php/component/content/article/94-monumentopaz/583-flamapaz.

Moraña, Mabel. "Maldita memoria." In *Los futuros de la memoria en América Latina: Sujetos, políticas y epistemologías en disputa*, edited by Michael J. Lazzara and Fernando A. Blanco, 25–37. Raleigh: A Contracorriente, Department of Foreign Languages and Literatures at North Carolina State University, 2022.

Moreiras, Alberto. "The Aura of Testimonio." *The Real Thing: Testimonial Discourse and Latin America*, edited by Georg M. Gugelberger, 193–224. Durham, N.C.: Duke University Press, 1996.

Moreiras, Alberto. "The Quest of Cynicism: A Reading of Horacio Castellanos Moya's *La diaspora* (1989)." *Nonsite.org*, articles issue 13, October 13, 2014, https://nonsite.org/the-question-of-cynicism/.

Moreiras, Alberto. *Tercer espacio: Literatura y duelo en América Latina*. Santiago: LOM/Universidad Arcis, 1999.

Murphy, Kaitlin M. *Mapping Memory. Visuality, Affect, and Embodied Politics in the Americas*. New York: Fordham University Press, 2019.

"Museo Nacional de Historia Natural." Memoria chilena, Biblioteca Nacional de Chile. https://www.memoriachilena.gob.cl/602/w3-article-132485.html.

"Museo de la memoria contra la impunidad será llevado a Costa Rica." *100% Noticias*, December 6, 2019. https://100noticias.com.ni/nacionales/97039-nicaragua-museo-contra-impunidad-dictadura-uca-mad/.

Museo de la Memoria Histórica de Arcatao. https://museohistoricodearcatao.blogspot.com/.

Museo Rabinal. http://www.museo.rabinal.info/index.html.

"Museum of the Revolution Part I, Perkin Morazan El Salvador C.A P I." Posted on YouTube by Youtubero Salvadoreño, August 5, 2014, https://www.youtube.com/watch?v=bqQ8EMgc8GI.

Naas, Michael. *Derrida from Now On*. New York: Fordham University Press, 2009.

Nancy, Jean-Luc. *The Inoperative Community*. Edited by Peter Connor. Translated by Peter Connor, Lisa Garbus, Michael Holland, and Simona Sawhney. Minneapolis: University of Minnesota Press, 1991.

Nelson, Diane M. *Reckoning. The Ends of War in Guatemala*. Durham. N.C.: Duke University Press, 2009.

Nelson, Diane M. *Who Counts? The Mathematics of Death and Life After Genocide*. Durham. N.C.: Duke University Press, 2015.

Nichanian, Marc, "Mourning and Reconciliation." In *Living Together: Jacques Derrida's Communities of Violence and Peace*, edited by Elisabeth Weber, 191–210. New York: Fordham University Press, 2012.

"No hubo genocidio en Guatemala, sostiene presidente Pérez Molina." *La Nación*, January 7, 2015. https://www.nacion.com/el-mundo/politica/no-hubo-genocidio-en-guatemala-sostiene-presidente-perez-molina/HYPK23SSGJFSBAVFCVIESW5X2Q/story/.

Nolasco, Alejandra. "Los ausentes." Posted on YouTube by Alejandra Nolasco, February 28, 2020. https://www.youtube.com/watch?v=P_0Ofa0Khfw&t=1s&ab_channel=AlejandraNolasco.

"Nombrar calles como d'Aubuisson viola DD.HH., dice Procuraduría salvadoreña." *Los Angeles Times*, April 30, 2015, https://www.hoylosangeles.com/noticias/elsalvador/hoyla-els-nombrar-calles-como-daubuisson-viola-ddhh-dice-procuradura-salvadorea-20150430-story.html.

Nora, Pierre. "Between Memory and History: Les Lieux de Mémoire." *Representations*, no. 26 (1989): 7–24.

Nora, Pierre. "From *Lieux de mémoire* to *Realms of Memory*." In *Realms of Memory: Rethinking the French Past of Memory*. Vol. 1, *Conflicts and Divisions*, translated by Arthur Goldhammer, xv–xxiv. New York: Columbia University Press, 1996.

Nora, Pierre. *Pierre Nora en* Les lieux de mémoire. Translated by Laura Masello, Santiago: LOM, 2009.

Oglesby, Elizabeth. "Educating Citizens in Postwar Guatemala: Historical Memory, Genocide, and the Culture of Peace." *Radical History Review* 97 (2007): 77–98.

Orellana, Óscar, dir. *El Mozote nunca más*. Gobierno de El Salvador, December 13, 2017. https://www.facebook.com/GobiernoSV/videos/754601514734104.

Orellana Calderón, Carlos Iván. "Discurso oficial y reparación social." *Estudios Centroamericanos* (ECA), no. 649/650 (2002): 1067–91.

Orozco, Andrea, and William Cumes. "Ministro Degenhart dice que PNC debe participar en manejo del archivo de la Policía Nacional." *Prensa Libre*, May 27, 2019. https://www.prensalibre.com/guatemala/justicia/ministro-degenhart-dice-que-archivo-de-la-policia-nacional-debe-pasar-a-manos-de-la-pnc/.

Ortiz Wallner, Alexandra. "Claudia Hernández: Por una poética de la prosa en tiempos violentos." *LEJANA: Revista crítica de narrativa breve*, no. 6 (2013): 1–10. https://ojs.elte.hu/index.php/lejana/article/download/65/58/.

Ortiz Wallner, Alexandra. *El arte de ficcionar: La novela contemporánea en Centroamérica*. Madrid: Iberoamericana, 2012.

Ortiz Wallner, Alexandra. "Las batallas por la memoria: La novela centroamericana como lugar de sobrevivencia." *Istmo: Revista virtual de estudios literarios y culturales centroamericanos*, no. 15 (2007). http://istmo.denison.edu/n15/proyectos/batallas.html.

Ortiz Wallner, Alexandra. "Narrativas centroamericanas de posguerra: Problemas de la constitución de una categoría de periodización literaria." *Iberoamericana: América Latina—España—Portugal*, no. 19 (2005): 135–47.

Ortiz Wallner, Alexandra. "Una escritura más allá de las fronteras: La narrativa f(r)iccional de Eduardo Halfon." *Hispanorama* 144 (2014): 34–38.

"Otto Pérez Molina asegura que no hubo genocidio en Guatemala." *La prensa*, March 20, 2013. https://www.laprensa.com.ni/2013/03/20/internacionales/138978-otto-perez-molina-asegura-que-no-hubo-genocidio-en-guatemala.

Padilla, Yajaira M. "Setting 'La Diabla' Free: Women, Violence, and the Struggle for Representation in Postwar El Salvador." *Latin American Perspectives* 35, no. 5 (2008): 133–45.

Padilla, Yajaira M. *Changing Women, Changing Nation: Female Agency, Nationhood, and Identity in Trans-Salvadoran Narratives*. Albany: State University of New York Press, 2012.

Padilla, Yajaira M. *From Threatening Guerrillas to Forever Illegals: US Central Americans and the Cultural Politics of Non-Belonging*. Austin: University of Texas Press, 2022.

Paredes, Juan Pablo. "La 'Plaza de la Dignidad' como escenario de protesta: La dimensión cultural en la comprensión del Acontecimiento de Octubre chileno." *Revista de humanidades de Valparaíso*, no. 17 (2021): 27–52.

Perdu, Vanessa. "Experiencias del exilio en el cuento guatemalteco: 'Los exiliados' de Mario Monteforte Toledo, 'Ningún lugar sagrado' de Rodrigo Rey Rosa y 'Mañana nunca lo hablamos' de Eduardo Halfon." *Península* 11, no. 1 (2016): 155–73.

Pérez, Yansi. "El poder de la abyección y la ficción de posguerra." In *Hacia una historia de las literaturas Centroamericanas III: (Per)Versiones de la modernidad. Literaturas, identidades y desplazamientos*, edited by Beatriz Cortez, Alexandra Ortiz Wallner, and Verónica Ríos Quesada, 49–72. Guatemala City: F&G, 2012.

Pérez, Yansi. "Historias de metamorfosis: Lo abyecto, los límites entre lo animal y lo humano, en la literatura centroamericana de posguerra." *Revista Iberoamericana* 79, no. 242 (2013): 163–80.

Pérez, Yansi. *Más allá del duelo: Otras formas de imaginar, sentir y pensar la memoria en Centroamérica*. San Salvador: UCA Editores, 2019.

Pérez, Yansi. "Memory and Mourning in Contemporary Latin American Literature: A Reading of Claudia Hernández' *De fronteras*." *La Habana elegante* 55 (2014). http://www.habanaelegante.com/Spring_Summer_2014/Invitation_Perez.html.

Perkowska, Magdalena. "Del militarismo y la melancolía al sujeto inclinado y la ética del cuidado." In *Escritura(s) en femenino en las literaturas centroamericanas: ¿Una cuestión de género?*, edited by Magdalena Perkwoska and Werner Mackenbach, 126–48. Raleigh: A Contracorriente, Department of Foreign Languages and Literatures at North Carolina State University, 2022.

Perkowska, Magdalena. "Infancia e historia: Actos de la memoria en *Dios tenía miedo* de Vanessa Núñez Handal y *Mañana nunca lo hablamos* de Eduardo Halfon." *Revista de Estudios Hispánicos* 51, no. 3 (2017): 595–620.

Perkowska, Magdalena. "La foto que suelta el secreto: El relato familiar, lo real y la fotografía en dos novelas latinoamericanas." In *Pensar lo real: Autoficción y discurso crítico*, edited by Ana Casas and Anna Forné, 33–52. Madrid: Iberoamericana, 2022.

Perkowska, Magdalena. "La infamia de las historias y la ética de la escritura en la novela centroamericana contemporánea." *Istmo: Revista virtual de estudios literarios y culturales centroamericanos* 22 (2011). http://istmo.denison.edu/n22/articulos/24_perkowska_magdalena_form.pdf.

Perkowska, Magdalena. "Los archivos del malestar: Estética y política de la infelicidad en la ficción centroamericana contemporánea (Ramiro Lacayo Deshón, Jacinta Escudos y Claudia Hernández)." *Revista canadiense de estudios hispánicos* 44, no. 1 (2019): 183–205.

Perkowska, Magdalena. "Silencios que hieren: La presencia espectral del pasado en la ficción centroamericana de la generación de *post*-guerra." In *Las posmemorias: Perspectivas latinoamericanas y europeas*, edited by Teresa Basile and Cecilia González, 433–54. La Plata: Universidad Nacional de la Plata, 2020.

Perkowska, Magdalena. "Una nación imposible: El *Bildungsroman* e imaginarios culturales en *El misterio de San Andrés*, de Dante Liano." *Istmo: Revista virtual de estudios literarios y culturales centroamericanos*, no. 24 (2012). http://istmo.denison.edu/n24/articulos/25.html.

Perkowska, Magdalena. "When Does Central American Literature Become Global? The Extraordinary (or Predictable) Case of Eduardo Halfon." In *Central American Literature as World Literature*, edited by Sophie Esch, 81–99. New York: Bloomsbury, 2023.

Peterson, Anna L., and Brandt G. Peterson. "Martyrdom, Sacrifice, and Political Memory in El Salvador." *Social Research* 75, no. 2 (2008): 511–42.

Pfosi, Nicholas. "Protesters Tear Down Christopher Columbus Statue in Saint Paul, Minnesota." *Reuters*, June 11, 2020. https://www.reuters.com/article/us-minneapolis-police-saint-paul-statue/protesters-tear-down-christopher-columbus-statue-in-saint-paul-minnesota-idUSKBN23I04X.

Picardo Joao, Oscar. *El humor social y político, cosmovisión e ideología de los salvadoreños*. San Salvador: Universidad Francisco Gavidia Editores, 2023.

Pineda, Alexander. "Jueza retrocede y anula segunda orden de arresto en contra de Rubén Zamora." *Elsalvador.com*, March 13, 2024. https://www.elsalvador.com/noticias/nacional/juicios-politicos-ruben-zamora-orden-de-captura-san-francisco-gotera-proceso-judicial/1129302/2024/.

Portillo, Denni. "Exigen que DOM respete el monumento a víctimas del Mozote." *La prensa gráfica*, March 8, 2022. https://www.laprensagrafica.com/elsalvador/Exigen-que-DOM-respete-el-monumento-a-victimas-del-Mozote-20220307-0083.html.

Portillo Peña, Nelson Antonio, Mauricio Gaborit, and José Miguel Cruz. *Psicología social en la posguerra: Teoría y aplicaciones desde El Salvador*. San Salvador: UCA Editores, 2005.

"Presidenta hondureña Inaugura Museo de la Memoria." Telesur, June 29, 2023. https://www.telesurtv.net/news/presidenta-hondurena-inaugura-museo-memoria-20230629-0002.html.

Pridgeon, Stephanie. "Silences Between Jewishness and Indigeneity in Eduardo Halfon's *Mañana nunca lo hablamos*." *Revista canadiense de estudios hispánicos* 42, no. 1 (2017): 99–121.

Pridgeon, Stephanie. "Jewish Guatemalan Fiction in a Global Context." In *Teaching Central American Literature in a Global Context*, edited by Gloria Elizabeth Chacón and Mónica Albizúrez Gil, 180–90. New York: Modern Language Association of America, 2022.

Rabinbach, Anson. "From Explosion to Erosion: Holocaust Memorialization in America Since Bitburg." *History and Memory* 9, no. 1/2 (1997): 226–55.

Ramsay, George. "FIFA Fines British National Teams $100K for Poppy Displays." *CNN*, December 19, 2016. https://www.cnn.com/2016/12/19/football/fifa-poppy-fine-england-fa-football/index.html.

Rappaccioli, Emilia Yang. "AMA y No Olvida: Collectivizing Memory Against Impunity: Transmedia Memory Practices, Modular Visibility, and Activist Participatory Design in Nicaragua." *International Journal of Communication* 16 (2022): 309–30.

Rauda Zablah, Nelson. "El estado hace oficial el número de víctimas en El Mozote: 978 ejecutados, 553 niños." *El Faro*, December 4, 2017. https://elfaro.net/es/201712/el_salvador/20953/El-Estado-hace-oficial-el-n%C3%BAmero-de-v%C3%ADctimas-en-El-Mozote-978-ejecutados-553-ni%C3%B1os.htm.

Rauda Zablah, Nelson. "Exsoldados del batallón Atlacatl declaran contra sus superiores en el caso de El Mozote." *El Faro*, November 2, 2019. https://elfaro.net/es/201911/el_salvador/23761/Exsoldados-del-batall%C3%B3n-Atlacatl-declaran-contra-sus-superiores-en-el-caso-de-El-Mozote.htm?fbclid=IwAR2l8FO7AlJobRPY-CSjuQnTkGqinLjKgbYMaLKS-100YBf3f0FA7F0EWMY.

Rauda Zablah, Nelson. "La nueva jueza de El Mozote cambia las reglas del juego." *El Faro*, October 21, 2022. https://elfaro.net/es/202210/el_salvador/26437/la-nueva-jueza-de-el-mozote-cambia-las-reglas-del-juicio.

Renan, Ernest. "What Is a Nation?" In *Nation and Narration*. Edited by Homi K. Bhabha and translated by Martin Thom, 8–22. London: Routledge, 1990.

"Resolución de la Corte Interamericana de Derechos Humanos de 28 de noviembre de 2018: Caso Masacres de el Mozote y lugares aledaños VS. El Salvador; Supervisión de cumplimiento de sentencia." Corte Interamericana de Derechos Humanos, https://www.corteidh.or.cr/docs/supervisiones/norincatriman_28_11_18.pdf.

Rey Rosa, Rodrigo. *El material humano*. Barcelona: Anagrama, 2009.

Rey Tristán, Eduardo, Alberto Martín Álvarez, and Jorge Juárez Ávila. "Las limitaciones de la paz en el caso salvadoreño: Memorias confrontadas y víctimas permanentes." In *Las luchas por la memoria en América Latina: Historia reciente y violencia política*, edited by Eugenia Allier Montaño and Emilio Crenzel, 273–96. Madrid: Iberoamericana, 2015.

Rey Tristán, Eduardo, and Pilar Cagiao Vila. *Conflicto, memoria y pasados traumáticos: El Salvador contemporáneo*. Santiago de Compostela: Universidad de Santiago de Compostela, 2011.

Ribas-Casasayas, Alberto, and Amanda L. Petersen. "Theories of the Ghost in a Transhispanic Context." In *Espectros: Ghostly Hauntings in Contemporary Transhispanic Narratives*, 1–11. Lewisburg, Pa.: Bucknell University Press, 2015.

Richard, Nelly. *Crítica y política*. Santiago: Palinodia, 2013.

Rickels, Laurence A. *Aberrations of Mourning: Writing on German Crypts*. Detroit: Wayne State University Press, 1988.

Ricoeur, Paul. *Memory, History, Forgetting*. Translated by Kathleen Blamey and David Pellauer. Chicago: University of Chicago Press, 2004.

Ridgeway, William. *The Origin of Tragedy with Special Reference to the Greek Tragedians*. Cambridge: Cambridge University Press, 1910.

Riehn, Astrid. "Las vidas ficcionales de Eduardo Halfon." *Tiempo Argentino*, February 11, 2023, https://www.tiempoar.com.ar/cultura/las-vidas-ficcionales-de-eduardo-halfon/.

Rincón-Chavarro, María Catalina. "De violencia, de normalización y *De fronteras*." *Catedral Tomada: Revista de crítica literaria latinoamericana* 1, no. 1 (2013). https://catedraltomada.pitt.edu/ojs/index.php/catedraltomada/article/view/27/34..

Ripa, Valentina. "Esperando el amanecer con los personajes de Jorgelina Cerritos." In *Venimos de la noche y hacia la noche vamos: XXXVI Convegno Internazionale di Americanista; Salerno (Italia), 14–16 de mayo de 2014*, edited by Rosa Maria Grillo, 65–83. Salerno: Oedipos, 2015.

Rocha Cortez, David. "El teatro como topografía del pasado: 'Ensayos sobre la memoria' de Jorgelina Cerritos." *13703. El misterio de las utopías*, by Jorgelina Ceritos, 7–16. San Salvador: Índole Editores, 2017.

Rocha Cortez, David. *Convergencias: Una mirada a la poética de Roberto Salomón*. San Salvador: Índole Editores, 2021.

Rodríguez, Ana Patricia. *Dividing the Isthmus: Central American Transnational Histories, Literatures, and Cultures*. Austin: University of Texas Press, 2009.

Rodríguez, Ana Patricia. "Mozote Homeland: Diasporic Memories of the Salvadoran Civil War in Testimonial and Filmic Narratives." *Istmo: Revista virtual de estudios literarios y culturales centroamericanos*, no. 13 (2006). http://istmo.denison.edu/n13/articulos/mozote.html.

Rodríguez, José Napoleón. *Muerte en la consagración o la consagración de la muerte*. San Salvador: Dirección de Publicaciones e Impresos, 2015.

Romanska, Magda. Introduction to *The Routledge Companion to Dramaturgy*, edited by Magda Romanska, 1–15. Abingdon: Routledge, 2016.

Romero de Thoma, Martha Verónica. *Verónica decide vivir: Libro histórico de las experiencias no contadas, que se vivieron en nuestra patria de El Salvador; En el conflicto armado salvadoreño (1980–1992) y la construcción de la Comunidad Segundo Montes*. San Salvador: Talleres Gráficos UCA, 2018.

Roque Baldovinos, Ricardo. "Duelo y memoria: Sobre la narrativa de posguerra en El Salvador." In *Niños de un planeta extraño*, 172–83. San Salvador: Editorial Universidad Don Bosco, 2012.

Roque Baldovinos, Ricardo. *La rebelión de los sentidos: Arte y revolución durante la modernización autoritaria en El Salvador*. San Salvador: UCA Editores, 2020.

Rosenzweig, Roy, and David Thalen. *The Presence of the Past: Popular Uses of History in American Life*. New York: Columbia University Press, 1998.

Rostica, Julieta. "The Naturalization of Peace and War: The Hegemonic Discourse on the Political Violence in Guatemala." In *The Struggle for Memory in Latin America: Recent History and Political Violence*, edited by Eugenia Allier-Montaño and Emilio Crenzel, 183–200. New York: Palgrave Macmillan, 2015.

Rubio, Francisco. "'Tengo a mi hijo libre, pero muerto.' Entierran a joven que murió en el penal de Mariona." *Elsalvador.com*, June 10, 2023, https://www.elsalvador.com/noticias/nacional/entierran-reo-muerto-penal-mariona-regimen-excepcion/1067346/2023/?fbclid=IwAR1dKES77GU2cVkcJ_1PeSClXmuHurCB50J5gMRzLFpDkdrFhyqsiu6SyUE.

Salamanca, Elena. *El Salvador: Monumentos y Esculturas del Rincón Mágico; Monuments and Sculptures*. San Salvador: Banco Agrícola de El Salvador, 2013.

Salamanca, Elena. "40 Years Without Roque Dalton: A Body in the Postwar Period." *Dichos de un bicho*, May 10, 2016. dichosdeunbicho.com/40-years-without-roque-dalton-a-body-in-the-postwar-period/.

Salamanca, Elena. "Lugares sagrados en la ciudad moderna: San Salvador, 1911–1928." *Anales del Museo de Antropología Dr. David J. Guzmán*, no. 57/58 (2017): 298–313.

Salamanca, Elena. "Último viernes." In *Último viernes*. San Salvador: Dirección de Publicaciones e Impresos, 2008.

Salamanca Villamizar, Carlos Arturo. "Los lugares de la memoria y de la acción política en Guatemala: Justicia transicional, políticas del reconocimiento y ficciones de secularismo." *Revista de Estudios Sociales* 51 (2015): 62–75.

Salomón, Roberto. "Theater in El Salvador During the Eighties." *Latin American Theater Review* 25, no. 2 (1992): 173–80.

Salomón, Roberto, and Alejandro Córdova. *Teatro: Análisis de la situación de la expresión artística en El Salvador*. San Salvador: Fundación Accesarte, 2015.

"Salvadorans Observing 3 Days of National Mourning as D'Aubuisson Receives State-Honors Burial." *Deseret News*, February 23, 1992. https://www.deseret.com/1992/2/23/18969270/salvadorans-observing-3-days-of-mourning-as-d-aubuisson-receives-state-honors-burial.

Sanford, Victoria. *Buried Secrets: Truth and Human Rights in Guatemala*. New York: Palgrave Macmillan, 2003.

Santos Cid, Alejandro. "Guatemala juzgará a nueve militares acusados de crímenes contra la humanidad por el caso Diario Militar." *El País*, May 6, 2022. https://elpais.com/internacional/2022-05-07/guatemala-juzgara-a-nueve-militares-acusados-de-crimenes-contra-la-humanidad-por-el-caso-diario-militar.html.

Sarmiento, Ignacio. "Claudia Hernández y la escritura de la precariedad." *Boletín de la asociación para el fomento de los estudios históricos en Centroamérica* (AFEHC), no. 69 (2016). https://www.academia.edu/27572399/Claudia_Hern%C3%A1ndez_y_la_escritura_de_la_precariedad.

Sarmiento, Ignacio. "Comunidad y catástrofe en la narrativa salvadoreña contemporánea." *Transmodernity: Journal of Peripheral Cultural Production of the Luso-Hispanic World* 6, no. 1 (2016): 16–34.

Sarmiento, Ignacio. "Frecuencias de lo (in)visible: La guerra civil salvadoreña en la narrativa de Claudia Hernández." *Pandora: Revue d'études hispaniques* 13 (2016): 115–27.

Sarmiento, Ignacio. "¿Qué hacer con los muertos? Claudia Hernández y el trabajo del duelo en la postguerra salvadoreña." *Revista canadiense de estudios hispánicos* 41, no. 2 (2017): 395–415.

Sarmiento, Ignacio. "Trabajo, etnicidades y figuraciones de la pobreza en la literatura salvadoreña." In *Estéticas de la precarización: La pobreza en el imaginario latinoamericano actual*, edited by Stephen Buttes and Dianna Niebylski, 295–317. Santiago: Editorial Cuarto Propio, 2017.

Schneider, Arron. *State-Building and Tax Regimes in Central America*. Cambridge: Cambridge University Press, 2012.

Shea, Maureen. "*Una mujer en la selva*, de Hernán Robleto: Precursora de la ecocrítica centroamericana." *(Re)Imaginar Centroamérica en el siglo XXI*, edited by Maureen Shea, Uriel Quesada, and Ignacio Sarmiento, 273–87. San José: Uruk, 2017.

Shear, M. Katherine. "Grief and Mourning Gone Awry: Pathway and Course of Complicated Grief." *Dialogues in Clinical Neuroscience* 14, no. 2 (2012): 119–28.

Sherlock, Peter. "The Reformation of Memory in Early Modern Europe." In *Memory: Histories, Theories, Debates*, edited by Susannah Radstone and Bill Schwarz, 30–40. New York: Fordham University Press, 2010.

Sierra Becerra, Diana. "Historical Memory at El Salvador's Museo de la Palabra y la Imagen." *Latin American Perspectives* 43, no. 6 (2016): 8–26.

"Silenciando la memoria." *No Ficción*, January 3, 2020. https://www.no-ficcion.com/projects/silenciando-la-memoria-ahpn.

Sobrino, Jon. "De una teología solo de la liberación a una teología del martirio." *Revista Latinoamericana de Teología*, no. 28 (1992): 27–48.

Sodaro, Amy. *Exhibiting Atrocity: Memorial Museums and the Politics of Past Violence*. New Brunswick, N.J.: Rutgers University Press, 2018.

Solan, Peter, dir. *The Boxer and Death*. Bratislava: Studio Hraných Filmov. 1963.

Solano, María Gabriela. "El teatro documental en Latinoamérica: Un escenario para la presencia simbólica y emotiva de comunidades y personas desaparecidas." PhD diss., University of Wisconsin–Madison, 2016.

Sprenkels, Ralph. *After Insurgency: Revolution and Electoral Politics in El Salvador*. Notre Dame, Ind.: University of Notre Dame Press, 2018.

Sprenkels, Ralph. "El trabajo de la memoria en Centroamérica: Cinco propuestas heurísticas en torno a las guerras en El Salvador, Guatemala y Nicaragua." *Revista de Historia*, no. 76, (2017). https://www.revistas.una.ac.cr/index.php/historia/article/view/10046/24978#toc.

Sprenkels, Ralph. "La guerra como controversia: Una reflexión sobre las secuelas políticas del informe de la Comisión de la Verdad para El Salvador." *Identidades*, no. 4 (2012): 68–89.

Sprenkels, Ralph. "Roberto D'Aubuisson vs Schafik Handal: Militancy, Memory Work and Human Rights." *European Review of Latin American and Caribbean Studies* 91 (2011): 15–30.

Stein, Ben. "In Class Warfare, Guess Which Class Is Winning." *New York Times*, November 2006. https://www.nytimes.com/2006/11/26/business/yourmoney/26every.html.

Steinberg, Michael K., and Matthew J. Taylor. "Public Memory and Political Power in Guatemala's Postconflict Landscape." *Geography Review* 93, no. 4 (2003): 449–68.

Stelian Rusu, Mihai. "The Politics of Mourning in Post-Communist Romania: Unravelling the Thanatopolitics of Grievable Deaths." *Mortality* 25, no. 3 (2020): 313–31.

Stelzner, Uli, dir. *La isla: Archivos de una tragedia*. Berlin: Iskacine, 2009.

Stern, Steve. *Remembering Pinochet's Chile: On the Eve of London 1998*. Durham, N.C.: Duke University Press, 2004.

Stoll, David. *Rigoberta Menchú and the Story of All Poor Guatemalans*. Abingdon: Routledge, 1998.

Stuesse, Angela, Beatriz Manz, Elizabeth Oglesby, Krisjon Olson, Victoria Sanford, Clyde Collins Snow, and Heather Walsh-Haney. "*Sí hubo genocidio*: Anthropologists and the Genocide Trial of Guatemala's Ríos Montt." *American Anthropology* 115, no. 4 (2013): 658–66.

Suffern, Ryan, dir. *Finding Oscar*. Brooklyn, N.Y.: FilmRise, 2016.

Szafran, Eleonora. *Mistrz. Tadeusz "Teddy" Pietrzykowski*. Warsaw: Ringier Axel Springer Polska, 2021.

Taum, James. *The Mourner's Song: War and Remembrance from the* Iliad *to Vietnam*. Chicago: University of Chicago Press, 2003.

Taylor, Diana. "Trauma and Performance: Lessons from Latin America." *PMLA* 121, no. 5 (2006): 1674–77.

Tejada, Nubia. "Ráfagas de historia, patria y cultura." *Diario El Salvador*, March 20, 2022. https://diarioelsalvador.com/rafagas-de-historia-patria-y-cultura/205189/.

Tello, Andrés Maximiliano. *Anarchivismo: Tecnologías políticas del archivo*. Buenos Aires: La Cebra, 2018.

Till, Karen. *The New Berlin: Memory, Politics, Place*. Minneapolis: University of Minnesota Press, 2005.

Tobar Serrano, José Apolonio. "Aportaciones de la Procuraduría para la Defensa de los Derechos Humanos de El Salvador para la preparación del Informe del Alto Comisionado de las Naciones Unidas para los Derechos Humanos de conformidad con la resolución 42/17 del Consejo de Derechos Humanos sobre 'Derechos humanos y justicia de transición.'" Instituto Nacional de Derechos Humanos de El Salvador, October 11, 2021. https://www.ohchr.org/sites/default/files/2022-01/INDH_El_Salvador.docx.

Torres-Rivas, Edelberto. "La justicia, la verdad, el castigo y las estrategias del mal." In *Conflicto armado y denegación de justicia: Guatemala memoria del silencio*, 11–50. Guatemala City: F&G, 1999.

Traverso, Enzo. *Left-Wing Melancholia: Marxism, History, and Memory*. New York: Columbia University Press, 2016.

Valencia Caravantes, Daniel. "Funes pide perdón por abusos durante la guerra." *El Faro*, January 16, 2010. http://www.elfaro.net/es/201001/noticias/932/Funes-pide-perd%C3%B3n-por-abusos-durante-la-guerra.htm.

Valtierra, Ana. "Las plañideras." *Adiós*, no. 106 (2014): 22–23.

Vázquez Enríquez, Emily C. "Companion Species in Border Crossings: *Mediodía de fronteras* by Claudia Hernández." *Ciberletras*, no. 42 (2019): 120–32.

Vega y Ortega Báez, Rodrigo. "La vida pública del Museo Nacional de México a través de la prensa capitalina, 1825–1851." *Tzintzun: Revista de Estudios Históricos*, no. 59 (2014): 94–138.

Velásquez, Eugenia. "Escultura del mayor Roberto d'Aubuisson fue incautada por la Fiscalía." *Elsalvador.com*, April 25, 2022. https://www.elsalvador.com/noticias/nacional/arena-fiscalia-incauta-escultura-mayor-roberto-dabuisson/949766/2022/.

Velásquez Estrada, Ruth Elizabeth. "Grassroots Peacemaking: The Paradox of Reconciliation in El Salvador." *Social Justice* 41, no. 3 (2015): 69–86.

Velis, Carlos. *San Salvador después del eclipse*. San Salvador: Dirección de Publicaciones e Impresos, 1999.

Villalobos-Ruminott, Sergio. "La ficción de lo real: Horacio Castellanos Moya y la pregunta por la historia." *Crisol* 25 (2023). https://crisol.parisnanterre.fr/index.php/crisol/article/view/510/580.

Villalobos-Ruminott, Sergio. "Literatura y destrucción: Aproximación a la narrativa centroamericana actual." *Revista Iberoamericana* 59, no. 242 (2013): 131–48.

Villalobos-Ruminott, Sergio. *Soberanías en suspenso: Imaginación y violencia en América Latina*. Buenos Aires: La Cebra, 2013.

"Visita su tumba en Morazán, Madre de internacionalista chileno." *Farabuntera*, February 22, 2010. http://valquiria-enbsquedadedignidad.blogspot.com/2010/02/visita-su-tumba-en-morazan-madre-de.html.

Von Vogt, Maggie. "Oraciones incompletas: Una colaboración para preservar la memoria histórica de las y los sobrevivientes del conflicto salvadoreño." *Groundswell: Oral History for Social Change*, June 11, 2019. http://www.mail.oralhistoryforsocialchange.org/blog/2019/6/11/oraciones-incompletas-una-colaboracin-para-preservar-la-memoria-histrica-de-las-y-los-sobrevivientes-del-conflicto-armado-salvadoreo-2.

Vrana, Heather. *The City Belongs to You: A History of Student Activism in Guatemala, 1944–1996*. Oakland: University of California Press, 2017.

Wade, Christine J. *Captured Peace: Elites and Peacebuilding in El Salvador*. Athens: Ohio University Press, 2016.

Weld, Kristen. *Paper Cadavers: The Archives of Dictatorship in Guatemala*. Durham, N.C.: Duke University Press, 2014.

Westlake, E. J. *Our Land Is Made of Courage and Glory: Nationalistic Performance of Nicaragua and Guatemala*. Carbondale: Southern Illinois University Press, 2005.

Wieser, Doris. "Masculinidad y violencia de género en la novela negrocriminal nicaragüense." *Badebec* 4, no. 8 (2015): 205–32.

Wilkinson, Daniel. *Silence on the Mountain: Stories of Terror, Betrayal, and Forgetting in Guatemala*. Durham, N.C.: Duke University Press, 2004.

Williams, Paul. *Memorial Museums: The Global Rush to Commemorate Atrocities*. Oxford: Berg, 2007.

Winter, Jay. *Sites of Memory, Sites of Mourning: The Great War in European Cultural History*. 1995. Cambridge: Cambridge University Press, 2014.

Witcomb, Andrea. *Re-Imagining the Museum: Beyond the Mausoleum*. London: Routledge, 2002.

Wolf, Sonja. "El Salvador's State of Exception: A Piece in Nayib Bukele's Political Project." *LASA Forum* 54, no. 4 (2023): 34–41.

Yates, Pamela, dir. *500 Years*. Skylight Pictures, 2017.

Yates, Pamela, dir. *Granito: How to Nail a Dictator*. Brooklyn, N.Y.: Skylight Pictures, 2011.

Young, James E. "The Counter-Monument: Memory Against Itself in Germany Today." *Critical Inquiry* 18, no. 2 (1992): 267–96.

Yúdice, George. "Testimonio and Postmodernism." *Latin American Perspectives* 18, no. 3 (1991): 15–31.

Zardetto, Carol. "Arte y posguerra en Guatemala." In "Recordar el pasado para imaginar otro futuro: Artes y políticas de la memoria en Centroamérica," special issue, *Revista de Historia* 36 (2019): 99–109.

Zamora, Marcela, dir. *El cuarto de los huesos*. Mexico City: La Sandía Digital, Trípode Audiovisual. 2015.

Zamora, Marcela, dir. *Las aradas: Masacre en seis actos*. San Salvador: El Faro, 2014.

Zamora, Marcela, dir. *Las masacres de El Mozote*. San Salvador: El Faro, 2011.

Zamora, Marcela, dir. *Los ofendidos*. San Salvador: El Faro, Kino Glaz, 2016.

Zamora, Marcela, dir. *María en tierra de nadie*. San Salvador: Ruido, El Faro, Idheas, 2011.

Zegers, Mariana. "Sitios de Memoria en Chile." *El desconcierto*, December 14, 2017. https://www.eldesconcierto.cl/2017/12/14/sitios-de-memoria-en-chile/.

Žižek, Slavoj. *Violence: Six Sideways Reflections*. New York: Picador, 2008.

Zoodsma, Marieke, and Juliette Schaafsma. "Examining the 'Age of Apology': Insights from the Political Apology Database." *Journal of Peace Research* 59, no. 3 (2021): 436–48.

INDEX

ABOUT THE AUTHOR

Ignacio Sarmiento is an associate professor of Central American and Transborder studies at the California State University, Northridge. He is a coeditor of *Central American Migrations in the Twenty-First Century* (University of Arizona Press, 2023) and *(Re)Imaginar Centroamérica en el siglo XXI* (Uruk Editores, 2017). Sarmiento's research focuses on postwar Central America and the Central American diaspora.